D1029026

Love, Intimacy, and Sex

SOCIOLOGICAL
OBSERVATIONS

Series Editor: **JOHN M. JOHNSON,** Arizona State University

"This series seeks its inspiration primarily from its subject matter and the nature of its observational setting. It draws on all academic disciplines and a wide variety of theoretical and methodological perspectives. The series has a commitment to substantive problems and issues and favors research and analysis which seek to blend actual observations of human actions in daily life with broader theoretical, comparative, and historical perspectives. SOCIOLOGICAL OBSERVATIONS aims to use all of our available intellectual resources to better understand all facets of human experience and the nature of our society."
—John M. Johnson

Volumes in this series:

1. **THE NUDE BEACH,** by Jack D. Douglas and Paul K. Rasmussen, with Carol Ann Flanagan
2. **SEEKING SPIRITUAL MEANING,** by Joseph Damrell
3. **THE SILENT COMMUNITY,** by Edward William Delph
4. **CROWDS AND RIOTS,** by Sam Wright
5. **THE MAD GENIUS CONTROVERSY,** by George Becker
6. **AMATEURS,** by Robert A. Stebbins
7. **CARETAKERS,** by David R. Buckholdt and Jaber F. Gubrium
8. **HARD HATS,** by Jeffrey W. Riemer
9. **LOVE AND COMMITMENT,** by Gary Schwartz and Don Merten, with Fran Behan and Allyne Rosenthal
10. **OUTSIDERS IN A HEARING WORLD,** by Paul C. Higgins
11. **MOMENTUM,** by Peter Adler
12. **WORLDS OF FRIENDSHIP,** by Robert R. Bell
13. **CHRONIC PAIN,** by Joseph A. Kotarba
14. **INVISIBLE LIVES,** by David R. Unruh
15. **SOCIAL ROLES,** by Louis A. Zurcher
16. **THE REHABILITATION DETECTIVES,** by Paul C. Higgins
17. **AGING CRIMINALS,** by Neal Shover
18. **THE ALCOHOLIC SELF,** by Norman K. Denzin
19. **THE RECOVERING ALCOHOLIC,** by Norman K. Denzin
20. **LOVE, INTIMACY, AND SEX,** by Jack D. Douglas and Freda Cruse Atwell, with John Hillebrand

Love, Intimacy, and Sex

Jack D. Douglas
and Freda Cruse Atwell

With the assistance of
John Hillebrand

SAGE PUBLICATIONS
The Publishers of Professional Social Science
Newbury Park   Beverly Hills   London   New Delhi

For information address:

SAGE Publications, Inc.
2111 West Hillcrest Drive
Newbury Park, California 91320

SAGE Publications Inc.　　SAGE Publications Ltd.
275 South Beverly Drive　　28 Banner Street
Beverly Hills　　London EC1Y 8QE
California 90212　　England

SAGE PUBLICATIONS India Pvt. Ltd.
M-32 Market
Greater Kailash I
New Delhi 110 048 India

Printed in the United States of America

Library of Congress Cataloging-in-Publication Data

Douglas, Jack D.
    Love, intimacy, and sex.

    (Sociological observations ; 20)
    Bibliography: p.
    1. Interpersonal relations. 2. Love. 3. Intimacy
(Psychology) 4. Sex. I. Atwell, Freda Cruse.
II. Hillebrand, John. III. Title. IV. Series.
HM132.D69   1987   306.7   87-20658
ISBN 0-8039-2605-7
ISBN 0-8039-2606-5 (pbk.)

Contents

Preface 7

Acknowledgments 15

1. The Sexual Modernist Revolt
   Against the Myth of Victorianism 17

2. Learning to Love/Not to Love 47

3. Becoming Insecure/Becoming Secure 88

4. The Development of Love 129

5. Falling In-Love and Lust 166

6. Falling Out of Love, Divorcing, and
   Starting Over 228

"Prologue": The Eternal Quest 273

Appendix: The Freudian Theory of
   Incest and the Jealous Child 277

References 292

About the Authors 303

Preface

Love is one of the most overworked words in our vocabulary. There is hardly a field of human activity in which the word is not worked to death. It is not restricted to expressing an emotion between the sexes, but also expresses the emotion between members of a family. It signifies the feeling for your neighbor, for your friend, and even for your foe, for the whole of mankind, for the home, social or racial group, nation, for all that is beautiful and good, and for God Himself. It is almost incredible that it can be equal to its many tasks. "L'amour" in French comedies is obviously not the same as "love" in the Holy Scripture.

Its diversity of meaning, its adaptability and its capability of quick change are astonishing . . .

The subject which is most talked and written about remains a mystery. It is experienced every hour everywhere on this globe and it is still unknown. That everybody has experienced it does not make its understanding easier. What happens every day often stays unknown . . . love is an unknown physical power, its origin not yet discovered, and its character not yet understood. If it is true that science is the topography of ignorance, as Oliver Wendell Holmes once said, then the region of love is a vast white spot on the map.

Theodor Reik

"Love is a many splendored thing," as one of America's thousands of popular love songs puts it. Parental caring love, adoration love, friendly love, romantic love, Erotic love, love possession (daimonic love), sexual obsession, and the many dimensions of pseudolove are only the most obvious of the many types of "love" distinguished in commonsense discourse today. These and the vast number of other dimensions of human experience that are interdependent with them are the emotional foundations of human life, the hard, yet flexible bonds that hold us together. The many dimensions of love bond us emotionally to our families—the universal social groups that shape the senses of selves and the values of all human beings. Though less obviously so, they are also the emotional foundations of the webs of production and marketing relationships, of military relationships, and of political relationships, all of which depend profoundly on the bonds of loving friendship. If they are to prevail over the many harsh conflicts in life, these vital emotional bonds must be supported by the shared ideas and moral obligations of culture and by community action based on those.

With rare exceptions, the advancement of individual lives is inseparable in our thinking and feeling from the advancement of those with whom we identify our selves in loving partnerships. (Throughout the book, we shall use the words *partners* and *partnerships* to refer to attachments that involve identification of the sense of self with the other, that is, a feeling of fusion or union of selves. The popular term *relationship* will be used to refer to interactions that may not involve this fusion, such as the casual sexual affair. The great importance of this distinction will become clearer.) Shorn of the powerful bonds of love that undergird our everyday lives and that unite us in memory and imagination with our ancestors and our progeny, almost all of us would find our lives meaningless.

Though love partnerships are generally the wellsprings of our greatest joys and senses of fulfillment, there have always been painful conflicts and other problems in the realms of love, intimacy, and sex in all societies. In recent years, however, these problems have reached epidemic proportions in the Western world, especially in the United States, among our most educated young people. The official statistics of love miseries have grown for decades, sometimes reaching a plateau (or even taking a gentle dip), but thus far returning inexorably to their upward trends. Neuroses, depressions, anxieties, phobias, narcissistic panics, wife batterings, child batterings, husband batterings, aged parent batterings, emotional abuses, abandonments, divorces, custody battles, kidnappings by noncustodial parents, FBI investigations of parent kidnappers, extraditions, failures of support, illegitimacies, abortions, single-parent impoverishments, venereal diseases, herpes, chlamydia, AIDS—onward and upward soar these official litanies of our crises of love, intimacy, and sex. The most exuberant doomsayer surveying the rising divorce statistics in the 1890s could only be further

inspired by these official litanies of misery to believe that the modernization of "love" has produced an "immiseration" of the "masses,"
especially of the college-educated and financially well-off "masses," who
used to be much safer than the less fortunate from such catastrophes.

The official figures on divorce, the most closely watched official
index of love misery, give stunning testimony to the farsightedness of
those distant doomsayers. Yet anyone with much experience in our
society today knows that the official indices of misery vastly underestimate the general trends of misery. While the official rates of legal
divorces show that approximately 50% of new marriages will end in
divorce, the real rates of *emotional divorce* (of what we call "unbonding")
have soared far beyond that. The dissolution of legally contracted
marriages may on average be more painful than the dissolution of
common-law marriages and other lesser degrees of love partnerships
and sexual relationships, especially because legally contracted marriages are far more likely to involve children. But unbonding from
anyone with whom you have fallen in love, especially from someone
with whom you have also shared the intimacies of Erotic ecstasy,
produces protracted anguish and insecurity. Though officials keep no
direct figures on these unbondings, most of us are painfully aware that
our social landscape is littered with many more depressed and grieving
"love zombies" than the official figures indicate. Our own very rough
guess from our many contacts with young people is that the average
graduate from our "elite" universities now goes through months of
misery and depression from two real divorces before ever getting legally
married. Many of these love unbondings are far more excruciating for
their victims than later legal divorces are, simply because earlier loves,
before the lovers have developed defenses to protect themselves against
the losses of lovers, are often the deepest. While they almost never have
children, and the great miseries they add to legal divorces, these couples
contribute far more than their share of abortions to the national total of
1.3 million a year. While many women seem to endure only short-lived
depression over abortions, many others suffer prolonged agony from
guilt or loss. Most abortions also injure a romantic love, so that misery
from the abortion is compounded by feelings of betrayal, desertion, or
rejection and by lasting "emotional scar tissue."

There always were some broken hearts and broken love dreams
among the young and unmarried. There always have been some
unmarried pregnancies, adoptions, and abortions. But few older
observers with much experience with the young over the last several

decades will doubt that young people today are suffering a massive epidemic of love misery by comparison with those in the 1950s. Young people may have been more lonely and sexually frustrated in the 1950s, but, if so, those were minor pains by comparison. In the 1950s, our major universities had clinical and counseling services to help students through emotional crises, but few students showed up, and when they did love misery was only one of the many possible problems on their minds. Today, university psychologists are nearly swamped by a rising tide of love miseries. At the same time, students were turning college counseling on love and sex misery into a growth industry, the graduates were turning our society into "the therapeutic society" in which roughly 2000 forms of psychological therapy have been exploding. Love problems were the overwhelming majority of problems driving people to these generally expensive and time-consuming forms of psychic dependency.

Our primary purpose in doing this work has not been that of reversing the rising tide of love miseries. Such a task would demand the rhetorical skills of the politician and the extrarational skills of the prophet rather than those of the scholar and scientist. Nor has our primary purpose been that of directly helping individuals who have extreme problems. On the contrary, though our work draws upon all forms of clinical and other attempts to help people with such problems, we do so only when we can put them in the context of our own work, which is focused more on the normal and brighter sides of love, intimacy, and sex. Inevitably, our own work has included a great deal of investigation of problems, because all normal and brighter love partnerships and sexual relations involve serious problems at times, but the probers into the nether reaches of misery have already provided us with a mass of fine material on extreme problems. We have tried to right the balance by focusing away from those and putting them into the greater context of normal and happier human lives.

We have tried, especially in Chapters 1 and 2, to sketch an overview of the powerful currents of sexual modernism that have played such a major role in producing the rising tide of love confusion and thus of love problems. It is necessary to see in general how cultural relativism, biological determinism, sexual behaviorism, Freudianism (especially the "pop-Freudianism" of the mass media), and many other streams of sexual modernism have grossly distorted the contemporary under-standing of love. In doing this, we have also tried to show what deeper forces have been at work in our Western cultures over the centuries to inspire these great political conflicts over love and Eros and, thereby, to make the objective study and analysis of them so problematic. Severe space limitations forced us to keep these historical and theoretical arguments to a minimum, which can make our sketch of major conclusions look like dangling assertions to readers unaware of the rich mass of historical and analytical work being done on these. Jack Douglas will publish books on the whole history of sexual modernism, and on the centuries' long development of the anthropological ideas about the sexual life of "savages" and the use of these to "disprove" any ideas about human nature. But Chapters 1 and 2 only put this book in that complex historical perspective. The detailed history of sexual modernism and the full explanation of love problems in our Western societies are not our primary concern in this book. Our primary purpose and the main focus of this work has been that of providing the general model of love, intimacy, and sex in human life that is necessary for understanding them and their fundamental places in human life. We believe this general model is the necessary beginning for any successful attempts to understand the vastly complex particulars and to understand our rising tide of love miseries.

Though we expect that some of our findings and ideas will be original discoveries for scholars and scientists, we do not see that as the primary value of this work. None of the basic truths of the social sciences is something totally unknown to previous human beings. Basic truths such as the law of supply and demand in economic exchanges and the related law of reciprocity in friendly exchanges were clearly stated thousands of years ago and have probably been understood in some taken-for-granted manner by human beings of all ages. Because all human beings spend much of their lives thinking intensively about love, intimacy, and sex, and because most great thinkers of all ages have written about them, bright new discoveries about them are rare. Social scientists improve on such basic understandings by making them more precise, but they hardly discover them for the first time. The greatest value of social science comes from providing a more general model that systematically relates such basic truths to each other to show how they interact. The lack of such a systematic model is the greatest weakness of common sense and of Western intellectual thought about love. The sexual modernists, as we shall see, greatly exacerbated this weakness by radically reducing all of the complex dimensions of love and Eros to "sexual libido" or "sex." "Erotic" has now been transmogrified through the lens of political rhetoric into "merely sensual sex." Our focus in this book is presenting a true and systematic model of all the basic dimensions of love and Eros.

Most earlier social science works that have dealt with love, intimacy, and sex in their natural settings have tried to show that these often fall into certain "natural types"—such as "best friends" or "best friend lovers." This is true, but such an approach does not offer much hope of ever providing a fundamental theory of love, intimacy, and sex in human life. As earlier scientists would have said, it does not provide a *fundamentum divisionis*—a system of fundamental dimensions of the phenomena being studied. That is what we try to do first. Only then are we able to show the major systematic interdependencies among the dimensions. This approach has certainly been taken by many earlier scientists and scholars, most notably those following the ethological perspective on child development first proposed by John Bowlby (1971-1979, 1979) and his many coworkers. (Herbert Spencer, 1890, made a brilliant beginning in analyzing them well over a century ago.) We have incorporated their ideas and tried to show that there are many other dimensions involved than they realized. Significantly, we have tried to show that there are a number of interdependent dimensions of basic insecurity and security in the sense of self that are overwhelmingly dependent on the early experience of children in their *love-duets* with their mothers and that normally have profound effects on later love partnerships, especially on the failures to build such partnerships. Though neither our knowledge nor the space available to us will allow us to explore all of the relations among these, we have tried to consider the ones that seem to us to be the most important. In the process, we try to show that each person's love experience constitutes a unique *love gestalt*, that is, an integral whole of interdependent perceptions, emotions, cognitions, evaluations, and actions—a vastly complex, ever-shifting, and revitalized symphony of conscious and subconscious strains of experience. While many of these are similar enough to be dealt with commonsensically as "natural types" of love experience without greatly distorting the phenomena, most cannot.

Our primary purpose, then, is to establish a systematic scientific model that will give us a generally valid understanding of love, which will help in solving our many love miseries. Without a systematic model of all the major dimensions of love and their interdependencies, analysts can spin out endless minitheories (*petitio principii*) about each piece of the elephant's ear or tail, and wind up with endless contradictions and misunderstandings in concrete instances. Our goal here is to present the holistic picture of the elephant.

It would be absurd in the small space allowed us for this book to try to deal with all the jungles of facts and theories in this vastly complex realm of experience. We have not tried to do so. Nor have we tried to exhaust the mountains of factual and analytical work with which so many thousands of our dedicated colleagues have provided us. That would be useless pedantry in the present state of analysis. We cannot even present much of the massive evidence from our own life studies, some of which would be many thousands of pages long. Severe limitations of space allow us to use them only to illustrate some of our major points. We must first have the basic truths and the right model and methods for getting more truth. We have dealt in previous works, especially in *Investigative Social Research* and *Creative Interviewing* (Douglas, 1976, 1985), with the methods involved. We hope to present some of the detailed findings in later works.

If we have succeeded in our theoretical work, we are confident that the thousands of other dedicated researchers probing these depths of the human heart and soul will also forge ahead with the new work required.

—Jack D. Douglas
La Jolla, California

—Freda Cruse Atwell
Del Mar, California

Acknowledgments

Our intellectual debts to the many people who have shared their lives with us in our cooperative searches for mutual understanding will be obvious on every page of this book. Our greatest debts are owed to our many loving friends who have communed with us over the years about their lives and ours. We owe a special debt to John M. Johnson for his devoted communing and his editorial work. This book is their work as much as ours, for better or worse.

1

THE SEXUAL MODERNIST
REVOLT AGAINST THE
MYTH OF VICTORIANISM

Alfred Kinsey . . . represents most perfectly the anti-Romantic impulse in sexual modernism. He is not so unqualified a sexual materialist as was the Marquis de Sade, but he sought above all else to separate human sexual experience from its elaborate emotional associations. Those associations, he believed, placed unnecessary restrictions on the expression of an innocent physical need. Only when repressed did sexual urges threaten emotional stability, and thus a rational society, he implied, would seek to promote not only a positive but an essentially casual attitude toward sexuality. . . . [In the work of Masters and Johnson], on the one hand there is the clinical, some would say heartless, subjection of human sexual behavior to laboratory scrutiny and manipulation, and on the other hand there is the repeated insistence on the need for communication in sexual relationships and the implicit critique of all sexual encounters devoid of serious emotional content. It would seem that they belong neither to the party of Keats nor that of Sade.

The almost schizoid character of Masters and Johnson's thought exactly reflects the unresolved tensions of the modern sexual tradition as a whole. As moderns, we remain permanently divided between a Romantic past, whose repressions we would gladly rid ourselves of, and a deromanticized future, whose emotional emptiness we fear even while we anticipate its greater freedom. It is precisely in this antithesis of Romantic and anti-Romantic impulses that the distinctly modern element in sexual modernism is to be located.

Paul Robinson

The mistaken ideas about love, intimacy, and sex that are now so common in the mass media and in intellectual analyses have sprung overwhelmingly from the social movement of sexual modernism. Sexual modernism (Robinson, 1976) and neo-modernism (Libby and Whitehurst, 1977) are the body of twentieth-century research and thought intended to revolutionize the very complex Western ideas about love and Eros by replacing them with radically reduced ideas about "sex" or the "sexual libido" and to revolutionize traditional practices by replacing them with "rational and scientific" ones, which, it is supposed, will end repressive misery and usher in happiness. The movement as a whole is like a great river with many currents and cross-eddies that stem from many headwaters, most beginning with the French Revolution and the utopian socialists of that era, and now flow in somewhat different but interconnected directions. Some streams of sexual modernism are openly revolutionary, most are only moderately and secretly so and use the Fabian methods of protracted cultural conflict and evolution to achieve the revolutionary goals. Anyone with much knowledge of the multitude of works in this tradition must have a healthy fear of being engulfed by its complexities. (Historians have barely begun to study it. See Robinson, 1976.) We have no intention of trying to provide a detailed map of it in this book. Because so much thought about these matters today is partly inspired by the proclamations of the modernists and by reactions to the movement, however, we feel forced to give a brief overview of it and of the historical facts about the commonsensical ideas and practices against which the modernists have been revolting. In our brief overview of modernism, we have excluded the extremes of the movement, the great mass of hate-filled demagoguery that began with the Sadists, the Saint-Simonians, the Fourierists, and the Owenites. (For these utopian roots of sexual modernism, see Manuel and Manuel, 1979; Billington, 1980; and Lauer and Lauer, 1983.) We consider only the scientific work of people like Havelock Ellis, Sigmund Freud, Margaret Mead, and Bronislaw Malinowski. We try to show that their general theories are quite wrong, especially in their secretly revolutionary thrusts derived from the utopians, but we certainly have learned valuable details from their scientific work, as will be obvious in succeeding chapters. Most especially, we consider Ellis the best of all sexual researchers. It is tragic that his work is now almost totally unread. Our analyses of the modernists will seem harsh only to those who do not know the wealth of historical material brought to light in recent years.

Even the best works of this massive social movement normally present it as a revolt against Victorianism and either imply or assert that the Victorians were guilty of an unprecedented repression of sexuality (see the treatment of this in May, 1980; and Robinson, 1976). None of the extreme charges against the Victorians is true, except that of public prudishness and hypocrisy. The sexual modernists were struggling against some real official and unofficial barriers to discussing basic sexual facts of human life, but their real problems and their political zeal led them to mythologize, stereotype, and stigmatize their Victorian enemies. They wound up rebelling against a myth of the "ancient regime" inspired by their own revolutionary zeal. Just as political revolutionaries the world over see their opponents as monsters, and just as rebellious teenagers often create images that portray their parents as great repressors when actually they are models of patient tolerance, so the modernists greatly distorted the realities of our Victorian ancestors. We in turn must be cautious not to "o'erleap the mark" in reacting against the overzealous mistakes of the modernists. We obviously have no interest in returning to prudery or hypocrisy, but we do intend to retrieve the truths that were thrown out with them.

There is always a wide gap between what is publicly visible about love and sex and what is going on in private. (This secrecy makes them among the most difficult to study of all human activities. See Douglas, 1976, 1985.) These gaps between the public fronts and the private realities have almost certainly waxed and waned far more than any of the private realities have changed. As we shall see, the realities of individual feelings and actions in this realm are highly primed by genetic inheritance (human nature), so they normally vary only within a narrow range. The so-called Victorians were normally prudish and hypocritical in their public behavior and statements about sex, but in their private lives they were not nearly so repressive. Crane Brinton's wise "guesstimate" seems best: "I think it extremely likely that on the whole there was, in the nineteenth century West at least, less sexual promiscuity of all sorts, less deviation from the moral code in this respect than in the immediate previous centuries, the usual difference of a few percentage points" (1959, p. 363). In matters of love and intimacy, the Victorians were far more publicly supportive than people are today in the same nations, but the evidence makes it clear that people today are actually far more loving and intimate than the casual sex-talk in the sex manuals of our colleges and in the mass media would lead one to believe.

The evidence now being carefully sifted and assessed by Gertrude

Himmelfarb (1986), Peter Gay (1984-1986), Michel Foucault (1980), and other historians makes it reasonably clear that the public-private sexual gap was a yawning abyss in "respectable" British and American society in the middle 1800s; that there probably were slightly more sexually repressed individuals, especially more severely repressed "bourgeois" women who developed symptoms of "hysteria" and other sex-related problems; that the sexual behavior of most people was probably not greatly different from that of most people in the same nations today, except in realms such as birth control and abortion; that there were plenty of privately promiscuous people at all times in the two most Victorian nations, Britain and the United States, including rampant promiscuity among the aristocrats, such as the parents of Winston Churchill (Manchester, 1983); and that we have a long way to go before we shall be very sure about how much repressiveness there actually was in the Victorian Era. Our own reading of that evidence, combined with our own life studies and those of many others, leads us to conclude that today people are somewhat more repressed in love and intimacy, that there has been an evolutionary increase in premarital intercourse among college students and graduates (Bell and Coughey, 1980, review the evidence), and that strong majorities of young people are seeking love and intimacy (Blumstein and Schwartz, 1983), often in gropings befuddled by the basic distortions of love taught them by the sexual modernists.

SEXUAL STIGMATIC
WARFARE AND
PURIFICATION RITUALS

The myth of Victorianism and the stigmatization of the Victorians are only the latest in the long history of sexual myths and sexual stigmatic warfare in the Western World (see the massive history of sexual demythologization in Crosby, 1985). The underlying cause of this extreme mythologization has been the *politicization of sex*, which began in a serious way in the fourth and fifth centuries AD (Lecky, 1869/1955; Brinton, 1959). The members of all cultures (at least on average) see the Erotic as tremendously important and generally potentially dangerous, always posing some danger of pollution, if not in itself then at least when the Erotic rituals are misperformed. The Greeks were no exception to this rule, but most of them were among the more relaxed and tolerant about physical desire and action—sexuality. (See Flaceliere, 1971; and Rougemont, 1940, 1963. Licht, 1934, presents a sensual picture of the Greeks). Many of the educated, however, became devotees of Eastern dualism, which saw the spirit—the realm of light and Godly virtue—as locked in mortal combat with the materialistic body—the realm of darkness and Satanic pollution. The Platonists, who shared this dualism, became the dominant philosophical influence on Christians (see Brunner, 1947; Bullough and Bullough, 1977, chap. 2).

The Christian sects competed against each other and defended themselves against their outside enemies in good part by trying to stigmatize their opponents while trying to avoid stigmatization of themselves (Bullough and Bullough, 1977, p. 18). When the Church became very powerful in the third and fourth centuries, the empire was being destroyed by invaders. Roman leaders often accused the Christians of undermining the Roman will to fight and of polluting the city with foreign gods. As the Christians came to be seen by the Roman elites as a threat to their entire society, even some of the most intelligent and educated Romans circulated stigmatizing myths about the Christians. As Norman Cohn (1975) has shown, these included some myths of horrendous sexual pollution, including those of parent-child incest.

In spite of their roots, early Christians, though ambivalent and ambiguous in statements about physical desire (Bullough and Brundage, 1982, pp. 1-21), were still relaxed and tolerant toward sexual matters, at least by comparison with later Church doctrine and practice, possibly because of the early non-Platonic Greek influences and the need to appeal to outcast groups. (Christ himself had set the example by washing the feet of a former prostitute.) But the growing stigmatic warfare launched against them by the Romans and their sectarian competitors, especially the Gnostics, put tremendous pressure on them to defend themselves with the "breastplate of righteousness," that is, to defend themselves by trying to appear purer than their stigmatizers (Humphreys, 1970). As the Empire entered its death throes and sectarian civil wars engulfed Christians in the fourth and fifth centuries, the stigmatic warfare over sexual pollution and the craving for purification became ever more intense and threatening. The Church leaders responded by becoming ever more "puritanical" (that is, purifying) in their rhetorical counterattacks on their enemies and in their public practices. They purified themselves to contrast with the supposedly rampant sexual pollution of their Roman and sectarian enemies (Kiefer, 1934). (The decline and fall of the Empire, which involved tremendous violence and dread, would have called forth purification rituals even without this political conflict. Earlier historians, such as W.E.H. Lecky, 1869/1955, emphasized this factor. But the work of Cohn, 1975, and others make it clear that the political conflict was also very important.)

In the fifth century, Christianity's most powerful intellectual systematized and burnished the breastplate with which to defend and advance the faith. Augustine himself was torn by ambivalence. His sexual lust and Erotic love led him to take a mistress and have a son, but his youthful Manichaeanism filled him with revulsion for this materialistic pollution. As he revealed in his moving *Confessions*, by middle age he was becoming profoundly disturbed by his fleshly corruption. In his account of his final conversion to Christianity, he shows that the battle to purify himself of the corruption of the flesh, especially the awful corruption of the sexual lust (*libido*, in Latin), was the very heart of his struggle to be Godly. In the full flush of the conversion experience, he opened the *New Testament* and read in the "Letter of Paul to the Romans": "Put on the Lord Jesus Christ, and make no provision for the flesh, to gratify its desires" (*Romans* 13:14). Many years later when he wrote his most influential work, *The City of God*, he described in vivid terms the awful shame anyone should feel who indulges in the sexual passions and, he presumed, demonstrated to all the world that the recent sack of Rome by the invading Visigoths could not possibly be due to the polluting effect of such a puritanical religion. The extreme puritanism of the age is even more obvious in the fact that Augustine spent much of his life as a Churchman defending the Church against even more extreme puritans. Like most reigning political hierarchies, the Church staked out a middle ground between extremes, but this compromise position, which became Church dogma thereafter, was far more antisexual than the ethos of most cultures.

In almost all cultures, the Erotic forces of life are felt to be expressions of the vital, creative forces of the God(s) and of Being. Sexuality is seen to be only one part of these creative, sacred, and magical forces of the Erotic. Because of this, it is common for priests or other agents of purity (such as virgins) to perform public Erotic rituals, even in rare instances, public intercourse, as a way to commune with the magical or godly forces of creation and Being, of earthly fertility and human fertility. Sexuality is seen as potentially dangerous, precisely because of its great sacred power, which can become terribly destructive if incorrectly channeled by mistakes in the rituals. The Erotic is holy and awesome, the opposite of "casual." (Even the best recent anthropological studies of sex generally fail to consider this vital distinction. For example, see Suggs, 1966, pp. 170-171.) The Greek god Eros involved this idea of the sacred power, and thus the potential danger, of sexuality, at least when the full heat of daimonic passion was unleashed (in "mania"). From the time of Augustine, Western Christian cultures presented sexuality in public discourse as dangerous for the opposite reason, because the satanic materialism of all aspects other than that of marital procreation were seen as inherently polluting. There have, however, always been great variations in the public sex lives and some variations in practices of different Western groups. And the private lives of the "earthy" masses has always retained a worship of Eros (see Bullough and Brundage, 1982). Over the centuries, this idea of sexual pollution became so totally taken for granted in public settings in Western cultures—and the idea of sex as sacred so repressed from public view—that Christians who first encountered cultures in which public Erotic rites were sacred rites professed to be profoundly shocked. Some eighteenth-century English explorers reacted to the Tahitian Erotic rituals as if they were forms of devil worship. (Bougainville, 1772, the first French discoverer of Tahiti, was astounded, but also intrigued, showing once again the pluralism of Western societies.)

The degree to which Christians have decried sexual pollution and tried to purify themselves and the world by beating the breastplate of righteousness and repressing sexuality has varied widely. As a general rule, however, we can say that the more threatened Christians have felt, the more they have decried sexuality as polluting and the more they have sacrificed sexual expression as a form of ritual purification to ward off the threats. One of the most threatening things in life is intense political conflict and the warfare it so often produces; and the most intense and threatening form of warfare is commonly civil war. Given the central place of sexual purity in Christian purification rituals, sexual purity has been a powerful weapon in the internecine struggles within the Western world, and the various Christian factions in these struggles have often resorted to arms races in sexual purity, just as Augustine did with his Roman and sectarian enemies.

When the Catholic Church launched its first great crusade against internal enemies in the twelfth century, it branded these dreaded heretics—the Albighensians and Cathars (some of whose ideas of the Erotic go back to the Gnostics)—as sexual polluters. The Albighensians more than returned the favor with fiery denunciations of the impurities of the Church. The Church soon launched a great self-purification program, including the systematic enforcement of its old celibacy rules for priests. By the fifteenth century, after several centuries with little internal religious competition, the Church drifted into rampant sexual deviance clearly visible to the public (though probably not on the massive scale charged by enemies such as Machiavelli and Savanarola). Sexual pollution thus became one of the major stigmatic charges launched against the Church by the protesters of the Reformation in the sixteenth century.

The Protestants in general, including the extreme Puritan Protestants, were not against Erotic sex. On the contrary, they argued that human nature and the fallen state of mankind was such that the Erotic was inevitable and a vital part of all life. They wanted only to channel and "chasten" its expression into the purer state of married life and argued that the futile attempts by the Church to repress it would only lead to further pollution (Leites, 1986). The Church, however, launched its own depollution war. The Counter-Reformation imposed stern measures against sexual pollution within the Church and denounced the Protestants as sexual polluters of the worst order. Though it is unlikely that so-called Victorianism ever existed in any Western society, sixteenth-century Counter-Reformation Spain probably came closest.

The sixteenth and seventeenth centuries saw the most intense warfare, including the most intense stigmatic warfare of sexual pollution charges, between the Reformation and Counter-Reformation forces and then between the more moderate and more extreme Protestant forces. It was an era of intense sexual purification rituals. But, once again, we must keep constantly in mind the great difference between these public rituals, which are always presented brazenly for all the world to see, and the private realities that were carefully shielded from view by the breastplate of righteousness. *The Diary of Samuel Pepys* (Pepys, 1970), a man of great respectability who made his way to the top in government service in the very vortex of Puritanical England, serves as a monument to the hidden private realities of all ages of public repression.

The eighteenth century was a period of public reaction against the extremes of these purification rituals. Though *Fanny Hill* can hardly be considered a realistic and representative portrayal, its great success is a good indication of the non-Puritanical tastes of the era in England. The discoveries of the Polynesian islands, with their robust public displays of Eroticism and their traditions of casual prostitution, created mass sensations and gave birth and wing to the full panoply of utopian myths of the bliss of casual sex as the natural condition of mankind. (There is a vast literature on these "primitivist" myths.) The French Revolution in 1789 involved a utopian revolution against sexual repression in any form. Every idea of sexual liberation, sexual casualness, polymorphous perversity, and sadomasochism that we have seen explode in our modernist century was first proclaimed in that revolt against the repressions of the "ancient regime" (Billington, 1980; Manuel and Manuel, 1979; Lauer and Lauer, 1983). Victorianism was partly a generalized reaction against this earlier "libertinism," the utopian experiments going on, and the rising tide of revolutionary socialist politics, which made "free love" one of its major goals. But Victorianism was probably inspired most of all by the attempts of the embattled middle classes to present themselves in public as purer than the aristocrats and the rising socialists, both of whom scorned them as crass and vulgar and attacked them in class civil war from above and below.

THE REAL VICTORIANS

The bourgeoisie's own ambivalence about themselves, which Peter Gay (1984-1986) has shown pervaded their public lives, was probably the most powerful force behind this defensive and arrogant display of the breastplate of sexual purity. The bourgeoisie suffered from ambivalent insecurities on several fronts (see Chapter 3 on insecurities). Being devoted to making money, and thus subject to the eternal temptations of the mortal sin of greed, they were necessarily at odds with their own fervently felt Christianity. (No amount of Calvinist denials or intellectualizations of materialism could completely hide their "sinfulness" from their ever-vigilant consciences, which was very likely one reason why they were also the most charitable people in all of history.) At the same time, from the eighteenth century on, they were continually under emotional attack from the aristocratic elites, who branded them as "vulgar merchants and mechanics" to fend off their growing political threat. As the century wore on, the laborers became an ever-greater threat to their growing political power and social respectability. In Anglo-Saxon nations, the "bourgeoisie" called themselves the middle classes, symbolizing their feeling caught between the two extreme classes. Finally, as if fighting defensive wars on three fronts were not enough, political reformers and revolutionaries increasingly turned the liberals' own value of liberty against them. By carrying that value to "libertine" extremes in proclamations of "free love" and attacks on marriage, some came to seem a threat to all family life and thus to all social life. The extreme feminists among these inspired the intensely ambivalent figure of the "femme fatale." These androgynous beauties, most alluring and most frightening, promising both heaven and hell, are the most striking figures of high-Victorian art (Bade, 1979). Given their religious backgrounds, and the whole history of stigmatic warfare and purification rituals in the Christian world, it is not too surprising that they defended and puffed themselves up with puritanical diatribes and arrogance in their public campaigns.

In spite of all these grounds for arrogant pronouncements against sin, the growing political power of the middle classes was rarely used to increase the social repression of sexuality until the latter half of the nineteenth century. Even then, the enforcement of both old and new laws was normally like that of today. It was normally quite relaxed, but was punctuated by short periods of politically inspired repression, which is what researchers in this century came to call the "lid-on, lid-off" approach. Most of the time the enforcers left the great majority of prostitutes, homosexuals (normally called "sodomites" at that time), and pornographers alone, enforcing laws and local morals only against more infamous cases. But political campaigns and mass media campaigns often produced both opportunities and pressures that led politicians and enforcers to "put the lid on," until the opportunities or pressures waned. Charles Winnick and Paul Kinsie (1971) have shown that the legal repression of prostitution in the United States was very weak until the 1920s in most states and was far more severe and effective in the 1960s than in the early part of the century (also see Waterman, 1932; Reckless, 1933).

The many studies done of prostitution in almost every Western nation from the 1840s onward shows that there were many thousands of prostitutes and millions of customers in the cities, as there always have been in Megalopolises (Brinton, 1959, pp. 362-365). The studies began in earnest only in the 1840s for reasons that had little to do with increased prudery or repressiveness in the Anglo-Saxon nations. In fact, the major studies were long done mainly in the nations most relaxed about deviant sexual activities, especially in France, the most relaxed of all. The most famous works on prostitution published throughout the entire century were organized and edited by Parent-Duchatelet (1836), a French public hygienist. Though he and his co-authors showed most of the standard Christian attitudes (and naivete) toward their subject, they were not inspired primarily, if at all, by moral repressiveness. They were deeply disturbed by the public hygiene implications of prostitution.

It was only in the nineteenth century that the scientific-technological, industrial, and urban evolutions led to explosions in the populations of Western cities. With the growth of massive cities came an explosion of diseases produced by the tremendous increase in the communication of germs and viruses (McNeill, 1976) and the increase in public filth in an age when sewage systems were themselves a revolutionary innovation. (The earlier sewage systems going back to ancient Rome were used only for draining rain or flood waters. In the nineteenth century, the massive sewage systems were a symbol of the vitally important developments in medicine and public hygiene, but this symbol of the age has been replaced by railroads, perhaps because sewers are not so romantic as steam engines.)

The great epidemics produced a background of dread of deadly contagion from casual contact in urban settings. First came the mysterious spread of the awful "consumption" (tuberculosis), then cholera raged through the cities, and typhoid struck intermittently, killing even Prince Albert. In the 1850s, John Snow demonstrated that a London outbreak of cholera was caused by contamination of the water supply. A few years later, the discovery of the role of bacteria in spreading disease led to a rapid increase in the dread of urban contagion-pollution. Though the official figures were highly unreliable, by the late nineteenth century it was clear to all medical hygienists and to all informed citizens that the venereal diseases were exploding right along with the explosion of urban populations and that promiscuity, especially that represented on a massive scale by prostitution, was the primary cause of this explosion. Havelock Ellis was very aware that "in the eyes of many people, the question of prostitution is simply the question of syphilis" (1936, vol. 2, p. 319). Even the most famous aristocrats and political leaders of the day were not immune to the terrifying and mysteriously dehumanizing ravages of syphilitic paresis. Randolph Churchill, the father of Winston Churchill and one of the most powerful politicians of his day, was only one of the multitude who died a slow and agonizing death caused by these diseases communicated almost entirely by casual sexual contact. Most European nations responded not with the massive legal repression of prostitution, but with attempts to control sexually transmitted disease by requiring medical examination and certification of prostitutes. At the turn of the century, an American doctor, Abraham Flexner, surveyed these European efforts and concluded that only a minority of prostitutes bothered to register.

The standard picture presented by sexual modernists depicts a few lonely culture heroes, especially Havelock Ellis and Sigmund Freud, suddenly launching a revolution against massive Victorian sexual repression. This picture is completely false. Havelock Ellis built his great work on a mass of earlier scholarly and scientific work, all carefully footnoted. Though he hid most of his sources, Freud drew almost all of his major ideas from Ellis and other researchers and from literature and philosophy (see Ellenberger, 1970; Kern, 1973, 1975; Sulloway, 1983). There were specialized journals of sexual research, case studies of every conceivable form of sexual activity, and for every article or book proposing repression there was generally another proposing the opposite and several proposing something in between. What is striking, by contrast with our own day, is how lively and undogmatic the massive controversies over sexuality were. It is only late in the century that the leagues for "decency" became important and by then the dread of venereal disease had produced a massive clamor, not for repressing information about sexuality, but for the exact opposite. By then almost all doctors, educationalists, and popular writers were thunderous in their calls for sexual education of the young to prevent venereal disease and the other social problems associated with casual sex, especially divorce and illegitimacy (Peter Gay, 1984-1986, p. 326).

It is easy to forget how realistic it was to be filled with dread by the urban epidemics in a day when there was no defense against their ravages and when the official figures showed soaring numbers of victims and carriers. It is common now to look at those panic-stricken calls for sexual education as merely another symptom of sexual repressiveness, rather than expressions of reasonable fears based on all the facts known to the best medical experts at the time. (Even Peter Gay, 1984-1986, p. 326, fell victim to this anachronistic interpretation of their lust for sexual education.) Now that we have seen millions of Americans, including some of the most "liberated," becoming nearly hysterical in public statements and actions about the acquired immune deficiency syndrome (AIDS), we are better able to understand their sense of dread. Thus far the number of victims of AIDS is small by comparison with the proportion of people killed, maimed, and otherwise victimized by venereal disease alone in the nineteenth century, only one of many plagues Victorians dreaded. Moreover, we have immensely more hope of finding medical solutions to the problem before it becomes a massive epidemic killing millions. Yet already we have hysterical proclamations in the news media.

It now seems likely that even the modernist interpretation of the famous Victorian dread of masturbation is more an expression of the modernist dread of the myth of Victorianism than anything else (Hare, 1962; MacDonald, 1967; Robinson, 1976, pp. 11-15 ff.). Victorians were actually highly divided in their opinions about masturbation. Havelock Ellis's own work on the subject, *Studies in the Psychology of Sex* (1936, vol. 1), drew on many earlier sources that took all possible positions on it. It was quite common for doctors to claim that the symptoms of paresis and other forms of madness could be caused by masturbation and this was why they and the general public became anxious about masturbation, not only in the more repressive Britain and the United States, but also in the less repressive European nations. This delusion might well have been the result of a simple correlation between the observation of masturbation and the observation of the symptoms of paresis and madness. Both governments and private groups began to build insane asylums in the eighteenth century and greatly expanded these in the nineteenth. As a result, psychiatrists attending the patients could for the first time observe cases of "madmen," including those with the psychotic and paralyzing symptoms of syphilitic paresis, in all of their daily activities. In the mental institutions of the day, the patients had no privacy. Moreover, they were systematically denied sexual intercourse (just as they are today, at least officially). As a result, mental patients were for the first time observable in all their sexual activities and they undoubtedly resorted to masturbation for both sexual outlets and for general self-reassurance. (Havelock Ellis noted that masturbation was the most observed form of autoeroticism because doctors observed it in extreme form in insanity and allied conditions; 1936, vol. 1, p. 163.) Thus, for the first time ever, doctors directly observed people masturbating on a massive scale and the people they saw doing so were insane and often paralytic. There was a very high correlation in this biased sample and their inference of a causal relation is hardly surprising in view of their general lack of knowledge of statistical sampling and the problems of inferring social causality. Once convinced by such faulty research methods that they had discovered a cause of madness and paralysis, even the most dedicated autoeroticist would probably urge the world to stop masturbating—and try to kick the habit. Even the revolutionary Havelock Ellis (1936, vol. 1) admitted masturbation could cause nervousness, though he systematically shows that the evidence of worse effects was completely false. Nevertheless, he apparently kicked the habit. The "revolutionary" Freud was convinced as late as 1893 that masturbation almost invariably led to neurosis.

THE SEXUAL REVOLUTIONARIES

The euphemisms and squeamishness in which nineteenth-century writers cloaked their works on sex published for the general public were only intensifications of the censorship of "obscenity" that was generally practiced in Christian nations, with considerable variations from one era and locale to another. The Victorian middle classes merely went further than most earlier Christians in beating their breastplate of righteousness. But an episodic exaggeration hardly constituted a revolution of sexual repression. Publications for the general public had for centuries been carefully censored, normally by Church celibates who were careful to purify everything in sight. (This was probably a result of the stigmatic warfare of the Reformation. Medieval Europe was pretty free of official sexual censorship. See Bullough and Brundage, 1982.) Even in the bawdy age of eighteenth-century France, Rousseau was ordered by the lieutenant of police in Paris to cease reading the manuscript of his *Confessions* to small audiences in private salons and it was not published until long after his death; yet his confessions are prudish by the standards of underground Victorian novels (such as the "autobiographical" tomes of *My Secret Life*, Anonymous, 1966) and not so sexual as some scenes in some Thomas Hardy novels published above ground. (There is little comparison at all with legal publications in France in the nineteenth century. Even *Madame Bovary* was declared legal.) Scientific studies were almost never repressed until they were seen to be part of a revolutionary movement and even then what could not be published in Britain could often be published in the United States. By the height of the Victorian era, the respectable medical journals were routinely publishing articles on almost every form of sexual activity, including homosexual anal intercourse, with little squeamishness.

It was not so much the average Victorians who changed their sexual behavior or their behavior toward sexual activities by others. They continued responding within the range of variability normal for Christians over the centuries. They became anxious about sexual promiscuity, especially prostitution, with far better reason than Americans who are doing so today. They became deeply fearful of some forms of sexuality, especially masturbation, for the same wrong reasons Americans have recently been so filled with dread of all contacts with the victims of AIDS.

What changed was the explosion in the number of sexual revolutionaries and their apparent threat to 1500 years of Western cultural traditions, especially the entire complex of Augustinian Christian traditions about the Erotic and love. The sexual revolutionaries normally, though by no means always, carefully presented fronts of scientific objectivity and were normally cautious in their proposals for reform. The strong reactions against the utopian socialist sexual revolutionaries showed how dangerous sexual revolution could be. But the facts are that they were often extremely revolutionary in their goals, that the most dedicated and influential of them were often stigmatized violators of the ancient rules they sought to overturn, that much of their "scientific" evidence presented to promote the revolutionary goals was not scientific, and that at least some of their opponents rightly suspected these facts.

Freud was the least revolutionary of them in his actual pronouncements and may have been a secret Victorian, but there is plenty of evidence of his secretiveness and deviousness (Sulloway, 1983; Masson, 1985; Malcolm, 1984) to justify suspicions he may have been secretly extremely revolutionary. William McGrath's (1986) argument that Viennese political realities, including virulent anti-Semitism, drove Freud into his inner life as an escape may be true, but, if so, Freud's youthful political radicalism returned from the netherworld to inspire a theory that was profoundly subversive of traditional Western values and practices. As Peter Gay, a Freudian devotee, has said: "Freud was an irreproachable bourgeois who fashioned for himself an unmistakable bourgeois environment but who, at the same time, developed theories about human nature and human conduct as subversive as any set of ideas in history" (1978, p. 60). Aside from the immense subversiveness of such ideas as the universality of the Oedipal syndrome of incestuous lust, Freud offered mankind a claustrophobically dismal picture of human life trapped between murderous rage and suicidal self-hatred, with no hope of redemption and salvation.

Havelock Ellis, who was by far the best scholar, scientist, and writer of them all, clearly fell into this revolutionary pattern, though he was only moderately subversive by comparison with Freud, whose theory of incest he firmly rejected. He was himself an extreme fetishist (a devotee of "golden showers"—that is, urination), impotent with his lesbian wife, and a sufferer from premature ejaculation (Grosskurth, 1985). He knew very well that he was revolting against the Christian tradition, and not simply against some supposed repressiveness of Victorians, but he could hardly be expected to announce this fact. The entire success of the revolution hinged on hiding this revolt against Christianity, for any widespread recognition that this was their goal would certainly have led to a far more massive counterrevolution against them.

In her recent biography of Ellis, Phyllis Grosskurth (1985) has revealed letters exchanged between Ellis and Bronislaw Malinowski, one of the moderate leaders of the modernist movement in anthropology. Exhorting Malinowski not to "cringe to the obscene mob" (p. 382), Ellis insisted it is

> quite necessary, as you say, to avoid any temptation to shock, "épater le bourgeois", because, although it may be good for *him*, it prevents oneself being taken seriously. . . . I seek to express the shocking things in a quiet, suave, matter-of-course way, sugar-coating the pill. (Some of my shocking things have never been discovered!). . . . Only when used, it must not be visible [pp. 384-385]!

Malinowski agreed wholeheartedly with Ellis, and when Ellis saw Malinowski's manuscript for *The Sexual Life of Savages* (1929), he wrote: "I shall begin to suspect that you are a moralist in disguise and that you aim to follow up Diderot with a 'Deuxième Supplement au Voyage de Bougainville'" (p. 384). Diderot's work became a rallying cry in the late eighteenth- and early nineteenth-century sexual revolution, though he might have been shocked by this.

Ellis knew his fellow sexual modernist well, but he did not expose Malinowski's "disguised" purpose in the preface he wrote to *The Sexual Life of Savages* (1929). Instead, he extolled "the scientific outfit, the sensitive intelligence, the patience in observation, the sympathetic insight" (p. x) of Malinowski and concluded in sugarcoated terms, "We may even find that in some respects the savage had here reached a finer degree of civilization than the civilized man" (p. xiii). In what respects had they reached a finer degree of civilization? Surely not in their stigmatization of masturbators as "idiots" (p. 470); nor in the branding of homosexuals, bestialists, fetishists, and exhibitionists as "bad" and "fools" (p. 469); nor in their "supreme" taboo against showing the slightest affection between brother and sister (pp. 518-520 ff.); nor in their generally "sluggish" sexual feelings that are much less than

Western man's (pp. 476-477); nor in their "keen sense of delicacy" about sex that makes roundabout allusions to it natural (p. 283); nor in their usually less intimate marriages and frequent jealous conflicts, wife-batterings, "Puritanical" public pronouncements, and chiefly polygamy (pp. 109-132 ff.); nor in their usually tragic sense of sex lives (p. 283).

What "aspect" of their sex lives could the modernist Ellis possibly have seen as more "advanced"? The only possibility was their greater sexual *casualness*, especially in early adolescence, the complement of their less intimate love at that time, which corresponds roughly to the period of "boy craziness" and "girl craziness" of the early teens today. Sexual casualness was the very heart of the modernist sexual revolution and anything that seemed to advance that cause was likely to be seen as "advanced," "progressive," and "civilized." Malinowski's factual reports on the Trobriand Islanders did not really fit the modernist picture of casual sexual bliss, but he did not reject their misinterpretations, except in the matter of Freud's specific theory of the universality of the Oedipal syndrome, which he firmly rejected (see Spiro, 1982). By his silence, Malinowski lent his considerable professional reputation to the mass media modernists who used the "scientific" evidence of anthropology to "prove" there is nothing in human nature to prevent our achieving a casual sexual utopia.

There were many other anthropologists anxious to support the modernists actively through proclamations in the mass media. Margaret Mead launched her career in 1928 as the spokeswoman of the casual utopia with the publication of *Coming of Age in Samoa*, which became the most famous and widely read of all anthropological works. As early as 1934, J. D. Unwin showed that Mead was wrong about the Samoans, quite confused, and was merely repeating earlier errors (1934, pp. 64-65). His massive review in *Sex and Culture* of all the major evidence available led him to conclude that Erotic ritualism, sexual moderation, and repression—not sexual casualness—are universal in civilizations and possibly so in all but the most "savage" societies. This massive work was totally shunned by professionals and journalists (as noted by Pitirim Sorokin, 1956, pp. 108-110).

After decades of students had been trained to believe in Mead's bright visions of a casual sexual utopia, and to believe they too could vault into bliss by merely joining the growing ranks of the sexual modernists, Freeman (1983) showed in minute detail what Unwin had noted in 1934. The anthropologists could not deny the basic truth of his indictment, but they almost unanimously attacked the messenger of these sad facts of the abuse of science, not the perpetrators. Freeman was soundly attacked for having misinterpreted Boas's works done 75 years before, while complicity in the miseducation of a whole civilization for 50 years about the cornerstones of human nature was excused as unfortunate but understandable. Anyone taking up the cudgels against the Victorian "repressiveness" could hardly do any wrong, and no amount of evidence would save those who disagreed. The most balanced appraisals of the controversy agree with much of Freeman's argument about Mead's study of Samoa, show that he in turn made mistakes, especially about Boas, but do not consider the modernist illusions that Mead did so much to advance through the mass media (see Levy, 1983, 1984).

THE FREUDIAN AND
BEHAVIORIST REVOLUTIONARIES

Creating a vivid and plausible image of the evil repressor was a vital tactic in unleashing the revolution against the ancient regime of Christian love, intimacy, and sex. But, just as in the great political revolutions of our century, the creation of this stigmatic image had to be complemented and potentiated by many other tactics. None was more crucial to the success of sexual modernism than the creation and purveying of a sexual-newspeak in which sacred and powerful words with ancient meanings were expropriated, their ancient meanings poured out, and revolutionary new meanings poured into the sacred ancient symbols. *Sex*, or "sexuality" in the modernist sense of mere physical biological desire and action, was apparently first used by the utopian socialist Charles Fourier and was adopted by revolutionaries to replace the ancient Erotic with the merely physical. The sexual modernists progressively appropriated the ancient words of "love" and transmuted them by the magic of "scientific" rhetoric into *sex*, devoid of any form of love. The Freudians and the vastly more popular pseudo-Freudians of the mass media—the most powerful cultural assault force of the modernist movement—stole the most sacred words of all love vocabularies—"mother and child love"—and transmuted them into "incestuous lust." (Theodore Reik, 1944, analyzed Freud's "magnificent mistake." Bruno Bettelheim, 1983, has shown how Freud's mistake was vastly magnified by the purposeful English mistranslations in which *Eros* was transmuted into *sex*.)

Most competent members of our culture today are still able to distinguish different types of love. Most people do not really think that a three-year-old's love for his mother is the *same* as a nineteen-year-old's romantic lust for his date. But these distinctions must now be made by specifying the context or else by linguistic elaborations. The word *love* standing alone, without any context specified, now denotes sexual love and even has a powerful connotation of plain and simple "sex." *Making love* means "making sex," with or without any love feelings distinct from sexual feelings. Today, even a ten-minute "trick" between a prostitute and a "John" is routinely referred to as "making love," by newsmen, not by prostitutes. Eros has been transmuted by cognitive castration into a mechanistic twitching of genitalia and *erotic* often refers to films or books pervaded by murderous sexual assaults, the exact opposite of the creative drive that is the soul of Eros. Today, most people take these things for granted and assume it has always been so in our culture. This is the opposite of the truth and hides one of the many cognitive crimes of our tortured century.

We shall see in the next chapter that the experiences of love have been very problematic—"mysteries"—for all human beings, and we shall explain that this is because there are many overlapping dimensions of love experience that interact in vastly complex ways that no one has yet been able to present in rational analyses. The great complexity of total love experiences has led some peoples to make very clear and categorical linguistic distinctions among the major permutations and combinations of these dimensions. (The American Indians were reported to make linguistic distinctions among approximately 600 types of love experience. See Daniel Brinton, 1886.) In Western cultures, it was commonplace, especially for those with any education, to distinguish four major types of love: filial love (between parents and children), friendly love (*philia*), godly love (*agape*), and Erotic love—the primeval urge to unite in the creation of embodied Being (see Rougemont, 1940, 1963, especially pp. 3-38; Maurois, 1944; Hunt, 1959; Lewis, 1960; May, 1969; Norton, 1970; Tennov, 1979).

Though these linguistic distinctions certainly made it easier for them to keep clearly in mind the different forms of love experience intended than our current impoverished love-talk does, this was not a very detailed set of linguistic categories. Possibilities of confusion seem always to have lurked in our love language. (We shall elaborate on this below and in Chapter 6.) But in earlier centuries, the word *love* itself denoted and connoted a predominance of nonsexual experience and certainly not what we would now call "sex" (the feelings and actions of sexual lust divorced from anything else). This does not mean that they did not experience lust devoid of love and devoid of the rest of the Erotic. We shall see in succeeding chapters (especially Chapter 2) that the available evidence indicates that the basic emotions of human beings are universal. This linguistic difference indicates a very great difference in the ways of thinking about these emotional experiences and this difference has helped to produce differences in actions. Specifically, our relative lack of categorical distinctions is a linguistic index of our strong tendency to confuse love with sex, to reduce all of love and the Erotic to sex, and greatly encourages this confusion and sexual reductionism.

The sexual modernists were by no means the only cultural force acting to bring about this love confusion and sexual reductionism. The Social Darwinists and behavioral psychologists greatly reinforced the sexual modernists' ideas about sex. Operating on the reductionist idea that mating, thus "perpetuating the species," is all our biological life is concerned with, the Social Darwinists commonly saw sex as the only reality and the vastly complex emotional experiences of "love" as rationalizations and cultural myths of Christianity. Freudians of the mass media then combined this behavioristic and biologistic assumption with the Freudian idea of the sublimation of repressed libido to argue that any ideas of romantic love, enduring commitments of the self, and the Erotic are mere sublimations of repressed sexuality—that is, neurotic symptoms (see Marcuse, 1966).

The modernist works made scrupulous and extreme use of all the rhetoric of science, ranging from the biologism of the Freudians to the statistical tables of Kinsey's "outlets," and the sex labs of Masters and Johnson. This made them look morally respectable and gave their work the aura of absolutely objective truth. Certainly many of the more empirically based and commonsensical ideas in Freud's work are true and were greatly improved by his creative analyses. But his general model of human nature, and especially the unique aspects of it such as the Oedipal conflict, were neither true nor treated by him and his followers in a scientific way. Rather, they were treated as a sacred canon to be defended against infidels and heretics by beating the breastplate of scientific righteousness. Many historians have noted this extreme disjunction between the Freudian rhetoric of biologism and the realities of their actual methods and procedures (Sulloway, 1983). Paul Johnson has summed up this indictment:

As Sir Peter Medawar has put it, psychoanalysis is akin to Mesmerism and phrenology: it contains isolated nuggets of truth, but the general theory is false.

Moreover, as the young Karl Popper correctly noted at the time, Freud's attitude to scientific proof was very different to Einstein's and more akin to Marx's. Far from formulating his theories with a high degree of specific content which invited empirical testing and refutation, Freud made them all-embracing and difficult to test at all. And, like Marx's followers, when evidence did turn up which appeared to refute them, he modified the theories to accommodate it. Thus the Freudian corpus of belief was subject to continual expansion and osmosis, like a religious system in its formative period. As one would expect, internal critics, like Jung, were treated as heretics; external ones, like Havelock Ellis, as infidels. Freud betrayed signs, in fact, of the twentieth-century messianic ideologue at his worst, namely, a persistent tendency to regard those who diverged from him as themselves unstable and in need of treatment. Thus Ellis's sublimated form of "resistance." "My inclination," he wrote to Jung just before their break, "is to treat those colleagues who offer resistance exactly as we treat patients in the same situation." Two decades later, the notion of regarding dissent as a form of mental sickness, suitable for compulsory hospitalization, was to blossom in the Soviet Union into a new form of political repression [Johnson, 1983, p. 6].

The early sexologists set the scientistic tone by hiding their own vested interests and real goals behind fronts of scientistic rhetoric. Freud carried these measures to something of an extreme with his austere, Victorian model of the aloof scientist who was, it was supposed, so uninvolved with his patients that they could not even see him while he probed their souls to find ways to release and summon forth the sexual energy (the libido) that had been damned up by the Victorian Repressors. It now appears from the records that are slowly leaking out of the secret Freud archives (Masson, 1985; Malcolm, 1984) that Freud did not really act in this way at all. If he had, he probably would have been a dismal failure as a therapist. Recent revelations by one of his patients, Princess Marie Bonaparte, show that he dealt with her in a very friendly manner, exchanging intimate details of his own life for hers and generally behaving in ways that lately would have gotten him excommunicated from the professional sanctum (see New York Times News Service, 1985). But the aloof, cold, totally objective pose was a vital part of the myth of the scientific hero. And hiding the "scientific" records, in an inner sanctum closed to everyone not initiated into the official sect, was vital to protecting Olympian truths.

The ancient and universal myth of the hero was the cultural archetype on which this scientific myth was built (Campbell, 1968). Frank Sulloway (1983) has shown in massive detail how Freud and his disciples carefully constructed this myth of the hero, partly by conscious design (such as Freud's twice burning all of his papers and correspondences with scientific colleagues to hide the roots of his great "discoveries") and partly by unconscious inspiration springing from the cultural archetype of the hero available to us all. Like all heroes, Freud was presented as the lonely man of courage who faced almost insuperable odds and conquered by the force of his will. Most accounts of this hero portray his descent into the netherworld of his own unconscious through his self-analysis, his desperate and nearly fatal struggle with his inner demons, and his wresting of the truth from his own entrails. When he returned to the upper world of rational discourse, he brought with him almost all of the distinctive ideas of his later theories. As Sulloway has shown, Freud actually took these ideas from earlier works by other people, and when he entered his netherworld he merely carried them with him to give them a more heroic birth scene. (Havelock Ellis traced these sources in minute detail because he resented having his ideas and those of his predecessors expropriated.) But none of that was known to most of those who believed and worshipped the myth of this hero.

Entrusting the myth to a Freudian Church was also a vital factor in its success. The devoted disciples provided pseudoindependent sources of testimony on behalf of the myth, thereby helping to convince others of its truth. The Freudian chorus became a wondrous source of miraculous revelations for the mass media and they in turn were bathed in glory by the mass media accounts of their closeness to the hero. No sycophantic account of the greatness of a prophet outshone the glowing accounts of Freud by the disciples of the pantheon. To this day, they are protecting the hero's papers from rude assaults by nonbelievers (Masson, 1985; Malcolm, 1984).

Far more important than all of these factors, however, was the relative simplicity and sweeping universality of Freud's theory that made it easily salable by mass mediation in the first age of the mass media before people understood how the mass media work. The controversial-yet-respectable angle of Freud's theory gave it access to the mass media and gave it great potential for catching the mass attention at least briefly. (It is this attention-getting potential of the controversial-yet-respectable that led journalists to make it a standard "angle" for their stories. See Altheide, 1976.) But it could never hold that attention for long, and thus could not continue to get mass media attention, without being simple and striking, even shocking, yet scientifically respectable. The same has always been true of scientific theories, and this imperative of mass opinion is one crucial reason why even inherently more simple ideas, like Newton's theory of gravity, have almost always been remembered in terms of absurdly simplistic myths, such as the myth of the apple falling on Newton's head. (All myths operate in this way. In political myths, for example, a very simple and striking incident comes to stand for a man's entire character. Thus George Washington's character becomes symbolized by telling the truth about chopping down a cherry tree and Honest Abe's by walking miles to return pennies.) Freud's theory was simple by comparison with those of his major competitors, such as those of Havelock Ellis, especially when it is noted that Freud presented his theory as an explanation of almost everything of importance in all societies for all times (see Robinson, 1976, pp. 40-41).

Yet Freud's theory did not go too far. It is simple, but, as Popper and Johnson argued, not so simple as to be falsifiable by scientific research. There are enough pieces to Freud's theories and his methods of analysis are flexible and complex enough that anyone very tempted to believe in them, not to mention any true believer, can always find a way to stretch them to fit almost anything. (Fisher and Greenberg, 1977, have done this on a comprehensive scale.) Popular psychohistorians have now spun out enough "pop-Freudian" analyses of the most diverse phenomena and individuals throughout history to make Freudian theory look like a "monomyth," that is, a myth that pervades an entire culture (Jewett and Lawrence, 1977). Like all such monomyths, the pop-Freudian secular religion of sexual liberation could never have achieved its success without being simple enough to be dramatized in the mass media of the day.

Freud would now hasten to remind us that behind every myth there is a wish and in this instance he would be entirely right. The great source of energy inspiring mass faith in the Freudian myth was the millennial craving for ecstasy in this world. As Bruno Bettelheim (1983) and others have shown, Freud's own ideas about sex were partly grounded in traditional, even conservative ideas and were ultimately tragic for civilized man. (They, however, overlook or downplay the crucial role of biologism and mechanistic behaviorism in Freud's work, in spite of the important part these played in leading to the heresies and excommunications of his most brilliant disciples, especially Rank, Reik, Adler, and

Jung; see Roazen, 1975; Sulloway, 1983.) Freud believed civilization itself is not possible without some moderate degree of repression and repression inevitably means neurotic conflict, suffering, and symptom formation (including the valuable sublimations known as the creations of civilization). Freud himself declared, near the end of his life, "My discoveries are a basis for a very grave philosophy" (Sulloway, 1983, p. 439). Just as the ideas of Christianity were stripped of most of their more gloomy aspects—such as Augustine's predestination, by which all but the few elect were doomed to eternal damnation—and sold through the mass media of the Church in a much simplified and jollied-up version, so did Freud's later disciples and the mass media conspire with the cravings of modern peoples for a secular millennium to strip grim Freudianism down to a model of "pop-Freudianism" that promised sexual ecstasy for one and all, with no bad afterthoughts of guilt or jealousy.

As Frank Sulloway (1983) has noted, one of the most remarkable aspects of the whole transformation of Freudian theory was the way in which his biological determinism was denied and replaced with a thoroughgoing environmental determinism in which inherited, constitutional characteristics played almost no role. And the most remarkable aspect of this is that Freud's own ideas became more and more biologically deterministic as his work progressed, while the social interpretations of them increasingly saw them as based on an assumption of environmental, cultural determinism (Sulloway, 1983, pp. 437 ff.). Freud apparently conspired in this transmutation to some extent, at least by not opposing the misinterpretations, but it was his later disciples who carefully interpreted them in this way for the mass media and, hence, for the public (see Bettelheim, 1983). In doing so, they were only repackaging the psychoanalytic product to meet a growing public clamor for cultural determinism, cultural relativism, and, hence, for a revolution that would transport mankind into a utopia of sexual bliss.

As long as Freud's theory was seen to be built on a foundation of Darwinian and pre-Darwinian Vitalist assumptions about inherited characteristics and stages of development, it could hardly support the growing craving for a sexual millennium. The more sexuality is inherited, the less change can be expected. Anyone hoping to produce a sexual millennium would obviously have to have a successful revolution against man's entire history and this sexual revolution could only be successful if there were no hereditary bounds to human sexual possibilities. Freud's model of the human psyche was overwhelmingly grounded in the Darwinian model of inherited characteristics that could change only very slowly over millennia (Sulloway, 1983). His works, such as *Totem and Taboo* (1953-1974e), made it obvious that he believed his model of human nature applied to all human beings and thus had to spring from universal biological heritage.

The most powerful of the "pop-Freudian" shibboleths in the service of the sexual revolution proved to be (1) the reduction of all human motivation and energy to sexual libido, (2) the Vitalistic-Freudian doctrine of the destructive consequences of repressing the sexual libido too much, and (3) the cultural and individual relativism of sexual morality, emotion, and action. Freud's reduction of all desire to that of sexual lust is ultimately grounded in an ancient Western, Augustinian model of desire that involves some rather complex ideas and an overriding linguistic confusion (see Augustine's analysis of "libido" in *The City of God*, 1950, Bk. XIV, chap. 15, p. 464). The ancient model and the Freudian model derived from it are actually grounded in powerful and complex ideas about the creative life forces believed by Western peoples to permeate all of being and ultimately to flow from and yet remain coterminous with God. (The same basic ideas are found in the ideas of magical forces and magical shamanism that appear to be part of human heritage in all cultures. An excellent example is found in Richard Katz's analysis of *Boiling Energy*, 1985, among the bushmen of the Kalahari.) As we noted, the classical Western ideas were commonly called Eros. They are the forces of life-giving, of creating and propagating in general. What is now called "sex" is only one important part of this whole complex of creative, vitalizing energies. In Freud's day, the classical ideas were known at least vaguely by almost any educated person. The so-called maternal and paternal drives are even more powerful dimensions of Eros in most people. And the general lust to create, to explore, to build, and to expand are other dimensions that become more powerful as the sexual and parental cravings are fulfilled. The ancient ideas became the foundation in a simplified and rationalistic form for the model of Vitalism, which permeated nineteenth century psychology, but they were also revived in most of their original form in works such as those of Henri Bergson on the "vital force" (*élan vital*) and Friedrich Nietzsche on the Dionysian. Freud's idea of the libido was really very much that of Nietzsche's Dionysian, but translated into the language of biological determinism. As his model developed, he became more and more concerned with the opposition between the struggle between the amalgamated forces of the life-urge, or Eros, and the death-urge, or Thanatos, which finally led to a religio-poetic vision of this universal struggle between good and evil that was remarkably like the ancient Manichaean dualism that had inspired Augustine and pervaded some of Nietzsche's work. Most of Freud's ideas are bio-logistic translations of Nietzsche's poetic-philosophical insights. Lou Salome was the direct personal link between Nietzsche and Freud's work after 1911. In 1909, she published a Nietzschean work, *The Erotic* (see Heller, 1966; Pfeiffer, 1972; Binion, 1968; Reik, 1944).

Freud's open-ended extension of the term *sex* to all forms of desire, that is, to the entire "libido," was one of the most powerful opening wedges in the modernist transformation of Western thinking about love. In doing so, he at least maintained—at times—some of the meaning of Eros in his conception of Eros-libido. But the later sexual modernists found many ways to drive the wedge ever deeper into our collective consciousness. Some of his own disciples did so by draining Eros of all meaning other than "skin sensations," thereby producing neo-Freudian sexual behaviorism. The sharpest wedge was the method of rigid experimental controls and statistical analyses imposed by behaviorists on the study of "sexual outlets" and physiology. Freud himself had done the exact opposite. He insisted that the truth about the deepest human emotional experience could only be gotten by allowing the patient to talk about whatever she felt was important—"free association." He was attacked by medical experimentalists for supposedly reverting to methods of everyday life. (He was actually carrying on the phenom-enological methods developed by Franz Brentano. See McGrath, 1986.) The sexual revolutionaries who came after him were even more keenly aware of the tremendous power of the rhetoric of "hard science" in our society, presumably because the power of this rhetoric was growing. They made use of ever-more rigidly experimental methods of studying sex, including those of questionnaire surveys and the sex labs. Their methods thus progressively eliminated almost everything but the physiology of genital sex and other "erotogenic" zones from their studies.

Alfred Kinsey (1948, 1953) asked questions and analyzed their answers statistically in ways that *assumed* that *all* forms of "sexual outlets" are scientifically equivalent and that any other meanings, values, emotional powers, consequences, or everything else associated with "outlets" is irrelevant to the science of sex. (Kinsey was an entomologist who had spent his entire earlier career studying wasps. He simply applied his methods of studying wasp mating to human beings.

This sexual reductionist program was applied, though less relentlessly, to other animals and other human cultures by F. A. Beach, C. S. Ford, and their many collaborators. See Ford and Beach, 1951; Beach, 1965, 1977.) In his behavioristic metaphysics, the number of orgasmic "outlets" alone has *any* meaning. His revolutionary zeal knew no bounds. His casual pronouncement on animalism shows this assumption carried to the extreme: "The elements that are involved in sexual contacts between the human and animals of other species are at no point basically different from those that are involved in erotic responses to human situations" (Kinsey, 1948, pp. 676-677).

What could be more logical? Once nothing else has *any* meaning, *any* relevance, then "erotic" bestiality is exactly the same as the Erotic love between a human couple intent on creating a new human being to love and develop. Sex is no longer even meaningful as the basis of "mating" and "reproducing." Logically, there is no difference between human outlets and the stickleback who blindly emits sperm into the water when perceptual cues trigger his automatic response. In Kinsey's metaphysics, Havelock Ellis's orgasmic responses to urination are every bit as "Erotic" as "making love" with a dog, or, presumably, the raping of a human infant.

Kinsey recognized, five years after stating this position, that its logical conclusion could have unfortunate consequences, such as making mass sadism conceptually equivalent to all other "outlets" among "consenting" adults (1953, p. 476). This, however, was only a temporary lapse from the courageous stance of pure science devoid of humanistic concerns. After all, if "consent" is necessary, then expressed "intention" becomes a modifier of "outlets" and the floodgates of subjectivity would be breached. Kinsey recoiled from such a breach of pure scientism. As Paul Robinson (1976, p. 118) concluded:

> Not only did Kinsey lack Freud's sense of the demonic element in human sexuality, he was also as untainted by romanticism as any major sexual theorist we can think of, with the possible exception of the Marquis de Sade. Not even Masters and Johnson approach his purity in this regard. Indeed, no one else has more consistently associated sexual experiences with dispassion.

William Masters and Virginia Johnson (1966, 1970) do not focus their attention as relentlessly on "outlets," partly because their medical focus on sexual dysfunction led them to see that "outlets" can become highly problematic. But their method of studying sex in sex labs is even more relentlessly behavioristic and reductionist than Kinsey's precoded and presupposed interview method in isolating sex from every possible form of love and intimacy. Their behavioristic experimental method involves the study of sexual "outlets" in a laboratory setting in which the sexual "subjects" are carefully and minutely watched by a team of scientist-voyeurs, filmed for posterity, and their physiological responses (or unresponsiveness) recorded by electrodes attached to the sex organs and other parts of the body. Needless to say, they got an extremely biased sample of sexual gladiators who self-selected for these studies. But that bias seems small by comparison with the other effects of the method. However useful the sex lab may be for studying sexual physiology, it is almost inconceivable that this public sex-arena could become the scene for exhibiting loving, intimate, or Erotic acts. The method excludes from study anything but the physiology of sex as found in sexual gladiators. Sex in and for scientific observation is guaranteed by the method of the sex lab, in spite of their occasional references to the importance of lasting and loving relationships. In that particular situation, masturbation is probably the most satisfying sexual activity, because it is the least embarrassing—and possibly the only form of sexual outlet some sexual gladiators can manage in the arena. That is exactly what they found:

> Understandably, the maximum physiologic intensity of orgasmic response subjectively reported or objectively recorded has been achieved by self regulated mechanical or auto-manipulative techniques. The next highest level of erotic intensity has resulted from partner manipulation, again with established or self-regulated methods, and the lowest intensity of target-organ response was achieved during coition [Masters and Johnson, 1966, pp. 63-64, 133].

THE SEXUAL
MODERNIST CONFUSION

Among the most educated, sexual modernism transformed the fundamental ideas and meanings of our ancient language for talking about love, intimacy, and sex. It took the words and phrases of everyday life, which had accreted meanings over millennia of practical experience, scornfully emptied out those rich meanings, and poured in the newspeak of casual sex. This modernist sexual newspeak cut away all the ideas of profound mystery, passion, intimate communings, and of self-fusion and commitment embodied in our ancient language of love and Eros. *Love* itself was transformed into a three letter word—sex— and sex became in behaviorist and neo-Freudian behaviorist terms "a peculiarly pleasurable sensitivity of the skin to the self- or other manipulation" (Grosskurth, 1985, p. 409). As Freudian Marie Jahoda thus concluded, "Any apparent reason for requiring a partner of the other sex drops away" (Grosskurth, 1985, p. 409). And the path leads straight to Masters and Johnson's revolutionary discovery that in the sex lab the electrode-linked bodies find their ultimate "ecstasy" in self-masturbation. Freud took some of the biggest steps down this drab and dusty path to repressing all the ancient commonsense truth about love, intimacy, and sex and replacing it with modernist sex-talk. But, as Bettelheim has argued (1983), even his language and ideas were purposefully and systematically mistranslated more easily to pour the new and deadening wine of sexual modernism into them.

The result of this cognitive transformation has not been to revolutionize our ancient cravings for love and intimacy. Rather, it has produced a pervasive and monstrous misunderstanding and confusion among the most miseducated about some of the simplest realities of love and has made it nearly impossible for those drilled in this modernist newspeak to understand the vast complexities of life built on those simple cornerstones. It is common today to find college students who think they are merely having a casual sexual affair when in fact they are very much in-love and to find people who think they are no longer in-love because the "thrill" is gone when in fact they are extremely fused with the other and care frantically for them. These people often make terrible mistakes that produce love-agony all around, not because they are really unloving or crave Freud's polymorphous perversity or Kinsey's bestiality, but because they have been misled by the myths of sexual modernism into a morass of love-confusion. Maxine Schnall's confessions (1981) of her own descent into this modernist confusion and misery is probably the best yet done. Her opening cry greatly exaggerates the scope of the problem (because she did not discount the sampling error inspired by living in New York City) but strikes the pure chord of the modernist love-confusion:

> *Where did we go wrong?* I hear that question from everyone these days, as if we are all victims of a massive shipwreck. Awash in the debris of our cultural values, the survivors struggle to keep from drowning in a limitless sea of options.

Desperately lonely people in bars and discos search hungrily for intimacy and find only another dreary one-night connection. Joyless pleasure-seekers and self-improvers obsessively take courses, quaaludes, cocaine, EST, Life Spring, silicone injections and trips to Club Med in a vain attempt to dispel their inner emptiness [Schnall, 1981, p. 3].

In retrospect, she realizes that her revolt against "Victorianism" and her reliance on misunderstandings of experts was a crucial mistake:

Somewhere past the straits of Victorianism on our way to the brave new world, we went out of control. We disregarded the navigator in our heads yelling "No! Don't! You can't!" because some of us were sick of hearing those words all of our lives, and the rest of us, having never heard them didn't know what they meant. So we crashed through the boundaries of freedom and sailed into chaos.

The crash had been coming for a long time. As our quest for personal and sexual freedom gathered momentum in the Sixties, it set us on a blind collision course between rising permissiveness and collapsing values. Our biggest mistake, other than our gross misapplication of Freudian concepts, was in thinking of human freedom as a thing apart from our connectedness to a world order [p. 4].

She also recognizes that her exclusive pursuit of the thrills led unknowingly to a destruction of loving intimacy and communion:

With gratification as our only guide, the sexual revolution fails to promote greater intimacy but separates people from genuine contact and becomes a revelation in mutual masturbation [p. 6].

The thrills quickly evaporated and left her with the miserable realization that,

in the seventies, I fell under the spell of the myth of romantic divorce: It led me to believe that I had found the final solution to all problems in relationship.... For myself, I can say only this. Despite the discrepancy of interests and the discordance of roles, the glue that held my former husband and me together in the good old days of our marriage has become almost irreplaceable in our culture as it is today. If I could have that back again with a new partner—that same constancy, that same self-less devotion—I would *never*, not for a galaxy of moments of passion, trade it in again [pp. 301-304].

2

LEARNING TO LOVE/
NOT TO LOVE

We are moulded and remoulded by those who have loved us; and, though
the love may pass, we are nevertheless their work, for good or ill.

François Mauriac

All such interaction, it is well to remember, is accompanied by the
strongest of feelings and emotions, happy or reverse. When interaction
between a couple runs smoothly, each party manifests intense pleasure in
the other's company, and especially in the other's expressions of affection.
Conversely, whenever interaction results in persistent conflict each party
is likely on occasion to exhibit intense anxiety or unhappiness, especially
when the other is rejecting . . . the internal standards against which the
consequences of behaviour are appraised by both mother and child are
such as strongly to favour the development of attachment: for proximity
and affectionate interchange are appraised and felt as pleasurable by both
whereas distance and expressions of rejection are appraised and felt as
disagreeable or painful by both. For no other standards of appraisal in
man are more clearcut from the start, or more environmentally stable. So
stable indeed are they as a rule that for babies it is taken for granted as
intrinsic to human nature. As a result, whenever during the development
of some individual these standards become markedly different from the
norm, as occasionally they do, all are disposed to judge the conditions as
pathological.

John Bowlby

There is love, or whatever we call that group of sentiments which
surround the biological need for intercourse. A [Lesu] woman in love is

lost to the world; she neglects her everyday duties, and thinks and dreams of no one except the beloved. All of which is not so different from the picture of a woman in love in any other part of the world. Beside love and passion, there is also affection, which is seen in the relationship between mates, and which comes out so clearly in times of illness or other crises. Thus in the sexual life of these Melanesians occurs the interplay of instincts, emotions, and sentiments which appear to be universal.

Hortense Powdermaker, on the Lesu

The young mother approaches her baby with outstretched arms. He hears her coming and immediately turns his head toward her. His eyes lock onto hers and they both smile faintly. He throws his arms up toward her as she reaches down and swoops him up. She holds him up and stares into his eyes with the looks of joy, excitement, and adoration. They both begin cooing and babbling. She serenades him with the rhythmic, high-pitched but low and tender voice of the universal baby talk. Then she cuddles him to her soft, warm body and begins rocking him back and forth, intermittently cooing, gurgling, babbling, singing, laughing, and sometimes "tearing up" with joy.

What's going on here? You know immediately what it all means, the mother knows, and even the one-year-old baby knows, all without ever uttering one meaningful word. The mother and baby are loving each other. Putting it as precisely as we can in language, the mother and her son are *adoring* each other completely in the *primal scene of loving*. (Stern, 1977, gives detailed case descriptions of various "styles" of these mother-baby duets.) *Adoring love* is one of the most powerful and enduring of all the positive human emotions and one of the most powerful components of the vastly complex mother-child love partnership. The behavioral patterns springing from these powerful emotions and in turn inspiring them are, as John Bowlby argued (1971-1979), among the most genetically primed and situationally invariant patterns in human life. The primal scene of mother-child loving can be seen in all cultures and its meaning will be immediately known to any competent human being, though its full emotional significance will not be fully grasped by those unfortunate enough not to have experienced it fully as a baby (Bowlby, 1971-1979; Ainsworth, 1967; Wagner and Stevenson, 1982). John Bowlby (1971-1979) and most psychologists of child development (e.g., Stern, 1977; Lamb and Campos, 1982; Greenspan and Greenspan, 1985) estimate that "attachment behavior" is normally learned between the third and sixth months. The core of *parent-child attachment* is mutual self-identification, adoration love, caring love, a complex set of "fun" emotions involved in playing together, and a complex set of dependency emotions.

MONKEY LOVE AND ADULT COMPETENCE

The primates that are closest to us genetically show the same basic patterns of mother-child attachment. (See Eibl-Eibesfeldt, 1970; Michael and Crook, 1973; Rowell, 1972. Wilson, 1975, gives the big evolutionary picture of parental care.) This suggests even more clearly what Bowlby argued: Our inherited genes prime us very strongly to focus our attention on certain crucial communications from a mother figure of our own species; to respond in certain emotional and behavioral ways to these communications; and thus we are guided genetically to learn how to behave throughout life as competent (whole) members of our species' society. Thelma Rowell (1972, p. 134) has summarized the general conclusion about the way the genes of monkeys prime them to recognize their own kind and to focus on these vital social communications in infancy:

Monkeys are adapted to live socially just as they are adapted to live in trees, or to eat a certain type of diet. For all these adaptations, in the life of the individual monkey, some aspects are genetically programmed, so that each grows the right sort of limbs and teeth and makes the right communicative gestures; and other aspects the individual learns as it develops, like how to run on lianas, how to recognize food, or how and with whom to communicate. There is no hard line that can usefully be drawn between learned components of behaviour on the one hand and innate ones on the other: some things are much easier for a monkey to learn than others, showing that there are innate "guidelines" for which responses will be acquired. For example, monkeys learn to recognize other individual monkeys more quickly than they learn to distinguish geometrical shapes.

Rowell's point is that the genetic priming of particular emotions and patterns of behavior varies greatly. Holding the situational inputs constant, the stronger the genetic priming, the more probable a given response is (see Wilson, 1975, 1984; Dawkins, 1976; Bonner, 1980). Though our later social lives diverge markedly from those of our primate relatives, as our central nervous system and our cultural learning develop further, the basic patterns of mother-child emotions and behavior are remarkably similar, including the vital primal scenes of adoration love:

> Like all mammals, the infant monkey is totally dependent on its mother for some time after it is born, and it is essential for its survival that certain interaction patterns are immediately established between them. Mother monkeys carry, feed, and clean their newborn infants, and defend them if necessary, and the infant must cling and nurse, and indicate any discomfort by movements and noises. In these processes, which lead to the infant's healthy physical growth, it is quite possible for a human caretaker, or even a carefully prepared nursery cage, to replace the functions of the mother. But a monkey also peers intently into her new infant's face, touches its face with her lips, cuddles it and croons to it, and with these activities she starts the learning processes through which the infant develops into a psychologically normal adult [Rowell, 1972, p. 134].

Loving motherly care must be received without too many conflicting signals within the first year or so (the vital "genetic window") or the child will never learn adequately to bond socially and mate. A *genetic window* is the period during which an organism is highly primed to perceive, interpret, and respond to certain cues. These responses in turn will trigger or reinforce certain of the individual's developments. Once the window "closes," no amount of cuing will produce the fully integrated development, though extensive *fragments* of the emotional and behavioral system are developed. The human genetic window for language development appears to be roughly from six months to several years. If the integrated linguistic cues are not received within this period, the person may develop only fragments of language and never learn fully to interpret and use the deep rules of language (Lenneberg, 1960; Lamb and Bornstein, 1987). Primates must experience the close attachment and bonding with a mother or other surrogate of their species within the early months of their lives or they will never *fully* develop the basic patterns of attachment, bonding, mating, or any other interactions with members of their species. As Rowell (1972, p. 137) found:

Many primates are captured as infants and hand-reared as pets, then transferred to zoos when they get older. Attempts to use such animals as breeding stock have a very low rate of success: typically these ex-pets show little or no mating behaviour, and the females do not care for their infants, which are then hand-reared, thus creating the breeding problems of the next generation. The histories of these zoo animals are of course varied, and the fact that some of them do breed suggests that one might be dealing with quite short critical periods during which social experience is necessary. This was investigated in the rhesus infants. Isolation for the first three months produced no permanent effects, if the infants were then placed in a group, but isolation for the whole of the first year destroyed all social ability. The period between three and nine months seemed to be critical for establishing normal social behaviour, although the communicative gestures have nearly all appeared in the first three months.

Jane van Lawick-Goodall (1971) found that the young chimpanzee may not even be able to live without his or her mother. Regardless of how adequate the food or how much help and protection there is from caring siblings, the very young orphan may go into depression, reach despair, and die.

THE SIGNS OF LOVE:
THE FEELS, SOUNDS, AND LOOKS

The behaviorist revolution in American academic psychology reduced all of the emotions of mother-child attachment to a few obvious biological requirements, just as they reduced all of the vastly complex emotions of adult love to the obvious biological necessity of sexual mating. By the 1950s, behaviorist social scientists routinely asserted that the full panoply of the mother-child love partnership was built on the slender biological need of the child's pleasure in suckling and eating and the mother's tension-release resulting from lowering the milk pressure within the breast. Because most American mothers at the time were not suckling their babies, but were following the advice of "experts" to bottle-feed them, yet neither showed the slightest diminution in love for the other, the whole idea was absurd. Yet even the most empirical of social scientists glibly generalized this behaviorist assertion to all human beings—with no consideration of empirical facts (see, for example, Burdock, 1949, pp. 9-10).

The classic work of H. F. Harlow and his colleagues at the University of Wisconsin (Harlow and Harlow, 1965, 1969) soundly refuted the idea that feeding and other forms of behavior that merely meet the physical needs of infants are sufficient to produce attachment and to raise competent adults. Their original goal was to isolate infant monkeys from mothers and other members of their species to determine precisely how they developed, independently of what they could learn from their mothers and other members of their species. They found the same things van Lawick-Goodall later found with chimpanzees, Bowlby and others found in their studies of human children, and most of us have found by observing our own and other children. Very young monkeys separated from their mothers very quickly started crying in the startled, high-pitched voice of distress and showing every other sign of the universal "separation anxiety." If the separation continued, in time the young became depressed and might eventually despair. The Harlow team found that they could pacify the isolated monkeys by providing them with a soft cloth to which they clung as they would to a mother when she was returned after a separation. They then devised a simple but ingenious experiment to show that feeding in itself does not produce attachment behavior.

They constructed two types of "substitute" mothers, each made of wire mesh. The one wire-mesh "mother" had a nipple from which the infant could suck all the milk needed to thrive physically. The other wire-mesh "mother" was covered with a soft cloth but had no nipple or milk. The infants quickly learned to go to the wire-mesh "mother" to suckle for milk when hungry. But then they would return to the cloth-covered "mother" and cling to it except when exercising or when hunger returned, at which time they would return to the wire-mesh "mother" and repeat the pattern. Whenever they were distressed about anything, they would immediately run to the cloth-covered "mother" and cling to it, until they were calmed. It was quite obvious that the wire-mesh "mother" that fed the infant did not produce attachment behavior, or what Harlow called "affectional bonds." The cloth "mother" produced attachment behavior *without providing any milk*. Nourishment and whatever rudimentary forms of love these infants felt were quite separate.

Monkeys raised in this way in isolation from other monkeys developed quite well physically. At first they seemed to develop all right emotionally, though they did cry more than infants raised by their real mothers and they did suck their fingers, toes, or penises much more. Compulsive masturbation by young children is an especially strong indicator of emotional distress arising from disturbed relations with parents. In this intensive work over many years with extremely distressed human children, all of whom had severely disturbed relations with parents, Bruno Bettelheim (1950) and his colleagues found that, even though the masturbation was treated quite permissively, it declined in direct proportion to the decline in the pathological conflicts in their relations with parents and others.

Theorists who believe that punishment of the young, and intermittent rejection of them for "bad" behavior, have bad effects emotionally and socially would clearly expect these isolated monkeys to develop better emotionally, because, unlike those raised by their own mothers, they were *never* punished by their substitute "mothers" and lived in a totally permissive environment making no demands on them. But, as soon as these physically healthy but isolated monkeys were allowed to rejoin a group of monkeys that had been raised by their mothers in the normal ways, they were discovered to be severely disturbed and socially retarded. In fact, they were total social incompetents. They either behaved extremely aggressively or else they withdrew as much as possible from their peers. That is, they either became "enraged" or "coldly aloof" (the same two alternatives Bowlby, 1971-1979, and others found in young human children who are long separated from their mothers). They did not show any of the normal patterns of friendly behavior (which in other primates consists largely of mutual "grooming" behavior), nor did they know how to take part in the patterns of mild threat behavior so vital in primate groups to establishing one's place in the dominance-submission (social status) hierarchy. It also soon became apparent that these physically totally indulged monkeys were totally incapable of performing normal sexual behavior. The males were especially incompetent sexually, never learning the normal patterns of behavior necessary for mating. Some of the females were successfully mated by normal monkeys, but they then did not know how to take care of their children and, in fact, normally completely rejected their newborn infants.

Harlow and his team demonstrated conclusively that feeding does not establish attachment behavior and that mere physical care, even the most indulgent care possible by a mechanical "substitute," will not produce emotionally mature adults. They also showed that a material soft to the touch will produce some minimal attachment behavior, even when it is completely divorced from any nourishment. This, of course, fits exactly what we might expect from our own experience. Soft, gentle caressing is the touch of human love (just as it may be the touch of the primate friendly "love" involved in mutual grooming, if the other primates have the same emotions associated with the same patterns of behavior). The soft, gentle caress by the mother is a source of joy to the baby.

It has been shown that human infants from the earliest days are genetically primed to move toward what is soft. (Brazelton, 1963, 1980; Brazelton et al., 1974, 1975, did much of the classic work on mother-infant interaction and bonding. Desmond Morris, 1977, has presented a wealth of such findings.) When a tender, soft pressure—such as that from a soft, caressing hand or breast—is applied to the cheek of a baby, the baby turns his or her face toward the pressure to bring him- or herself more into contact with the source of the caressing. But a harsher pressure leads the baby to pull his or her face away. A mother expresses her love for her baby, especially when the baby is distressed and she wishes to calm him or her, by softly, gently holding the baby to her body and caressing and patting. She may caress almost any part of the baby, but she focuses her caressing on the child's head, especially the cheeks and hair. (Caressing the top of the head and the hair is strikingly like grooming behavior in other primates.)

The ability of a soft substance to soothe a distressed baby is obvious enough to most mothers. A high percentage of babies soon develop a deep attachment to a soft blanket or other cloth material and rub it against their cheeks or suck a finger while holding the blanket whenever they are distressed, especially when they are punished or feel rejected by the mother. One of Jack Douglas's daughters became so attached to her pink blanket that "pinky" became her almost constant companion, always in reserve for when she might feel anxious and rejected. The soft wool was not nearly as important as the silky seam, whose softness was almost exactly like that of her mother's soft, hairless cheek. After years of desperate use, "pinky" became worn and tattered and slowly fell apart. But this disintegration proved to be a blessing. As she got older, having a "pacifier" became more embarrassing, so she started carrying a piece of it, including a piece of the vital seam, hidden in a pocket or some other item of clothing. When she started school, she was more distressed than her siblings by separation from her mother, so she secretly carried "pinky" with her and would suck her thumb with it wrapped around the thumb when she put her head on her desk.

We do not lose our attachment for softness as we grow older, though it probably grows weaker in comparison to other components of loving behavior. Adult human beings still love soft materials, like silk. And nothing is softer and more tender than the feel of a baby's skin, especially a baby's cheek rubbing against our own. "As soft as a baby's skin" is the human standard for softness and for desirability in touch. Though adult men in our society dislike soft male hands because of the association of softness with females, they love soft female hands and soft baby hands. Softness and tenderness constitute the universal touch of love. The baby's softness and tenderness encourage us to touch him or her and our soft and tender touching of the baby encourages him or her to touch in response. Attachment and loving in general are reciprocal, interdependent—giving and receiving; and the giving of love encourages the receiver to love in return. Almost all human emotions are contagious: love is very contagious.

Developmental psychologists have found that the newborn infant is just as responsive to sound as to touch. A sudden loud noise causes an immediate startle response from the very beginning of postpartum life; and the startle is followed by the sudden, high-pitched wail-of-distress crying that signals the mother to rush to and protect the baby. A sudden, loud noise inspires fear and, later, hatred and aggression (as we can all see when a sudden backfire, clap of thunder, or sonic boom destroys our peace of mind).

Soft, gentle, and rhythmical sounds are the sounds of peacefulness, reassurance, and love. When the human infant is born (and probably while in utero), the infant is genetically primed to respond with reassurance to the soft, gentle beat of the human heart. If a metronome is set to beat softly at the same rate as the human heart at rest, the baby is calmed by it, though not nearly as much as by the sound of a restful heart beat. It seems that the baby when cuddled and suckled can respond emotionally to the reassuring heart beat of the mother and others at the same time he or she responds to the soft, tender caressing.

Human vision is not clearly focused in the first several weeks and the infant learns to focus visual attention and distinguish visual patterns only slowly. First the child focuses attention on light and colors. Because pattern recognition involves immensely more complex neural processing of information, it is not surprising that this develops more slowly. But, from what we have already seen about the vital importance of the development of attachment, it is not too surprising to find that among the first visual patterns that a baby learns to recognize and respond to are those of the human face. First the baby recognizes the eyes and focuses attention on them, especially when they are brought near his or her own. Then the baby recognizes the rest of the face and begins to explore it with his or her own eyes. The child begins to show flickering patterns of smiling on his or her own face. Sometime between two and four months old, the child is able to recognize the complex pattern of facial expression we call a smile. Then the child begins to respond to the smile by smiling. Then the child smiles independently and elicits a smile in response. Smiling is one of the best-studied infant expressions (see Spitz and Wolf, 1946; Bowlby, 1979, pp. 37-40). For cross-cultural evidence of the strong genetic priming, see Landau (1977) and Super and Harkness (1982). Blind babies initially smile like seeing babies but, of course, do not develop the smiling response to adoration. Smiling is the beginning of the look of love. And it is the look of love that is the most convincing communication of love for human beings.

Any human experience that is vital to our survival and development normally makes use of several channels of perception and communication. This high "redundancy," or repetition, of love messages makes it far more likely they will be received and understood. Lower animals, as we are all aware from our close experience with dogs and cats, make far more use of taste and smell than we do. These remain important in our lives. It is even possible that they are far more important in building our early love partnerships than developmental psychologists have yet found. We are all aware from everyday experience that they are important to us adults sexually. But hearing and vision are far more important in human life than taste or smell. They are certainly the dominant senses in perceiving and communicating love. We have already seen how important the sound of love, especially the tone of love, is in human life. The looks of love, as perceived through vision, are even more important. The looks of love speak far louder to us than words, even louder than the very meaningful tone of love.

Feelings are the soul, the heart, the inner core of the human being. Feelings are of vital importance to us in themselves, but feelings also tell us most reliably what others will think about us and do toward us. If they love us, they will do all they can to help us. If they hate us, they will do all they can to hurt us. (Of course, situational perceptions and estimates of "interests" also affect our actions, until our emotions reach "passionate" levels and sweep away reason and self-control.) We need desperately to know how they feel about us. Our eyes are our most dependable means of determining what they feel toward us and all other signs of their feelings, such as their tones of voice, are generally interpreted in the context of what we see their feelings to be, at least once vision is fully developed (during the first year; see Plutchik and Kellerman, 1980; Ekman, 1972; Ekman et al., 1972; Izard, 1971, 1980).

Just as our eyes are the primary means by which we see their feelings, so their eyes are a primary means by which we perceive their feelings. Their eyes are the first important portal into their own souls. This is why writers have always seen the eyes as "soulful." Think how common it is to hear statements such as, "I could see from his eyes that he didn't mean it." Authors often talk about eyes "clouding over" when the person is angry, or "brightening" when they are joyful or loving. Regardless of whether there is a general darkening or brightening of eyes, the black pupil of the eye expands and contracts in response to our emotions. We subconsciously respond to those pupil contractions and expansions. When we are joyful or positively excited in any way by a person we are looking at, our pupils expand; when we are angry at them, our pupils contract. While we are not normally consciously aware of these pupil movements, our own feelings respond to them. When we see pupils looking at us expand, we respond more positively toward that person than we would otherwise have done; and when we see pupils contract, we feel less positive toward that person (Morris, 1977.) The baby's eyes, like his or her entire body and his or her basic patterns of action, are different from those of adults in ways that will elicit love from adults. The baby's pupils are larger in proportion to the eyes' total size than they will be when he or she grows up, thus eliciting more favorable emotional response. It may also be significant that babies often have lighter-colored eyes than when they grow up, because the lighter color sets off the black of the pupils.

Most of the information given off by the eyes about the feelings of the person do not come from the eyes themselves. Rather, the information comes from the gaze behavior of the eyes and, above all, from the facial expressions around the eyes, especially from the movements of the eyelids, the corners of the eyelids, and the eyebrows. Gaze behavior tells us when someone is paying attention to us and a great deal about the nature of this attention. The eyeballs of other primates are dark. The human eyeball is white. This, of course, sets off the pupils, allowing us to determine better whether they like or dislike us. But it also allows us to tell far better what the exact directions of their gazes are. We can track the movement of a viewer's eyes extremely rapidly and accurately. By doing so, we can tell just how long they look at us, whether they look us in the eye or look at some other part of our body (some being quite revealing, as when someone stares at your breasts or pubic region), whether they "stare" or look "shifty-eyed" (and all variations in between), whether they look intimate (close) or distant, and so on. An immense amount of information is conveyed about a person's feelings, thoughts, and intentions by gaze behavior. Consider, for example, Desmond Morris's example about a man looking at a beautiful woman and her looking back in return:

> In ordinary conversation, it is the moments where the eyes make brief contact, at the point of handing over the speaking role, that the variations in attention make themselves felt. It is there that the amorous male holds on a little too long. As he answers the beautiful girl's last statement he begins talking and reaches the point where normally he would turn away, but instead he is still staring at her. This makes her uncomfortable, because she is forced either to lock eyes with him, or to look away from him while he is talking. If he continues to talk and stare while she deflects her eyes, it puts her into the "shy" category, which she resents. If she boldly locks eyes with him, then he has forced her into a "lover's gaze", which she also resents. But the chances are that he will not go this far. He will only increase his gaze-time by a tiny amount, just long enough for the message to get across without creating any embarrassment [Morris, 1977, pp. 75-76].

Gaze behavior is very important in communicating love. Someone who looks "shifty-eyed," looks "off into the distance," or "averts" the eyes from you entirely is not communicating a sincere love. (A shy lover may stare downward, probably at his or her feet, and dart a quick glance up at your eyes every now and then to see what you're feeling; but even that is not really being "shifty-eyed." It's honest enough; it's simply an insecure love.) The mother who loves her baby securely shows the full-faced, steady-eyed look of love, often "gazing" for 20 seconds or more (Stern, 1977, p. 18). As we described it above in our depiction of the primal scene of love, the mother often holds the baby's face directly in front of hers at just the right distance (approximately a foot away) so that she can focus her eyes completely on the baby's eyes and she looks fully into the baby's eyes with complete intimacy, that is, for the longest period of unblinking eye-fixation on the other's eyes found in human experience. She and her baby are looking into each other's souls. They are *communing* with each other, expressing and receiving adoration love and the sense of self. But, as important as gaze behavior is, it is not as important as the full facial expression. The look that the mother and child use to communicate their feelings of adoration love to each other involves this full gaze into each other's eyes, the eyelids, the corner of the eyelids, and the corner of the mouth. All the rest of the face (the eyebrows, forehead, the corners of the nostrils, and the cheeks) is loose, largely expressionless.

Consider the general expression of happiness or joyfulness, such as you might show a friend or even a new acquaintance of whom you think well. The *look of friendly greeting* is a full smile, a "happy face." The full smile is a very distinctive human facial expression. Other primates obviously feel and express good feelings to their fellows, but the human being does so far more and does so in this very distinctive way, which indicates that expressing joy toward and with other human beings is far more important for us than for other primates. Our guess is that all primates that have very extensive patterns of friendly and cooperative behavior will be found to have some similar means of expressing their joy-in-the-presence-of-others.

The joyful smile involves pulling the lips back wide (with lips either parted or closed) and the eyelids wide. As the intensity of the joy increases, the lips are pulled back so far the mouth opens, and the corners of the eyelids are pulled back so far that the eyebrows and forehead begin to crease. At the extreme, the whole face may "light up" and the joy be vented by laughter. This happy face is the one we see most of the time when mothers are playing with their babies. It expresses their common joy in each other, but it is not the look of adoration love.

The look of adoration love is rarely seen in photographs because it is *inherently linked* (as an undertone—see below) to the feeling and state of intimacy, and thus is inherently so private that it is nearly impossible to show it in full public view to strangers. It occurs very rarely by itself in movies and then almost always fleetingly. When it does occur in movies, it is almost always combined with sexual excitement in the look of Erotic love, which we shall come to next.

The look of adoration love relaxes the happy smile. The muscles that pulled back the lips and eyes in the look of joy are relaxed so completely that the eyes become languorous, possibly even sleepy, and the lips show only a faint smile or, at the extreme, may even turn down slightly. This is a look of adoration-love. We can see this look of love most clearly in Western paintings of the Mother of God or others adoring Christ or other children, as, for example, in Leonardo's "Virgin of the Rocks." (The smile of the Mona Lisa is enigmatic because the eyes show moderate adoration, but the mouth is smiling too much, and with a hint of coy flirtation, to communicate adoration-love.)

The look of sexual excitement involves a parting of the lips but still with relaxed muscles at the corner of the mouth, and an uplifting of the eyelids (and dilated pupils) at the far corners. This look can be made a sexual stare, or even an aggressive male look of sexual attack, by pulling the mouth down at the corners, jutting the jaw, knitting the brow, and tensing the muscles under the eyes. But it can also be made a look of adoration-love-and-sexual-excitement (that is, Erotic love) by showing the look of adoration love and adding the open mouth and a slightly tensed stare. This is the look that Marilyn Monroe and her Hollywood managers exaggerated slightly in the sexual direction (suggesting a somewhat more aroused sexual state and less adoration feeling, as happens during intercourse). When combined, it is a look of *Erotic love.* Sexual (lustful) arousal without adoration love looks aggressive, not adoring and intimate.

The look of sexual orgasm or ecstasy involves an even more open mouth (even of the tongue jutting out), the eyelids pulled down but the eyebrows up, and the eyeballs rolling toward the forehead (giving the appearance of sinking into oneself). This is a look of total joy, plus adoration love, plus sexual excitement with the glazed, rolling eyeballs added, but with the eyelids almost closed. The look of happy peacefulness that follows ecstasy is the face almost completely at rest, as in quiet, happy sleep.

Psychologists have shown what novelists and others who have closely described our everyday life emotions and patterns of behavior have always known: human beings have immensely complex and subtle facial expressions, tones of voice, and touches that communicate our immensely complex and subtle emotions to other human beings. By the time we become adults, our conscious minds are concentrated far more on our verbal forms for communicating emotions, because consciousness is largely specialized for processing verbal behavior. But our vastly more complex subconscious minds are still continually processing and using these vastly complex body-language messengers of emotions to experience others for their own sake (when they are intimates) and to help us decide how others really feel about us, how they will really act toward us, what we can really count on their doing because they are emotionally committed to doing it. We all take it for granted that words can easily lie, but that the body language of emotions, while it can be manipulated too, is far more reliable as signs of our feelings and emotional commitments, so we rely on them as the sources of our most important information about our relations with other human beings.

We all know the implications of what one young woman told us: "He always said he loved me and he did all the right things sexually—he was a real sexual technician, right out of the sex manuals. But whenever he said 'I love you,' I looked in his eyes and there was nothing there." If we had asked her what the look of love is, what it was she was looking for in his eyes, she would not have known what to say and, in fact, would probably have thought it bizarre that we would feel the need to ask. She knew subconsciously what the look of love is and she knew how vastly important it is. But, like almost all human beings, she would not know how to express the look clearly in words.

Small children without much language know how their mothers feel toward them, though with the problems inherent in "reading" such a vastly complex and ever-shifting congeries of messages, by "reading" their vastly complex body language of emotions, especially by reading the look of love (or its absence) in the primal scenes of the mother-child duets. They are primed genetically by somewhere around six months to one and a half years to watch for, recognize, and then slowly learn to respond through the body language of love and thus to receive and give love. As Anna Freud and Dorothy Burlingham (1943, 1944) concluded from their years of work with very young children: "The child has instinctive understanding of whatever emotion moves the mother; he watches her face and through imitation reproduces her facial expressions."

The child is ready, highly primed, to respond to the body language of love. The child will even show spontaneous bits of the language and behavior before the mother gives her love, especially if the child is separated from the mother before he or she is ready to recognize it. But this is "vacuum" behavior without the inner emotions, thoughts, and intentions associated with the appropriate body language and patterns of behavior. The child must first receive the communication of love and the behavior associated with it or else he or she will not learn fully how to love others. *Human beings must be loved and perceive this in the communion of the emotional language before they can fully love either themselves or others.* This is the same as learning to smile or talk. A baby can babble and gurgle all the 16 consonants contained in the full range of human language before adults teach him or her to talk by imitation. But the baby must receive talk from them or he or she will never be able to talk beyond fragments. Recent evidence shows that these fragments of meaningful language are quite extensive and so highly primed geneti-cally that even mute children can produce extensive gesture language without learning it. But learning is obviously crucial to the development of fully integrated language use (see the review of the evidence in Lamb and Bornstein, 1987, pp. 271-299). The sparse evidence from the few children almost totally isolated from adults from birth, so-called wild children, indicated that they must be talked to and imitate the talk within the first few years or they will never be able to learn the "deep" grammatical structure of language necessary to communicate more than a few words (Lenneberg, 1960).

This dependence of the child on the adult initiation of the love partnership was most strikingly illustrated by the children Freud and Burlingham (1943, 1944) worked with. These were children who were separated from their families, and, being in the first few years of life, were in the period when they were highly primed to recognize, receive, and give love. In every case, they found that the children responded almost desperately to any expressions of love feeling for them by attaching themselves to the adults, *but the adult had to show the feeling of love first*:

> We have shown before how quickly the latent parent-child relationship becomes manifest, for instance, when opportunity is offered through formation of artificial family groups. These inner urges of the child do not always wait for carefully thought out arrangements. They arise in answer to actions of the grown-ups: whoever merely takes care of a child for any length of time in a motherly way, may easily become the chosen foster-mother of this child. But children choose their foster-mothers too where no previous action on the part of the grown-up has provoked the process; it seems at first sight as if they choose at random. Closer investigation of every such occurrence shows that these apparently spontaneous attachments of the children really arise in answer to a feeling in the adult person, in many cases a feeling of which the adult was not aware in the beginning, or the reasons for which only became apparent after some searching.
>
> A young nurse for instance felt attracted to one of the liveliest little boys in the nursery. When questioning herself she found that he resembled the favorite brother of her childhood. Another nurse felt attracted to a child whose tragic loss of his parents reminded her of her own tragic separation from her family. Another one felt specially drawn to small girls whose family constellation reminded her of her own position in her family with all its consequences, etc. In all these instances the children answered this hardly conscious attitude with violent attachments from their own side. It seemed as if the emotion that lay dormant in them had only waited for an answering spark in some adult person to flare up [Freud and Burlingham, 1944].

CARING LOVE

Our discussion of the primal scene of mother-child loving does not yet include all the dimensions of mother-child loving. We started with adoration love because it is the half of mother-child love that is generally taken for granted or actually overlooked by students of attachment behavior. (We have found no study of adoration love in the mother-child partnership, though psychologists often "lapse" into common sense and speak of the "adoring baby." See Greenspan and Greenspan, 1985, p. 65. Dorothy Tennov, 1979, has studied adoration, which she calls "limerance," in romantic love.) The second major dimension of motherly love includes the traditional concern with feeding and protection ("caring") behavior that psychologists once thought was the entire basis of a child's love for his or her mother or any surrogate who did those things for him or her. This dimension is *caring love* and it is what we have in mind when we say that the mother "takes care of" her baby because she "cares for" the baby. Far more than mere feeding and protecting, it includes the mother's caring for the entire development of her baby.

Dorothy Tennov (1979) has an excellent analysis and some case material (pp. 39-41) showing the independence of both caring and adoration from sex and the complex ways in which adoration can be associated with fantasies of caring. It is crucial to see that adoration and caring trigger undertones of each other and that *adoration love triggers undertones of Erotic love* that can be extremely powerful. (Undertones of emotion are dealt with below.) *Human life is inherently embodied and the adoration of a human being is inherently embodied.* The adoring lover adores the beautiful body of the beloved (and extreme adoration love *mythologizes* the perception of that body so that it is presented to consciousness as beautiful; see Chapter 5). Erotic love, however, is directed toward ("intends") the creation, support, and enhancement of the entire body and life space—the biosphere—of the beloved. Sexual feelings are only one dimension of this complex of interdependent Erotic feelings and, when not triggered by the complex cues of the primary and secondary sexual characteristics of adults, the sexual feelings remain only an undertone of the other erotic feeling and are not directed into sexual craving and behavior. The infant and young child has no lust feelings or cravings, but only the fragments of genital skin sexual feeling. (We shall deal further with this major issue in Chapter 4.) The baby who adores his or her parents does not have undertones of sexual craving, but clearly has adoration feelings for the body of the beloved. The baby *in-love* with his mother "loves" to caress her hair and every part of her beautiful body. Parents adore their baby's beautiful body, have powerful Erotic feelings about him or her, and caress his or her beautiful body to commune in-love. But the baby's *infantile characteristics trigger an inhibition of any undertone of sexual feelings in direct proportion to their caring love for him or her.* (We call this the *Westermarck principle* in honor of Edward Westermarck, 1921, 1934a, 1934b. And see Shepher, 1983. Westermarck first recognized that incest inhibitions vary directly with prolonged closeness during early childhood. We merely add that caring love and infantile characteristics are the immediate triggers of the inhibition in adults. Caring love for the parents and anyone else is probably the trigger of the child's inhibitions. Someone who does not feel caring love might be stimulated sexually by closeness as the child develops the sexual characteristics that trigger sex drives. See Chapter 4 for further details.)

It is vitally important in all discussions of love to remember that our English word *love* covers all degrees of adoration love (including, as we shall see, *friendly liking*), caring love, Erotic feelings and behavior, communings between selves, self-identifications (fusions), and even emotional dependencies (see Reik, 1944; Rougemont, 1940, 1963; Solomon, 1981). All of these combined is what we call *overall love*. As we have just argued, there are some vital interdependencies between Erotic feelings and adoration feelings. The sexual feelings and behavior are so different from adoration and caring that it is relatively easy for adults to distinguish among them. *Adoration* and *caring*, on the other hand, trigger strong undertones of each other and, consequently, the two words overlap each other far more in their actual meaning than *adoration* does with *sex*. They overlap even more in their expressions in behavior (because each triggers a strong undertone of the other), so that it is often extremely hard to clearly distinguish between them.[1] This partial similarity of feelings and the linguistic confusion led Freud into a fatal confusion about human feelings, cognition, and behavior in general.

Over and over again, we've found people who said they "loved" someone very much but did not find them exciting, or wanted to divorce them to marry someone else, and so on. If one thinks they're talking about adoration love, which (in combination with the Erotic, intimacy, and the fusion of selves) is the core of romantic love and being in-love (see Chapters 5 and 6), their statements must be mistaken. But, of course, they were talking about caring love. It is entirely possible, and all too common, to care very much for someone but to have only a low undertone of adoration feelings and little or no sexual feelings for them, and thus not to have romantic feelings about them.

In addition to its own distinctive patterns of adoration behavior, adoration love leads to much of the same kind of behavior—-taking care of—that caring love does. When we adore a child (or anyone else, or anything), we want very much to keep him or her (or it) in good condition, so we take care of him or her (or it). If we adore a car, we carefully wash and wax it. If it gets "hurt," we feel bad because of our loss. But, of course, there is a great difference in the way we feel when our child or other loved one gets hurt. We do not merely feel bad because we have lost something we adore. We feel horrified, crushed, and we mourn. We feel hurt ourselves. If someone who injures our car repays us for it with damages for the time and hurt it costs us, we may even feel better because now we can more than replace the car. While we might be recompensed for the injury to someone we adore, we cannot possibly be recompensed for injury to someone for whom we care. Injury to someone we care for hurts in and of itself and it makes us grieve for the one we care for, in proportion to the injury, and feel anger for the source of the injury. Note, for example, the tremendous difference in "fan" response to an injury to a "sex symbol" and a response to an injury to a "star" that a fan identifies with and for which he or she develops caring. The "sex symbols" are always astounded that people who seem to "adore" them can also pull their hair out just to "preserve" some little piece of them. Fans will do anything to get close to them, including jumping on them and nearly killing them. Of course, when the symbol disappears for any reason, the fans feel a loss. But their sense of loss is very different compared to the grieving the fans felt when John Lennon was murdered. Some observers felt that Lennon fans were grieving for themselves and concluded that they were "merely" displaying their grief for publicity. They were indeed grieving for themselves, but not out of some supposed "self-display." Most of them were grieving for themselves in the same way we grieve for anyone we care for and with whom we identify ourselves. They felt *caring love, which involves the distinctive caring love feeling and identification with the person so loved.*

Nature has built some vitally important redundancy into our feelings and behavior toward our children and others. Just like the fans of a sex symbol, a mother who feels only adoration for her baby will not be the most reliable caretaker. If she adores the child when it's being cute and darling, will she still do so when the child cries and gets dirty? A mother who only adores her baby's good parts would be like a "sunshine friend" who adores you when you are on top and forgets you when you are on your way down, or like someone who feels "endless love" (lust or pseudolove) for you during the summer's bright days and forgets you when he or she returns to college. (As the old song asks plaintively, "Will you still love me in December as you did in May?") So nature has endowed us with caring feelings as a kind of fail-safe set of emotions and identifications: *No matter how unadorable the baby may be, and no matter how distressed or even mad she might be about having to get up in the middle of the night in response to the baby's wailing, the mother will do so as long as her caring love feelings are great enough.* (Stern, 1977, p. 29, discusses the case of the "ugly" baby; and Bolton, 1983, discussed the many problems and conflicts that arise when babies do not respond with the signs of love, as in the cases of blind or premature infants. Also see Taylor, 1980; Lewis and Rosenbaum, 1974; Hofer, 1975.)

Like adoration love, caring love has distinctive forms of communication. The touch of caring is pretty much the same as adoration, though perhaps even more soft and tender. But the sounds and looks of caring are quite different. They show sadness—grieving of some degree—over the suffering of the one cared for. The voice becomes sad, plaintive, supportive, uplifting, even crying in mourning if the threat or injury is bad enough. And the look of care is an unhappy face, ranging all the way from showing concern to agonized mourning (or even horror followed by mourning). If the lover wants merely to show caring love when there is no real injury or threat to the loved one, he or she shows caring playfully, perhaps even with a superimposition of self-mockery. The looks of caring involve more dimensions of expressions of feeling than the looks of adoration love and sexual excitement. (Consider, for example, how complex the look of "being touched" is.) In general, though, the major looks of caring are pretty much the opposite of those of the happy faces. Instead of pulling the mouth, cheeks, and eyes up into varying degrees of a smile, caring pulls them down into the looks of sadness.

Caring love is our modern phrase meaning very roughly what the ancient Greeks meant by *agape*, the Romans by *caritas*, and Christians translated into English as *charity*. When the Christians said that faith, hope, and charity were the greatest virtues, and charity the greatest of these, they meant that the caring love such as God, through Christ, feels for all human beings is the greatest virtue and originally was the force that created the universe and man. This is why they often resorted to the short motto, "God is love." The subject is really far more complex. After Augustine, Christian thinkers normally thought human beings capable at best only of an impure form of *agape*, which Augustine called "amor." In recent centuries, the Latin peoples, especially the French, have sexualized this Latin root (such historical details are not a major concern here, but see Flaceliere, 1971; Rougemont, 1940, 1963; Lewis, 1960; Maurois, 1944).

The crucial differences between adoration and caring can be seen most clearly in situations in which the dimensions of shame and pride and guilt and self-respect are varied. Shame is the emotional reaction to failing or being submissive in the eyes of others (in terms of their values). Pride is the opposite end of the same emotional dimension, the emotional reaction to succeeding or being dominant in the eyes of others. Guilt is failure or being submissive in your own eyes. Self-respect is the opposite. When one's child, with whom one is identified, fails in the other's eyes, the parent feels shame. When the child succeeds, the parent feels pride. Adoration love is highly interdependent with both pride and self-respect. When the child does something that makes the parent feel shame, he or she does not adore the child and may feel some of the opposites, hatred or contempt. But this very failure of one's child makes the parent feel intense caring love for the child, if he or she identifies with and has caring love for the child. This caring love normally completely dominates any hatred or contempt that may result from the shaming. A parent who only feels adoration for the child, without caring, or whose adoration sweeps away any caring, will feel the hatred or contempt when the child fails in other's eyes and show them by facial expressions or by actions-denunciations, rebukes, even physical attacks. These reactions are extreme when the parent does not really feel adoration, but only pride from social association with the successful, beautiful, or dominant child. This pride from social association is a *halo effect* and leads to *adulation*, not adoration. One can adore a child who fails in others' eyes but succeeds in the parent's and child's eyes—for example, when the child acts courageously against the "mob." In this situation, the parent can feel and truthfully say, "Son (or Daughter), I'm proud of you, even though you've also caused the family some shame in the eyes of the motley crowd." The parent who feels only adulation does not *love* the child and will abandon him or her to the mob, unless obligations or material interests intervene. Adulation is *pseudolove* that actually *uses* the one supposedly loved. The movie or political celebrity who mistakes it for adoration will find him- or herself *abandoned* when attachment and caring are most needed. Like the star, the child may be quite confused by this pseudolove that so closely mimics adoration love and even caring love (as long as the sun is shining). The child who learns self-adulation from his or her parents, rather than self-adoration and self-caring, becomes hostage in her basic sense of self to the whims of crowd reactions and thus to terrible insecurities. (We believe this is one origin of many cases of self-pseudolove known as narcissism; see Chapter 3.)

Caring love, like adoration love, is a distinctive emotion, as we can see from the distinctive and universal human facial expressions for it. Caring love is the extreme of a continuum of caring feeling. Pity is the minimal caring, sympathy is in between, and caring love is the maximum caring. When we "care" without any empathy we call it *pity*. *Empathy* is simply "feeling with," putting yourself in the other's shoes, that is, imagining yourself in that person's situation (see Parkes, 1984, pp. 51-54). If you think about your experiences of pity, say your feelings of pity for an injured dog or cat, you'll know exactly what it is. It is a powerful feeling in people who have not had it repressed or distorted beyond recognition by terrible experiences early in life. It develops early in life, like all our love feelings. Anna Freud and others who have worked with institutionalized children have seen it in full-blown form by about the second or third year. By that age, even children who can barely talk, and children who have severe problems of caring more fully (see below), will often show sad expressions of pity and do all they can to help another child who is injured or sad. In his study, *Chimpanzee Politics* (1982, pp. 48 and 194), Frans de Waal and his colleagues saw chimps put on "pitiful" displays to get the help of other chimps.

When we feel pity and we empathize with the other person's situation and suffering, then we feel to some degree as if that person's suffering is our own and we say that we have *sympathy* for that person. Similarity breeds comparability and identification, which breed empathy. Empathy allows us to feel sympathy. Only pantheists feel much pity for a tree that is cut down (though we may feel a real loss), but most of us feel pity for animals that are hurt and some feel sympathy. The difference is that few of us can empathize with trees, but the greater similarity of animals to us encourages us to empathize with them; and the more like us we feel they are, especially in their feelings and behavior, the more we empathize with them and feel sympathy. Dogs and monkeys elicit the most empathy because they seem by their behavior to have the human feelings of love. Dogs are man's best friend because they are man's most loving animal. Some people whose love feelings toward human beings have been blocked by early experiences love animals passionately, though not normally in the Kinsey sense. Their animals, who may be called "the kids" or "darlings," may become their most intimate and loving friends and family.

Caring love involves pity plus empathy (sympathy), but it also involves some major degree of identification of the self with the other person, some major fusion of the sense of self with the sense of self of the other. This is a vital difference between sympathy and caring love. It is this great identification of your self with the other person that guarantees that you will feel hurt when you know the other is hurting. In a real sense, a spiritual sense, *when someone you care for gets hurt it is you getting hurt.* And when someone you care for profoundly dies, you *lose much of yourself* and you have to re-create yourself into a new self to be able to go on living. When we mourn for someone we have cared for deeply we feel like a vital part of us has literally been torn out of us (see the moving description of this by C. S. Lewis, 1980).

But that is looking at caring love only from the loss side. Caring love also leads us to advance the positive interests and the development of the self of the other person as if it were ourselves, precisely because we identify with that person. Some social scientists have tried to explain our social lives, including our love lives, entirely on the basis of selfish motives, of giving only to get in return. This "reciprocal altruism" is true of most of our economic lives, but in any literal sense that is absurd when applied to our love lives, especially to our caring love lives. (Sexual modernists have been extremely partial to *exchange theories* of love. See Huston, 1974, pp. 43-44, 128-130, 225-229.) Certainly any overall love partnership involves reciprocal altruism as well as love, and will at times degenerate into selfish demands, but it is absurd to reduce any of these to the others. Even when we simply feel adoring love for someone, we will give them things because we want what we adore to be better off. *Giving without reciprocity* is a universal sign of adoration, caring, the Erotic and overall love. But when we feel caring love for someone, then giving is as good as, or maybe better, than receiving. *If you identify with someone in caring love, then giving to them, bringing pleasure to them, gives you the same pleasure, in proportion to the degree of your identification.* There are in fact some people who either feel more caring for the one they love than they do for themselves, or they largely "lose" themselves in the other (identifying more with them than with their own innermost sense of selves). These people become extremely self-sacrificing, even masochistic, giving anything to the others and living largely through them (see Norwood, 1986). *Overcaring* can breed overdependency and "spoiled" demands for more, but it can also breed guilt in those who care for and identify with the overcarer. In the *survivor syndrome*, the guilt springing from accepting overcaring often pervades the rest of life as a powerful moral insecurity (see Chapter 3).

The *overcaring lover syndrome* is well recognized by psychiatrists. It consists of giving so much that the dependency bred in the other person actually causes them to become weaker, less able to do for themselves. The overcaring wife may actually encourage her husbands' alcoholic spiral downward at the same time she is desperately trying to stop it. Most people want to give and receive from the people they care most deeply for in more or less equal amounts. The more you care for someone, the more you give to and do for them as long as it seems to be in their best interest. (Giving them too much may make them weak and "spoiled," unable and unwilling to care for themselves, and will prevent their being effectively caring.) Giving to and doing for are the action-expressions of caring love, until they "o'er leap the mark" and retard the development of the other person (see Douglas, 1983; Peck, 1978).

A woman normally identifies with and cares for her baby in imagination before he or she is even conceived. Once she knows she is pregnant, the woman normally feels a sudden surge of caring for her child-to-be. As the baby grows, the caring feelings grow (see Bolton, 1983). The baby comes to feel more and more like exactly what it is—part of the mother. It is in good part this growing identification with and caring love for the baby that makes the abhorrence for abortion grow as the baby becomes more human in appearance. Some developmental psychologists have argued that by the time of birth the mother has undergone an "implosion" by which she becomes totally focused on herself-and-baby and subconsciously no longer distinguishes between herself and the baby. At the least, it is obvious that at birth the mother is very self-possessed and very identified with the baby.

If the birth goes all right, the child is healthy, and the mother conscious, in most cases there is almost immediately a sense of joy and happiness, even ecstasy. And this joy involves intense adoration for the baby. (For many years, some psychologists thought this *postpartum bonding* was necessary for the development of maternal bonding, as it is in some mammals. But this is not true. See Lamb and Campos, 1982, pp. 172-174.) Up to that point, the feelings are normally mainly caring, perhaps because the inevitable tinge of fear over birth and the well-being of the child restrain adoration. Once the adoration feelings explode, they multiply (potentiate) the caring feelings and the mother feels intensely in-love. (If the child is born deformed in a major way, the emotional overtone is normally that of extreme caring-mourning.)

We have already seen the touches, sounds, and looks of adoration love. A few further words about caring touches, sounds, and looks are in order. The universal looks of sadness, distress, and fear on a baby's face trigger the mother's caring feeling. The two distinct types of cries a baby makes are also universal signals triggering caring feelings in the mother. The low-pitched, slow buildup of the hunger cry makes the mother care, but not intensely and with no anxiety or dread. The high-pitched, sudden wailing of the frightened baby frightens the mother, thus preparing her (with adrenaline) for sudden exertions and arouses intense caring feelings. Mothers thus aroused are ready to do almost anything to protect their children. We've probably all seen some instance of this in animals, which normally act far more extremely than human beings.

Fathers-to-be normally go through roughly the same development but at a much lower level, rarely identifying as closely with the child as the mother until later years. This is one major reason why so many men become increasingly anxious and even jealous as the pregnancy develops. As the mother withdraws into herself-and-baby, the father is almost bound to feel some sense of being "left out" of the feelings of the woman he has loved and with whom his self is partially fused. If he does not understand what is happening, he may feel a mysterious anxiety; and, if he is quite insecure and dependent on the woman, he may become jealous and enraged. (John Johnson notes, in a personal communication, that about 10% of physical assaults by husbands or "lovers" against women take place during pregnancy.)

Traditional forms of bureaucratized medicine almost completely shut the fathers out, thus almost guaranteeing at least some sense of fatherly loss. The various forms of natural childbirth now used, normally in some combination with medical care, try to prevent this alienation and all of the implications it can have for the future family life.

Of course, this is all very different if the pregnancy is unwanted. Though we shall not be very concerned here with this tragic situation, it is important to keep in mind. In almost all the cases we have observed closely, women who for any reason feel they cannot—must not—have the baby develop the same kind of caring feelings toward their children-to-be. These are sometimes repressed and then suddenly explode into consciousness at the point of abortion or birth, or remain hidden only to explode later in feelings of anxiety, depression, and guilt. But normally the women are aware of them and do everything they can to minimize the ambivalence. If they've decided not to have the baby, or to adopt it out, they try not to think of it as a human being—a "thou"—and, once born, it is very important for them not to see the baby at all (see Buber, 1970).

Once the child is born, there are a great number of genetically highly primed and interdependent cues and emotional and behavioral responses between mothers and their babies, many of which in human beings are tied in with the touches, sounds, and sights of love. Behavioral biologists, anxious to avoid attributing human emotions to animals, have called these *attachment cues* and *attachment responses*, the dual aspects of *attachment relations* (Bowlby, 1971-1979, 1979). They are found profusely and redundantly in all higher mammals and seem to vary directly with the degree of dependency of the newborn on the mother for survival and development (Wilson, 1975, p. 347). The human infant, being completely dependent on others for survival for several years, enters this world with a massive armory of infantile attachment cues that call out to the mother (and, to less degree, others) for adoring and caring feelings and the responses that they both lead to and reinforce. Some of these are what in our society are called "cuteness" and are possessed by all but the deformed babies (Stern, 1977, pp. 24-26).

Cuteness refers to the overall, archetypical form of the baby's face and the head, which forms the background for the face. The baby's head, forehead, and face are much larger in proportion to the body than they are in adults. (In fact, an adult with such a proportionally large head, forehead, or face would be seen as deformed.) The baby's eyes are proportionally much larger than the face, compared to adults. The baby's nose and lips are smaller proportionally. The cheeks are fatter, the nose more up-turned and buttony, the lips more pursed. Judged by the standards of adulthood, babies are ugly, a point that has often been noted by nonparents, especially by men who have not yet become fathers. But adult criteria of beauty are felt by almost everyone to be irrelevant and each loving mother tends to see her own baby as beautiful, or, at least, as divinely cute. This is not an accident, nor the result of central planning by some higher culture council. (Desmond Morris, 1977, has presented the evidence and beautiful pictures to illustrate the findings.) The same general criteria of cuteness are found in the other mammals, and at least some of them may be found even in fish or birds. Relative smallness, softness, cuddliness, and "pitiful" helplessness seem to be extremely general attachment cues for the newly born. This is why baby animals are more loved by humans than older ones and why baby stuffed animals, which are also given cuter characteristics than their real counterparts, evoke far more loving than realistic reproductions would do. In addition, the baby has the softest and smoothest of skins and hair and the whole body is soft and "cuddly." The baby has the in-born repertoire of cries, coos, and sighs that elicit adoring and caring responses in mothers. Most of these cues elicit pleasure in the mother in and of themselves. Some elicit caring, and, when the caring is done and the baby responds contentedly, are replaced by cues that elicit pleasure directly. As George Murdock (1949) and almost all nursing mothers are aware, the baby also provides the mother with the pleasure of sucking her full nipples and relieving the pressure in her breast. Soon the baby adds new cues that greatly increase the mother's excitement and joy at being with him or her—being attached to the baby. The smile is probably the most extensively studied and understood of all the attachment cues and their effects. It is a complex and highly patterned form of behavior in the mother-baby duet that is clearly universal.

Behavioral biologists argue that all of this massive armory of in-born baby cues and maternal responses has the effect initially of "attaching" the mother to her baby. Clearly they do have this minimal effect of keeping the mother with or close by the baby, which is obviously very important in her caring for and advancing the development of her baby in the first few years. But "being attached" is only the initial requirement for the mother-baby partnership to work its genetic destiny. A mother who merely became attached to her baby and hovered over while the baby screamed in agony from hunger would hardly fulfill the survival and development needs of her baby. "Attachment" is actually a hand-me-down concept from the days when the behaviorists dominated the study of child development.

Attachment itself is biologically useless unless it evokes the communing, identification, caring and adoring love, and the vast repertoire of play and practical activities that lead to and reinforce the multifarious forms of behavior that protect and advance the development of the baby. These general dimensions of love appear to be necessary both in motivating the mother to perform the adoring and caring forms of behavior and in *organizing* the complex relations among the many forms of behavior in ways that lead to the normal development of the child's own emotions and general sense of self, which in turn are vital to the child's later development of the normal human partnerships that lead to effective mating and parenting.

In human beings, the giving and receiving of the feelings of love and of intimacy are of crucial importance in themselves, independently of how they affect the behavior of the mother and the child. The human mother who hears her baby cry in the sharp and piercing cry of distress does not sit down and calculate a lifetime schedule of payoffs to determine whether it is to her benefit to help. The cry "pierces her to the heart" with caring and dread, so she dashes to care for the baby. It is presumably because emotions are important in and of themselves that human beings evolved facial expressions for communicating these emotions and use these and other forms of love communications with the baby profusely in those quiet periods of rest and play when no other form of caring or practical development behavior is being performed.

Academic psychologists in recent decades have only rarely referred to "love" between the mother and her child. Presumably as a result of this, they have also rarely referred to the "looks of love" exchanged by mothers and babies. On those occasions when they do, the reference is normally couched in terms of what everyone understands common-sensically. Thus both child development psychologists and psychologists studying facial expressions of emotion have rarely, if ever, noted the universality of the caring and adoration looks of love exchanged by mothers and babies, but they are obvious in any observations of their intimate everyday behavior.

UNIVERSAL EMOTIONS, THEIR INTERACTIONS AND INDEPENDENCE, AND THEIR EXPRESSIONS

The scientific study of the emotions and the bodily expressions of them, especially the facial expressions of them, was first undertaken by Charles Darwin, who published *The Expression of the Emotions in Men and Animals* in 1877. Darwin demonstrated the striking similarities of animal expressions of emotions with those of human beings. This was, he thought, clear evidence of the evolutionary origin of human emotions and their related patterns in animal emotions and behavior. While biologists now recognize that such similarities need not indicate a common origin, Darwin showed that there are certainly remarkable similarities in some of the expressions of emotion, even between human beings and wild mammals that have not been selected for their human characteristics. The "snarl" of the angry animal "threatening" to attack, which involves pulling the lips back to bare the fangs while staring intently with narrowed eyes at the offender or prey, and the deep growling accompanying it are basically the same in enraged human beings.

The behaviorists assumed our inherited (primary) emotions were very simple, very few, and very obvious. Thus they devoted little time to studying them. As the failures of the behaviorists became ever more apparent in the 1950s and 1960s, psychologists rapidly devoted themselves to "cognitive models" and the vast majority gave up any study of the emotions. In fact, some (e.g., Mandler, 1980) outdid the behaviorists in radical reductionism by asserting that emotions were not independent variables in human life at all, but merely vague, undifferentiated organic states with specific effects on actions only when they are rationally labeled. One whole school of child development psychologists has adopted this form of behavioristic rationalism and attempts to reduce all forms of mother-child experience that we recognize commonsensically to be emotional to cognitive forms of behavior. These extreme cognitive models have been well critiqued by other child development psychologists (see, especially, the excellent analyses of the different theoretical perspectives in Lamb and Campos, 1982; Lamb and Bornstein, 1987).

The vast evidence available to us about human life shows that there are many basic, partially independent dimensions to it and that each of these basic dimensions has a great number of subdimensions. Rather than seizing upon one basic dimension and pretending it is the whole thing, it is vitally important to the understanding of all experience of love, intimacy, and the Erotic (and all the rest of human life) to see that perceptions, emotions, cognitions, moral values, senses of selves, decision-making processes, willing, and behaviors and consequences are all independent basic dimensions or variables that also interact with each other (and thus are partially dependent on each other) in vastly complex ways in concrete situations.

While we shall continually be concerned with one or more specific

aspects of experience, we must always keep in mind that all but the
simplest forms of behavior in real situations involve all of these basic
dimensions. When we analyze adoration love, we are focusing our
attention on a specific dimension of emotion. In real life situations,
individuals can and do at times focus on that or any other particular
dimension of experience, but normally we experience each dimension in
relation to many others in vastly complex ways. When you feel
adoration love for someone at a particular time, your perceptions of that
person and the situation have great effects on some other emotions (e.g.,
seeing a loved one excites us); when you see or think of your loved one,
you think at the same time of many things you know about him or her
(e.g., that she will most likely want you to kiss her in a very specific way
to show how you love her); when you adore someone, you wish to see
him or her and, when you see him or her, your love affects your
perceptions of that person (e.g., through the mythicizing "pink lens
effect" we consider in Chapter 5); and so on and on. No one would
imagine commonsensically that it is possible to understand what
someone will do without knowing what their emotions are, what their
thoughts (cognitions) are, what they are perceiving at a given time, their
plans for the future, and so on.

The basic dimensions of emotion, their interactions, and their modes
of bodily expression, especially facial expressions, are universal in
human life. Every culture, and to some extent every cohesive group and
every individual, gives somewhat different emphases and de-emphases
to them. In some cultures, men normally try to hide or "mask" all the
emotions expressed by crying or weeping, but are capable of expressing
such emotions and of recognizing what the expressions of them mean.
Cross-cultural studies (Ekman, 1972; Ekman et al., 1972; Izard, 1971,
1980) have shown that the facial expressions of the basic emotions can
be clearly recognized even independent of the situations in which they
are aroused and expressed, though knowledge of the situation provides
information of great value in doing this. Considering how highly
situated most of human life is, and how much we normally rely on
complex interplays between situational cues and cues from bodily
expressions, this relatively high degree of situational independence of
the facial expressions of emotions is very striking and indicates how
basic these emotions and their expressions are to human life.

There is a great deal of controversy over exactly what the basic
dimensions of human emotion are (see the excellent essays in Plutchik
and Kellerman, 1980). Some theories try to show that there are only six,

eight, or some other small number of basic emotions and that all the others are compounded *meldings* of these. These theories certainly see far more complexity in the independent dimensions of emotion than the Freudian theory of the all-encompassing sexual libido, but they still greatly oversimplify our experience. These theories, for example, commonly try to show that an emotion such as sexual lust is actually made up of or constituted by more basic emotions, such as excitement and joy. It is clear from introspective analysis of our emotions that sexual lust is normally associated with a number of other emotions, including the more general dimensions of excitement, tension, and craving (before orgasmic release) and joy and peacefulness (afterward). But it also seems clear, as best we can tell from introspective observation and from discussing sexual experiences with other people, that there is a specific feeling of sexual lust that is associated only with sexual excitements of the adult and no other excitements. Sexual lust is not merely the genital skin pleasures that even infants can feel. Sexual lust is a melding of that with the *cravings* for sexual excitement and orgasmic reactions, which begin only in prepubescence and develop fully in pubescence.

There also are situations, however, in which otherwise nonsexual, exciting stimuli can make us feel sexually aroused. Some people, for example, are very aroused sexually by concerts, others by committing burglary. But the point is that they recognize that the feeling in these strange situations is sexual, even though there are no normal sexual cues to this effect. This is an example of what sexologists, such as Havelock Ellis (1936), called the "irradiation" of one emotion by another. It is a spreading of one emotion to another. It is a vital part of emotional experience, and very important in understanding how other emotions such as aggression can arouse sexual lust in some people. But it is also vitally important that we can tell, though sometimes with uncertainty, when one emotion has given rise to another. From such analyses it seems clear that there are many more basic emotions than psychologists normally believe. They are probably related in some way to the dozens of different "neurotransmitters" that have already been identified in the central nervous system.

The independent dimensions of emotions can be experienced alone, but normally a number are experienced together and then they normally interact with each other. Some emotions seem to be linked in set ways with others, so that when the one is experienced it triggers the other. Sexual lust triggers excitement and great excitements can trigger sexual lust in some people in some situations. When one emotion triggers another, it is (at least initially) the dominant *overtone-emotion*, and the one triggered is the subordinate *undertone-emotion*. For example, intense sexual lust seems to trigger an undertone of adoration, which seems to be why orgasmic and obsessive sexual relations, even those of the briefest duration, trigger at least a fleeting feeling of adoring "specialness" about the sex partner. Rollo May (1969) noted this even in his most casual sexual modernist patients. Undertones are far more easily repressed from consciousness so many sexually casual people are not aware of feeling such adoration and may even be aware only of the feeling of contempt for the "conquered" that soon follows the conquest.

Emotions in fact are generally paired *against* each other in complex ways to maintain some rough emotional balancing that prevents our getting stuck in a self-destructive rut. Consider, for example, the paired opposition between hunger and satiation. There are actually two separate centers for these in the hypothalamus that psychophysiologists can stimulate or excise experimentally. As the blood sugar level goes down, the hunger feeling is increasingly triggered (by sensors in the hunger center of the hypothalamus). As we eat, the blood sugar level increases and this increasingly triggers the satiation feeling, which *counterweights* (opposes) the hungry feeling, so we decrease our eating. If something physical or psychological intervenes to break this simple feedback system involving the two counterweighting feelings, the result can be a catastrophic drift or plunge in one uncounterweighted direction. The domestic horse, for example, has lost (through the domestication process) the satiation counterweight to hunger. Thus he will eat and eat until he founders and dies. Human beings in whom this counterweighted balance has been severely disturbed can become totally anorexic and starve themselves to death, become bulimic and swing from one extreme to the other, or gorge themselves into immense obesity. Normally, the human being recognizes rationally what is happening and intervenes with conscious, rational decision making to stop the drift toward catastrophe. (In some extreme cases of anorexia, however, the individuals seem to suffer such an extreme sense of insecurity about the whole self, which is so completely *embodied* in the perception of the body, that they see themselves as fat when they are extremely thin. We deal with the way very powerful emotions mythicize thinking and even perception in Chapter 5.) We shall see (in Chapter 3 and beyond) that individuals subconsciously and consciously counterweight their own emotions to decrease their suffering or to maintain control of themselves. "Whistling in the dark" to arouse feelings of courage or martial aggressiveness, which counterweight a feeling of anxiety that threatens us with being swept away by panic, is a simple example. Arlie Hochschild (1979) and many other sociologists of emotion refer to this as "emotion work." We shall see that there are very complex subconscious and conscious counterweighting interdependencies among our dimensions of insecurity and security that are of vital importance in coping with the vast problems of love, intimacy, and sex.

Some emotions aroused independently of each other interact in a very special way to produce a great intensification of each other, or of the dominant overtone-emotion. We call this multiplication effect emotional *potentiation* because it is exactly like the well-known potentiating effect some drugs have on each other. Some "uppers" and "downers" when mixed together produce a far greater "high" than the two separately would do. Amphetamines and opiates potentiate each other in this way.

Whenever the separate dimensions of emotions are experienced simultaneously, in addition to such specific interactions among them, there is an overall interaction that leads us to experience all of them together as a uniquely integrated whole, an *emotional gestalt* experience. When we listen to a symphony, we can focus our attention on and thus hear each major instrument playing, but our experience of the symphony is an experience of all of the independent sounds melded together into a whole sound. The same is true of *emotional melding* (gestalt). Izard (1971), Ekman (1972b), and other psychologists generally focus on the discrete dimensions of the melded emotions. In everyday life, we normally focus on the overall gestalt of emotions, but in some situations, such as those in which we experience conflicting or ambivalent emotions, we may focus intensely on the separate dimensions and insist our emotions are confused or that we do not know how we feel.

Every love experience is made up of a number of these independent dimensions of emotions and the other basic variables of human life; their specific interactions with each other; and their overall, uniquely experienced meldings (gestalts). There are many dimensions of love, intimacy, and the Erotic; and in any particular love experience all of the ones present interact and meld together to produce a *love gestalt*. There are certain very common meldings of love dimensions into love gestalts, and these are the elements on which analysts of love commonly concentrate (see, for example, Lasswell and Lobsenz, 1980; Goldstein et al., 1977; Schwartz et al., 1980; Walster and Walster, 1978). These are *natural cultural gestalts* (or types) of love, which are commonly recognized in a culture. "Best friend lover" is a good example today in our culture. While it is sometimes useful to deal with these natural types, it is very confusing to talk about them as if all love experiences fit into them. There are as many love gestalts as there are combinations of the independent dimensions, which is certainly a huge number. Each culture conceptualizes and names these natural types somewhat differently. Though most of the differences are not important enough to concern us, every individual's love experience is somewhat different from that of everyone else and even from his or her own love experience at other times in other situations.

Far more important than the natural cultural gestalts of love are the natural *genetic love gestalts*, which are the genetic foundations of love on which the members of cultures build to elaborate their cultures. The natural genetic love gestalts are made of the basic, genetically highly primed dimensions. They are gestalts of love dimensions that are so highly interdependent by genetic priming that they are common in all cultures. How highly primed and thus how common in different cultures varies greatly, but we shall be concerned only with the most highly primed. These are maternal and paternal love, a child's love for parents and siblings, friendly love, romantic love, Erotic love, obsessive Erotic love (daimonic love), and sexual obsessions.

A few additional distinctions will help clarify this and are very important in our whole argument. *Romantic love* (designated with lower-case letters) is a genetic love gestalt found in widely varying degrees and frequencies in all cultures. It is a gestalt made up of *at least* adoration love and the Erotic. Each culture then elaborates on this genetic gestalt, emphasizing some dimensions and downplaying others, and generally adding some other dimensions of experience. Some cultures, such as our modernist subculture, give powerful (even exclusive) emphasis to sexuality, but cannot normally fully repress the rest of the gestalt. Others, such as all earlier periods of our Judeo-Christian Western cultures, give far more emphasis to the procreative and creative dimensions of the Erotic. Victorians deemphasized sex in order to emphasize the procreative and creative. Again, the people of Lesu (Powdermaker, 1933/1971) obviously have romantic love, emphasize sex for early life and the Erotic after marriage, and greatly emphasize the sense of fatedness and being out of control of one's will, felt when in the grip of these passions potentiating each other (hence their use of love magic on a massive scale). Most very poor societies see romantic love as disruptive economically and thus often as dangerous. They generally oppose the free choice that leads to romantic love. *Romantic Love* (capitalized) is the distinctive Western cultural elaboration of the genetic gestalt, developed mainly from the fourteenth to nineteenth centuries (with earlier inputs from the tradition of Courtly Love). Western Romantic Love, and the closely related cultural patterns of other civilizations, have emphasized individual uniqueness, fatedness, the fusion of souls, and the potentiating conflicts of the lovers with the rest of society. Romantic Love is still common in our society, as we shall see in some cases, but it is waning. Today the emphasis in our culture is on the adoration and sexual dimensions, with a growing emphasis on the fusion of selves. When there is a high degree of fusion of selves in romantic love, the lovers are said to be "in-love" (hyphenated), a vital distinction we shall use throughout this work.

Romantic love today tends, then, to be very *duetistic*, emphasizing the isolation, exclusiveness, and supremacy of the fused lovers over all else, even their children, because the sexual is emphasized over the rest of the Erotic. This cultural gestalt promotes dependent love as a way of counterweighting the growing insecurities over feeling unlovable (see Chapter 3), which produces a craving to be loved, rather than a craving to love, which is what an individual feels predominantly when secure in his or her own sense of lovability. We have no doubt, however, that our vast, pluralistic, and individualistic culture has members who share every genetic gestalt and almost every cultural gestalt found around the world. Civilization in general involves vast subcultural elaborations of the genetic and cultural dimensions of love, intimacy, and sex, just as with most other dimensions of life. "Primitive" cultures have neither sadomasochist subcultures nor the Romantic Love fantasies of Gothic novels, but similar subcultural forms are found in most of the civilizations, at least underground.

THE SHIFTING EQUILIBRIUM OF ATTACHMENT AND INDEPENDENCE AND THE DEVELOPMENT OF INSECURITY AND SECURITY

As we saw above, the communications of the emotions of love are vital in and of themselves, independent of any effects they have on the other emotions, behavior, or aspects of the mother-child relationship.

Though there are probably many ways in which they are vital in themselves, which we do not yet know about, certainly one of the most important is their powerful effects on the child's own feelings of love and other basic feelings about him- or herself. Though some developmental psychologists may have exaggerated in arguing that the baby comes to identify him- or herself completely (or almost so) with the mother's self, there can be little doubt that the baby does identify with her to a very high degree in the first year of life and then progressively de-identifies with her, even at times dis-identifying with her (i.e., rebelling *against* her) as the baby develops his or her independent and individuated sense of self. Normally, there remains a large degree of identification with parents throughout life, but this is progressively diminished from about one year. One of the crucial things children absorb from this identification with the mother, probably beginning somewhere around the sixth month of life, is their own feelings toward themselves. Normally, the mother communicates love for the baby and the baby absorbs this love of him- or herself, both caring and adoring, thereby becoming basically self-loving. If, however, the mother hates the baby or is indifferent or rejecting, the baby absorbs these feelings. If the mother is ambivalent, or alternates from one to the other, the child's self-feelings will presumably be ambivalent. As far as we can determine, nothing much is known from detailed observations of what the complex relations might be between various mixes of loving and hating (and other emotions) because psychologists have not been observing them systematically. It is only these broad outlines that seem clear. (Bowlby, 1979, has summarized and systematized the findings.) We shall return to them in the next chapter.

Beyond their importance in themselves, the communications of love, pride, and other emotions between the mother and her child inspire a mutual and generalized state of intense positive emotionality, which powerfully affects and reinforces almost everything experienced at the time. Every adult who has ever fallen deeply in-love is aware of this generalized and intense state of emotionality. When we are fully possessed by it, firmly in the grip of the "magical spell of love," we feel like we are "walking on air," like we are "soaring," like we could "climb the highest mountain," like we have magical powers, like this unique moment is timeless and eternal. We are all aware of how intense the memories of those moments can be, even many decades later. Every detail relevant to our love—which often means merely the face of the loved one—is emblazoned or "imprinted" eidetically in our memories.

The learning that comes from this generalized state of intense emotionality is quite comparable to the "imprint learning" observed in some animals. (For a survey of the massive evidence and theories see Hess, 1973, especially pp. 324-350.) The memories of some experiences can be so intense, so minute, and so unchanging compared to other memories that psychologists sometimes call them "light bulb learning," referring to the way in which the memory is so intensely lighted while all else is darkness, lost in forgetfulness. While grownups will not normally remember these scenes with their mothers before the age of about three years, most people have some very vivid memories at that time of the intense excitement and joy felt in their loving duets with their mothers. It is very easy to see how powerful the effects of these emotional scenes are by watching any baby "playing" with a loving mother (see Chapter 4).

The learning that takes place under this generalized state of intense emotionality is what learning psychologists now commonly call *observational learning* (imprint learning is an extreme form of it). This form of learning does not depend only on so-called classical or operant conditioning or on trial and error learning, in which successes are reinforced by the pleasures associated with the success. They are normally going on at the same time as observational learning, but observational learning comes directly from observing, though it may also be the preliminary to *learning by observing-and-doing* (which is then reinforced by positive and negative feelings attendant on the outcomes of the doing). The crucial thing is that the child (and, to a less extent, the mother) *learns by observing an entire scene*, so that the learning is a global learning that includes both a general context and many particulars. This *scene learning* is a form of *gestalt learning*. (We shall examine its importance further in Chapter 4.)

When securely engrossed in this primal scene of love with the mother, the child can be catapulted into an ecstasy or cast into despair by the mere change in the mother's facial expressions of emotions. Every mother has seen this happen many times (and some can remember with a sense of despair the instances in which they unintentionally precipitated their babies into despair by showing the wrong facial expression). Mothers are no doubt far less affected by these facial communications of emotion from their babies, because they have a vast repertoire of previous experience and a whole life context into which they put such experiences. Nevertheless, they can be profoundly affected by their babies' failure for any reason to respond to their loving expressions with loving expressions. Mothers of babies born blind, and thus unable to see their loving expressions, normally become depressed and begin subconsciously to reject their babies, unless they learn to understand the nature of the problem and to emphasize nonvisual forms of communication.

Psychologists have not yet devised any means of studying the effects on global or *scene learning* produced by mother's communications of love, pride, and other positive emotions expressed in the primal scene. But they have devised some excellent experimental methods for demonstrating the powerful effects of the mother's facial expressions of specific negative emotions on specific actions. For example, babies who crawl to a realistic painting of a cliff (which triggers the genetically primed fear of heights) will look to their mothers' faces for emotional signs of fear or reassurance (Lamb and Campos, 1982, discuss these in great detail).

Bronislaw Malinowski has provided an excellent example of the way in which facial expressions of emotions (presumably by parents) seem to have the most powerful effects on the long-run development of a child's character. Among the Trobriand Islanders, the toddler is greatly indulged in almost every wish by a loving mother, father, and other relatives. The one major exception is that brothers and sisters are not allowed to play together because of the dread of brother-sister incest and the consequent training from toddlerdom onward of the two to remain at a great emotional distance. The infant boy is taught to keep his distance from his sister (*luguta*), not by physical punishment, but by emotional punishments meted out by facial expressions (and, presumably, oral expressions supporting the facial):

> Above all, the child experiences an emotional shock when it becomes aware of the expression of horror and anger on the faces of its elders when they correct it. This emotional contagion, this perception of moral reactions in the social environment is perhaps the most powerful factor in a native community by which norms and values are imposed on an individual character [1929, p. 520].

The mother's loving of her child is roughly orchestrated to keep her own emotions and interactions with the child in key with the child's own genetically primed development. Their entire *duet of love attachment and interdependent development* slowly evolves. Children develop new abilities that enable them to become independent of their mothers and develop new emotional primings that push them toward increasing independence—individuation from the mother. At the same time, the mother both encourages this and discourages overindependence. It is remarkable how closely interlocked their mutual developments are. At first the child is almost totally dependent on the mother and, as we have seen, it is she who is emotionally primed, both from within herself and by the armory of adoration-love-cuteness cues and caring-love cues her baby emits, to remain "attached" to the baby. The evidence available so far indicates that babies add greatly to their armory of love-cues as they become more able to roll over, inch along, and do other things that might hurt if the mothers did not become more attached to them. Then, as babies develop the ability to move around, thus doing things that could injure or kill them, they begin to develop their own powerful repertoire of emotional primings that attach them to the mother. At precisely the time the baby is becoming ever-more able physically to wander away from the mother, and is being primed by developing emotions to do so, the baby is developing emotional primings of love for the mother and anxieties about the unknown world and people beyond that pull and push him or her back toward the mother—"attaching" the baby to the mother at the very time he or she is slowly moving away and at the very time the mother might be increasingly attaching herself to a new baby.

The baby's identification with the mother, the growing adoration for her, and later the caring for her, make her important to the baby in every way. Just as with adults in-love, the baby's whole life is affected by or partially *depends* on her. This is the *love dependency* that is a *necessary* consequence of being in-love. Somewhere around six months, the baby develops anxieties, especially the anxiety about strangers, which push him or her back to the mother for help in dealing with these insecurities. This *insecurity dependency* is what people normally mean by "dependency," a concept that has been subject to great confusion. Insecurity dependency is also a normal part of love partnerships. It is only overdependency—clinging dependency—that prevents the further development of the sense of security necessary to develop a more independent sense of self. If all has gone right in the baby's development, and love with the mother has endowed him or her with a feeling of basic security (see Chapter 3), the baby's conflictful emotions and actions, and those of the mother, will continue to shift slowly toward independence from the mother, he or she will develop an ever-more independent sense of self, will slowly and partially de-identify and fall out of love with her, and will begin the many years of falling ever more deeply in-love with other people that will eventually lead him or her to reproduce this great shifting equilibrium of dependency and independency, of attachment and individuation.

The mother becomes the rock of security around which the baby explores the world. The more secure the baby feels in the love partnership with her, the more secure he or she feels in exploring all the exciting possibilities raised by a new mobility. At first, the baby routinely keeps her presence in mind and checks to make sure she is there and that she does not signal danger, as we saw her do above in our discussions of the cliff-drawing experiments. As the baby gains more feelings of instrumental security from successful experience, he or she moves further away and becomes ever more independent of the mother (see Bowlby, 1979).

Around one year of age, children enter a phase of *infant rebellion* that is very similar to the rebellion they will later experience in adolescence. Parents, especially mothers, begin making major demands on children at this time, though the degree and types of demands obviously vary greatly from culture to culture (see Mahler, 1975). Children probably feel more betrayed by these demands than adults feel when their lovers try to reform them in some way. Children differ greatly in how "headstrong" they are in resisting these demands and insisting on doing what they want to do, but all of them resist, as all mothers are aware. "Overconformity" is likely a sign of great insecurity.

As long as the love partnership with the mother has been firmly and securely established before this, the child will compromise with her demands if they are made persistently and with love as the foundation for them. But infant rebellion begins the many years' long process of partially falling out of love with the mother, which is necessary for the child to develop fully his or her own sense of self, to become independent, and to develop fully love feelings for others. There can be little doubt that the normal child by this time, about one to two years old, has a clear recognition of his or her self as independent from the mother and, from this time onward, develops his or her independent sense of self in direct proportion to becoming independent in the world. All of this development of the independent sense of self depends profoundly on the degrees of security and insecurity felt (see Chapter 3).

NOTE

1. In fact, we've found that most people do not yet do so clearly and consistently. And the failure to do so can be a disaster, contributing terribly to confusion over what love is

and is not. Probably because of their fundamental importance to all human life, the core meanings of love have also been *extended* metaphorically to cover feelings and actions similar in some ways to those of love proper. Someone who says "I *love* fried chicken" means the taste of fried chicken is extremely pleasurable, possibly even triggering some undertones of excitement and joy, as adoration love does. This does *not* mean this lusty eater is a lustful eater who has sexual feelings for fried chicken legs. "Love" can be extended metaphorically to cover almost anything that gives us great pleasure, especially if this is a persistent pleasure involving excitement (see Solomon, 1981).

3

BECOMING INSECURE/
BECOMING SECURE

I don't understand myself, am dissatisfied with myself and everybody else. In the condition I am in now, I am absolutely good for nothing. I can work hard 1 to 2 days a week, and for that I am mortally weak the next day. I constantly have the feeling that I'm going to collapse. Does it come from my longing for "her and him"?? From the irritating and so fatiguing daily excitements with Father here?? From sympathy with Mutti?? Because I see Mother suffering, or from my own occupations, in which I am perhaps not yet quite at home? Je ne sais pas, for I have not overworked myself as yet [in English]. If only I could work the way I would so much like to. Perhaps it's only a weakness of will that makes me succumb so often to my headache, limpness, lack of courage and desire? No, that shall not be: I will now be stronger than this other complaining me: I will.

> *Karen Horney* (*Adolescent Diaries*, 1980)

There's no such thing as love . . . is there?

> *25-year-old prostitute*

Love is nice, but I don't know if it's necessary.

> *Lisa* (studied by Maxine Schnall)

I'd rather be alone by myself than feel alone with someone else.

> *Susan Strassberg*

Insecurity and security are recognized commonsensically to have profound effects on our entire lives. In discussions of love experience, it is common to hear teenagers, especially those with a bit of painful experience, make comments such as "He's so insecure that he's always dependent" or "He's one of the most secure people I know and my friendships with other guys just don't threaten him." As these teenagers are well aware, it is impossible to understand love experience without understanding insecurity and security.

Most of the attempts by depth psychologists to understand the general phenomena of love, especially the painful problems people so commonly experience with them today, have drawn heavily upon these commonsensical ideas. For example, Erich Fromm's popular work *The Art of Loving* (1974) accepts the distinction between immature-insecure love and mature-secure love. There is a core of very important truth to these commonsense ideas, but they are not very detailed or systematic. Because almost all of the depth psychologies were forged in clinical attempts to overcome extremely painful and incapacitating feelings of being unsafe—anxious, depressed, phobically fearful, filled with dread— they concentrate a great deal of attention on insecurity. This is normally dealt with in terms of "neurotic fears," "phobic obsessions," "paranoid dreads of retribution resulting from guilt feelings and projections," "borderline syndromes," and so on (see especially Horney, 1950, 1980; May, 1977; Nicholi, 1978; Yalom, 1980). These analyses are more developed and contribute more to our understanding of love experience, but they commonly fail to see all of the basic dimensions of insecurity and security and their many interdependencies.

The Freudians have focused most of their attention on insecurities supposed to have been caused by Oedipal conflicts and the repression of sexuality. Most insecurities have nothing to do with these and most sexual insecurities spring from more basic insecurities—especially that of feeling unlovable—which produce dread of intimacy and lead to rejections of potential loves and many other patterns. Karen Horney (1950) saw this and was excommunicated for her departure from existing orthodoxy. Her work made great contributions to understanding insecurities in the senses of dominance and competence, but failed to provide the systematic theory needed to understand the great complexities of insecurity and security in our everyday lives. By focusing on insecurities, and failing to see those in relation to the senses of security that are dominant in everyday life (but see Erikson, 1963), the work of the depth psychologists cast a neurotic pall of despair over

human life in general (Douglas, 1984a). The close partnership forged in
recent years by clinicians, developmental psychologists, and even some
naturalistic existential observers has alleviated some of the problems
(see Bowlby, 1971-1979; Garmezy and Rutter, 1983, 1985; Parkes,
1984). Most of this work, however, remains at a low level of analysis.
Our work is aimed predominantly at providing a more comprehensive
understanding of the many dimensions of insecurity and security.

The basic ideas captured by the commonsense ideas of insecurity and
security are that each individual has

(1) a more or less generalized *feeling* of being unsafe (or anxious) or safe (or
    peaceful), which may be dormant until triggered and then leads to
(2) more or less generalized *expectations* of pains or pleasures, failures or
    successes, and thence to
(3) a more or less generalized *readiness to respond* defensively or hopefully,
    and
(4) a more or less generalized system of many *tactics and strategies* to defend
    the self (*defense mechanisms*) or to open and expand the self in the
    biosphere (*iniative mechanisms*).

It is vitally important to keep in mind all four of these major dimensions
of the idea: feeling, expectation, readiness to respond (i.e., attitude or
motivation), and action.

Psychologists who have considered only some of these dimensions
have been easily led astray into simplistic ideas. E. H. Erikson's (1963)
theory of "basic distrust" and "basic trust" is probably the best known
and most widely used of all the psychological theories of insecurity and
security. Basic distrust is a generalized expectation of disappointment,
pain, or failure from others, which leads to a generalized readiness to
respond defensively to them. Almost all psychologists of love and child
development recognize that these two core dimensions of insecurity and
security are very important, but Erikson's failure to emphasize the
feelings that can give rise to and organize these and later cognitive states
of readiness to act and action states generally prevents their seeing the
most important sources of insecurity and security and seeing that there
are a number of interdependent dimensions of them. For example,
Lamb and Campos (1982, pp. 226-232) have shown how child development psychologists have been led by Erikson's theory to see the mother's
schedule of reinforcements of the child as crucial in their development.
Erikson's theory leads psychologists to expect that caretaker consis-
tency is vital in producing basic trust, or basic "effectance" (Lamb and

Campos, p. 232), and inconsistency in producing basic distrust, or basic "ineffectance." They have generally failed to see that inconsistency is a basic part of human life, at least in the sense that situations are different and problematic, and must be dealt with differently and creatively if one is to be successful—and safe—in life. All parents must deal continually with the need to teach their children this inherently problematic and situated nature of life. The scenario so well known to all parents runs something like this. The child does something that upsets the parent. The child protests in the best spirit of absolutist moral outrage: "But you told me that . . ." And the parent, undeterred by this wounded abstract rationalism, responds, "Yes, I did, but this is a different situation and you'd better find a new way to deal with it or else."

The matter of crucial importance to the child and to the parent is feeling involved in such "training exercises." It is the feeling overtones and undertones that focus and organize the next crucial bits of information, those of good intentions and bad intentions, which are crucial in inferring the trustability and untrustability of others. Most important, as long as children feel that their parents love them across all situations (as an unconditional background to all actions), then even massive inconsistency need not produce generalized distrust, as long as its reason is understandable and any misunderstandings cleared up. Children are not simpleminded computers who register "Fatal Error" and go into a lifelong stall or spiral downward into total distrust just because all parents seem sometimes very inconsistent. Even the most hypocritical parents, who consistently say one thing and do another, can raise very secure children, if they are loving hypocrites. Because cognitive and moral factors have important independent effects in life, however, we can confidently predict that a loving hypocrite will have more trouble doing so than a loving parent who consistently tries to act honestly (except in those situations in which love demands that massive "white lies" be told, such as on Christmas Eve).

We are predominantly concerned with the emotional dimensions of insecurity and security. They are the most important; but cognitive expectations, readiness states, and actions are always assumed here to be important. We shall especially argue that one cognitive factor is extremely interdependent with emotions, especially early in life. The feelings of insecurity and security develop complex interdependencies with the "cognitive" factors of *pictorial images* (eidetic pictures of *world scenes*) of how others feel and act toward the child and how he or she feels and acts toward them (Bowlby calls these "representational models," 1979, pp. 126-160, but this does not capture their *pictorial* essence). These pictorial images and feelings also develop complex interdependencies with *action systems*. Any one of these three general variables can change independently and trigger the others, which then react back on the triggering variable to modify it. For example, it is most common for the very early feelings and images of adoration love-duet scenes to lie dormant and unconscious until the adolescent or adult falls deeply in-love for the second time. As the adoration love feelings, intimacy, and dependency increase, they trigger those dormant images of such love scenes, which then trigger feelings of insecurity and security that were involved with the images. Thus the individual with a dormant scenic-expectation of abandonment and betrayal by a lover may have no idea of this until falling in-love triggers a panic of jealousy. But, once triggered, this "conjugal paranoia" (as some psychiatrists call it) becomes an independent factor weighting the interpretations of newly perceived scenes so that even expressions of love can be distorted into deceit intended to hide betrayals.

Insecurities and securities vary in the degrees of their *relevance* (or salience) to situations in life and thus in their *situational pervasiveness*. They can be relevant only to one situation or generalize across situations until they *pervade* all of life (as happens in *panic* reactions). They also vary in the degrees of their *embeddedness* (or *rootedness*) *in the sense of self*. Embeddedness is the strength of the hold a sense of insecurity or security has on an individual. The more embedded, the more difficult it is to change. Very early senses of insecurity and security tend to be so embedded in the basic sense of self that they cannot be changed, though they may be *dominated* (*overridden*) by very powerful situational overtones of insecurities or securities, and they can be situationally *evaded* and *counterweighted*, which is what most behavioral modification therapy now tries to do, with considerable success.

Researchers have shown that the Freudian theories of early oral and other "traumas" and "overindulgences" were quite mistaken. No monocausal, mechanistic, or linear theories of insecurity and security fit the vastly complex, interdependent, and changeable human experience (Sameroff, 1975; Sameroff and Cavanaugh, 1979; Kagan and Zelazo, 1978). Growing recognition of these facts has led most developmental psychiatrists and psychologists to adopt the multivariate risk model to explain relations between earlier and later experience (Masten and Garmezy, 1985). This is a very practical model for the arts of clinical work, but it errs in the other extreme and leads to an abandonment of any detailed theory. Most of the evidence for the relative lack of importance of early experience for later comes from the study of cognitive factors like IQ. These are far less affected by early experience than emotional factors, but even there the argument was overdone (Lamb and Campos, 1982, p. 233).

In general, we find that early experience is a vastly complex, ever-shifting system of duets ("dyads") in which infants and emotionally important others interact to affect each other, especially to affect emotions. Even emotionally traumatic early experiences (such as "birth traumas") may not have much effect directly on later life, but will generally do so by leading family members to organize their long-run, interactional emotional lives around it. *The long-run effects of early experience are overwhelmingly the result of vastly complex, cumulative factors, which produce situationally generalized senses of emotional insecurity and security so embedded that they are experienced as aspects of the sense of self itself when they are triggered by later experience.* Because of their powerful, pervasive, and embedded nature, basic (see below) senses of insecurity and security pervade cognitions, attitudes, and actions, weighting and organizing these in distinctive ways that have high probabilities of producing *self-reinforcing consequences*, especially in the emotional reactions of others. Thus these early basic emotional insecurities and securities generally lead to long-run *drift (stochastic) processes* reinforcing themselves. These are called *autocatalytic drift processes* by economists (see Douglas, in press). Except (possibly) in the most extreme cases (of "borderline" and "schizoid" reactions), these early (basic) senses of insecurity and security may be counterweighted (even overridden) by later (situated—see below) senses of insecurities and securities. They may also be *cognitively* managed (discounted, evaded) and generally are increasingly evaded as cognition develops and the individual learns by trial and error how to do so.

The self defends itself against the too intense pains of insecurities (those above a threshold of normal self-control and coping) by progressively developing a complex *system of defensive tactics and strategies*, and opens itself to the pleasures of greater securities by progressively developing a complex *system of initiative tactics and strategies*. At any high level of insecurity, the defense system overrides the initiative system, but normally the two are used jointly as interdependent parts of the progressive development of a *system of coping-and-growth* tactics and strategies for projecting and incorporating the self into the world, with an *optimum of safety and riskiness* in relation to the inherently problematic balance of threats and opportunities. This *creative life-thrust* is motivated by the *Erotic cravings* of the innermost sense of self. As Western people have known for eons, the lust for the creative growth and expansion of life—Eros—is the heart of our innermost sense of the self.

It is very important, as we shall see in detail, that the individual defends his or her sense of self in part by *counterweighting* dimensions of insecurity with achieved dimensions of security. Some of these patterns of counterweighting are highly primed genetically and by nearly universal experience in life, so those dimensions appear to be inherently interdependent in those ways. Such interdependencies of insecurity and security are now well recognized in the forms of "compensations" and "overdriven strivings." But our life studies show that these are far more complex and important than has commonly been recognized.

PRIMARY, SECONDARY, AND TERTIARY INSECURITY AND SECURITY

For our purposes, we shall distinguish three levels in the senses of insecurity and security. *Primary general insecurity and security* is apparently derived predominantly from one's first few years of interaction with the mother and other extremely close partners, almost always in the family in our society. No doubt genetically primed *temperament* can make major initial inputs (see Gittelman, 1985). Some babies are born more anxious or anxiety-prone; but mother-child duets modulate all temperamental factors. We shall shorten primary general insecurity and security to *primary insecurity* or *primary security*, depending on which side of the continuum one falls. We must always keep in mind, however, that the degree of either is very important. Life is a matter of degree, not of either-or. The feelings of insecurity and security that are developed at this earliest stage of life tend to be powerful, pervasive, and embedded because this is the stage in which the individual's sense of self is being developed; the feelings of insecurity and security become highly embedded aspects of the sense of self itself; and the individual has not yet developed most of the powers of discrimination, compartmentalization, disattending, repression, and other cognitive tactics of the system of self-defense that he or she will eventually have. The feelings of insecurity and security that come from the communing (or failure to commune) with the mother thus tend to be highly embedded in the child's whole sense of self, thus pervading all life, and to be as powerful as the feelings about the mother and the self.

The normal human condition seems to be one of a low degree of primary security in feeling hopeful, lovable, good, dominant, and successful (see Figure 3.1). This is very much the assumption of common sense in the Western world, but there are great variations in this from culture to culture and from individual to individual within our own culture. As depicted in Figure 3.1, the feeling of dread of death or hope of life is the most powerful, pervasive, and embedded dimension of insecurity and security. In early childhood, it appears to be highly interdependent with feeling hated or loved by the mother and other partners. Hatred—as communicated by body language, voice tone, rejection, and physical abuse—inspires obsessive dread.[1]

In early life, being hated or loved is by far the most powerful, pervasive, and embedded of the dimensions of insecurity and security for the vast majority of people. This experience begins much earlier than the others (by around six months) and, as we can see from the arrows in Figure 3.1 depicting emotional undertones triggered by one dimension in others, this dimension has profound influences on the others. The infant who feels securely lovable has a strong tendency later to develop feelings of being a good person, dominant, and successful (potent).

The great majority of people develop a moderate degree of self-adoration and self-caring from their communings with their mothers and thus have a moderate degree of primary security in feeling lovable. Almost everyone experiences enough conflict with his or her mother, and other close loved ones a little later in life—especially in the difficult phase of *infant rebellion* (about one to four years, see Mahler, 1975) against early child training—to have at least some secondary insecurity (see below) in some situations of life, however, so that such situations later in life that involve rejections or other signs of indifference or hatred of them produce secondary self-hatreds (see Chapter 6). Those who have received the most unalloyed adoration and caring from the mother and other close family members are the unusual individuals whose lives are pervaded by warm caring and friendly feelings, except in the most traumatic situations.

Secondary general insecurity and security (*secondary insecurity* and *secondary security*) come later, though commonly in the first several years of life, and are built over the already existing sense of primary insecurity and security. When there is an inversion in the relations

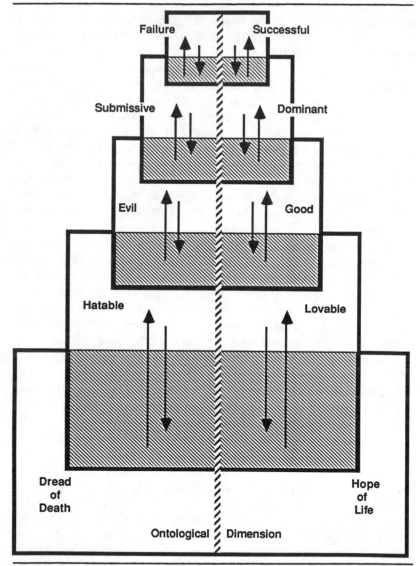

Figure 3.1:   Dimensions of Insecurity and Security, and Their Major Interdependencies

between the two levels, then the ambivalence in feelings of insecurity and security can be great and the individual can rapidly swing from one to the other, from soaring hope to plummeting despair from one situation to another. This condition is commonly seen, for example, in individuals who have had very loving partnerships with their mothers in the first few years of life, thus developing strong senses of primary security and a strong sense of self, but who then feel rejected or abused by the mothers, or feel very badly treated by others who wholly or partially replace the mothers in their lives, such as fathers or siblings who assume greater control of the children. It is this pattern of ambivalent insecurity and security that is normally observed in clinical studies (e.g., Henderson, 1974; Parkes, 1972). Bowlby (1971-1979), Henderson (1974), Parkes (1973), and others have noted the importance of *discontinuities in attachment bonding* in producing *anxious, ambivalent attachment*, which leads in later life to ambivalent love-hate relations, craving love while fearing it, overcaring while rejecting romantic love, and many other "neurotic" symptoms.[2]

Some estimate that as many as one-third of Americans and British now suffer from these early insecurities (Bowlby, 1979, p. 136). This, for example, is the pattern of early life that is extremely common in the most compulsive gamblers (Dickerson, 1983; Holden, 1985). Their mothers have normally been loving toward them, but they have also been highly dependent and submissive to emotionally and physically abusive fathers who become more important in determining what happens to the child, especially the male child, after the first year or so. The gamblers have intense feelings of having been rejected and abused ("pushed around," "beaten," and so on). But what the psychologists have not generally noted is that these individuals have not withdrawn, broken down, given up, become totally dependent addicts (though a high percentage are addicted to some drugs), or so deeply depressed they are unable to function. They normally have enough primary sense of security to get jobs, get married, become extremely manipulative, be trusted enough to get huge loans or embezzle great sums of money, and so on.

The key to understanding them is that they have a secondary insecurity (an undertone) that partially counterbalances the primary sense of security (the dominant overtone). Their overall ambivalent sense of insecurity and security leads them to swing easily from one extreme to another, from soaring optimism to crashing despair, but the dominant sense is the positive one of soaring hope, which is potentiated by the secondary dread or despair. It is this soaring hope, born of the primary security potentiated by the secondary insecurity, that leads them into massive mythical expectations of the "Big Score." Almost all of them are trying desperately to become extremely rich, powerful, and famous to overcome their secondary insecurity. We shall show below how this insecurity-counteraction works.

While the compulsive gamblers are a fine beginning for studying these profound ambivalences and their effects, because they are "writ large" in these extremes, they also obscure the complexities normally observed. There is a remarkably large number of people who suffer from secondary insecurity in our society. This includes large percentages of people who had no major love problems at home but who at a very early age, before they can make the distinctions and compartmentalizations necessary to understand and deal emotionally with the conflicts, find themselves stigmatized by most of the people around them for racial, religious, ethnic, or other reasons. At the extreme, stigmatization and ostracism by the general community, even in mature adulthood, can produce a traumatic ontological (Being) insecurity so extreme that defenses are overwhelmed and the individual dies. Less extreme forms of secondary "self-hatred" pervade the entire lives of many subjected to such early stigmatization and ostracism.

The great majority of people who suffer from secondary insecurity do not fall at the extremes of the compulsive gamblers and most of them do not become involved in games of compulsive gambling such as horse racing and cards, or do so only at one or more periods in their lives when situational insecurities greatly exacerbate their secondary insecurity. Later situations, individual constructions of the meanings of these, and individual choices of action have a great effect in *channeling* them into *protracted drifts* into gambling or into alternative forms of behavior. Those who have this secondary insecurity and primary security ambivalence often are channeled by emotionally explosive, *turning-point experiences*, such as a "Big Win" or other stroke of "luck" or "fate," which imprints their potentiated optimism on that experience. Most of them take their great risks in what are socially defined as more "realistic" activities, such as the stock market or love affairs (in which they may play *Erotic roulette* by having intercourse without contraception in a desperate lunge for love and marriage happily ever after) or revolutionary political activity. We observed the maniacal craving and Quixotic quest for the "Big Score" and the "fast life" in almost all big-time drug dealers, who were casting their fates on each big deal (Adler, 1985).

We call this the *Fyodor Dostoyevsky syndrome*, because he was probably the greatest analyst of it (see Mochulsky, 1967; Payne, 1961; Peace, 1971; Yarmolinsky, 1957). Dostoyevsky's partnership with his mother appears to have been a loving one with few complications, other than her inability or unwillingness to prevent the father from imposing his stern and rigid life-mold on the boy at an early age. We suspect that Dostoyevsky and most people with this experience have some suppressed ambivalent feeling of betrayal and resentment because they believe the mother *chose* not to stop the attacks. If, however, she was the victim of attack, especially the primary victim, then she may be completely absolved of guilt, thus diminishing the ambivalence the child feels in his or her sense of insecurity and security. We have observed this in several of our life studies, one of whom has an unalloyed love for his victimized mother. He identified overwhelmingly with her from the earliest years, began playing dolls at an early age, feels that his innermost sexual-self is female, and has become almost exclusively "gay" in his twenties.

Dostoyevsky's secondary insecurity seems to have been exacerbated as well by the fact that he experienced his father as ambivalent toward him, both loving and hating, so that he was continually subjected to "mixed signals." From his early years, he was highly aware of the two selves that lived inside his body, one loving and one hating, and the two together making partnerships with people highly ambivalent and tortured. His first novel, *Poor Folk*, depicted the agonizing futility of loving anyone, experienced by the stigmatized poor and weak who depend on others for their very existence. His second novel, *The Double*, depicted the ravages caused by the split personality: the innermost self—the dominant overtone—loving the self, and the outer self—an undertone sense of self—projected from within that hates the overtone sense of self and is out to destroy the overtone self.

Dostoyevsky's later novels, especially *The Brothers Karamazov*, were often concerned with murderous rages that have been suppressed and then suddenly explode, sometimes resulting in the murder of the father, combined with a deep but hopeless love for a loving woman who is predominantly good but is marred by her own evils. His early love affairs and his first marriage were extremely ambivalent struggles between love and hate, which drove him to tortured distraction, and to a protracted period of soaring hopes and plummeting depressions involved in compulsive gambling (all carefully depicted in *The Gambler*).

Though he probably never completely escaped the early ravages of secondary insecurity, he did finally overcome most of them. He broke the pattern of love and hate relations, married a woman who adored and cared for him and his work, loved her unambivalently, and completely broke his gambling compulsion. In fact, as with most ambivalent people who overcome one extreme pole of the ambivalence, he swung to the other extreme and became extremely conservative and cautious in politics and in his everyday life. Because Dostoyevsky was one of the most honest self-analysts and one of the most creative artists who have depicted the depths of human experience, his description and analysis of primary security and secondary insecurity ambivalence is the best ever done. Our only addition is that of putting it into a more general theoretical analysis, thus, it is hoped, adding to our general understanding of it.

Tertiary situated insecurities and securities are distinguished from the others by their relative lack of pervasiveness (their situatedness) and by generally being much less embedded (easier to change). Situated insecurity and security are felt by everyone, and even the individual with the greatest sense of primary and secondary security can be thrown into a situated panic by noting that the airliner's engines are on fire or by a "Dear Jill" letter that violates her basic trust of the world by announcing that her deeply loved husband has just run off to Tahiti with her deeply loved sister. The difference is that the individual with insecurity that is merely situated will rarely be thrown into an abyss of despair, and will normally spring back much sooner and with fewer lasting scars. This is why phobic reactions that have occurred after the primary and secondary senses of security have been established can be extinguished relatively easily by counteractive learning experience, called "behavior modification" by psychologists, but actually an ancient commonsense technique for overcoming phobias. G. Gordon Liddy (1981) has given a striking description of how he overcame a generalized phobia as a young boy by taking increasing risks.[3]

Because the infant first develops his or her general sense of self from the communing duet with the mother, her general feelings toward the infant largely become his or her own feelings toward him- or herself and, thereby, the mother has an overwhelming effect on all of the dimensions of primary feelings of insecurity and security. We do not mean, however, that the mother has a total effect in the first year or so. The evidence from child development studies, which have been greatly aided by the use of film and video-taped records, has steadily pushed back the age at which infants are believed to develop emotionally and cognitively. The evidence has also shown ever more clearly the great importance of the genetic characteristics and thus of the wide individual variations primed genetically. The evidence also shows that the child greatly affects the mother, so theirs is a genuine partnership—a vastly complex, ever-shifting duet of intense perceptions, emotions, cognitions, motivations, and actions. It is quite clear that some children commune and identify far more with their mothers and for longer periods of time, apparently being far more affected in this way in their feelings of insecurity and security. Some children, especially some "rambunctious" boys, "push away from" their mothers far earlier and more intensely, even when their mothers are quite loving. Their greater independence probably makes them less affected by their mothers in their primary senses of insecurity and security. At the same time, some fathers or other close family members are far more important than most; and fathers in general seem to become very important emotionally to children, especially to boys, around the age of two or three. Most have great effects, as we can see in excellent biographies, such as those on Theodore Roosevelt (Morris, 1979) and Russell Baker (1984). Unfortunately, not much is known as yet about these factors (see Lamb and Campos, 1982; Lamb and Bornstein, 1987, pp. 36-45). The father, however, seems unable to substitute for the mother completely in the development of the optimal sense of primary and secondary security (that is, in the first year or so of life).[4]

SELF-HATE, SELF-LOVE, AND THE SENSE OF THE SELF

The dimensions of insecurity and security appear to be interdependent in complex ways, so that overtones in one can trigger undertones in others, and to have upper and lower thresholds beyond which new factors (such as defenses) are brought into play that add further complications. Figure 3.1 is our rough schematization of this model of insecurity and security. Some interdependencies are so great that we show the dimensions overlapping. We shall discuss here only those aspects of the model that seem important to the development of our whole theory of love, intimacy, and sex.

This model is a hierarchical model in roughly the same way as Abraham Maslow's (1962, 1970) famous model of the hierarchy of motives. Those at the base of the model, the more basic, have a more pervasive or generalized effect on our lives, that is, they affect more situations of life, they are more powerful, and they are more embedded. They also have greater undertone effects (symbolized by the longer arrows pointing upward) on the dimensions above them than those above have on the ones below. Unlike some of Maslow's motives, however, all of the dimensions of insecurity and security are always there, at least as background emotional force fields that may at any moment be triggered and hence organize our other feelings, cognitions, values, perceptions, and actions in concrete situations. Thus they act continually to shape our decisions and actions, even in situations that outsiders would see as obviously safe. Most of the time, their organizing effects are subtle and we are not immediately aware of them, but they are always there ready to spring into full force when different situations *and inner states* engage—trigger—them (to varying degrees). Let us elaborate on some details of this model that are crucial in understanding love, intimacy, and sex.

DREAD OF DEATH VERSUS
HOPE FOR LIFE AND THE
HATED AND LOVABLE SENSE OF SELF

The dimension of ontological (Being) insecurity and security is the dimension of dread of death and hope for life. Though we have previously argued (Douglas, 1984a) that the "grim existentialists" have assumed we human beings are far more insecure in a primary sense than is normally the case in our society today, there can be little doubt that this dimension pervades all of life, at least as a dormant potential. Whenever life is felt to be threatened seriously and immediately, the dread of death is normally triggered and has effects on our whole lives, unless countervailing forces have completely counterweighted it (see below). This dread can instantaneously sweep away all other concerns and reorient us entirely toward dealing with *the* threat. The only reason this is not normally obvious to us is because in our culture most people feel far more secure than did those of earlier cultures, both because of the drastic differences in the realities that protect us and because of the many defensive measures taken to compartmentalize and hide death (see Douglas, 1984a). Nevertheless, it is always there ready to spring into life. Though this has not been a focus of our work on love, it seems clear from the general evidence about human beings that this dread is so powerful in most people and most cultures that it would make life impossible (paralyzed with dread) if it were not powerfully counterweighted by the religious rites, beliefs, and emotions that inspire the hope for life even beyond the fact of death. Figure 3.1 shows that there is an extraordinarily close relation between the ontological dimension and that of feeling hatable and feeling lovable.

The evidence indicates that a child must receive caring and adoring love from his or her mother within the first several years of life or the child will never be able to feel these for anyone in more than fragmentary ways. Just as language must be learned within the first several years, or the child will never learn more than phrases, so the feelings of love must be fully experienced within the first several years with his or her mother before the genetic window for them closes, or the child will have no more than fragmentary love feelings. The child cannot feel real self-love, but, instead, will develop defensive, narcissistic pseudo-self-loving, that is, the pride of self-adulation or vanity. The feeling of pride is often mistaken for love. It is the most common pseudolove. The child must, then, always feel insecure in the sense of hating him- or herself and, hence, expecting to be hated by others, though this will normally be repressed from consciousness by the counterweighting of defensive pseudoloving. Winnicott (1965, 1971) found in his studies of such children that they develop a "false self" as a general defense system against these terrifying basic insecurities, which involve a dread of death and non-Being. His argument actually implies that there is an inner-self that constructs and maintains this false-self to defend itself, but that the inner-self and outer-self cannot be integrated and thus remain fragmentary and give only a brittle order to life. These so-called narcissists crave adulatory priding of their false-selves, something we have seen often in our studies of insecure beautiful women.

The extremely close relation between the ontological dimension and the hate and love dimension is portrayed in the striking imagery of adult talk about love. Love is not only portrayed as giving ultimate meaning—directedness—to life, but as giving the very feeling of life itself. The contrast is most striking when one falls in-love or when one loses a love. Falling in-love makes everything come to life: Every moment is filled with the thrill of feeling alive. Falling out of love makes the whole world feel dead and the very self feel lifeless. At the extreme, the schizoid who cannot feel love, or any life-giving positive passion, often says that he or she is literally dead (Day and Semrod, 1978). Eros gives birth both to life and to the feelings of being alive.

Adoration love and the Erotic feelings trigger undertones of all the positive feelings and potentiate them to a maximum degree so that any experience that would normally give rise to some slight pleasure is transformed by love into a great joy. When one is most intensely in-romantic-love, experiences that are normally dull and lifeless, or even painful, can be transfigured into their opposites. The positive emotions are generally felt to be a part of the innermost sense of self, and love, which is so tied in with all of them, is at the very core of the innermost sense of self. The adult with the most completely developed powers of rational and analytical thought can be magically transformed into vibrant life by love. This is the story of Goethe's Doctor Faustus, the scholar who has searched for the meaning of life in lifeless books only to discover a deadly depression and who is transported back to life by his own feelings of love for an inner picture of perfection. We can all remember the intense emotions of childhood, a time when the beauty of a single blossom or the dancing colors of a fractured ray of sunshine can bring an exquisite joy that is never forgotten. We have forgotten the earliest joys of life-giving love we felt for our mothers, but most of us can remember times when we were three or four when we felt intense love for our mothers and the simple pleasures of reading a book with her, or being praised for some otherwise minor feat filled us with joyful and vibrant love for her and for ourselves. Those moments of intense joy stand out as spotlighted moments of intense light in the years of darkness that are our memories of our early childhoods.

Individuals fully inflamed by life-giving Erotic love feel that they have transcended death and merged with the eternal and the infinite. The great romantic tragedies of both the West and the East depict this transcendence of death by love in the suicidal merging of the lovers in a death that is the entrance to eternal bliss or the oneness of being (more emphasized in the East). Romeo and Juliet are the supreme exemplars of death-transcending love in the West. Japanese myths and popular stories commonly depict the star-crossed lovers leaping (falling) into the ocean, a symbol of the love-fusion of their selves and of fusing with all of Being.

This transcendence of death by love is a theme that appears in other realms of life as well. The love of God is the way to eternal life, necessarily through the grim portals of death. It is this love of God that produces the transcendence of death. This basic relation is seen in various ways and with various emphases in all the great religions. In the Eastern religions, the emphasis is placed on the merging with the

Godhead, with Being, by identifying intensely with Being and disidentifying with the self chained by desires in this world. In Christianity, the emphasis is so much on loving God as the way to eternal life that Christian mystics normally express themselves in the same terms as romantic lovers, even to making Erotic avowals (not sexual, but creative). The patriot is a man who loves his country, obviously not sexually, but in the sense of adoring, caring, and especially of identifying with the country as an abstract whole. He may die for the country and, thereby, receive undying love from his countrymen and live forever in their hearts. There are many other extensions of these basic ideas of love transcending death itself.

As we noted above, it is this inherent interdependency between the sense of dread of death or hope of life and the sense of being hatable or lovable that leads us to depict the two dimensions as overlapping in a major way. Loving gives life not only physically but spiritually. In fact, it is precisely because loving gives life spiritually that the lovers are inspired—filled with the breath of life—by Erotic love to give birth to new life. Erotic loving fills us with the breath of life, with the profound longing to create life that transcends our own deaths. Those who do not love in the full Erotic sense, but only lust or feel fragments of caring or adoration, do not feel inspired to give birth to life. Very sexual people may wish not to have children and may be shocked to find that when they finally fall in-love they are "seized" by a deep urge to have a child.

Even in our supposed secular age, most people continue to understand and take for granted in their everyday actions this great "mystery" of the intertwining of love and life and of hate and death. Even people who pride themselves on their sexual modernism find themselves drawn irresistibly, often kicking and screaming most of the way, toward creation of what is now routinely called a "love-baby." This name is especially used to designate a single child born to divorced people who have children from previous marriages. Their children from the earlier marriages, combined with their economic and emotional problems with their "exes," give them every rational reason in the world *not* to have a child together. The only force greater than every rational reason is life-inspiring Erotic love.

There are, however, many people today who have no inkling of this cornerstone of life until they actually experience the "mysterious" force stirring within themselves. They thus assume that having a baby is *merely* a rational decision that can be turned on or off as easily as one can turn on or off the computer terminal in the library. If you turn it on, then you will desire—even love—the baby; and, of course, what you will to desire or not to desire determines your emotions. These are the millions of people who almost offhandedly have an abortion because "it's the thing to do" in certain ill-timed situations, only to discover that no amount of cognitive willing away of love for the new life and dread and guilt for killing it can make it go away. And the millions who have steadfastly committed themselves to never having a child because it would disrupt their dominance striving, only to discover years later, perhaps when it is too late, that they are seized by emotions they willed away and that they cannot resist or still the powerful craving to have a child. And the millions who, never having felt the Erotic, decide after a "rational" weighing of the many costs and benefits that there are no "rational" benefits to having a child and thus have themselves sterilized to make "love making" more convenient, only to discover years later that their first experience of "true love"—an Erotic romantic love partnership—has inspired them with a tragic longing they cannot remove surgically. We have encountered so many of these people that we could fill great tomes with their often tragic stories—and their frequent triumphs over irrational rationalizations. But there is no need to do so. Everyone with much experience knows some of them, so they do not need more evidence, and today most of those with little experience in these matters would not believe any amount of this evidence.

THE EVIL SELF AND THE
GOOD SELF

The dimension of feeling evil or feeling good seems clearly to be the next most powerful dimension of insecurity and security. It is closely interdependent with the three interrelated negative feelings of shame, embarrassment, and guilt, and the positive feeling of pride. (As usual in human life, the negative feelings are more numerous than the positive and this helps to skew experience toward the insecure side, a point to which we shall return.) Almost everyone can remember some experiences from the third, fourth, or fifth years in which they were "mortified" by intense feelings of shame, embarrassment, and guilt and by the wonderful exhilaration of pride. Because of the mother's intense importance, she is by far the most apt to have been the source of the moral feelings about one's sense of self, though others soon become very important, first the father and siblings and then other children. Even when the child feels deeply loved by the mother, he or she can be haunted through life, perhaps unconsciously, with a morbid feeling of guilt that must be expiated in some way.

One of the very common patterns of intense guilt—of feeling the self is evil—has been that resulting from feeling that one caused the death of a sibling, parent, or other loved one. Jealousy of a new sibling is often so intense that murderous thoughts can be aroused in the young child, especially one who has been most intensely in-love with the mother before the interloper's arrival. In earlier centuries, the newborn had an extremely high probability of dying compared with today in the West. When the hated interloper died, the magical thinking of children, which associates the wish with the event, made many feel that they were guilty of the most terrible sin; and this feeling of being evil aroused dread in many of losing the mother's love, perhaps of being executed for the murder (see Chapter 4 on jealousy).

Shame, embarrassment, and guilt have been objects of special attack for sexual modernists and for cultural relativists in general. They are almost taboo topics in some educated circles these days and avoiding or overcoming guilt feelings—one form of "getting over your hang-ups"—has been a major segment of the therapy industry. As a result, they are often repressed from consciousness. A great many individuals suffer terribly from guilt—which is not communicated so tellingly in body language as shame and embarrassment are—without knowing that it is the source of their suffering. Some forms of therapy may actually inadvertently encourage people to do things that produce unconscious guilt. Because the cultural relativists commonly deny that there are any universal social rules whose violation might produce guilt, they have not bothered to look to see if in fact there are.

There certainly appear to be very strong and universal rules associated with the feelings of love, intimacy, and sex that are quite comparable to the universal rule of reciprocity in friendly relations. One of these rules is that the rule of strict reciprocity does not hold in the ultimate partnerships of love. As we have already noted, parents, especially mothers, have obligations the world over to love and care for their children independently of any possible returns. (As usual, each culture emphasizes some aspects of such relations more than others. Trobriand Islanders shift some of the caring responsibilities from the father to the mother's brother. But this is just an instance of the usual variation in cultural degree.) The strict rule of reciprocity (an eye for an eye, a kind act for a kind act, and so on) holds for most of the aspects even of close love and intimacy partnerships, but there are some special ones for which it does not. In these, the "silver rule" of strict reciprocity is supplemented by the extremely stern "golden rule" of doing unto loved and intimate ones as they should also do unto you—independent of the expectations of their actually doing so. The golden rule of loving and intimate partnerships consists of many more specific rules. A number of them are summed up in the stern rule of "loyalty." Though the particulars vary widely from culture to culture, probably the most important taken-for-granted moral rule of loving and intimate partnerships is that we must not act against the ultimate good of the loved one; we must not "betray" their ultimate good. The "ultimate" here is very important. It is obvious that parents have obligations everywhere to hurt a child's short-run interests, such as the pleasure he would derive from jumping into the ocean, in order to advance his long-run or ultimate interest. The "ultimate good" is not only the long-run interests but also the primary sense of security, including moral status. This is Aristotle's "summum bonum" (see Douglas, 1983).

No doubt there have always been many violations of the golden rule of love partnerships, including this all-important general rule of loyalty. The golden rule is stern indeed and often imposes immense losses of one's other satisfactions in life, so there are always great temptations to violate it. And yet there are remarkably few violations compared to the frequency of temptations, and the violations that do occur seem most commonly to be acts of retaliation against a loved one believed, rightly or wrongly, to have betrayed one, thereby seeming to abrogate the love partnerships and the stern rule of loyalty itself. Murder in a jealous rage seems to fit this pattern. But when we consider how intense and frequent arguments (and what we shall call "Arguments" in Chapter 6) are within love partnerships, and how common actual physical attacks are, it is striking how rarely they lead to murder. Rather, they seem to lead to thoughts of such betrayals of love and these alone can inspire intense guilt, especially in very young children who do not yet distinguish as categorically as adults do between thoughts and actions, between the wish and the deed.

It is probably a rare individual who does not feel some sense of shame, embarrassment, or guilt over some early "betrayals" of loved ones. Some of these betrayals of loyalty are real. Most are imagined or mythical, but they have all the sense of reality and show all the complexities that myths commonly do. They can become a haunting source of moral insecurity throughout life, especially when it is impossible to go back to undo the wrong or to go forward to a reconciliation and forgiveness. When the loved one dies at the point of such a betrayal, he or she cannot grant forgiveness and the survivor is easily left with permanent moral insecurity.

Survivors of the Nazi holocaust commonly feel this haunting, sometimes agonizing sense of moral insecurity over the "sin" of having survived when the loved ones died, even though they themselves could do absolutely nothing to save them. The same survivor guilt is sometimes seen in survivors of accidents, even when they were not there and had nothing to do with the accident. The survivors feel "It should have been me, not them!" It is as if there is a program of primitive magic at work in the mind, which tells us that the death is a form of sacrifice and that another victim is necessary as a sacrifice, so that, by not having made the sacrifice, they become guilty of intending to let that sacrificial death occur. Bowlby (1979) and others have found that highly insecure adults frequently had a parent who threatened to commit suicide, presumably because of some evil action (betrayal?) by the child. Killing oneself "on the head of another"—revenge suicide—is common around the world (Douglas, 1967).

By a similar process of mythical thought, children who are abandoned or left by one parent in a divorce very often feel guilty. Though adults see them as the victims who had nothing to do with the divorce, the children often feel that they were left because of something terribly evil they have done. The mythical program, which is strongly reinforced by popular fairy tales, tells us that good people win the love of the loved one and live happily ever after. When the loved one seems to reject the lover, the mythical program says, conversely, that the rejected one must be an evil person not worthy of love (see McDermott, 1970; Stuart and Abt, 1981, especially pp. 20-32).

Bruno Bettelheim (1976) has shown how fairy tales of this sort, especially "Cinderella," normally allow the child to feel that he or she can overcome the problem, that he or she will receive the love that is deserved. But when the loved one leaves the child, rejecting the child's love, haunting guilt may be an unintended misuse of fairy-tale enchantment. And, of course, this program is also reinforced by the feelings of guilty betrayal that can so easily arise over "evil thoughts" directed at a parent, almost always the father, who seems to be betraying the loved mother, with whom the child identifies, by fighting with her and then leaving her. Perhaps worst of all, the departing parent may be denounced by the abandoned one for "not loving your children enough to stay with them," thereby confirming the dreaded guilt. Departing parents commonly recognize this grave problem, however dimly, and try to reassure the children that they are not abandoning them and still love them, but actions have ways of speaking much louder than words to the magical programs of the subconscious mind.

A very high percentage of adults today are painfully aware of the guilt they feel over "abandoning" their wives, husbands, or children; over abortions; over not spending enough time with their children, or not loving them enough; and over many lesser evil deeds. Children who develop this sense of themselves as guilty of some evil at a very early age are commonly not aware that this is where it came from and it is extremely problematic to know when such early experience is the source. Even the extreme cases are highly problematic for anyone. Some forms of secondary narcissism are pervaded with a sense of guilt, of being evil in many specific ways or in no ways in particular. These are the kinds of individuals who are most apt to develop strong and rigid "ego-ideals," which are partially separated from the sense of self and are used insistently to judge the self from on high. Karen Horney (1950) was the greatest analyst of this syndrome and her adolescent diaries (Horney, 1980) reveal her to be a great sufferer from it.

Most people do not have clearly formulated and systematic ego-ideals, and certainly do not judge themselves in the abstract, rigidly and harshly in terms of it. Even when they do form very stern, specific rules for themselves, such as "New Year's Resolutions," most people back-slide repeatedly without feeling any dread of retribution from unknown powers or self-hatred that inspires self-punishment (or projection onto others and punishment of them for imagined evils). Narcissists with secondary guilt insecurity may do all this and worse, even when they have had quite loving parents, and probably especially when they feel that their evil will also lose them that cherished love. These are the anguished "perfectionists" who always seem to find a way to hate themselves for imagined failures, even when they are being highly successful in their own terms. They can be beautiful women (or would-be beautiful women who emaciate themselves with anorexia nervosa) who loathe themselves for gaining two pounds at Christmastime (ballooning up to 103 pounds), or counterphobes who unflinchingly court death on the battlefield (or the highway) to prove their courage and heroic dedication to ideals. Puritanical saints exorcising some unknown guilt may commit endless acts of evil (in terms of their own morals) in the pursuit of self-purification, as if sacrificing themselves and everyone else to expiate the unknown guilt. Their vanity over their sainthood—even over humility itself (Wilson, 1984)—can be an incongruous sign that their purification rituals are a desperate defense against this feeling of evil.

The close interdependence of the dimensions of hatability and lovability and morality lead to many patterns of striving for "over" security in one to counterweight insecurity in the other. The insecurity-driven striving to become more moral in order to overcome feelings of insecurity about one's lovability is seen starkly in the wish to be "worthy of your love." This phrase is little used today because it strikes the clear and shrill tone of Victorian moralism. As we noted in Chapter 1, at the very heart of Victorianism was an emphasis on being more pure, and by being purer proving one's superiority—dominance—over the less pure. Much of middle-class—"bourgeois"—behavior consisted of purification rituals used as weapons in this secular purification warfare. Rather than relying on the rod to train children, as laborers commonly did, the bourgeoisie came increasingly to rely on the use of shame, embarrassment, and guilt, thus instilling an intense sense of moral insecurity in most children and making them feel insecure about the love of their parents as well, the two greatly reinforcing each other. It is commonly overlooked that, in the vastly popular Horatio Alger stories of that era, Horatio achieved his worldly success by first becoming morally superior and, thereby, winning the esteem, love, and worldly help of a parentlike benefactor.

Though bourgeois moralism became the most loathed part of the myth of Victorianism, it was a crucial reality of less than mythical proportions. Because parents were especially prudish about childhood sexuality, which brought them into moral conflict with the inevitable, genetically primed sex play and development of the children, some of the children developed a great deal of shame, embarrassment, and guilt about sex. This in turn produced a good deal of dread, anxiety, impotence, frigidity, and other problems with sex. The problems were especially acute in women because they were subjected to more intense purification rituals.

The intense insecurity many people felt about their lovability and morality as a result of this socialization is quite sufficient to account for the sex problems, including the embodiments and displacements of such insecurities seen in the prevalent forms of hysteria, fetishism, sado-

masochism, and so on. The Freudian Oedipal conflict is quite unnecessary to account for any of these and is merely a more complex and
fanciful explanation that directly contradicts almost all the evidence.
The lifelong impotence, fetishism, and possible sadomasochism of a
Havelock Ellis is easy to explain in terms of his intense early feelings of
moral insecurity about sexuality in general and some early experiences
he had. He was quite aware of his early excitement about seeing his
mother's and nurse's public urination (leading, he said, to his obsession
with urinating). He had no intense conflict with his father, who was
away almost his entire childhood, and considered him largely irrelevant.
He had no conscious sexual lust for his mother and his lifelong self-
analysis would almost certainly have uncovered it, if it had existed.
(Freud is supposed to have uncovered his lust for his mother in one year
of self-analysis while still relatively young.) He most likely did not hide
any such thing, because he admitted obliquely his incestuous love for a
sister with whom he did not grow up and, as we noted, he was completely
aware of his excitement about his mother's urinating. He showed all the
signs of intense shame, embarrassment, and guilt about sexuality in
general and intense attempts to overcome those by being more lovable
and more dominant (famous). He showed no signs of repressed or
hidden Oedipal conflicts and those are quite unnecessary to explain all
of what was visible. His basic moral insecurity and (less) love insecurity
over sex made sex a source of anxiety. Because these insecurities—
including guilt about the evil witnessing of public urination by his
mother—involved his mother, he tended to feel very anxious about
sexuality with women and was, therefore, impotent.

Though it is commonly overlooked, this sexual moralism was
probably even more intense among middle-class Jews. Because they
bore the insecurities both of the status struggle and of religious (moral)
stigmatization, they tended to strive even harder to compensate by being
purer than the Christians did. (This was the social situation of so many
of Freud's women patients.) This pattern is found in many variations,
primarily in the forms of the "mama's boy" or the "spinster" who cannot
leave the loving parent who professes to need the child desperately.
Most manage eventually to find a situation they can combine with
enough rebellion or courage to escape physically, yet they often remain
trapped emotionally because the combination of love, parental need
summoning up caring, and guilt often subtly manipulated make it
impossible for the child to develop enough of an independent sense of
self to escape. Failure to "fall out of love" with the parent sufficiently to

free the sense of self to "fall in love" with someone else can be crippling in itself. (We shall see this in the *orphan syndrome*, illustrated by Dante, in Chapter 5.)

THE SUBMISSIVE FAILURE AND THE DOMINANT SUCCESS

The fourth and fifth dimensions of insecurity and security that appear to be universal are those of submission and dominance and failure and success. These are highly interdependent, especially today when a popular term—*loser*—means both a failure and one who is submissive, and another—*winner*—means the opposite. The drives for dominance and success seem to be universal and quite powerful in higher animals. Submission and failure produce powerful feelings of shame, embarrassment, and guilt. Successful dominance striving produces the intensely pleasurable feeling of pride. At the extreme, such as victory in war or sexual conquest of the greatest prize, this feeling is one of exultation and is almost orgasmic in intensity, while lasting much longer. The great effects of the love dimension on the dimensions of submission and dominance and failure and success do not become clear until the child begins to develop the first brittle "friendships" and comes into competition with other children in play and games. But the effects on one subdimension of the sense of successful potency become clear in the second and third years of life when the child begins moving away from the mother to explore and conquer the fearful world on his or her own. Because of lingering separation anxiety and stranger anxiety, and the inevitable pains of exploratory mishaps, the child normally feels some anxieties about these forays into the unknown. But the amount varies tremendously. Some of this is no doubt the result of genetic variations. But psychologists have concluded that most of it is due to the differences in the degree of "secure attachment" of the children to their mother earlier in life (Bowlby, 1971-1979, 1979).

Unfortunately, these studies do not normally distinguish the mother's giving of love from her fulfillment of more general attachment needs. But it seems clear from everyday life observations and other evidence that the child's sense of being loved, thus of being lovable, is the overwhelming factor here. The "clinging child" is recognized commonsensically to be the child who is "afraid of losing his mother," normally because the mother has left and made the child feel rejected. It is entirely possible, of course, that this is very much affected by a cognitive factor of "felt dependability" or "basic trust." Thus, for example, the child may feel secure about the mother's love, but feel that she is simply undependable when it comes to being there when the child feels frightened or hungry. This, however, is quite contrary to the commonsense experience of parents. On the whole, it seems to us that the child does not make such rational distinctions. The mother not there to comfort the child when he or she is frightened is very likely experienced by the child to be the mother who does not love him or her. This is why the child quickly goes into Bowlby's "loss" syndrome of rage or aloofness. "Rejecting the rejector," that is, not loving someone who does not love you and pushing away emotionally someone who pushes you away emotionally, is the standard program of self-defense for maintaining the feelings of being lovable. Bowlby's observation of this "rejecting the rejector" program in the child who has for any reasons experienced a loss of the mother (after establishing primary attachment to her) is a very good sign that the child is feeling the mother does not love the child and is rejecting the child's love.

As soon as such a child begins to interact and play with other children and adults, the sense of insecurity becomes apparent in all the signs of tentativeness, shyness, awayness, rejecting, or domineering (overdriven or counterweighting dominance striving) he or she shows toward them and the attendant "clinging" the child shows toward the mother when such contacts are anticipated or under way. These new situations always involve considerable risk for the child, because they are emotionally very important and their newness produces great uncertainty. The child who has gained from the mother a secure sense of being lovable as a person normally is carried along by the excitement and joy of the risky encounters with others. The child who feels that his or her self is not lovable to others dreads the rejections he or she anticipates, and the consequent shame and embarrassments they can cause, in general—independent of situations—because it is a psychic cornerstone of his or her very being. Those who are merely shy approach the strangers with ambivalence, happily excited yet miserably dreading rejection. Sometimes they show the most intense approach-avoidance ambivalence, advancing then retreating, smiling then looking embarrassed, saying hello but biting their lip so much it is hard to understand what they say. Some children literally "weave a circle around" the strangers, moving in closer toward intimacy, yet ever ready to pretend unconcern and awayness by disattending to them and even fleeing. The very insecure can hardly imagine being liked and will go to extremes of clinging, begging, crying, going into enraged tantrums, hiding, and running away to avoid having to feel the burning pain of shame and embarrassment that come from rejection.

Just as tentativeness is a tactic that allows the individual to advance while being in a state of maximum readiness to run away, and to be open to interaction while being ready on the instant to reject the rejector (thus maximizing the hope of friendly contact while minimizing the dreaded rejection), so awayness allows the individual to have some chance of friendly contact while putting the emphasis on minimizing the rejection that is expected. *Awayness tactics* involve "positioning" yourself so that anyone who wants to can initiate interaction with you, thereby accepting the onus of the risk of rejection, while avoiding such risks yourself. The highly insecure child sometimes literally approaches strangers, and even people they already know but from whom he or she continues to dread rejection, by "sidling up" to them at an angle with eyes averted, or even by moving forward backward, pretending all the time to be doing the exact opposite of initiating contact, such as talking with someone else while progressing backwards toward the hoped-for friendly contact. All of these can be seen in any nursery school and in the many movies about little children. They can also be seen throughout the rest of life in increasingly complex and hidden—deceiving—forms. "Chance" encounters that have been planned down to the last detail for weeks are common tactics used by insecure, would-be lovers. Given the high degree of risk of insecurity to the whole sense of self involved in any love-overture or sex-overture, even people with a high degree of primary and secondary security commonly make use of some degree of the *strategies of indirection* to hide their intentions. Indirection minimizes both the observability of the real intentions and the degree to which the individual is putting him- or herself "on the line" by making the overtures that expose him or her to rejection. Like all great generals, great seducers and insecure lovers are masters of indirection (see Liddell Hart, 1954; Douglas, 1984).

Anyone who has experienced or closely observed the use of these tactics and their outcomes in others is likely to have an intuitive sense of why primary and secondary insecurities are almost always perpetuated. They are largely self-reinforcing because they are largely self-fulfilling. Because there is a considerable degree of risk of rejection involved in any early contacts with others, even those with a high degree of primary, secondary, and situational security can easily be temporarily tipped into feeling situational insecurity about their lovability. Anyone who approaches new contacts with a defensive attitude is throwing the risk of rejection more on the other person, thus increasing their potential for situational rejections that trigger and reinforce insecurity. The result is that the approached persons easily feel rejected by the defensive person and quickly reject him or her in return by retreating into a defensive position to fend off the slings and arrows of shame and embarrassment. The expectation of rejection is thus very likely to be self-fulfilled and, hence, self-reinforced, so the insecurity is reinforced and becomes more embedded in the sense of self. This makes the next encounters even more risky, so the insecure child faces the danger of spiraling downward into isolation and a defensive tactic of pseudoproud aloofness and isolation. And that is exactly the tragic fate that befalls some of them as a result of this fatal flaw of love insecurity.

Fortunately for them, most who do not suffer from primary insecurities are saved by a combination of accidental factors such as literally "falling into" a friendship, or backing into a marriage—perhaps arranged by someone else; increased desire because of love-starvation or sex-starvation, which leads to a greater willingness to accept the risks of rejection; recognition of the emotional problems and forcing oneself by willpower to compensate for them or evade them; and being saved by other people who are not insecure and who may recognize the problems involved. One of our life studies was done with a young woman who was saved from the spiral downward by a happy family of remarkably secure people. Annette felt securely loved by her mother and generally secure about herself until she was about to enter adolescence. For some mysterious reason, at that time her mother became increasingly depressed and angry. She began a prolonged moral crusade of recriminations, debasements, and angry outbursts against Annette, often in the presence of others. A perfectionist about orderliness and cleanliness, she increasingly attacked Annette for moral failures in household chores. One of Annette's most mortifying memories is of her mother rushing into the kitchen, denouncing her for some supposed filth, and hitting her in the head with a heavy dish. When her mother attempted suicide, Annette felt sure she must be the cause of it, which greatly multiplied her feelings of being evil.

By the time she entered college, Annette was extremely insecure about her sense of self in general. She felt strongly that she was guilty of some unknown evils, that she was ugly when in fact she was extremely pretty, and above all that no one could like her and certainly not love her. She had partially counterweighted her insecurities by becoming a success at sports. A woman coach in high school, who believed in her and liked her, helped her begin her long struggle back to security, but when she entered college she still could not believe that anyone who acted friendly toward her could really like her. A friendly roommate was "tested" mercilessly until she broke down and fled to save her own senses of security. Her flight convinced Annette she had been right all along. By luck, she then fell into the care of a real heroine of self-security, a young woman from a happy family of extremely loving parents and siblings. She felt sure she could bring Annette "back" and dedicated herself to this labor of love. She introduced Annette into her family and they joined in a loving conspiracy. It took months during which our heroine almost broke down and fled, but Annette was finally convinced they had met the supreme "tests" of love she set for them. Over the ensuing months, her earlier sense of security seemed to be completely reestablished. Commonsense love-therapy through concrete action had apparently completely succeeded.

Because the sense of the self as a moral person has not commonly been seen as a basic dimension of personality, there has been little systematic observation and research done on it and its interdependencies with the other dimensions. Our argument that the sense of hatability and lovability greatly affects the sense of being immoral and moral, which in turn greatly affects the sense of submission and dominance and of being a failure or a success, is based predominantly on common sense and everyday experience. The interdependence of these dimensions of insecurity are almost palpably obvious in adults working through the shock of rejection by someone with whom they are very much in love. In fact, the dimensions are so aroused in this situation that it is commonly impossible to distinguish them clearly.

No matter how much the rejector tries to reassure the one rejected that "it's not because of anything wrong with you," the rejected almost always feels profoundly that it is the result of something wrong with him or her. The sense of being unlovable or hatable is commonly immediately translated into "wrongfulness." The sense of being immoral is experienced as "something I did wrong" or "something bad about me." The deepest depression comes from a combination of the unbonding of the sense of self from the other (see Chapter 6) combined with the feeling that one deserves to be rejected because of some immorality, some failure to live up to the ideals of the other person. The senses of failure and submission aroused are almost always transformed at the same time into an embodied insecurity. The rejected person is haunted by an anguished dread of being "ugly," just as Annette was.

"Ugly" symbolizes very well the way in which the rejection triggers both a sense of immorality and a sense of submissiveness. The ugly person has very low ranking in dominance status (negative ranking, because people disidentify with and distance themselves from the ugly). But ugliness is also an external sign of an internal immorality, a physical index of a soul "ugly as sin." The rejected person dreads being ugly within and ugly without. But even women who place tremendous emphasis on external beauty normally show the greater influence of the judgment about the internal state in this situation. At the very time they are dreading external ugliness, they commonly "let themselves go" and become ugly. The beautiful woman who suffers from a primary or secondary insecurity to begin with often becomes so insecure during the period of feeling rejected, thus hatable, that she commits "beautycide," which is normally an only half-conscious murder of her external beauty. The magical logic of the subconscious at work here is simple: "I am hatable. A hatable person is one who is evil and thus deserves to be degraded. Therefore, I will degrade myself by becoming ugly." Even when her beautycide only reduces her in the eyes of others to an attractive "7" ranking, her insecurities and magical logic lead her to see herself as ugly. One of the best signs that her insecurities are receding to more normal levels is that she works this logic of beauty and ugliness backward and resumes her demanding beauty rituals.

As can already be seen in some of our allusions, submission and dominance are closely interdependent from adolescence on in complex and subtle ways with sexuality. Aggression is one of the ways of pursuing dominance, though by no means a necessary one, nor the most commonly successful one. This is, presumably, why aggression has so commonly been seen, especially by psychoanalysts, as necessarily related in some ways to sexuality. But aggression is only a means to dominance, not an end in itself, except for those who are trying to overcome insecurity. The physical exuberance of passionate intercourse has often been mistaken for aggression, but there is a world of difference to the participants between a scratch or bite that is intended to hurt and a scratch or bite that communicates passionate abandon and a desire to potentiate the joys and excitements of lust with a small amount of pain. Aggression involves the emotion of hate, while the most physically exuberant lust involves love and the rest of the Erotic. Cold indifference can even be the most effective form of hate-filled aggression in some situations.

The dominance drive in human beings certainly appears to be universal, with the usual cultural and individual variations. But this universality is obscured by the different dimensions of dominance and by the many ways they can be pursued and achieved. There appear to be at least four broad dimensions of dominance in human beings—power, status, fame, and wealth. But there are some complexities to these. Influence over power-wielders, that is, indirect power, sometimes takes the place of direct power as a goal. Status is a ranking in terms of prestige. It obviously overlaps with fame, which is the visibility of and knowledge of someone. The importance of being seen, of all eyes looking at one, is further testimony to the tremendous emotional importance of vision and the eyes in human life. As we have seen, intimacy is in part being visible to the other. (Nathaniel Branden, 1980, mistakenly sees being visible as the essence of romantic love.) Wealth is probably the most recent of the dimensions, because the early hunting and gathering peoples apparently could not store much wealth and thus their genes may not have been selected for ability to get wealth. Wealth may, then, not be a genetically distinct dimension of dominance at all, but is of great importance in all civilizations in establishing power, status, and fame. On the other hand, in very poor hunting and gathering societies, rare bird feathers alone can be vitally important forms of wealth. Today, most rich Americans will pay vast sums to become powerful, upper class, or famous, but few will give up these just to become wealthy (though they may give up some of those in the short run to gain the wealth necessary to gain more of those). The power hungry will endure the most grinding poverty for a lifetime for the smallest chance of becoming a dictator, but will disdain any "money grubbing."

As schematized in Figure 3.1, those who suffer from the more basic insecurities generally try to counterweight ("overcome," "compensate for") them by becoming extremely secure morally (saintly perfectionists) or by becoming extremely dominant and successful. We began our study of beautiful women, of both those who are "stars" only in everyday life and those who are "Stars" professionally as well, largely in an attempt to deal with such questions. The whole study was launched to clear up the great mystery of "the immensely insecure beautiful woman." The high rate of great personal insecurities among these women was already well known among experts in the beauty industries, but it was shockingly contrary to our commonsense expectations. We found that only rare beautiful women have primary narcissism but many have secondary narcissism pervaded by situational insecurities that trigger and exacerbate those deeper insecurities. Probably the most important finding of all was that the early insecurities, especially secondary narcissistic insecurities of feeling hatable or evil, had led these women as girls or adolescents to focus their attention on developing their beautiful bodies as a way to achieve love, moral standing, dominance, and success. It was their immense insecurities that "drove" them to all the suffering and hard work it normally takes to be labeled as beautiful in our society today, because most of them have to suffer to be thin enough, many have to have painful cosmetic surgery, and all have to work endless hours on body care, dress, and comportment. These girls come to *embody their insecurities*, that is, to conceive of and defend against their insecurities in terms of their bodies. Their bodies become symbols of their emotional insecurities and the fortress of their main defense strategies.

Those who found early success in these beauty strategies found their dread, anxieties, depressions, shames, embarrassments, and guilts reduced situationally. Otherwise morally harsh mothers or fathers became caring and forgiving. This greatly reinforced their strivings for beauty. It has been found that compulsive gamblers, whom we have seen started with the same kinds of early insecurities, commonly begin their careers with a "Big Score" that is immensely exciting and acts as a near-imprint learning experience. From then on, they are "addicted," so that they pursue gambling compulsively, striving desperately to repeat and add to their big score and eventually to transcend all their inner dread (Holden, 1985). Only much later, if ever, do they come to realize that they are caught in a spiral of uncertainty and risk, which tends over the long run to exacerbate their early insecurities by creating new situational ones. Precisely the same sort of spiral captures the beautiful girls and winds up making their emotional lives hostage to the uncertain and conflictful opinions and actions of others—adulation. Their very success in the beauty games makes other women, some of whom earlier were their friends, afraid of their competition or envious, so they move away from them and often begin secretly attacking them ("backbiting," "stabbing them in the back," "cutting them"—the language of our high schools is a gold mine of the terminology of emotional warfare). This hurts the girls and soon begins exacerbating some of their deeper insecurities, but at the same time they are winning ever-more exciting attention, pseudolove (normally adulation that they mistake for love), and dominance from their dating and from the boys more generally. If they get into modeling, acting, the beauty queen circuit, or some other part of our massive beauty industries, they commonly win adulation (which they also mistake for crowd and fan love) and dominance, so they are further reinforced in powerful ways to embody their insecurities.

Thus they spiral (drift) upward toward the dizzying heights of exciting dominance and adulation—and situational insecurities that exacerbate their more basic insecurities. This worsening of their insecurities leads them to more frantic attempts at beautification and body victory. And on and on. Also like the gamblers, this compulsive behavior is very hard to break, in spite of growing recognition of the problems and growing desires to get off the autocatalytic spiral. Beauty addiction is a special form of the gambling addiction, made all the worse by the fact that the early winnings are more common than at the race track. The accumulating suffering leads most of them to find ways to get out of the beauty vortex and find ways to deal successfully with their insecurities. The most basically insecure strive ever more desperately to win the great beauty contest of life, until old age makes them all losers. Still, the "miracles" of modern surgery and the deceits of the camera arts, reinforced by the willing suspension of disbelief by some fans, are so great today that a few continue to project the image of the beauty and sex goddess into old age.

There have been almost no studies directed specifically at determining the early developments of the sense of being insecure or secure in dominance and success striving, because psychologists and others have been focusing their attention too steadily on the catchall cognitive dimension of general distrust and trust. (Erikson, 1963, recognized the importance of "autonomy," "inferiority," and other dimensions later in childhood.) Nevertheless, it is clear that this dimension is developed quite early in life, not in the first year, but within the first several years. Primatologists have been very impressed with the way in which the children of dominant parents develop a generalized set of attitudes and behavior that seems to give them a far greater chance of success in moving up the dominance hierarchy when they get old enough and strong enough to compete. The same kinds of attitudes and behaviors can be seen in human children in early "play friendships" and in associations in nursery schools. Some children are very confident in their dealings with other children and with adults (though, of course, less so). Others approach everyone with shyness and tentativeness, which show a generalized expectation and foreboding about being inadequate. Of course, it is difficult at this stage and in most situations to tell when they are showing a deeper dread of rejection (hatability insecurity) or of shame, embarrassment, and guilt over expecting to be stigmatized (evilness insecurity), as distinct from feeling insecure in dominance situations. But close observations can often make the distinctions.

The child's feelings of insecurity and security as a failure or success at instrumental activity, ranging from success at sports to success at school lessons, is inherently highly intertwined with success in dominance striving. Ability at sports—winning or losing—is always necessarily judged relative to that of others. The same is roughly true of school tasks. But, in our society, tasks are so highly specialized and objectified (with stop watches, official records, IQ tests, and so on) that children soon begin to judge themselves and to be judged by others against partially impersonalized standards not so directly subject to the criteria of dominance hierarchies. Moreover, the idea of absolute, universal standards is basic to our whole culture (and probably to all cultures in some ways) and underlie these partially objectified achievement standards. This makes it possible for the child, and far more for the adolescent or adult, to judge him- or herself partially independently of judgments of others. A child who feels quite a general failure in his or her dominance strivings, or even hatable or evil, can partially withdraw and build a compartmentalized wall around his or her sense of self-security by focusing on these partially objectified standards of achievement. This is, of course, an extremely common pattern noted in schools in the case of "teacher's pets," "brains," or "nerds." They may feel terribly shy and "clutzy" in any direct comparisons with others and yet feel like immense successes in their own world of achievement standards.

There appears to be an extraordinarily close interdependency between the sense of hatability-lovability and the subdimension of sexual dominance-submission, including sexual potency. This is the result of the direct interdependency that exists between the Erotic and adoration love in romantic love. The basic relationship is simple and well recognized in everyday life: The more dominant individuals feel sexually, the more lovable (adorable) they feel; and, conversely, the less dominant they feel sexually, the more hatable they feel. This dominance applies predominantly to people other than the sex partners, but it does apply as well to the sex partners, for both men and women. We find no evidence in nonneurotic people that women are any more submissive or masochistic than men, except when social pressures in those directions are stronger. Women are on average more caring, not more masochistic. The two are often confused, largely because of the power of the Freudian tradition.

It is very important in this respect to keep in mind that when individuals are "in-love" with each other they identify with each other; and to the extent to which they do identify with the loved one, dominance and submission become irrelevant because the "thou" and the "I" largely fuse and move up and down together in the human dominance wars. This union is, of course, symbolized in multifarious and sacred ways in the individual myths of love and in the marriage rituals found in all societies. The united lovers are judged as a unit in the dominance wars, pretty much in direct proportion to the degree of their mutual identification commonly found in a society. One of the strong bits of evidence to support this general connection is the often-observed fact that submission and dominance feelings and strivings are intense and permeate those sexual relationships that involve the least feelings of adoration and caring, the prostitute-customer relationships. The exchange of money is itself a vital aspect of this struggle for dominance: the more money given, the more submissive; the more money received, the more dominant. Prostitutes, being in the inherently more submissive end of these relationships (as long as they feel the social stigma of the acts as evil), are especially obsessed with "putting down" the customers, so that the very names used, such as "Johns" and "tricks," are commonly stigmas that "degrade" the self of the customer into an impersonal "it" (see Buber, 1970). This symbolic relation between giving and the sense of security is the exact inversion of that found associated with sexual acts in love partnerships. Because it is found pretty universally among human societies and even among closely related primates, the male's giving of gifts to the loved woman (perhaps in symbolic exchange for her "favors" or the children she "gives" the man) appears to be genetically primed. But the priming is clearly associated with the love felt, not the lust felt. The more a man loves a woman, the more he wants to give her, up to the near-union of their material goods in marriage, and this impulse is clearly greatly heightened by the sexual potentiation of the adoration in romantic love.[5]

Individuals who feel secure in their sense of lovability can compensate far more for insecurities in the sense of morality or dominance by success in love (thus "proving" in the logic of the subconscious that they are more lovable) than individuals can compensate for insecurity in the sense of lovability by success in the senses of morality, dominance, or success. The lovable failure may feel some great insecurities about his or her failures, especially in our highly competitive society, but he or she does not thereby suffer the agonies of narcissism. Moreover, a large proportion of people who feel lovable find they can be quite happily secure with themselves by achieving just a modicum of moral respectability, social dominance, and success. Women not subjected to the competition ethos commonly felt quite secure about their selves in their "Cinderella" dependency on husbands for worldly dominance and success, as long as they were loved and respected. It was when they found themselves facing rejection through divorce that they started feeling highly insecure and started overdriven strivings to succeed. Even men subjected to the achievement ethos have sometimes relaxed into a life of being the "playboy," as long as the ethos did not greatly affect the other dimensions of self-security.

In recent decades, the emphasis on giving "unconditional love" among better-off American families has led many parents to make few demands for achievement until adulthood. Loving parents commonly allow the children to do no chores, have no part-time jobs, skimp on schoolwork, and just enjoy childhood. As long as they are also affluent and thus have secure dominance among their peers, a high percentage even of males becomes "drifters" for many years, spending extra years in the extended "identity moratorium" of financial dependency and college life, then working the minimum necessary as a busboy or car-parker to spend the days riding the surf or the nights partying. Never having felt the lash of insecurity, they have no "fire in their bellies." Until they feel the need to make a higher income to support a family of their own, they often seem quite secure in their sense of self and assuage any feelings of incompetence or immorality by burnishing their image as a loving friend and sexy "lover." Their subcultures of similar friends provide them with feelings of dominance and success, if they "make it big" in the subculture. The most dominant and successful in the subcultures commonly resist "graduating" to the bigger "fishpond," where they will suddenly be transformed into "minnows" and "airheads." They often hang on to their past glories well into middle age, drifting into ever less meaningful and more insecure lives, which end semipurposefully in accidents and drug overdoses with high frequencies. The waning of the glory days of these adolescent subcultures are remarkably similar to the wanings of any erstwhile elites (see Anton Checkhov's "The Cherry Orchard," and Huizinga, 1956; compare them with the aging surfers who "hang on" in the famous surf movie "Big Wednesday").

THE GENERAL MODEL OF
HUMAN DEVELOPMENT

Human experience is far more complex, individually diverse, partially interdependent, and plastic than the early biologistic theories of development assumed. The early theories assumed children must develop through clearly defined and linear *phases* during *critical windows*, an age period that is highly genetically primed, in order to develop into *healthy* adults whose "healthiness" was assumed to consist of very clearly defined and narrow social roles. These critical phases were assumed to consist of very simple behavioral items (orality, anality, moral absolutism, and so on), which could be easily observed by behavioristic methods. They were also assumed to be arranged hierarchically, so that the earlier were more important than the later and each later one had to be built on the earlier ones, to eventually produce healthy adults. This *simple aetiological model* was built on the biological idea that life *unfolds* in a preprogrammed form that progresses linearly from the simpler to the more complex and that each organism must recapitulate the earlier development (see the critique of Freud's theory by Sulloway, 1983).

The *aetiological principle* (that early experience has profound effects on the individual sense of self and, hence, on later life) is true in general. Human beings have always assumed that "the child is father to the man" and that early socialization is crucial in developing adult character ("spare the rod and spoil the man"). There are also some *critical windows* of experience during which children are primed genetically and some obvious phases of development. After all, who has not known commonsensically that infants suck at birth but are neither inclined nor capable of walking until ten months or later, or that "you must crawl before you can walk" and "you must walk before you can run"?

The general assumptions were obviously true. But the simplistic behavioristic items and mechanisms seized upon by theorists led to very misleading ideas about human life in general. Focusing attention on oral and anal behavior—and thus away from loving communion and the sense of self—makes life simple and linear for the behaviorist. No competent mother doubts the impact of orality on infants, nor does she doubt its impact on her if she nurses. Nor does any competent mother doubt that the far more complex emotions of love and the securities of the sense of self are far more important in the development of the child into an adult.

There are a great many dimensions of early life fraught with great significance for later life, especially the many basic emotions embedded in the sense of self (or, far more important, rejected from the sense of self). Their effects on later life do not come from simple, linear, and phased causal processes. Some of these first appear during critical windows, but the competent adult emotions and behaviors do not spring full blown into life in phases. They first appear in fragmentary forms that can later be modified, elaborated, and integrated into more complex forms. It is very important that we do not normally grow beyond earlier fragments in a linear progress. In most cases, earlier fragments of emotions, cognitions, values, and behavior patterns remain important in themselves but also become important components of far more complex systems or gestalts. The pleasurable genital (sex) skin sensations develop in infancy, then become part of sexual lust in preadolescence and early adolescence. Both become part of Erotic romantic love in full adulthood, and all become part of the Erotic worship of Being later in life. Again, as Bowlby (1979) has argued so persuasively, attachment behavior does not disappear with infancy. Throughout life, we want a comforting, caring hand when we are sick, and a "Rock of Ages" when we are gripped by the dread of death. The passionate kiss of communing lovers is neither a "fixation" on infantile sucking, nor merely the same communing adoration first felt with their mothers. It is normally that same communing adoration become an integral part of the fuller Erotic gestalt that is possible only in adulthood. (Of course, the individual might never unbond from his mother, and thereby remain "in human bondage" to his primal love, as we see in the *Somerset Maugham syndrome* and the *orphan syndrome*. But those are rare.) The effects of the early basic senses of insecurity and security and of the sense of self come predominantly from their heavily weighting the choices of actions in each new situation in ways that tend to produce consequences that reinforce them. The basic sense of insecurity and security and the sense of self, then, set in motion generalized *drift processes*, which tend strongly to be cumulative and self-reinforcing (autocatalytic). In the realm of love, intimacy, and sex these drift processes are extremely complex. They even include time-outs, backtrackings, leaps forward, and so on, and show wide individual variations that result in many different patterns of competent func-tionings in adulthood. Daniel Stern (1977, pp. 71-75) has shown how the mother and infant, even at their level of minimal complexity, are continually missing, "messing up," adjusting, and changing their optimal ranges of interaction and seem to drift toward optimal development precisely because they risk mistakes.

NOTES

1. Though we cannot go into the controversial issues here, it is *possible* that such protracted dread leads to the most extreme defenses, the schizoid breaks and narcissistic detachments from emotional reality that involve a partial to wholesale exclusion of the basic emotions from the inner sense of self and the construction of a *defensive false world* (Day and Semrod, 1978), or a *defensive false self* (D. W. Winnicott, 1965, 1971).

The history of studies of autism, which in itself is a syndrome of cognitive problems, not of such emotional problems, must serve as a cautionary tale for such theorizing. For almost 30 years, the overwhelming conclusion of these studies was that autism was the result of great stress in infancy, especially of "refrigerator parents" (Kanner, 1943; Bettelheim, 1967; Schopler and Mesibov, 1984). Parents of autistic children were actually stigmatized as abusers of their children. Almost all recent studies have concluded that autism is caused by organic factors, disease, physical stress, and genes (see Schopler and Mesibov, 1984). The recent studies seem to be better, thus autism seems now to be initially caused by organic factors, which then produce great family problems (Cantwell and Baker, 1984). These studies may greatly underestimate family effects because of the powerful trend in the medical sciences against the earlier extremes of popularized psychoanalysis (Zigler, 1984). There are more likely to be complex interdependencies among genetic and family factors in extreme syndromes of emotional problems, but little is clear about these issues. Our own studies simply do not deal much with such extreme insecurities and defensive syndromes. In the normal range of people we have concentrated on, we rarely found people who remembered having been filled with dread of death or even thinking much about death as a young child.

2. Because the vast majority of people develop primary security in their love duets with their mothers, the case of primary insecurity combined with secondary insecurity is a special and extreme case likely to be found only in "schizoid" or primary narcissistic people, whom we do not study.

3. There are, however, some adult traumas that are so horrifying that even the most generally secure individual can be overwhelmed and made permanently insecure by them, though they probably do not feel this insecurity is embedded in their senses of self. The holocausts of the modern world have had this effect on entire cultures. Stalin's holocaust of the 1930s has left most members of the elites in the Soviet Empire with a lingering dread and a generalized cultural sense of "demoralization," which is an excellent commonsense term for this condition of "giving up" that affects people whose defenses have been overwhelmed by insecurities. It is a condition that has been observed over and over again in the people whose cultures have been overwhelmed by Western civilization. It can lead to a submissive, ambivalently adoring, and hating identification with the repressor, which Max Scheler called *Ressentiment* (1961), or to an outright identification with the repressor, such as was seen in some of the Jews in the Nazi death camps. When repression is extreme, it can lead to a spiral downward into depression, or into a violent and murderous rage against the repressor (as we see in the *Franz Fanon syndrome*). Any situation that produces a pervasive sense of uncertainty tends to induce great anxiety,

depression, and demoralization. If the situation combines extreme dangers—such as possible death—with these uncontrollable uncertainties, it tends to produce a sense of terror, paralysis, and extreme demoralization (see Yalom, 1980). *Randomized danger* is the weapon of terrorism. Its effects are vastly out of proportion to the number of deaths and injuries caused. When a great success (inducing a sense of certainty and joyful security) is followed suddenly and unexpectedly (uncertainly) by a great failure, the uncertainty and demoralization are multiplied in the *sudden reversal syndrome*. All of these are easily seen in Great Terrors and in warfare. The theory of *indirection* in strategy is based on these principles (see Liddell Hart, 1954).

4. Because few children in the first several years are attached only, or even primarily, to a father, we must be cautious. Many cases show clearly, however, what we call the *Helene Deutsch syndrome*. Helene Deutsch (Roazen, 1985) became a famous psychoanalyst of women. She was partially analyzed by Freud himself, but, because of his failure to understand the profound importance of the mother-child communion and loves, he hardly explored her overt hatred of her mother. Because she identified lovingly with her father, Freud probably thought she was a typical modern Electra (who has incestuous desires for the father and thus falls into jealous conflict with the erstwhile loving mother). But this sexual theme, whether present or not, would only trivialize Deutsch's basic insecurity.

She felt her entire life that neither Freud nor later psychoanalysts revealed her deep problem. She herself seemed not to understand it, probably because Freudian theory supported her childhood lack of memory or repression of its causes. She was only aware of a haunting, lifelong feeling of detachment, emptiness, loss, and failure. She was unable really to love others or herself, to open up and share herself with them. She seems to have fit her own brilliantly delineated picture of feminine narcissism. We suspect hers was only a secondary narcissism characterized by an ambivalent and partially fragmented sense of self stemming from her lack or loss of motherly love. She showed none of the hysterical dread, anxiety, depressions, extreme self-pity, love-craving, and other symptoms characteristic of the primary narcissist. She had an ambivalently true and false sense of self. She was apparently what we have called a *secondary narcissist*.

5. Thus far we have said very little about the effects of the upper (the lesser) dimensions of insecurity and security on the lower levels. The best known and best understood of these relations is that of "overdriven striving," or the attempts by individuals to overcome (*compensate* for) greater insecurities (lower in the schema) by achieving a sense of security on the lesser (higher) dimensions. (Alfred Adler, 1930, 1946, 1964, developed most of the early ideas on compensating for insecurities. The basic ideas of his "individual psychology" are quite in harmony with our work.) Overdriven dominance or success, the *Getty Syndrome* (Lenzner, 1985), is possible only because the dimensions are partially interdependent, and we must be clear from the beginning that this success in overcoming more basic insecurities by success at the less basic levels is always only partial and is less than can be achieved in the other direction. The *Don Juan (and Doña Juanita)* syndrome is the seeking of a sense of sexual or love security by counterweighting sexual or love insecurity with "conquests" (dominance). It is extremely common in politics and business because of the high degree of interdependency between sexual insecurity and security and the insecurities and securities of submission and dominance and failure and success. J. Paul Getty was an extreme Don Juan (Lenzner, 1985).

4

THE DEVELOPMENT OF LOVE

At first glance, it seems out of perspective to consider play and having fun as occupying such a key role in the social interactions between mother and infant. Where do loving and needing to care for and identifying with the infant come into view? These are powerful motivating forces that mothers feel deep inside, but we have barely touched upon them and don't quite know how to. Certainly no face-to-face play would ever occur if a mother were not activated by these deeper forces and the long-range goals that accompany them. Still the question arises: If the mother does love and feels the need to care for and identify with her infant, and they are sitting across from each other face to face, what will happen? How will those motives translate into what acts? How do you love your baby so that a social interaction emerges? It is here that playing and having fun come into operation. They are an already available and ideally suited set of human operations to effect the translation from the longer-range motives into the behaviors that constitute the interaction and provide guidelines for the flow of the whole process.

Daniel Stern

Friendship is love without his wings.

Lord Byron

All socially competent adults implicitly assume themselves to be individual selves separate in some fundamental ways from all other human beings, in spite of their partial identifications with loved ones (see Douglas, 1984a). The very young baby seems to be subsumed under the mother's self and father's self. The baby is the most socially incompetent human being, and competent adults agree with the implicit assumption that he or she is almost totally part of the parents. In our society today, it normally takes roughly 20 years for a child who stays in school through college to develop enough of a sense of an independent self to feel even moderately secure in situations of dominance and competence. A remarkably large minority do not make it by then and some always remain in "human bondage."

The child progressively develops an independent sense of self through a vastly complex, progressive, interdependent drift-process of partially falling-out-of-love, especially falling out of identification, with his parents and falling in-love and developing intimate friendships and then romantic and Erotic loves with others. If the child does not progressively fall-out-of-love and identification with the parents, he or she cannot become more intimate and loving toward others and cannot develop a fully independent sense of self. If the child is "suffocated" in attempts to become independent, he or she remains in "human bondage" to them and cannot develop fully intimate love partnerships with others. The "father on his back" syndrome, seen so starkly in the *Franz Kafka syndrome*, involves the suppression of an independent sense of self by the dread of losing love, the dread of becoming immoral by becoming "rebellious," or the dread of failure—even of self-annihilation—if one dares to try to achieve independent dominance. The "mama's boy" or "daddy's girl" syndrome involves the partial suspension of independence striving out of both the hope of keeping the love of the parent and the dread of losing it. The *Somerset Maugham syndrome* involves the extreme forms of this bondage in which the inner sense of self is still fully in-love with and identified with the parent, who is thereby completely idealized and too precious to dare losing by loving someone else. While most orphans do not suffer from this, many do, especially when they lose a greatly loved mother very early in life (see our discussion of Dante's experience in Chapter 5).

The child can only begin to become intimate with others and thus to love them fully after he or she begins to fall out of the powerful love for the mother. The intimate identification and love feelings for the mother are simply too pervasive, embedded, and powerful for the child to have much self left over for identification with anyone else or much emotional interest in anyone else. If the first full flush—the first "honeymoon"—of the mother-baby love duet were to continue in full force, the child would not develop the fully intimate and loving friendships necessary for the full development of an independent sense of self and he or she would never fall in-love Erotically.

In the normal course of human love partnerships, then, the child is destined to suffer the emotional pains of partially unbonding from the first and most true love. The unbonding process normally grows in direct proportion to the independence demands made by the mother on the child and the independence demands the child makes on the mother. The first little crises normally come somewhere around the first year of age when the child's physical development makes it possible for him or her to start wandering off and poking into everything, and the child's burgeoning curiosity—lust for new experience and new places to explore—motivate him or her to do those things ever more insistently. These developments launch in earnest what Margaret Mahler (1975) and others have called the "nay saying" period when the mother must curtail some of this independence striving by stopping the child from running in front of cars, jumping out the tenth floor window, turning the pot of boiling water over on him- or herself, and the myriad other disasters that ignorant curiosity so cheerfully courts.

Like all unbonding processes, this one necessarily involves some suffering for both parties. But the process need not be very painful for very long. It certainly is not normally traumatic, like some kind of "rebirth trauma." But it can become traumatic if either or both make demands on each other that are too threatening. The most likely source of trauma would seem to be an insecure mother who feels very threatened by the rejecting screams of denunciation the little prisoner may shower on her, or, of course, a duet of mutually reinforcing insecurity that has started earlier and is now inflamed by further threats to both insecure selves. The mother who becomes the "rigid disciplinarian" or who calls in the father to perform that role to "break the will" of the young ruffian in order to save him or her from a miserable life of crime will almost certainly create a Frankenstein, a child and adult driven by a severe secondary insecurity. Traumatic breaks can produce a lasting sense of betrayal and distrust, outrage, hatred, detachment and depression, and the full array of defenses against insecurities far more easily and completely than the unbonding of adults, because the child has probably not developed his defenses very well at this point and can hardly understand what is happening.

But these are unusual. Normally the great caring love of the mother leads her to put up with much infantile rebellion full of sound and fury signifying not only temporary rejection but also the development of her child's independent sense of self. For, unlike most adult unbondings, this first falling out of love is largely precipitated by the mother out of her caring love, which leads her to want her child to become independent and less submissive at a steady but undangerous pace. In the anguished battles with the young rebel, it is sometimes hard to keep in mind, but she does derive a sense of fulfillment and pride from the general direction of this rocky road to love-with-independence. Barring unforeseen catastrophes, this drift away from the mother will not lead to complete unbonding, but only to a lower level of identification and love commensurate with the development of the independent sense of self and new love communings and partnerships.

BUILDING INTIMATE FRIENDSHIPS

The first fragments of childish friendliness begin at the toddler age with the visual recognition and tracking of other toddlers (Greenspan and Greenspan, 1985). Infants ten months to about a year old seem to be interested in and then increasingly fascinated with other infants about the same size as themselves. Toddler sociability begins with this mutual "sizing up" while ensconced in shopping carts at the supermarket or crawling around outside the thatched hut in the Trobriand Islands (we can only assume). It is not clear how much is due to spontaneous interest and how much to parental encouragement of nascent friendliness, as parents sometimes initiate the whole matter and generally give warm, baby-talky reinforcements to any spontaneous interest. As usual in the very heuristically (open-to-the-situation) primed human being, the rudiments of sociability seem to depend on both, and either internal priming or external priming (directing attention and conditioning) can come first. When they come together, sparks of interest fly and, when the other infant returns the interest, the reciprocal eyeing begins the opening of the windows of intimacy onto the soul of the other, the "thou." The initial interest in the other child may even spring entirely from a misidentification of him or her with the self. It may be because the other is of the same size and general shape as the self that he or she is so interesting. Self-recognition begins earlier, as has been shown in studies of infants' mirror-viewing behavior.

In these early stages, the child seems to have no significant empathy for others. The child clearly expects their desires and other properties to be like, or the same as, his or her own. The child cannot yet abstract him- or herself from his or her own perspective and view him- or herself from the perspective of someone else. (Considering that this is difficult enough for us adults in the least impassioned of conditions, it is no wonder the infant is so egocentric.) Empathy and thus sympathy and intimate caring take many years and vast experience to develop. Those unfortunates in life who have not received enough loving as infants, or who have received it but had it followed by the conflicting messages that inspire great secondary insecurities, will never develop much empathy, sympathy, and intimate loving because they are so defensively locked into their obsessions with their own weak and fragmented senses of their selves.

The initial play sessions of very young children are almost entirely restricted to playing *in the presence of* the interesting other, with undertones of playing with the other. Each child probably assumes the other will fit into his or her expectations and thus into the playing patterns learned from the intensive play with the mother. They normally do not do so very well, because each mother-child duet drifts into distinctive improvisations on the universal play patterns (Stern, 1977). Early play experience must normally be closely supervised and at least subtly guided by adults to prevent baby carnage on a grand scale. Few mothers would agree with Rousseau or ultra-progressives who expect little children spontaneously to do good unto other children. Those who do have their self-centered and spoiled children expelled from nursery school for violent behavior. Little boys are obviously far less empathetic and far more violent than little girls, as any kindergarten teacher knows. But there are wide individual variations in this, as in most things, and much of it is the result of variations in insecurities.

Playing alone and with others is obviously highly primed genetically, given that it is universal and is everywhere highly developed. Playing with others grows slowly at first, but then rapidly accelerates around the age of three or four and soon shows all of the general properties of human play behavior. These include spontaneous creations of stories involving interacting partners, acting out dramatizations of these with others, and the development of intimate friendships that provide the support and feedback about the self necessary to the progressive growth of the sense of self and to the ever-more efficient interacting with the world.

The nature of play has been of great interest to social scientists since the late nineteenth century. Social thinkers before that generally had little to say about children, though commonsensically it has always been obvious that "the child is father to the man." In spite of the excellent initial work of Groos (1898, 1901) and others, the understanding of play soon took a bad turn, which misled generations of thinkers. As in so much else, the Freudian theories had a big hand in amplifying this misdirection, but they were built on the stooped shoulders of the ancient giant, Aristotle.

Aristotle argued that the primary value of drama (and, hence, by extension, of storytelling and play-acting out more generally) is that it gives its viewers an emotional catharsis. While he clearly thought of this in a broader sense that involved emotional *inspiration* as well, attention has focused on the "cleaning out" aspect, as seen in the idea of a cathartic. In this sense, catharsis is a *venting* or releasing of emotion. This sense tied in all too beautifully with Freud's adaptation of the vitalistic hydraulic pressure model of the human psyche. As emotions build up for any reason, especially because of repressive external forces preventing their venting, the increasing pressures must find some means of being vented or the entire system will tend to explode or, at least, collapse. This indirect, substitute venting of emotional energy—libido pressure—was what Freud and his disciples called *sublimation*. Sublimation could take place through alternative *acting out* (such as the scapegoat kicking of the cat when you are enraged at your mother but repress this rage for any reason) or through alternative (redirected) mental activity, that of dreaming, which comes in the forms of both sleep-dreaming and waking-dreaming, the latter including storytelling and artistic dreaming in general. Playing is, then, a combination of direct venting of emotions and indirect venting through acting out of repressed emotions and dreaming of both types.

This model, as we have seen before, certainly gets at some basic truths about human emotional life. Many basic emotions do build up in pressure for various reasons (spontaneous buildup over time, repression of venting, triggering by stimuli, and feedback loops) and are vented directly or indirectly in some proportion to the buildup of the emotions. This model is a powerful help in understanding otherwise mysterious phenomena such as scapegoating. Psychiatrists of many kinds have found the model very helpful in creating various forms of storytelling and acting-out play situations that provide great insights into the repressed emotions children or adults cannot talk about and in helping to bring these into consciousness and solving problems associated with them.

But Freud's understanding even of *venting play* was constricted by his too tight focus on interpreting night-dreams experienced by highly neurotic patients who almost certainly had repressed powerful emotions, especially sexual lust. It was this that led him to focus his attention overwhelmingly on the "wishing" for fulfillment of a repressed emotion seen in many such dreams. Even in these neurotic dreams, however, he was misled by his already developed pressure theory of venting. A very high percentage of neurotic dreams are not inspired by wishes but by dreads aroused by powerful insecurities. Dreading then inspires the natural mental defenses that either consist of or inspire wishing as a way of symbolically overcoming the dread. The mental images aroused by the insecurities (which often have been triggered by something that happened during the day before sleeping) do not vent emotion; they vastly increase dread, as we all know when we go to sleep feeling peaceful and are wakened by a horrible nightmare that causes the pounding heart, perspiration, and all the other bodily signs of dread.

The overall dreaming process is seen in waking dreams very clearly. As Bruno Bettelheim (1976) has shown in *The Uses of Enchantment*, the fairy tale is effective—and craved by the child—precisely because it triggers some dread or anxiety that is already lying dormant, generally a vague one that is given more specific, more realistic form by the fairy tale, but not so real that it would produce a paralyzing sense of terror. The child is usually feeling perfectly happy until the magical image of the Giant triggers his or her deeply embedded, pervasive, and powerful sense of submission and ontological insecurities. This dread triggers a wish for deliverance and the story provides it in realistic eidetic imagery. The wish fulfillment then pervades the child with a situational sense of security, which provides some increase in the basic sense of security by assuring him or her emotionally and, to a lesser extent, cognitively that even a tiny creature like the human child can make his or her way safely in this world of giant dangers. The fairy story (daydreaming) must first arouse anxiety and then vent it and replace it with powerful positive emotions—especially excitement, joy, relief, hope, and love—to be an effective catharsis for the child and, thereby, have a positive effect on the overall development of his or her sense of self. The child is commonly left with an unvented reservoir of positive feeling, which he or she partially acts out by jumping and dancing with joy, hugging the storyteller or him- or herself, and running off to play with other children.

The Freudian theory excludes from consideration the immense human effort that goes into the purposeful pursuit of increased stimulation of positive emotions (up to thresholds). The absence of other emotions produces a horrifying sense of depression, which human beings will try to counterweight even by inflicting severe physical pain (such as banging the head against the wall). The positive emotions all have optimal (or "satisficing") ranges of *intensity, duration,* and *alternation* (or time scheduling between episodes of the emotions). These vary somewhat for each individual. There are also cultural patterns of these preferences, as Ruth Benedict (1934) argued. Individuals drift in general toward an optimization of all these optimal ranges of intensity, duration, and alternation for positive emotions, which is a horrendously problematic and messy endeavor. (This may be why some people try to escape the whole "rat race" by trying to escape all desires. If they ever succeeded, they would be bored to death by their oversuccess.) Too little, too brief, or too infrequent emotion inspires action to increase it. Too much triggers a painful emotion of satiation ("stuffed," "drained," anxious, and so on) and leads to attempts to reduce it by reducing the stimuli or by venting.

Reducing all play to venting play is most distorting, however, because it completely excludes from consideration the even more important form of play we call *thou-engaging play.* Classical fairy tales, which is what Bettelheim was analyzing, engage the child in an emotional interaction with an already established sense of others' selves. (*Saccharine fairy tales* of the sort now so common in the mass media do not even do this because they do not first arouse dread. They provide only "fun" or "hap-hap-happy" feelings, which are effective only as diversions, because they are not emotionally powerful enough to affect the senses of security of the sense of self. Happy emotions must be tempered and potentiated by unhappy ones to be that powerful.) In this way, they do provide some testing out of the child's accumulated senses of others and can have some effects on his or her development of self-engagement with the selves of others. But the effects of this are pale by comparison with the effects of real-world play engagements of them.

But why "play engagements"? Why do children take part in such a vast amount of playfully engaging the senses of others? It is obvious that they do, though we must not overdo this difference between them and adults. All adults with reasonably secure senses of their selves engage others extensively in play, only proportionally not as much as children. Merrymaking, acting-out pretend roles, joking, mocking, teasing, and so on are pervasive in life. In general, they vary directly with the degree to which we are emotionally engaged with someone, but then decline precipitously in situations in which we are extremely emotionally engaged with them. This is clearest of all in love partnerships. Lovers play together so much that they literally feel they have become little children once again and are seen as childish by others (which is embarrassing, so they normally restrict their love-playing to very private situations). But when the emotions are most aroused—in jealous rage, frustrated anger, Erotic passion, caring, and so on—all sense of play immediately disappears and the senses of self are fully engaged in each other and in the world in all seriousness. Why? The answer for adults shows us why children are so prone to play engagements.

Playfulness puts a bracket of "let's pretend," of partially suspended reality, that is nonetheless quite emotionally relevant, around our behavior. *Playfulness involves willing a partial suspension of the attitude of realism and belief.* The partialness of this *willed suspension of belief* is of crucial importance. Play is suspended between the poles of the routinized and taken for granted on the one end, where there is little emotion, and the extraordinary and critically new at the other end, where there is very powerful emotion. If one's attitude shows too little engagement of the sense of self and of emotion—too much ho-humness—then one is not engaged enough to be successfully playful; if one's attitude shows too much engagement of the sense of self and of emotion, then one is too engaged to be successfully playful. The person who "plays" at the game with no real concern, only to please someone else, is not really "in play." He or she is only going through the motions. The one who plays in dead earnest out of greed, a lust for honor, sexual passion, or whatever is overdoing it and breaks the cognitive framework of play.

The dramaturgical analysts who believe "all the world's a stage," and that life is *only* playing, are wrong (see Goffman, 1959; and Fontana's critique, 1980). Life is both serious and playful, both engaged and disengaged, both real and unreal, closed and open, intended and unintended, determined and contingent. The "killjoy" is one who can only be serious and, thereby, destroys the vitalizing spontaneity of emotions in play. The "playboy" is one who is only "childish," only playful, and never serious, thereby making life an impossible dreaming, a utopia of fun, a madhouse. Sanity lies between the extremes and is maintained only by an ever-shifting balance of the counterweighted opposites of engagement and disengagement.

Play allows us to engage our real senses of selves emotionally in the world without doing so to such an extent that we are threatened by the triggering of our insecurities. By doing so, this *membrane of playfulness* casts a partial spell over us, which allows us to engage our senses of our selves to the maximum degree commensurate simultaneously with minimizing the threats to our feelings of self-security. Playfulness, then, allows us to engage, test out, and develop our senses of selves with each other to the optimal degrees because low degrees of threats to our self-security systems allow us to lower our systems of defenses. Play is not merely a "time-out" in a game or a "cease-fire" that allow us to lick our wounds and regroup our forces, nor is it a full "suspension of disbelief" such as we normally see in night-dreaming and in the performance of rituals. *Play is reality partially suspended and partially engaged within the bounds of security.* Play allows us to be intimate with others in activities that would make us feel insecure in situations of full realism.

Highly insecure people cannot really play with others because they dare not lower their defenses. The most insecure of all, such as the narcissists suffering the dreads of primary insecurity, are caught in a total web of playing within themselves, because they cannot even dare to be engaged in full reality within themselves. Their masks are first and foremost for themselves and secondarily for others. The less insecure, but still quite insecure, know they are using masks to hide their insecure selves, primarily from others but secondarily from the real inner sense of self. Masks in plays, in dancing, and other play situations are ways of hiding the real self while acting out new, potentially threatening possibilities that, if acted out in full reality with no hiding, would fully engage the sense of self, thereby putting the self fully "on the line" of danger. We know by intuition when someone has gotten "too serious," that is, when the framework and mask of play have been broken through by too much earnestness, reality, emotion. If play has been engaged in for the purpose—or hope—of moving toward a new reality by safely testing out ways of getting there, then the progressive breaking through of reality will be greeted with joy, as we see when childishly playful lovers romping on the bed move by little steps from tussling and wrestling to wriggling embraces and finally impassioned clasping. The step-wise, drift movement toward the full engagement of the sense of self with the thou and in the world allows engagements of the self a step at a time, so that an instant retreat to full play can be made if the other rejects the early steps, with no significant threat to the self caused by the rejection.

Play puts a magical screen of uncertainty between us and others, between our actions and their meanings, between the reactions of others and their meanings. It is one of the most important forms of our vastly rich repertoire of strategies and tactics for engaging reality indirectly by *manipulating the degrees of uncertainty* in our engagements. Dramatizations—plays—impose even more uncertainty upon what is observed and its relevance to the self. If you feel quite threatened, you may not see any relevance at all. The diplomacy that takes place during the time-outs in warfare has more certain meanings, including goals, than play generally does, but the deadly serious potential meanings are partially suspended by elaborate rituals, ceremonies, and celebrations that maintain some attitude of playfulness.

For children, play constitutes a progressive, step-by-step emotional engagement of the self with thous and in the world. The world engaged emotionally is both the imagined world beyond the realm of play, especially the imagined adult that the child normally yearns to become, and the selves of the other playmates. Much of the child's play involving the imagined world beyond is *venting play.* Like any unfulfilled craving, the child's craving to be and to do adult things, especially to be free to do as he or she wishes when he or she wishes, produces a buildup of frustrations. Much of play, such as the very aggressive attacks the child launches in war games, vents these frustrations and angers. The child wishes to join the adult world, but cannot, so he or she vents frustrations by playing at doing so and, thereby, gains the pleasures of imagined dominance and self-realization more generally; and, in some instances, the child fears or dreads some aspects of the world and acts out the defenses against them, thereby gaining increased feelings of security. (Beating up the bully is a very popular form of play, both with children and with adults.) Probably the most engaging and consequential form of this playful world-engagement is that involving self-identification with adult heroes and self-disidentification with adult villains.

The great power of observational learning comes from the immense amounts of information that are encoded in the sequences of eidetic images (scenarios), which are remembered and can be observed internally over and over again, like a movie being repeated over and over in the great theater of the semiconscious and conscious mind. The rationalistic argument that the human being's great adaptive advantage comes from the ability to create, learn, and manipulate symbols is wrong. Most people, other than intellectuals, do not do much important learning or thinking in words. The emotional and cognitive foundations of life are learned overwhelmingly before the child has many words to use and at the time when the words are understood and used by him or her predominantly as signs directly standing for world-scenarios which have been observed and recorded, rather than as abstract symbols. (The child is a primitivist, not an abstract symbolist.) Visual, auditory, olfactory, tactile, and emotional world-scenarios are highly developed in all mammals. We do not know whether the memory storage of these is more developed in human beings, though that seems likely. But the human being clearly has vastly greater abilities to process them—to call them up, manipulate them, mine them by doing close-ups and extracting details, enhancing and muting details, and endlessly comparing both the raw images and scenarios remembered and the infinite possible combinations, permutations, and imagined variations of them. The subconscious and conscious mind is ceaselessly encoding, creating, summoning up, manipulating, and processing these world-scenarios. Everyone from earliest childhood is his or her own tireless and impassioned movie producer, director, imagery-artist, actors, and audiences.

The human mind is overwhelmingly an eidetic imager and analyzer. We know this from our own experience and anyone can see it by watching the very young child act out complex imagery before he or she can say anything much in words. This is why the human being is so extremely ritualistic and why rituals have such a powerful impact in acting out basic emotional scenes. Most words used in rituals are "mumbo-jumbo" with little clear verbal meaning. They are themselves magical rituals that help to set the scene by arousing images. The most powerful love and Erotic rituals the world over are acted out in dances, music, and song. Each person who falls in-love feels the bodily impulse to act out these love rituals, if in no more complex forms than those of swirling around or chasing each other around, listening to "our music," listening together to the voices in the wind, and muttering ritualized words that speak to the heart of emotions and not to the mind of symbols.

Movies are the most powerful forms of story-seeing and storytelling ever invented and the most powerful fairy tales by far are movies such as The Wizard of Oz. The great inventors, scientists, and storytellers generally think in these vastly complex images and world-scenarios. The images and scenarios go on ceaselessly just outside of and on the edge of consciousness, relating to each other, developing into new forms to be tested, merging and separating, forming into ever-more complex possible scenarios; and when a relevant situation emerges in the world, these possible scenarios are normally ready for our rapid selection of the best to fit the world situation and our sense of self.

It is extremely difficult to learn how to do anything by words alone. Who has not created a tangled and misery-laden mess by trying to follow verbal instructions on how to assemble a child's swing set? Even when there are still, two-dimensional pictures simulating some of the vastly information-rich world-scenarios, we normally suffer terribly until we figure out by trial and error what the pictures *mean*, that is, *what scenarios are intended by the words and pictures*. It is immensely easier to learn by *observing* someone do it and then *doing* it ourselves. Even a simple form of learning such as learning how to drive to a given address shows the vast differences in these forms of learning. Following verbal directions is difficult at best, even when they are phrased in terms of world-scenarios such as "turn left at the red light," because we do not have the specific world-scenario in mind when we are told. If we do have that world-scenario in mind from previous experience there, then learning is very easy by comparison and mistakes are far fewer. If we are riding with someone and observe how they get there, we will find it much easier to remember how to get there than if we only learn abstractly by instructions how to get there. If we actually *do* the driving, there is a great quantum leap in how much we remember about getting there. Memory itself is so primed to encode world-scenarios in which we are actually engaged emotionally in *doing* things that we come to count on remembering how to get there when we are actually doing it, even though we could not tell anyone else how to get there. As we say, "I'm sure I'll remember which way to turn when I see it again."

Learning to live is inherently a vastly complex process of learning by observing, remembering world-images and world-scenarios, analyzing and testing out images and scenarios, acting them out and doing them. (An *image* is a still-frame memory, such as we have of a loved face. A *scenario* consists of "moving" images related to each other.) The infant begins by observing and remembering, at first quite passively. He or she is highly primed to observe and remember certain things, such as the facial expressions of emotion. Merely by observing images and scenarios, the infant rapidly becomes organized ("programmed") enough to begin to interact in certain limited situations quite effectively. We cannot yet be sure, but it seems quite likely that from very early in life the infant is already ceaselessly reviewing remembered images and scenarios.

By the age of two or three, the child relies more and more on the abilities to remember vastly complex eidetic scenarios and to test out possible lines of action in them. The child has entered the period when stories and, above all, movies fascinate him or her. He or she is now disturbed by the seeming reality of nightmares and must be reassured that "it's only a dream." The distinction between internal scenarios of the world—at least in their night-dream versions when the critical faculties of consciousness are suspended—and the directly perceived world is not yet clearly formed. But in wakeful states, the distinction is clear enough for the child to lose interest in "peek-a-boo" games, which fascinated him or her as long as he or she could not clearly understand how the face or eyes could disappear and yet still exist. Because the child is now relying so much on the internal processing of world-scenarios, he or she begins to tell his or her own rudimentary stories, at least to him- or herself, and begins "Let's Pretend" playing with others.

By the age of four or five, the child is heavily involved in acting out inner world-scenarios in play with others in everything from "playing house" and "playing mommy and daddy" to "playing cowboys and Indians" and "playing cops and robbers." The acting out of imagined world-scenarios of family relations is most indicative of how powerful, by this age, are the abilities to identify with highly complex world-scenarios of persons and their actions and to learn them progressively by acting them out. The first identification with a person, the love-identification with the mother, involved predominantly learning by observing the mother and only rudimentary learning by doing, by acting out. The child acted out only for rudimentary activities, such as patty-cake and peek-a-boo, or acted out observed facial expressions of emotion and, later, learned the rudiments of talk by observing and "copying" the mother's mouth movements.

In early family acting-out play, the child shows a great capacity to identify primarily with the external, physical aspects of others such as the father. The child adapts their ways of walking, dressing, eating, and doing many other things. Psychoanalysts and others were so impressed with this ability by this age to act like those with whom he or she identified that they talked of the child "introjecting" their values, their ways of acting, and even them as "objects." What the child actually does is form intensely emotion-laden world-scenarios of the parents and then considers making them part of him- or herself by testing them out internally and then acting them out progressively in play. The more the child acts them out, the more he or she moves toward doing them with a sense of full reality, thereby progressively leaving behind the sense of pretense that is inherent in playing, until they become a part of his or her real sense of self.

The hypotheses and theories about the development of the male sexual sense of self have suffered from every possible myth and mistake. Most of them were developed under the dark cloud of the Freudian model of biological determinism and of the incestuous and murderously guilty child. Consequently, they assumed that the sexual sense of self would develop very early, would be very simple (aimed just at sexual activity), and would be largely unchanging. Much work in recent decades has been concerned with showing that this model is wrong and that things are considerably more complex. That part was easy. Unfortunately, because these exposés, which sometimes degenerated into diatribes, were commonly undertaken to reach preconceived political goals, they generally threw masculinity out with the Freudian model.

It would be biologically most unadaptive to have the male or female sexual orientation, subsequent sexual behavior, and closely related forms of feeling and behavior depend entirely or even very strongly on cultural conditioning. Anything that is vital to biological adaptiveness is highly primed genetically. All cultures have profound effects on the specific channeling of our eating, drinking, and eliminative behavior; but no culture can long determine directly whether we eat, drink, or eliminate in biologically adaptive ways. Cultures can and do have great effects on the specific channeling of sexual emotions and behavior, though, as we have argued, this is far less than anyone would conclude by looking only at publicly visible sexual talk and behavior. But cultures probably have relatively little effect on the development of the individual into adult heterosexuality and procreativity. They may, but generally do not, have great effects on earlier developments of sexual behavior, but their effects on the daimonic Erotic urges are far less. Some cultures strongly encourage young male homosexual bonding, but this does not prevent the males from becoming husbands and fathers, and the encouragement is probably far less successful than we would be led to believe from the pederastic accounts of Plato. Even extreme subcultural situations such as the English public schools for boys do not succeed in channeling very many into adult homosexuals, though in the nineteenth century they probably helped to produce the obsession with the sadomasochistic fantasies of the femme fatale (see Bade, 1979). Those who were greatly affected were probably the most oriented that way in the beginning.

This, however, does not mean that the male sexual orientation was fully formed at an earlier age by identification with a loved father or father surrogate. The available evidence, from our own observations and those of others, clearly indicates that there is no great difference in the tendency to homosexuality among those boys raised without fathers, those raised with fathers, and those raised with fathers with whom they disidentified (see Adams, 1984). If being raised without a father close at hand to identify with does produce any insecurities about sexual orientation, it seems normally to be defended against by acting out aggressively male scenarios, such as we see in Don Juanism. The result then would be more masculine sexuality, not less.

There seem to be two reasons for this weak link between sexual orientation and early identification with a loved father. The first is simply that Freud was wrong. Sexuality is not born full-blown from the baby's crib, or from the working out of Oedipal conflicts in early childhood. Sexuality itself is of only minor importance in the early development of the sense of self. Sexuality develops slowly and probably more or less continually throughout childhood and then explodes during adolescence. The second reason is that sexual orientation and the Erotic are so highly primed genetically that the early developments need only minor observational learning, self-identification, and self-realization through playing and acting out (see Spiro, 1979). These apparently can be done at a distance and, in our society, there is never any lack of highly charged fantasy models in the movies and television, nor is there likely to be any lack of direct models when living with a heterosexual mother.

The evidence about girls is much more skimpy and ambiguous, because most of the work on this has been done in our society, where girls are almost always raised by the heterosexual mother or mother surrogate. (Nearly 90% of children are still in the custody of their mothers after divorce and the percentage is probably higher for girls.) Given that mothers are almost always much closer to their children than fathers are among mammals, it is entirely possible that the development of female sexual orientation relies on this far more intense partnership and self-identification. This seems especially likely because human female sexuality is more complex and more subject to repression than the male. Our "guesstimate" from our own observations is that severe problems between the mother and the daughter are far more likely to produce disturbances in sexual orientation and general development in the sexual sense of self than are similar problems between a boy and his father. Rejection by the mother and rejection of the mother by a daughter seem far more likely to produce homosexuality and any number of other disturbances in development, such as the Helena Deutsch syndrome.

More extreme situations seem to have similar effects on male sexual orientation, but not on sexual responsiveness. Extreme violence or other severe problems with a father can lead to a strong disidentification with the father and a corresponding identification with the mother, a fellow sufferer, which may affect the sexual orientation of the boy. (This might, however, only be temporary.) Disidentifications with fathers are not uncommon in our society today because there are so many family conflicts and dissolutions. These commonly come later and do not have much affect on the overall development of the sense of self, but, when they come very early in life and strongly encourage a boy to continue in his early identification with his mother, such disidentification with a father may lead to a later homosexual orientation. This was the pattern in one of our life studies of a gay male sadomasochist. His father was quite violent toward the mother, him, and his brother. The boy early began playing with dolls, which led to further abuse from the father. By adolescence, he was having intense sadomasochist dreams and was spending his summers hitchhiking around the country and taking part in homosexual relations. His sexual orientation, however, was not unidirectional. He married, divorced, fell deeply in love with a male lover, fell out of love, and entered the extreme cruising scenes of gays in Hollywood and Las Vegas, but always showed some sexual interest in women. He himself is convinced that he was "born gay" because it was such an early orientation. We suspect, however, that it was far more the extreme early situation of violence, disidentification with the father, and identification with the mother that led both him and his brother into gay sexual fantasies and play that make up the sadomasochist world. We also suspect that he may be one of those "totally" committed to the gay self who later drifts—however ambivalently—into heterosexual relations and Erotic partnerships. In life histories where there are no such extreme situations early in life and where the individual seems unambivalently oriented homosexually, the argument of Edward Wilson (1984) that there is a genetic basis for some homosexuality may be true.

This relative lack of effect of early self-identification on sexual orientation does not mean, however, that the progressive engagements of the child's sense of self in the world through identifications, playing, and acting out have no effects on the later sexual-gender sense of self. We must remember here that the sexual modernist program involves a radical reduction of sexuality to the activity of the sex organs and "erogenous zones" themselves, or even to mere "sexual outlets." This is done in the guise of experimental (laboratory) biology, but it is radically antibiological in that it is radically opposed to the Darwinian conceptions of organic adaptedness. Sexual "outlets" constitute only a tiny part of life's activities and in almost all societies, except our own, they make up relatively few of overall emotional engagements, except when they do not occur in a relatively routine manner. Biologically, sexual intercourse is a necessary part of masculinity, but it is only one of many parts and in all viable cultures it is normally of minor importance in terms of the emotional energy and time expended, especially in comparison with the daimonic urges of the Erotic. Except during the sporadic episodes of romantic love obsession, boys and men spend far more waking time and emotional engagement with other boys and men than they do with girls or women, just as girls and women do with other girls and women. Beyond some necessary minimum, sexual identification, play and acting out are not very important for developing adequate male sexual responses to women. In fact, after a man has this minimum needed for feeling sexual arousal and being potent with women, his sexual prowess probably depends far more on his ability to get along with and be pleasing in general to women than anything else, and this can probably be best learned by spending his youth with women. Even an impotent man may arouse passionate devotion in women, including sexual devotion, if he has learned early in life to adore them, to take them seriously, and to please them in general. Havelock Ellis is a perfect example of this, though his women with normal sexual orientations eventually drifted elsewhere for those fulfillments, thereby producing agonizing paroxysms of jealousy in this sexual modernist (see Grosskurth, 1985).

Just as girls in all cultures are immensely more concerned with learning through self-identification, playing, and acting out the immensely more complex and emotionally difficult activities of motherhood and economic work than they are with those of sexual outlets or even romantic love, so are boys immensely more involved in learning through self-identification, playing, and acting out the immensely more complex and emotionally difficult activities of fatherhood, work, and the warrior arts. In almost all cultures, boys and men have spent a very high proportion of their lives observing, identifying, playing at, and acting out in progressive self-engagements the immensely emotional, complex, and difficult arts of weaponry, hunting, attacking, defending, retreating, hiding, and many other demanding activities of warfare and hunting. Boys do not just grow by genetic priming into men able to run or march in close file as Masai warriors or Greek hoplites into the face of death and agonizing injury. They are not born as Australian aborigines with the genetic programs for the immense skills needed to cast a spear 200 yards with deadly accuracy. On average, boys are born everywhere with the genetic programs to become eventually far more aggressive than girls, in some rough proportion to the rise and decline of the male hormones, because male aggressiveness reaches its peak in young adulthood and in old age is not much more than that of women (see Wilson and Herrnstein, 1985). But developing this very raw genetic priming into the fine and deadly arts of hunting and warfare takes immense work. It also takes an immense amount of observing, self-identification, fantasizing, dreaming, playing, and acting out. Boys do not need to observe men involved in sexual intercourse to grow into effective sex partners. In fact, they almost never do in our society. Both they and girls learn perfectly well by fumbling and feeling their way. Most people immensely prefer spontaneity and the joy of un-self-conscious amateurism in their sex lives. Sex as work, which is the implicit ideal of the sexual modernist sex manuals, is seen as a repulsive perversion by almost all human beings. But hunting cape buffaloes or marching into a solid phalanx of hoplites with amateurish abandon is a sure way to exit quickly from the gene pool.

Sexual modernists routinely write as if the average person in our society approaches sex with a sense of dread. Just about the only people who do are those who have spent their time observing pictures of diseased sex organs in sexual modernist texts and obsessively trying to remember the 113 positions "necessary" for sexual fulfillment. As a popular old song says, sex is doing "what comes naturally," at least by comparison with warfare, hunting, friendship, and leadership in general. It is these complex and difficult activities that are so highly dependent on the boy's identification with grown men who already do them. These identifications are vastly more effective in their results when there is mutual love between the mentor and the novitiate, but the optimum of love is a different mix from the love-duet with the mother. The optimum mix involves intense adoration in the boy and intense caring in the father (and other mentors, both relatives and not; see the discussion of cooperative paternalism and maternalism in Douglas,

1983). But this love partnership has the practical goals of making the boy a competent man among men, a team player and leader. It is precisely the caring of the father that makes him demanding of the boy, though within the limits of his abilities to perform (or else the result will be successful rebellion or Kafkaesque submission). And these demands inevitably produce some ambivalence in the son and student, love mixed with some resentment and fear (especially if the adoration goes to the extreme of awe, which is especially common in the very young).

In most societies, the father and other older men also teach the boy to constrain his burgeoning sexual desires in the service of his higher commitments to the all-important military and economic activities on which the lives and freedom of everyone depend. Rather than serving as the identification models for his sexual activity, they normally serve far more as the models for the morality of chastity, which is nearly a universal norm among warrior and hunting bands when the sacred business is at hand. Sex is normally seen as polluting when big-game hunting or warfare is pending or under way, though this may well be because sexual desire and romantic love motivate the hunter or warrior to escape the dangers and sufferings he must face. In most societies, the initiation rites transforming boys into apprentice men involve symbolic sacrifices of sexuality in the service of the masculine bonds of teamwork necessary for effective fighting and hunting. The mutilation of his sex organ and the scarring of his body are marvelous symbols of this chaste sacrifice, but might be absurd symbols of becoming a sexual partner of women. They are symbolic sacrifices of the sex organs and body, at least in the short run, in the service of masculinity that goes beyond "organ performance." The same may well be true of the sacrificial rites of women in which older women initiate the apprentices in ways involving scarification, body distortions, and even sexual organ mutilations. These, however, seem to involve more complex motives than the male rites.

We do not mean that boys become aggressive through this process of observation, identification, and progressive engagement. On the contrary, rage and aggression are highly primed programs that appear early in infancy and childhood. Effective fathering is concerned with controlling, channeling, and modulating—"chastening"—the practical behavior of work, dominance seeking, and the closely associated aggressive behavior. Those without successful fathers or other adult males with whom they can identify seem to be far more aggressive and far more apt to act impulsively in "blind rage." Both male and female leadership in human societies, and in other primate societies, is the result of extremely complex and long-run patterns of interaction that rarely involve the actual use of violent behavior within the in-group one is leading (see Burns, 1978). Violence and, to a far less extent, any other form of very aggressive behavior (such as the arrogant degrading of others) within the human in-group is far more apt to lead to a rapid slide down the dominance scale than to lead to a position of leadership. One of the basic functions of leadership is to control, and largely suppress, aggression to make the in-group more effective in all of its coordinated tasks. The leader gives justice, peace, and order within the in-group, not violent injustice, internal warfare, and disorder. Learning to do so takes immensely complex, immensely problematic learning by observing, identifying, and engaging the self progressively in these patterns of interaction (see Douglas, forthcoming.) The relinquishing of the highly primed male patterns of aggression and the learning of these vastly problematic activities are greatly facilitated by the love partnerships between father and son and later mentors and apprentices.

The son does not relinquish incestuous lust for the mother and a consequent craving for jealous revenge against the father, as Freudians would have us believe. He simply comes to love and identify more with the father or other mentors as he slowly falls out of his obsessive love-duet with the mother. The father does not impose a harsh and repressive superego on the son. Out of his love and his identification with the father and other mentors, the son *chooses* to make their morality his and to try with the ambivalence born of fear of failure and self-suppression of desires to become like them. They in their turn provide him with the minutely phased, fearful challenges, the knowledge by observing and doing, the encouragement and loving support necessary to develop these abilities.

Of course, some fathers act in the exact opposite ways, generally because they themselves never learned these things effectively from their fathers and because they are defending against their own insecurities, perhaps with the dread that the son will outdo them (making them submissive), the very thing that most fathers want, out of love and identification with their sons. These failures at masculinity commonly become tyrants seeking to repress their sons or even degrade them. Rebellion is the most common outcome. If it is extreme, rebellion can become a life-consuming passion that may be extended to whole classes, races, or species identified with the repressor. At worse extremes, the repressor may break or repress the will of the child, as we see in the

Kafka syndrome. If it involves massive degrading, perhaps by comparison of the son with an idealized other son, the son who does not successfully rebel may even become self-hating and self-destructive, as we see in Vincent Van Gogh.

Girls normally learn in precisely the same ways the activities of effective female leadership, including those of the motherly leading of developing children. When boys or girls *cross-identify* with the parent of the opposite sex, they learn the opposite-sex patterns of activities, though probably with far more personal strain and insecurity because in any society they are brought into partial conflict with themselves and with what others expect and will tolerate from them. Helena Deutsch was a good example of the emotional cost exacted by such cross-sex identifications and activities. Of course, there are some boys and girls with more genetic priming to feel and act in such cross-sex ways (given that sex differences are just a matter of statistical distributions) and they are the ones who will most easily and with least long-run costs identify and develop cross-sexually.

THE DEVELOPMENT OF FRIENDSHIP

Loving fathers and mothers who sincerely care for and help to develop the increasingly adult sense of self of the child can never be fully loyal and supportive friends to the child, precisely because their love and identification with him or her is too intense and their caring responsibility for his or her moral and physical development too great. Because of their deep love and identification with the child and their maternalistic and paternalistic duties, they easily oscillate from being too accepting and supporting to being the exact opposite for the child's overall development, and from being too relaxed in their moral judgments, because they do not wish to hurt the child, to being too moralistic, because they are too concerned that he or she may be hurt by others far more for being deviant. Because the child loves and identifies with them so much, he or she is too self-conscious, too afraid of making mistakes, too risk-aversive, too easily hurt by well-intentioned criticisms, too morally upright, and generally too self-restrictive to be creatively playful enough with them. These are roughly the same reasons why adult romantic lovers cannot be the most intimate and supportive friends to each other until many years of progressive intimacy and mutual self-knowledge have brought them to a higher state of mutual development, acceptance, and compromise.

The optimum development of the child's sense of self in the world comes from a complex and slowly shifting balance in his or her intimate communings and love with parents, siblings, and other family members, and evolving sets of friendships and work relations. In the optimum development, the parents, being by far the most important people in the child's sense of self and biosphere, always set the general but shifting and evolving framework of his or her life, providing gentle, but sometimes harsh, guidelines. They gently, as indirectly as possible (because of the child's fear of failing in their august eyes), nudge the child forward, but remain ever ready to catch him or her when he or she falls. They discretely observe the child's misdemeanors but do little in minor instances, while remaining ready when necessary to punish the crimes. They support the child's efforts, but do not lie to make failures look like successes. They provide security, but do not hide the real and necessary situational insecurities of the human condition. They make progressive demands to temper and steel the child to meet hardship. Parents must act more or less as one on the vital matters, yet each provides some emotional backup for those times when the child has fallen out with the other. They must largely contain their own insecurities and hurt when they feel rejected by the child, yet they must not be unreal "plastic people," nor allow him or her to think that rejecting those one loves has no negative consequences.

"Gravely problematic" is far too tame a description of this most difficult and most perilous—and generally most rewarding—of human endeavors. Parents in our vastly complex civilization must navigate a sea of potential mishaps day in and day out; and they must do so while maintaining enough distance and hands off to encourage the optimal development of their child's sense of self, senses of security, and advances in the world. It is little wonder that so many make major mistakes, and the fact that most succeed so well may be testimony more to the genetic primings than to cultural learning or wise free choices.

Only when the child has developed an inner sense of self with enough basic senses of security can he or she begin to develop the sincerely loving and intimate self-fusings with others that we call friendship. Most children have done this with their parents and are ready to begin their ever-so-tentative explorations into the world of others by three or four, yet they begin in only the most rudimentary ways. Only slowly do they develop the empathy necessary to the development of real intimacy, the communing of their senses of self with each other in the world. And yet, as in most areas of life at this age, the child makes remarkably fast progress, as long as he or she has developed that basically secure sense of self. The child is ready and, as long as others who are also ready are at hand or can be found, he or she quickly takes off and makes rapidly accelerating progress. By the time the child is around six or seven, he or she is fully ready for the *group friendships and palling around* that will normally predominate until he or she is ready for fully loving and intimate friendships in adolescence. This "groupiness" of children is found the world over, wherever the situation allows for it. It becomes the foreground of the normal child's life and he or she and playmates (as they become by this time or soon thereafter) develop their own *kid subculture*, which takes off from and even diverges in some respects from that of the parents. The child is so taken up with the playmates and their kid culture that outside observers sometimes think—as the child him- or herself often does—that they are more important to him than the parents. This, however, is only true as long as the sun is shining on the little biosphere. The parents are still the all-pervading and only slowly receding background of the child's life and the outer props of an inner senses of security. A little whiff of crisis in the child's life sends him or her scurrying for their help, and a serious crisis within the family can have profound, if by now only secondary, consequences for the whole sense of self-security. Mother and father, and to a less extent sometimes brother and sister, can greatly assuage problems with playmates and burgeoning friends, but, try as they will, playmates and little friends cannot yet do much to assuage serious family crises. When families have failed to provide that strong background to the kid culture, as is often the case for boys when the father is completely absent or only a distant memory, the kid culture may become the substitute background, as we see in the "street smarts" of many gang boys, but it is a weak substitute that cannot prepare for dominance and competence in adult life.

These increasingly loving and intimate playmates and, finally, friendships allow the child far more freedom and diversity in playing at and acting out the self- and world-scenarios and thus in developing the child's sense of self in the child's biosphere. Sometimes a somewhat older child may serve as a temporary model of identification, but that is an aberrant situation that normally results from the older child not having developed beyond the sense of self of the younger child. Children have quite an aversion to "playing with babies." They identify upwardly and the entire thrust of their self-development is toward adulthood, not backward toward "regression." Regression tends to be precipitated by a crisis with which the child does not yet feel ready to deal. It is a withdrawal into play that allows the child to gather his or her strength—

"recoil"—to be ready to spring forward to meet and overcome the crisis.

The groupy period in most cultures normally begins for both sexes with fledgling friendly interests in both boys and girls. In our society, boys and girls play together un-self-consciously for the first several years. But with the passing of the years comes increasing identification with the adults of one's own sex, thus with the different patterns of behavior they enact, and the burgeoning flashes of romantic infatuations (see below) that necessarily make the members of the opposite sex too real, too emotionally charged—*dangerous* to one's senses of security—for ordinary friendships (for heterosexuals) and play. Western cultures have greatly emphasized this natural division of self-identifications and the development of the sexual senses of self. This extreme childhood sexual division was grounded in the extreme adult divisions of labor necessitated by the prevalence of warfare in feudal societies and by the very heavy labor of plowing in peasant families (in which about 90% of the population lived). It was greatly reinforced by the early Church's emphasis on sexual separation to build and maintain chastity and by the growing misogyny of the Church from about the fifteenth century. This sexual division reached its greatest extreme in the sexually exclusive Church monasteries and nunneries and in the schools that developed out of them.

John Hillebrand (forthcoming, and personal communications) has argued that friendship around the world has such powerful impacts on the whole development of the sense of self because it is open-ended, rather than clearly and powerfully bounded by social rules the way "role" relations are, including marriage, except when the marriage partners are friends or romantic lovers first and marriage partners second.[1] Friendships are open at both ends, at both beginnings and endings. Because the friendships involve more limited identification and emotion than family partnerships, especially in the younger ages when the child is far more vulnerable, this open-ended ("free market") testing and acting out gives the child an optimum of freedom with social feedback in developing the emerging sense of self—that is, to "find him- or herself," as it is very nicely put these days. As with all things in life, there is no absolute freedom of choice here. There are the constraining norms of loyalty and faithfulness in support of friends, and certainly there are the emotional constraints of affection. But the nonexclusive nature of friendships, even of what children call "best friends," allow for great freedom in starting new friendships, shifting the priorities of time and subject matter of discussions of old ones, and so on to achieve the mix of self-identifications, playing, testing out, acting out, critical feedback, and caring support that "feels right" to the individual at any time and that, we believe, is most likely to be the optimum mix for the developing sense of self in the world.[2]

The young child's criterion of "feeling right" or "feeling good" by which he or she navigates the development of self-realizations among shifting and evolving friendships has two potentially fatal flaws: it almost completely lacks long-run foresight and the empathetic ability to sense when "friends" are trying to manipulate the child for their own purposes, something most likely to be done by older "friends." These, of course, are the intuited reasons why parents feel they must hover above the evolving friendships to monitor their overall drifts and take discrete and gentle actions to nudge them into the right directions when they veer off course.

Indirection is crucial because even young children deeply resent these "interferences" in their "private" lives, that is, in their freely chosen self-development, and may for that reason alone insist more "stubbornly" on pursuing those friendships. (We might call this the *Huckleberry Finn principle*.) Parents are also aware intuitively of the aetiological principle, that is, of the greater importance of early experiences in the shaping of the sense of self, so they try to protect the child from taking the wrong courses in the development of the all-important friendships. Of course, in doing so, they take a risk of overprotecting and thus of producing a suboptimal development. Most parents seem to sense that the child's feeling of "rightness" has to be weighed heavily in balancing it against their greater foresight (which is still riddled with the inevitable uncertainties of life) and empathy. They normally pursue a strategy of prolonged waiting and watching until something clearly dangerous looms. As the child's sense of self, foresight, and empathy develop, they monitor ever more distantly, wait and watch ever longer, and "interfere" ever more indirectly. Those who do not are courting open rebellion, especially in our egalitarian and individualistic society. Almost all parents are aware of their complex strategies for monitoring their children and balancing indirect and direct interventions against freedom to achieve an optimum of development with security (see, for example, the mother's statements about sex in Sears et al., 1957, pp. 174-217).

On the surface and especially in their childhood beginnings, friendships are for "fun" and the exchange of "liking." But these surface emotions act very much like the ecstasy of sexuality acts in the development of romantic love, procreation, and family partnerships. They are the immediately conscious and short-run emotional reinforcements of patterns of behavior that have far more powerful, pervasive, and embedded outcomes in the development of the senses of self. Of course, some friendships, like some sexual relations and some romantic loves, do remain "good time friendships" or "fun friendships," dominated by merrymaking, fun-fun-fun, and hap-hap-happy talk. *Fun friendships* are valued because they allow us to share our good feelings when we feel like venting the exuberance of life and because they help to "pick us up" when we're "down." Some have a bubbly, externally oriented sense of self and seem to live largely in the world. They are wonderful as fun-time friends and terrible when one wants to be intimate. They are often especially prized by introverted people because their complementary thrust outward helps them to get "out of" themselves. But most friendships are far more intimate than that.

The important point is that friendships, like love partnerships in general, can be chosen and adjusted over time for their various dimensions, far more than the broad-based, emotionally highly charged family and romantic love partnerships can. If your partner or lover rejects your desire for intimacy and support, you cannot completely counterweight your sense of rejection and depression with someone else's intimacy and support, though you can certainly counterweight them partially by turning to your most loving, intimate, and supporting friends.

THE DEVELOPMENT OF
ROMANTIC LOVES

We have already argued that some degree of sexual feelings, certainly those produced by the gentle caressing of the sex organs, are obvious in infancy. This remains true during childhood, but the pleasures derived from such caressing do not normally seem to lead to significant masturbation (self-caressing) among the great majority of children until the preadolescence or early adolescence period when hormonal changes show themselves by the first appearance of pubic hairs. Masturbation does appear at quite early ages, and quite compulsively, in the very abnormal situations in which there is some great disturbance in the mother-child love-duet. It seems to be a counterweighting to the deep depression that such disturbances normally cause. As noted earlier, as the disturbance in the love-duet wanes, the masturbation wanes.[3]

Most of the childhood excitement associated with genital exposure and play in our society seems to be the result of the rules of genital secrecy that are sternly enforced after the age of a few years (though this varies with different ethnic and national groups). There probably are, however, some genetic primings that encourage the progressive development of increasingly organized fragments of sexual behavior, especially of sexual "mountings." These are standard patterns of behavior among primates and mammals more generally. Moreover, most complex emotion and behavior systems such as this are developed progressively over many years, with bits and pieces (fragments) being observed and acted out in play behavior long before the animal is ready to perform the full system in real-world activity. This progressive development has been observed in societies in which adult sexual behavior is far more observable to children (Malinowski, 1929; Powdermaker, 1933/1971). We cannot tell whether they are merely performing this sex-play as part of their more general program of playing at being adults or whether there are specific genetic primings for it, but the latter seems more likely.

It is quite obvious that, as children approach adolescence, their sexual interests, excitements, and behavior rapidly accelerate, unless these are severely repressed. In our society there has normally been enough shame and embarrassment involved with this to drive these developments underground where they are rarely visible to adults. These are obviously quite highly primed genetically among most males, so that drawings and pictures of nude females and sex acts have long been pervasive in the boys' late kid subcultures, and "circle jerks" are extremely common years before the boys can do more than fantasize about ejaculating. Heterosexual boys involved in "circle jerks" share their intense sexual fantasies about girls. Most of them do share genital pride, which is a fragmentary form of "phallus worship." Girls at roughly the same age develop an even more intense body pride and normally share this in many ways, ranging from play fashion shows to strip-poker games. Girls tend to focus their pride on the parts of their bodies they consider their "beauty characteristics" and become obsessive observers and fashioners of those characteristics. Mirrors become magical fetishes used to ward off "ugliness," the most dreaded adolescent disease. "Ugliness" is almost always an embodiment of other insecurities, commonly originating in family or friend problems. Those suffering such insecurities do not develop the normal rites of body pride and try to counterweight their embodied insecurities by becoming highly competent and dominant in schoolwork, which leads the envious to further stigmatize them as "ugly," "ungainly," "nerdish," and so on. Girls in our society are subject to more repressive pressure, but all the evidence available from here and around the world leads us to "guesstimate" that they are genetically primed at roughly the same or somewhat earlier ages to become excitedly inviting and fearful in the ambivalently potentiating pattern so familiar in *coyness* (which appears to be universal—see Eibl-Eibesfeldt, 1980) and far more concerned with their beauty and sexual attractiveness than males. (We shall see the standard expressions of these patterns by Leilani in the next section.)

Regardless of how sexual feelings and behavior develop, it is clear that heterosexual adoration love feelings and behavior develop in this progressive and accelerating manner, but apparently some years earlier, more or less in direct proportion to the degree to which the child drifts out of love and identification with the mother and father. Full-scale heterosexual infatuations with children of the same age are common from the ages of five to seven onward and sometimes with adults, especially in lonely children who have love and identification problems with their parents.

There does not appear to be any standard "latency period" in the development of adoration or sexual feelings. Their waxings and wanings seem highly situational and highly dependent on the developments of the individuals, very much as we see in the patterns of adults. There is obviously a great deal of shyness felt by almost everyone at some times. This seems to be predominantly the result of inexperience and a relative lack of empathy that leads the child to see far greater risk of rejection than actually exists, but the risk is inevitably high at this time and that justifies some shyness. Shyness is the result of an ambivalent conflict between desire and fear of rejection, with all of its attendant shame and embarrassment. Shyness soars in pre- and early adolescence because the craving for love and sex soar, while inexperience remains gross. Spiro (1979) found that, as girls in an Israeli kibbutz entered adolescence, they became extremely shy about the boys seeing them nude in showers, in spite of the fact that their parents socialized them in sexual modernism from infancy. Boys are less shy about their bodies, but only because masculine beauty is not as important. They are normally quite shy at first about being loved by those they are now adoring and over physical competence and dominance (see Dwyer and Meyer, 1976; Schoenfeld, 1969; Huston, 1974; Cook, 1981). The very intensity of the desire to have one's love accepted and to be loved in return makes the visibility of one's love, in the absence of obvious evidence signaling its acceptability and return, an inherently very risky business. Very importantly, as almost all children learn the hard way, the relative inexperience of children in adoration love with anyone other than their loving parents, their consequent lack of empathy in love matters, and their fear of being embarrassed even by the love someone else bears them makes them rather brutal in their quick rejections of any love they do not desire. By adulthood, most people learn at least to disattend to undesired love, and most eventually learn to "let someone down easily." But children can be brutal in rejecting undesired would-be lovers.

CRUSHES (INFATUATIONS)

Common sense makes a strong, even categorical, distinction between developing a crush, or becoming infatuated, and falling in-love, or being in-love. This distinction is seen, for example, in statements such as "I thought I was in-love but it proved to be just a crush," or, again, as a worried mother might put it, "You might think you're in love, little girl, but it's only a crush and will soon evaporate." Since commonsense ideas about love and sex represent millennia of accumulated experience, they should not be taken lightly. With this in mind, we studied crushes to find out what the big differences are between them and "real love." Because we were expecting to find a number of major differences, we wound up feeling very confused. We kept finding that there were no apparent differences at all between most crushes and most loves, especially loves at first sight.[4] In time, we came to see that the only major difference between a love and a crush is that *love lasts for a long time, but a crush does not* (see Bersheid and Walster, 1974). A crush is a quick flash in the pan, but love is "an ever fixed mark," as Shakespeare called it. A crush may burn as brightly (even with a searing heat!), but it is snuffed out by one of the first cool drafts of adversity. The difference is greater, of course, between a crush and being in-love.

But it is equally clear from commonsense experience and from our studies that some feelings that are first thought of as crushes turn out to be romantic love. All this means is that some loves that we first believe will quickly go away linger on, and linger on, until we are forced to recognize that it is love, that is, a relatively lasting love. If we look at several cases of "crushes," we can see how the crush shades into love and, in fact, comes to be seen as love that simply doesn't last very long. Let's consider first the most evanescent crush possible, the crush that cannot stand the slightest draft of reality. Laura was a beautiful example of the evanescent crusher. Laura comes from a family with a history of loving at first sight. Her father fell in love with her mother, a beautiful model, at first sight. (It took him many arduous months to convince her to even take him seriously, but he did make Fate come true.) She is now nineteen years old. Since her high school days, she has been an ardent crusher. She told us the following (reproduced from memory).

My crushes since high school follow the same monotonous pattern. Before this pattern I just had intense fantasies. But now I seem to be stuck in this pattern. You can see what I mean by looking at my "love" for Bill.

I first spotted Bill in one of my classes. I was bored with the class—the professor is super dull, a real champion of humdrum stuff—so I was looking around the class at the boys. And then I spotted this guy's hair. It was beautiful, fabulous. I was entranced by its color, by the wavy curls. They were tumbling down the back of his neck and he looked like an angel. I couldn't even see his face, but I knew he must be handsome.

So I focused all my attention on his hair and started daydreaming about what he must look like and what he would be like. I was already very excited.

And he really was handsome, kind of, when I could see his face. So from then on I started watching for him and finding reasons to have to stand where I could spot him when he left or returned to his room. I would get super excited and then I'd dream about what he must be like.

But I was really afraid to get to know him because I knew that it would be like all the others: once I got near enough to see what he was really like it would just blow up into pieces. My crushes are always shattered by the first bit of reality.

And that's what happened. I accidentally came across Bill at a school dance. He came over and asked me to dance. I said, "OK." And that was that. As soon as the dance was over I knew my crush was dead. I couldn't see what I had ever seen in a jerk like that. He was a lousy dancer. And that was not part of the dream.

Leilani's diary and life study reveal the typical adolescent crusher, with no primary or secondary insecurities and no hints of Oedipal conflicts or other traumas. At the age of 13, she began her new diary on January 1, 1960. Her first brief mention of boys was entered on January 2: "Oh—I'll never get Lee—Margaret has him hen-pecked. But I can still try." On January 4, she concluded resoundingly, "I love Harry and Dan and Stan. Davie is cute," and then lined up her loves and hates:

Love	Hate
Dan	Bates
Stan	Paige
Fish	Dianne
Harry	(Mr. Rickert)

Leilani is clearly in the "Boy Crazy" stage. Though she gets excited every day about numerous things (movies, ice cream, swimming, an "F" paper, snubs by other girls, and so on), most of her strongest statements are about her relations with boys (including her feelings for other girls as a result of their relations with various boys). She shows all the typical swings in adolescent situational insecurities about love and sex. (On January 6, she gives up boys because of a bad attack of acne: "Ugh is my face broken out!!! It looks like I have the measles! I like NO-ONE!!!! Surprise!!! I've given up boys for awhile.") Very importantly, and very typically for the "boy crazy" crusher, though her loves and hates show some degree of stability, she also goes though wild swings in her love and hate feelings, loving only one boy one day (January 7: "I love Harry, that's all!!!"), then adding a whole new list to the old one the next (January 8: "I love Dan, Bill, Harry, Less is OK (I guess)"), and a few days later dropping one of the most stable loves (January 13: "Got a letter form Stan. I REALLY WROTE HIM AND TOLD HIM OFF!!!!!"), and the next day drops an OK into the farthest depths of perdition (January 14: "Hate Lee—Gee, Lee unbuttoned my dress—he's number 1.ugly 2.mean 3.nasty 4.HORRIBLE!!! I HATE HIM").

One of the most volatile crushes, flying high and falling low in her esteem every few days, is Buddy, who first appears on January 9 ("Buddy had his gang over and so did Donnie. Curly [whom she normally thinks is Buddy's girl] was there. I'm jealous. I'm going to snub him [Buddy], the _____. I think he's going with Curly. Jealousy"). Then for several days Buddy does not even appear; then he reappears unappraised; then on January 20: "Buddy is OK." But on January 21, her clearest statement about the whole thing appears: "I love Buddy but I haven't got a chance." She generally hates Curly, out of jealousy, and tries to forget Buddy and be cool toward him so she won't run the danger of being rejected, or feeling rejected. Every now and then her confidence allows her to admit "Gee I'm lonely" and "Wish I could go steady with Buddy or Dan or Harry" (January 21), but then she soon must forsake all love because it is beyond her, "I love no-one" (January 31). Things soon got worse, especially over Buddy: "I found out Phyllis and Buddy like each other. They are having a slumber party. HUMPH!!!!! I hate Buddy" (February 5). Then they get even worse: "A slap to everyone of these boys [at school]. They're FICKLE!" (February 7). Then Buddy is the only target of her hate: "I wish Buddy was gone, I hate him. I'll never invite him to my party" (February 8). But slowly she rehabilitates him. He becomes OK, she then likes him, and soon, when she hears he's sick, she pleads, "OH GET WELL."

Her degree of commitment to Buddy grew over many months and, eventually, the feelings and actions of sex grew, step by ever more fateful step in the universal drift process of building up and developing the fully organized system of sexual emotions and actions (see Delamater and MacCorquodale, 1979). Leilani had felt love for Buddy for a long time. She tried to repress her feelings by trying to hate him, but she did this only because she felt she could not "get him." Her love for him and her fear she could not get him—rejection!—triggered feelings of intense situational insecurity, so she tried desperately not to love him. The more inaccessible he seemed, the more she feared rejection if she loved him, so the more she rejected him in advance with her denials and the more she repressed her love feelings with counterweighted, "psyched-up" feelings of hatred. But whenever there seemed any chance she might get him— might be accepted, validated, loved by him—her love exploded.

Just like most lovers in the early stages of adoration love, her hopes and fears inspired by her love led her rapidly to interpret and reinterpret every situation that arose, so she went through rapid alternations in her love and hate reactions. She was tormenting herself and her love feelings were becoming embedded in her sense of self, building up under the tantalizing alternation of hopes and fears, loves and hates. By the time she really had a clear chance to get Buddy, she was in-love both intensely and with considerable fusion of her self with his. This was no crush. She was moderately in-love and had a moderate commitment of her self to him. When she was "forced" to leave Buddy by her family's move, she suffered a great deal of lovesickness. But, it might be objected, she did leave him, so maybe she was only "in crush," not in love, after all. It is quite true that there are girls even at 14 or 15 who will run away from home to elope with a lover. These girls are normally very angry at their families, want desperately to leave, and are very insecure. They are normally very insecure because of the conflicts with the family, and rather easily fuse their selves with the new lover, becoming very dependent on him. Leilani did not feel that way about her family and, in the succeeding 20 years of her life, she has never fused herself very much with that of a lover, nor become much more dependent than she did with Buddy. She has loved more deeply and with more commitment. Very importantly, she has become more caring, though not procreative. But Buddy was a first love.

Situational factors are very important in preventing most crushes from developing into loves. In spite of the most intense feelings of fatedness that are commonly triggered by our feelings of adoration and by our hope, most romantic loves do not develop beyond the earliest stages. Most of the time, the other person simply doesn't cooperate. Either they fail to love us in return or they refuse to be the kind of person we hoped—and too often believed—they were when we started to love them. So our love wanes and evaporates. (And we normally forget that fate did not work the way we felt sure it must, so we're ready to believe in the sense of fatedness the next time love strikes.)

But there is a secret force at work in many people that makes them largely incapable of developing the fusion of self and the intertwining of their lives with that of another that would be necessary to develop the intense love of the crush into the love fusion necessary for the crush to become love. This force is insecurity. The more insecure an individual feels about him- or herself, the more fearful he or she is of committing herself to a love. (This fear of making a commitment of the self actually leads to a buildup in the craving for love that can make the insecure lover a hysterical lover. See Chapter 5.) This fearful, insecure lover may develop very intense feelings of love and yet recoil from committing him- or herself to the other person. He or she has a strong tendency to misinterpret things the lover says or does to make them look like rejections, put-downs, lack of love, deception, and infidelity. The highly insecure lover is the lover very apt to push the loved one away, thus producing the very thing he or she fears. The insecure lover thus tends to run unintentionally through a series of crushes rather than building a lasting love partnership.

We have already seen this at work in Leilani. As Leilani became less insecure about herself in the last year of the diary, largely by discovering through experience that she was quite attractive to boys, she was able to make more commitments and to develop somewhat more lasting relations. But some people remain so deeply insecure that they cannot do this and develop one wild and evanescent crush after another over many years.

The extreme form of the insecurity and crush syndrome is seen in the fantasy love. Scenic Fantasies are a very natural aspect of any intense romantic love, as, indeed, scenic fantasies are a natural part of any intense emotion (see Tennov, 1979). So we think over and over again about all the possible situations, actions, and outcomes relevant to this emotion, thus preparing ourselves to take the best possible actions when the time for action comes. The fantasies also provide us with substitute but partial gratification of the desire when the time for action has not come. This prevents us from getting too depressed over our frustrations or from acting desperately. We fantasize—daydream—until we see the situation allows us to act reasonably to achieve our goal. When we are in-love, but must be away from the loved one at school or at a job, we fantasize constantly—we are *love-obsessed*, or by love *possessed* (see Tennov, 1979). Our hope inspires happy daydreams; our fears inspire unhappy ones. Both prepare us for action and give us some partial gratification when we cannot be with the loved one. Lovers who are highly fused with someone but cannot be with them find some consolation (partial venting and fulfillment of love) by imagining that their loved ones are with them. In the nineteenth century, Clover Adams, the wife of Henry Adams, always remained deeply loving toward and dependent on her father. When he died, she became deeply depressed and finally took potassium cyanide. Henry was deeply in-love with her. He recovered from the grief and led a "normal" life, but many years later, in a letter of consolation to Henry Cabot Lodge when his wife died, he revealed that he had always been carrying on a fantasy life with Clover:

> You have got to endure what I have endured for thirty years. . . . I have gone on talking, all that time, but it has been to myself—and to her. The world has no part in it. One learns to lead two lives.

The very insecure lover commonly develops fantasies that are quite divorced from reality, simply because the insecure person feels so incapable of dealing with reality. The very insecure girl not only develops all kinds of fantasies about the loved one without knowing anything much about him, often without even having spoken a word to him, but also sometimes protects her fantasies by refusing to get to know the loved one, or by choosing to love only someone who is so distant and inaccessible that her love can never be put to the test. The extreme fantasy love is one that is so cut off from reality that there is almost no direct threat to the girl. Sometimes a fantasy love of this kind helps the insecure girl most of all in a time when her insecurities are being triggered by her fears of rejection, or by actually being "put through the ringer."

These love fantasies are almost always for a real person who might love us in return, but they're so distant that the probability is minuscule. We feel safe, so we test out our love feelings and actions. A beautiful case of this is Cheryl, the young high school girl studied in great detail by Gary Schwartz and his coworkers (1980). Like millions of other girls, Cheryl and two of her friends, Nora and Lisa, each fell in fantasy-love with a Beatle. They then did intensive studies of the fan magazines to determine everything they could about their fantasy-lovers. Everything had to feel "real" or it wouldn't work:

> Every detail of my daydreams is set. I once had a daydream that Ringo and I were married. I was getting out of bed, putting on a little makeup and combing my hair, and then I went down to make some breakfast. But I couldn't continue the daydream because I didn't know what he ate for breakfast. Everything has to be exactly right. Lisa and Cheryl are like that too. We start having a daydream and right in the middle we say no, it can't happen this way, so that one won't work [Schwartz et al., 1980, p. 101].

The three friends built a world of their own out of these realistic fantasies and tested out their love feelings and ideas on each other. Cheryl's fantasy about their dream encounter shows all the substitute gratification of love fantasies, but also the reality orientation of many of these precrush love fantasies. Her fantasy-love for George went on intensively for over a year. She even exchanged many letters about George with his mother. Then it faded, just as her first real romance dawned.

NOTES

1. Friendships have been universally valued, and although the literature in modern times is unsystematic, consensus exists that the everyday definitions of specific friendships are ones that are largely unspoken. Hillebrand argues that friendships are custom tailored

by unspoken agreements reinforced by practical criteria: Friends are those who live up to a mix of often diffuse expectations, while role relations revolve around sets of expectations. Other authors concur (see Pogrebin, 1987; Reisman, 1979).

2. In adult friendships, the vicissitudes of everyday life lead lasting friendships to be highly valued precisely because the continuing development of the self is accommodated and, through the feedback friendship supplies, evaluated and validated by a loved, trusted other. Friendships thus uniquely accommodate personal and situational change, their great flexibility accounting for the common observation that friendships overcome great obstacles and conflicts better than other loving relations do (see Hillebrand, forthcoming).

3. The assertions of the normalcy of childhood masturbation generally make no such distinctions and today are almost always made in works with clear political goals and other modernist preconceptions. (For example, see Stevi Jackson, 1982. She does, however, have a good critique of the Freudian ideas about childhood sexuality.) We do not believe this great infrequency of masturbation and other full-scale patterns of sexuality is the result of socialization practices. Socialization does not stop children from creating their sexual netherworlds for mutual exposure and discussion. Sears et al. (1957) found that even quite restrictive mothers sometimes discovered their children in these "shocking" netherworlds of mutual exposure. Why would it prevent the far more secretive practice of masturbation? And certainly socialization does not stop masturbation from exploding underground in preadolescence, even in the form of "circle jerks" among boys before they can ejaculate.

4. This confusion was made all the worse by our attempts to find differences between "crushes" and "infatuations." We eventually decided that, while some individuals make distinctions between a crush and an infatuation, most people today use the terms interchangeably. *Infatuation* was the more common term some years ago, while *crush* seems to be the common one today. The difference is one in the changing fashion of words, rather than in changing experiences or ideas. Some people who make a distinction see infatuation as largely a feeling of pride at possessing, or hoping to possess, the other's beauty status, wealth, and so on. In that sense, it is an important pseudolove.

5

FALLING IN-LOVE AND LUST

Stahr did not answer. Smiling faintly at him from not four feet away was the face of his dead wife, identical even to the expression. Across the four feet of moonlight, the eyes he knew looked back at him, a curl blew a little on a familiar forehead; the smile lingered, changed a little according to pattern; the lips parted—the same. An awful fear went over him, and he wanted to cry aloud. Back from the still court room, the muffled glide of the limousine hearse, the falling concealing flowers, from out there in the dark—here now warm and glowing. . . .

Stahr's eyes and Kathleen's met and tangled. For an instant they made love as no one ever dares to do after. Their glance was slower than an embrace, more urgent than a call. . . .

Her eyes invited him to a romantic communion of unbelievable intensity.

F. Scott Fitzgerald

The literary ideal of Romantic Love is still the dominant model in the thoughts, dreams, hopes, and fears of many people in Western cultures. But this seems to be declining rapidly in the affections of most people because of the spreading epidemic of love problems. Social scientists have found that, even in the traditional Midwest, there are several alternative models used in love talk (Schwartz et al., 1980). The most extreme form of Romantic Love, desperate love at first sight, does still happen in today's world of trivialized sexuality. Lesser forms of hysterical love (see below) are quite common. But they are certainly not the most common patterns of falling in-love today. They are found far more commonly in the very young, the very lonely and the very insecure who are highly primed and have few memories of love miseries. The great majority of them do not develop any high degree of self-identification—fusion—with the real self of the loved one, so they escape extreme love miseries. Nevertheless, most of them soon suffer enough to become far more cautious.

As we have argued from the beginning, there are a number of basic dimensions involved in love partnerships and the number of standard combinations and permutations of these is extremely large. It is quite impractical for us to try to deal with all or even a large percentage of them. Fortunately, there are a few standard patterns and variations of them that make up a large percentage of partnerships and relationships today. We shall focus our attention on them. Anyone concerned with other patterns can easily see how they are related to these and can analyze them in terms of our basic theory.

SEX-DOMINATED "LOVE"

Most "true love" today is not very true. It is only a partially true love shrouded in the confusions of sexual modernism (for an excellent example, see Albert Ellis, 1962). That, of course, is why the vast majority of "true loves" soon prove themselves false by producing misery, flight, and hatred. Most of these "love relations" are not mere pseudolove, such as excitement triggered by status symbols. Rather, most involve some adoration and, though much less, some caring love and fusion of the senses of selves. But those are not the dominant emotional themes of the relations. Sex is most often the dominant theme and the others, especially the rest of the Erotic, are nonexistent or merely subordinate themes. Because sexual excitation short of sexual obsession quickly runs its course once its goal is achieved, these sex-dominated relations would normally run down much more quickly than "true love" in any event. But there are more nettles on this sex-led path to true love than that. Lust, especially in its male variant, easily triggers selfish, posses-sive, and aggressive motives, especially in the insecure. When these are not counterweighted by powerful feelings of adoration, caring, identification, and the other dimensions of the Erotic, they precipitate bitter and often spiraling conflicts.

A constant theme of the great romantic love myths and stories around the world is the prolonged *tantalization of love and sex*. *Tantalizing* is merely the ancient word for "teasing." (Tantalus was punished by the gods by being bound and having both water and food come near his mouth repeatedly only to be snatched away at the last moment.) As we are all aware commonsensically, tantalizing intensifies desire to its peak. Since the ancient world, professional dancers and courtesans wishing to peak sexual desire have used the principle of tantalization. Rather than simply revealing the sexually desired parts of the body, they first veil those parts and only slowly and suggestively reveal them. Such practices build on the genetically highly primed patterns of behavior known as "coyness." Coy female birds drive male birds into a frenzy in their mating dances and coy female human beings drive their suitors into a frenzy of courtship.

Experience leads most of us eventually to grasp the principle of tantalization. Great salesmen, such as Ben Feldman (Thompson, 1969), are well aware that they must continually ratchet-up their goals to "psych-up" the sense of excitement that is vital to maintaining their maximum effort. The point is to keep the goal just a bit beyond present possibilities, so that it is almost within reach, but not quite. If it is so far away as to seem impossible, then it does not excite and may actually depress the salesman who wishes to achieve it. If it is too close, it is easily reached and interest quickly subsides into boredom. Parents use the same intuited application of the principle in training their children—at least, successful ones do. Behavior modification psychologists have made it more explicit than we do commonsensically, but this may be partially self-defeating. *Optimal uncertainty* is the vital component of the principle in operation. It is optimal uncertainty that combines with the positive (hoped-for) and negative (feared) payoffs to produce the excitement that drives us onward. Anything that removes that uncertainty removes the excitement. The stripteaser who tells you in advance that in the end she will bare all and then does so will likely soon find herself faced with a somnolent and dwindling audience. In fact, the greatest stripteasers never do bare all. In our study of the casual sex scenes at California's nude beaches, we found that even wild-eyed novitiates soon adapted to the mass nudity and calmed down (see Douglas and Rasmussen, with Flanagan, 1977).

The principle of tantalization is well enshrined in common sense.

"Playing hard to get" and its related "jealousy games" (intended to arouse the fear of losing the desired one) are standard phrases of our adolescent subcultures. "Always keep him guessing," "maintain an air of mystery," and "develop new interests to become a more exciting person" are clichés of the self-help literature that resound in our life studies (see Tennov, 1979, pp. 48-57). Since the romantic love novels of ancient Greece, the "man of mystery" and the "exotic woman" have always been far more exciting, precisely because of their unknownness and their tantalizing air of strangeness and mystery. In romance, the "tried and true" may be highly valued as an anchor, but it is the very opposite of the "untried and who knows whether true or not" that peaks sexual excitement. Mystery, ambiguity, the unexpected, veils, masks, the exotic, the dark, the unknown—these are the many faces of uncertainty that produce a maximum of tantalization in sex and romance. As our life study Katarina says archly, "Teach men to expect the unexpected."

Tantalizing emotions not only raises them to a peak intensity, but, when these peaks of emotion are reached repeatedly in different situations and are maintained for relatively long periods, they tend to become embedded and pervasive in the sense of self. That is, they are no longer merely responses to the situational stimuli eliciting the emotions, but become independent (endogenous) motives in the individual's own sense of self that can lead him or her to seek out the stimuli. *It is precisely the sharing of repeated and prolonged excitements of adoration, the Erotic and lesser emotions (such as fun) complementing and potentiating them that produce the romantic fusing of the senses of self. When this fusing is pervasive, as it is when individuals achieve the peak of intimacy we call communing, then each self becomes an integral part of the "thou" in the state of being in-love called "true love."* Psychiatrists have found that prolonged and intense depression tends in the same way to become "endogenous," that is, an emotion and motivation largely independent of the situation of the individual, pervasive and embedded in the sense of self. They call the process by which it becomes endogenous "kindling." This is seen in drug experiences and results in "craving" the drug. The individual who gets high repeatedly over long periods comes to crave the drug high independent of the fear of the withdrawal symptoms, so that long after he or she has been detoxified— "dried out"—and has no withdrawal symptoms, he or she still craves the high and will go to extremes to get the drug. The individual is pushed by a longing from within, not by any dread of withdrawal symptoms or by desire stimulated by the sight or smell of the drug. At the extreme, the drug becomes a part of the sense of self and he or she "communes" with it as if it were a sentient lover, as we see in *The Man with a Golden Arm*. Shakespeare imagined of Cleopatra, "She leaves hungry where most she satisfies." In terms of Freud's tension-release theory of emotion and motivation, which underlies the whole modernist theory of sex and love, that must be the opposite of the truth. She can only satisfy by venting his tension and then there can be no desire left, no craving, no obsessive and protracted longing to unite with her in romantic communion. But, as any true lover or obsessed sex fiend knows, Shakespeare knew whereof he spoke. (After all, he was driven to the peak of maddened craving by a "Dark Lady" who repeatedly promised all—and then coyly withdrew it just beyond his reach.)

The obsessed sexual modernist sees all of this coyness, mystery, and courting as nothing more than the neurotic self-tortures resulting from repressions. (See Albert Ellis, 1962. Contrast his analysis with the classical analysis of Romantic Love in Rougemont, 1940, 1963.) Sex is "natural," so it should be "gratified" in the same unproblematic, straightforward way that any "natural" physiological drive is. At the extreme, the sexual modernist looks at sex—and love, supposedly its sublimated symptom formation—as just another "bodily function," one more bodily pressure to be released by finding any "outlet" available for it. Actually, the competent human adult never just finds any "outlet" for any of his or her bodily pressures. The nature of the "outlets" for urination matters greatly in all cultures. And bodily functions such as eating are a simple matter of releasing the hunger pressure on any available nutrition only when people are starving, if then. In civilizations, it is routine for people not in danger of going hungry to put great effort into being chaste in fulfilling the hunger drive (given that being fat is the alternative), tantalizing the hunger and taste with vastly complex spices, herbs, and appetizers, and stopping short of satiation in order to maintain the future craving for good foods. How strange that the same people who systematically develop the most primitive of desires, that of hunger, into a vastly complex art of chastity and tantalized taste insist that gorging oneself on random sexual outlets is the only "natural" way to go. Actually, they themselves are merely blind to all of the devices they use, from wispy lingerie to videotapes, to tantalize their sexual appetites.

In classic romances, the tantalizing of sex and love is prolonged in several ways. The ambivalent desire and anxiety of the coy maiden combined with the same emotions of the young man—who is shy because of his fear of rejection and also fears being trapped into premature commitments—provide built-in forward and backward movements that optimize tantalization. The more she withdraws, the lower the fear, so the more the desire can push her forward, until the nearness of consummation peaks the risk and leads to withdrawal to think it over. And back and forth they go. Their situations also posed severe problems that held them at arms length from consummation. Some cultures have instituted courting practices that allow the young man to come very close, but not quite close enough. The ostensible purpose of courting, as we see in our culture, is commonly that of "getting to know you," both to determine whether the potential partners can get along well (that is, are "compatible") and whether love develops between them. There is no disputing the importance of those, but an unspoken effect of courting is to give the tantalization principle full sway.

The great intensity of the emotion subject to tantalization is crucial to its pervading and becoming embedded in the sense of self. The young man who "scores" a coolly casual sex triumph will normally feel a momentary ecstasy and a lingering glow of pride over his triumph, but he is far from the state of *romantic delirium* and *floating ex-stasis* that may seize the heart of the one subjected to the repeated and subtle "piercing of the heart" resulting from the masterly artistry of coyness to which each untutored young woman is heir. (Eibl-Eibesfeldt, 1980, has shown that "coyness" is cross-cultural.) *Ex-stasis*, from which "ecstasy" is derived, is the ancient term for "getting outside of oneself." When in a state of ecstasy, we literally feel dazed and outside of ourselves. We "transcend" ourselves without feeling any sense of depersonalization. When in the grip of the state of ecstasy, we feel an intense happiness and carefreeness. The defensive boundaries of the sense of self are relaxed without arousing a sense of insecurity. The mystical experience of adoration and communion with God and the conversion experience, whether seen in the Bacchanalian *coroboree* or the "born-again" religious experience, involve this transcending of the sense of self. Transcendental ecstasy is vital in creating the new sense of self that emerges from the experience. In the very same way, romantic love ecstasy produced by tantalization is vital to the transcendence of the separate senses of self and the emergence of the new, enlarged senses of self that incorporate the sense of self of the loved one. In the full grip of romantic communion and ecstasy, we feel ourselves completely realized and fulfilled because our being is filled with the love for and by the other and by the very self of the other. In the state of romantic ecstasy, we merge ourselves with Being itself and become part of the eternal and infinite. Romantic ecstasy transcends place and time, and death itself.

It is clearly possible for sexual passion alone to result in a *sexual delirium*, at least a partial transcendence of the sense of self, and a prolonged craving for a specific sexual partner. These *sexual obsessions* have long been called "grand passions," especially in France. (We must be careful, however, to distinguish real sexual obsessions from the histrionic or hysterical sexual obsessions, which contain a large component of exhibitionism. It is often quite difficult to distinguish real grand passions from histrionic grand passions in the self-publicized lives of such Frenchmen as Balzac.) Sometimes these obsessions seem to occur quite rapidly, without much apparent tantalization before the passions are consummated. We suspect, however, that these are most apt to follow upon prolonged failures to achieve sexual fulfillment, which provide an intense frustration and anxiety that produce a long period of self-tantalization (self-"psyching-up"—see Adler, 1981) and that potentiate the orgasmic pleasure when it does come. In our society, most adolescents go through a considerable amount of this sexual frustration, tantalizing by others, and self-tantalizing before their first intercourse. This seems to be the reason for the intense and prolonged effects of "the first time" and what is often a lifelong, if muted craving for "the first one." Experienced sexual seducers are often extremely wary of having intercourse with virgins precisely because of the dangers to them of producing such sexual obsessions. "Love affairs" often kindle these emotions. The anxiety over "being found out" combine with the sexual excitement of the new to produce an ambivalent—"wild"—oscillation back and forth. This is especially common when one of them is "rebounding" (see Chapter 6) from a dying marriage. As some of our life studies said, "She made me feel like a teenager again," and "I didn't know I could still feel this way."

It is entirely possible that a very intense sexual obsession and the addictive craving that comes from it will be more intense and tend for that reason to be more pervasive and embedded in the sense of self, thus more prolonged, than a tepid or lukewarm romantic love. Some people cannot break their addictive craving for a sex partner even when they come to fear or hate them and will return again and again for the sexual excitement and fulfillment, in spite of the battering that may entail. Sexual "athletes" sometimes become experts in controlling such sex addicts. (One of the popular theories purporting to explain the control pimps have over their "girls" involves the idea that they purposefully make them sexually addicted and then refuse to satisfy their craving in order to keep it at a fever pitch. While not true, this is a tantalizing theory.)

When we first met Katarina, she was 20 and living with Egon. She told us,

> Egon is the perfect speci"man." He's beautiful to look at and ah' so wonderful in bed. He's really totally insecure though. He goes out on me all the time and never fails to make me feel like it's somehow all my fault. I don't know what I'm doing wrong. He tells me that I need help [psychiatrist] but I don't think that I'm crazy. One day he even made an appointment for me and convinced the secretary for the office to call me at my work and tell me that I needed to come in.

Egon made Katarina feel that his physical as well as his mental abuse was somehow her fault. Yet she felt lucky to be with such a "beautiful" man who was so good in bed. She continually swung between leaving him and returning to him for his sexual prowess and good looks, despite broken ribs, busted lips, trips to the hospital, and eventually marrying someone else.

Most sexual obsessions, torn out of the context of love and the Erotic, are pervaded by intense conflict. As we have noted, sexual desire alone is one of the most selfish and aggressive drives, especially in insecure men. Sex is closely tied to the dominance drive and the success drive. It appears that, in people with normal ranges of insecurity, the dominance drive is triggered as an undertone of the sex drive, clearly so in men and possibly in women. Those with more intense insecurities tend to have strong desires for dominance in their sexual relations, if for no other purpose than to "control" the person from whom they fear rejection. (There are also some highly insecure people who adopt the opposite defensive strategy, that of propiative dependency. This "masochistic" defense is the complement to the "sadistic" strategy of defense.) Because individuals who are highly insecure about their sense of lovability are precisely the ones most apt to develop sexual relations with little or no love involved, they are also the ones most apt to be seeking dominance in their sexual activity. These are the Don Juans and Doña Juanitas who seek to conquer the Mount Everests, the most beautiful, most popular, most rich, most famous status symbols. A very sexual but unloving person is very apt to be seeking domination and possessive control over the sex "object" and this is very apt to produce intense conflict, thus leading in time to the end of the relationship. As Americans have become more insecure about their lovability, they have become far more aggressively sexual without love to counterbalance their insecurities with feelings of dominance and success—conquest. Even the most addictive, sexually satisfying relationship of this sort tends to be highly explosive and eventually self-destructive, doubly so when both status-objects are seeking dominance over the other. The extremely insecure "love relationships" of this kind are literally "masks of hatred" (Holbrook, 1972a, 1972b).

THE PINK-LENS EFFECT AND
SEXUAL ENTRAPMENT

One of the most powerful factors encouraging young people to fall into the trap of sexual relationships that they mistake for love is their own *pink-lens effect* (the focusing of attention on good characteristics). Almost everyone with much experience of the powerful emotions of love and sex are quite aware of what is commonsensically called the *pink-lens effect* and somewhat less aware of the *gray-lens effect* (the focusing of attention on bad characteristics) that sets in when love turns to hatred and sexual desire to repugnance. As one of our cultural clichés puts it, "Love is blind." Love-induced and hate-induced "blindness" are merely examples of the far more general phenomena of mythical distortions of thought so easily produced by all great emotions.

Bronislaw Malinowski and students of mythical thought since have argued that human beings create and believe in myths in some direct proportion to both the degree of uncertainty and the degree of anxiety experienced in a situation. Jack Douglas (forthcoming) has tried to show that this theory has to be extended to cover all powerful emotions and to recognize that certain emotionally held beliefs—convictions or impassioned stereotypes—can be themselves powerful arousers of emotions that inspire mythical thinking. In addition, individuals vary widely in their "reality testing" abilities ("ego strength"). Anyone who comes through experience to recognize these myth-inducing effects of powerful emotions may be able partially to discount their effects, much as Ulysses overcame the effects of the siren calls on his emotions by having his sailors tie him to the ship's mast. Love, the Erotic and the many other powerful emotions commonly associated with them, such as pride and jealousy, easily produce the most powerful mythical thinking effects, especially in young people who have little previous experience to inspire them to discount their effects.

It is also very important to recognize that emotions and uncertainty potentiate—or multiply—each other, just as certain emotions such as sexual lust and adoration love potentiate each other. Consequently, even moderate doses of sex and love mixed with moderate doses of uncertainty about someone can produce powerful effects in mythical thinking. Because we are normally ignorant about most people for whom we develop sexual feelings, we are normally quite uncertain about them, and this "newness" can potentiate any sexual feelings toward them.

The common relations among emotions, uncertainty, and mythical thinking can be illustrated in a simple graph, as in Figure 5.1. Each individual will vary in these relations, depending on his or her general degree of reality testing and the specific convictions that he or she brings to the situation. These cannot be represented in the graph, but must always be kept in mind. Uncertainty and emotion multiplied together constitute what we know in everyday life as risk. In Figure 5.1, we see that low levels of risk are associated with little or no effect on our thinking. As our uncertainty and emotions about something increase, we first experience a considerable increase in our degree of realistic thinking about it. The reason for this is very simple. When we think we know all about something (no uncertainty) and have little emotional reaction to something, we feel uninterested or maybe even slightly bored with it, so pay little attention to it and are very apt to be quite mistaken about it, even to limp along on outmoded clichés about it. As our uncertainty about it goes up, our curiosity is aroused and we focus more attention on it. As our feelings about it go up, we also focus our attention on it. This focusing of attention gives us more real information about it. Once our multiplied uncertainty and emotions are at high levels, however, our attention becomes so focused on those aspects of the phenomena that are relevant to the gratification of our emotion that we unknowingly disattend to—become blind to—most of its properties. This focusing of our attention by emotion is what Stendhal (1957) called the *crystallization [of attention] effect*. As he argued, when we fall in love with someone—or fall in lust for them—we focus our attention more and more on their beauty—or sexy—characteristics, that is, those that are relevant to—and confirm—our love or lust for them. This is why love turns our perceptions of an erstwhile ugly-duckling into a

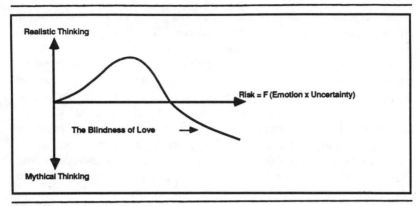

Figure 5.1:   Mythical Thinking

beautiful swan. (W. C. Fields proclaimed love wonderful because it can transform a bellhop into a hero.) Love, sex, and other powerful emotions combine with our uncertainty—ignorance—about something to produce a magical transformation of it. Of course, if our emotions toward the person change, or we become more knowledgeable about him or her through contact, then our focusing of attention also changes (see Tennov, 1979, for an excellent discussion and cases of Stendhal's "crystallization effect").

The mere increase of familiarity—decreased uncertainty—will decrease our focusing of attention on good characteristics, unless love or the Erotic increases our focusing on good characteristics as much or more. (Familiarity may thus in and of itself breed nonidealization, but not contempt.) Thus, if we begin to hate the one we once loved, then we focus on his or her bad characteristics—in the "gray-lens effect"—and he or she becomes more and more unattractive. Over the full cycle, an ordinary person may be transformed by love and lust into the most beautiful person in the whole world; by familiarity and the satiation of love and sex into an ordinary person; and by hate into an ugly duckling. As Stendhal also realized, we may even subconsciously remember the bad aspects at the very time we are focusing on the good, so that when we fall out of love or lust we may remember "I always knew she had warts, but I paid no attention to them—until she betrayed me, then all I could see were the warts!"

As our overall emotion and uncertainty about someone or something increases even more, our emotions rapidly increase their weighting—

distorting—of our whole reality testing system. At these airy levels we not only focus our attention but unconsciously change our analytical procedures to satisfy or confirm our emotions. The person at this stage is commonly considered to be *swept away* by the emotion, that is, quite incapable of thinking rationally. Anyone in the full grip of passions and a modicum of ignorance can believe the most farfetched things and lead others not sharing those emotions or ignorance to think of them as "mad," hence the "madness" of love and lust—and jealousy and hatred.

Great passions, then, have this built-in *self-confirming mechanism*. Anyone deeply in love and lust with someone, even with someone they know well, can easily "persuade" himself that "I know she loves me—she has to, because I love her so profoundly!" Great love is *self-confirming*, that is, inspires conviction that the one loved returns the love (see Tennov, 1979, pp. 57-62; de Beauvoir, 1961, pp. 620-621; Goode, 1959). Anyone trying to escape someone swept away by love normally finds it extremely difficult to convince him that she does not love him. The slightest act of everyday kindness or simple decency will be taken as a "magical sign" that she loves him and him alone—eternally, no less. In the same way, anyone in the grip of great sexual passion easily convinces himself that his casual date is equally inflamed and that her pleading "No!" really means "Yes! Take me, I'm yours forever!" This is one reason why "date rapes" are so common in situations in which great passions are aroused.

This self-confirming nature of powerful emotions is aided and abetted by the *contagious* nature of emotion. We are all painfully aware at times that even a moderate emotion like sleepiness or boredom expressed by a yawn can lead immediately to a spread of the emotion and its expression by yawning in others. As we can all see, and as the great observers of crowds always have, emotions can quickly sweep through a huge gathering of people, making them feel uneasy, agitated, excited, expectant, angry, frightened, or almost anything else, even without their having any basis other than the contagious response to emotions others are expressing. (Normally, there is some focal point of a crowd's attention, or at least of some segment of the crowd's attention where the emotion first begins and spreads outward. But this focal point is not necessary.) We are also aware that even the partly simulated excitement and optimistic cheerfulness of cheerleaders can spark a crowd's excitement and this in turn can spark excitement in the players on the field, thus giving them energy and motivation to play harder. It is much easier to be "psyched-up" by others than to "psych-up" ourselves, precisely because of this contagion factor. In the same way, when we do psych-up ourselves, we do so overwhelmingly by imagining the bodily expressions of emotions by other people, rather than by using the rationalist's "power of positive thinking" in words. Words, in fact, are extremely useful in depsyching or deemotionalizing ourselves, as we see in the hypnotic repetition of words as "mantras" or prayers to soothe our disturbed emotions. Even these uses of words, however, get much of their emotive effect from the intensity, rhythm, and pitch we use—all of which appeal directly to the emotions, as we see most strikingly in their use in music to produce emotions. Counting sheep with the intensity, rhythm, and pitch of a war chant would hardly put us to sleep, whereas the low, slow, and dull monotony of counting can certainly help to lull us and hypnotize us. When someone shows hatred, contempt, or anger toward us, we feel an immediate inclination to return the favor. The same is true of love, from the very beginning when the baby of six months first mirrors the mother's faint smile of adoration. Sexual excitement—and boredom—seems to be far more contagious than love, so that the bodily and auditory expressions of sexual lust are vital stimulants to the partner's feelings of lust. This is one of the reasons a sexually excited partner is so desirable—and a cold fish so dampening of the hottest ardor.

An inflamed lover tends, then, to communicate and arouse these emotions, at least situationally, in the loved one. And the mythically self-confirming nature of powerful love or sex leads us to seize on the slightest, most situated expression of love or sex as "absolute proof" of undying ardor, which then lures us ever onward into our own self-made emotional trap. Because love is commonly aroused only slowly (see the next section), love itself does not commonly lead us down this path to self-entrapment (unless we are hysterical lovers or transfer earlier love to a new person). Because of its far more contagious nature and its readiness to be inflamed by the most passing image of sexy beauty, lust is far more commonly the beginning of our self-entrapment, and the slower growth of love then comes in as a reinforcement of the already sprung trap.

Once fully inflamed by lust, it is easy to deceive ourselves about the "ideal" characteristics of the lustee whom we hardly know. This self-mythification induced by lust is extremely likely in our society because of the great responsiveness of lust to newness. It is precisely the stranger—the exotic, sexy beauty—who most inflames passion, while love is aroused more than other emotions by sharedness and similarity.

And it is precisely the stranger about whom we are almost totally ignorant (uncertain), thus about whom the most able to deceive ourselves with mythical thinking. In the small and highly conservative communities in which almost all human beings grew up and mated before the past 50 years, this inflammatory, self-confirming, and self-mythicizing nature of sexual passion worked to bond the newly married, or soon to be married, couple together by reinforcing the bonds of love. The reason is simple: The couples generally knew each other long before they became involved sexually or knew a vast amount about each other from others and they commonly shared most of their basic values and beliefs together (see below on similarity). They thus had all of the basic ingredients of budding love partnerships *before* they were inflamed by sexual passion, even in societies that allowed considerable premarital sexual experimentation. Moreover, once they were married and lust was fully aroused for both, there were numerous other ties and obligations that tended to bind them together when emotions like jealousy erupted and produced massive self-mythifications that, left to themselves, could easily destroy a partnership. The marriage contract also had very sharp teeth and no one could escape without extreme cause.

Today, the standard situation of young "lovers" is exactly the opposite of those in which our genetic primings and basic patterns of cultural behavior originated. In a mass society with such vast cultural pluralism as the United States, almost all potential sex partners we encounter are relative strangers. That very strangeness makes them potentially exotic and sexually arousing—and the ideal targets for mythical thinking. Our casual dating pattern, which began in small Puritanical communities where they were not at all casual by present standards, now make it remarkably easy (almost unheard of in most parts of the world) to get sexually close to complete strangers and, hence, to be almost instantly inflamed about almost complete strangers. From there on it's an easy and short slide into a self-mythicized "true love" and a high probability of marital misery and dissolution. This is why researchers consistently find that the more distant and less knowledgeable marital partners are about each other before marriage, the more likely they are to be unhappy in marriage and to get divorced. Certainly there are other major factors contributing to our astronomical love misery and divorce rates today, but this is probably the most important. Dating and mating patterns that worked fine for John and Abigail Adams in eighteenth-century Braintree can hardly be expected to work well for John and Jane in twentieth-century Astro-City—but couples lit up by lust and mythical thinking routinely overlook this and assume they are going into an eternal orbit when in fact they are merely taking a quick epicycle into misery. This epicycle is commonly shortest and the plunge deepest for those who are lured into the sexual-mating trap by beauty, which instantaneously triggers passion, which inspires the pink-lens effect.

FALLING IN LOVE AT FIRST SIGHT

Falling in love at first sight is an article of faith in the tradition of the Myth of Romantic Love. The most compelling stories of Romantic Love include a crucial scene in which one of the lovers or both of them are *stricken with love*, completely beyond their will or self-control, at the first sight of the loved one. The vision of perfection is a sign of the most profound soul-communion between the lovers. In the fully developed story, the lover knows from that first vision of beauty perfection that somehow, somewhere, this love must be fulfilled, regardless of what anyone wishes. Fate has struck and will work its iron destiny, even though at the same time the lover often has the opposite feelings of dreadful doubt that it can work, a conflict that helps to produce the agonizing ambivalence and thus the *self-tantalization* of romantic lovers in the early stages of love's buildup.

Dante's love for Beatrice in fourteenth-century Italy, which has been called the most famous love affair of history, set the stage historically for the images of Romantic Love in the Western world. Dante was only 9 years old when he first spotted 9-year-old Beatrice at a May Day party. When he was 18, he described this moment in *The New Life*:

> Her dress on that day was of a most noble color, a subdued and goodly crimson, girdled and adorned in such sort as suited with her very tender age. At that moment I say most truly that the spirit of life, which hath its dwelling in the secretest chamber of the heart, began to tremble so violently that the least pulses of my body shook therewith; and in trembling it said these words: Behold a deity stronger than I, who, coming, will rule me. . . . From that time forward Love quite governed my soul.

He seems not to have seen her again until they were 18, at which point he was once again transfixed, spellbound:

It happened that the same wonderful lady appeared to me dressed all in pure white. . . . And passing through a street, she turned her eyes thither where I stood sorely abashed; and by her unspeakable courtesy . . . she saluted me with so virtuous a bearing that I seemed then and there to behold the very limits of blessedness. . . . I parted thence as one intoxicated.

The call of Fate was once again a miscue, for Dante was never to get closer to Beatrice and she died at 24. But her love-inspired, poetic image has struck the true chord of Romantic Love down through the centuries.

The love poetry of Dante and his fellow Italian poets, especially Boccaccio and Petrarch, had a profound influence on the later literature of love. In the fourteenth century, Geoffrey Chaucer took most of his own ideas about love from them and immortalized them in English poetry in *Troilus and Criseyde* and in *The Canterbury Tales*. His beautiful description of Troilus's rapturous love for the beautiful Criseyde became a lasting and deeply moving image of love at first sight.

The ultimate expression of the myth of Romantic Love, Shakespeare's *Romeo and Juliet*, includes the most beautiful and compelling example of falling in love at first sight. In the earliest scenes, Romeo has spent all his words in proclaiming his eternal devotion to a girl who has given her heart to Celibacy, and thus forsworn Romeo to the depths of despair. He goes to the dance at Juliet's home only because of the pressure from his friends, but at the first sight of Juliet he is absolutely fascinated and struck with all the excited, ecstatic, and tormenting longings of romantic love:

O, she doth teach the torches to burn bright!
Her beauty hangs upon the cheek of night
Like the rich jewel in an Ethiop's ear;
So shows a snowy dove trooping with crows,
As yonder lady o'er her fellow shows.
The measure done, I'll watch her fellow's shows,
The measure done, I'll watch her place of stand,
And, touching hers, make blessed my rude hand.
Did my heart love till now? forswear it, sight!
For I ne'er saw true beauty till this night.

As Juliet suffered the same harsh blow of fate, the die is cast: There is no way they can stop themselves, they are swept away by love, and by the cruel conflicts between their families, to their star-crossed destinies.

In the late eighteenth century, the theme of love at first sight was enshrined as the ultimate symbol of the ultimate form of love, of soul union, which is both sanctified and kindled by their domination over sexual lust. Shelley's *Epipsychidion* is a beautiful evocation of this ideal of Romantic Love. This image of Romantic Love at first sight is also enshrined in Goethe's *Faust*. Goethe saw Love and its inspiration, Beauty, as the attractive forces that bind the world together to create and sustain life. Union through love is the eternal quest of us all. It drives us like a blind feeling of Fate that we cannot understand or control by our feeble reason and will. Love uses the voice of magic and poetry to work its will. Love is at its purest and most intense in first love, because that is the only love that partakes of eternity and infinity. (He once noted that only in the first love can we truly feel the conviction it will last to eternity, because, after that fails, we must suspect any new love may also fail.) And first love wells up within us as a divine mystery that transfixes heart and soul in love at first sight.

It is clear from the many instances of falling in love at first sight we've found that the intensity of love can vary along the entire continuum from zero romantic love to intense romantic love. It does not appear that anyone is seized by the most intense degrees of romantic love at first sight, at least as long as the new lover is not mistaken completely for an earlier one. There always seems to be some major reservation in the *intensity* of love feelings. And, even more important, there is a far greater reservation in the degree of commitment of one's love emotions to this new person and no real fusion of the sense of self with the new love. No matter how *intense* these emotions are, if they do not continue to develop through experience with the other person, then the lover is not very committed emotionally nor fused. Thus, if Fate does not decree a further encounter with the new loved one, the symptoms of love sickness will be minimal or nonexistent when the love is not returned. We're convinced that the classics did overdramatize their memories of their loves at first sight. Even Dante does not say he was much depressed over not seeing Beatrice for nine years after his first sight of her, a sure clue to a lack of fusion of selves. These symptoms are normally restricted in this situation to feelings of confusion (How could Fate misfire? How could the Muses be so wrong?) and craving.

It is also possible for the other aspects of the ideal of romantic love to appear separately, without the specific adoration love feelings. In fact, this is far more common than falling in love at first sight. As we have seen, most people who think they have fallen in love have merely fallen

in lust. If they have not really been in love before, they do not know what
adoration love feels like and they can easily mistake the undertones of
adoration triggered by intense sexual excitement for "the real thing."
The same thing happens with love at first sight, especially among very
young people who have not been seized by lust before: They see someone
who excites their newborn sexual feelings, repress any thoughts of sex,
and think they are feeling only "true love." People with more experience
with sexual feelings can also fall in lust at first sight to such a newly
intense degree that they think this is love at first sight. Most people,
however, have enough experience with sudden seizures of lust for
strangers, especially the stunningly beautiful stranger, not to mistake
this for love. They are far more apt to mistake the lust for love when it is
accompanied by some other major dimension of love, especially the
fascination that accompanies the obsession of romantic love and some
sexual cravings.

If the experience is one of full-blown fascination, it is normally
accompanied by some feeling of fatedness, even if there are only the
earliest stirrings of love. This is what we see in the fascination at first
sight that Susan experienced. In fact, in her case, we see fatedness writ
large. Even the fascination was largely in response to the feeling of
disbelief inspired by the feeling of fatedness:

> I still don't know how it happened. I know all the details—how can I
> forget? But it still doesn't make much sense.
>
> I'd been really in love with Jim right through high school. I knew it could
> never work, because he just didn't have much ambition, he was just a
> drifter going nowhere and I want to go somewhere. But I loved him and it
> took forever to break it off. . . .
>
> But I did and I still wasn't over all the misery after all those months. So I
> didn't want to go to any parties, but my friends dragged me to this one.
>
> And soon after I got there I noticed this guy sitting alone across the room.
> And I just felt, Oh, no, Jesus! I can't! I'm too young for this. But I knew
> right from then on that it had to be—HE had to be. I don't know what it
> was or why. Tony wasn't really handsome. . . . He looked attractive, sure,
> but it wasn't his looks. I guess there was something about him. Maybe an
> air of mastery. It was special and I could never get over it. He was like a
> magnet to me and I couldn't escape. I knew I was too young, but I couldn't
> do anything else. It wasn't long before we were living together.
>
> It wasn't even really love, exactly. I mean there was never a lot of love
> feelings for him and the sex was just all right—nothing much, but nothing
> bad, just not much.

We made it for six years, then one day he said he was moving out to marry some woman I'd never heard of. I think he couldn't make it with a career woman. . . . He wanted a stay at home type, . . . but somehow I still can't believe it [Written by us at the time].

Susan was depressed for months. We talked with her every week or so for well over a year. Some weeks she'd be fine, not happy, but also not depressed. Then she'd "go down, down, down" and it was almost impossible to get her to see that there was any hope in life. She still seemed to be fused with Tony. Hers was the closest case we can remember of almost pure fatedness and possession. She hardly even seemed to have the compensation of feeling the fearful joy of a star-crossed love at first sight. She simply felt possessed and fearful. She was a lady in confusion, never understanding how it happened to her.

Tess was a very different study in fascination. Now an ex-business-woman of 40 who made enough money to retire to an academic career, she's extremely insightful about her own emotions and about those of others. She's also extremely articulate and open, all of which made her one of the finest explorers of love to help us chart these dark waters. Though she's an extremely caring woman, her quiet manner easily hides her passionate side. She has always been a diligent, meticulous student, driven by the demons of personal insecurity to be a perfectionist in everything she tries. (Her mother was a moralist, but one who, rather than moralizing against Tess, always considered her to be perfect. Knowing she was not perfect, but feeling strongly that she must be, Tess has always felt a terrifying need to achieve the impossible.) She did very well in college, but left with little clear idea of where she was headed. She had only minor romances during college and in the immediate period of work after college. Having no love life to hold her back, and craving something more exciting in life, she joined the CIA and was trained very carefully over many months to be a foreign agent. Once her training was completed, she was assigned to the agency headquarters in a large foreign country. Soon after she arrived:

I can see it now. . . . It's such a vivid memory I can see all the details, as if it were right here in front of me. It's a vision that will always be with me.

I was standing in my office. (The offices all ran along a central corridor and the top half of the walls was all glass, so you could look out into the corridor from the office.) I looked down the corridor and there, standing in front of the drinking fountain about to get a drink, was this strikingly handsome man. I'd never seen him before and I was absolutely fascinated with him. I knew from the very beginning. It's as if all the pieces had to fall into place, as if they had no choice, as if the normal chance element of life were suspended by a higher power.

I don't believe I was actually in love from that first moment, but I was certainly fascinated with him and I knew that love would follow, that I must love him. And that he would love me. And I did and he did. . . .

I soon discovered that he was my section chief, so it was easy to get to know him, in fact, impossible not to. We worked beautifully together from the very beginning, our love grew—or mine did, then his seemed to respond. Soon we were doing stake-outs together, debriefing the beautiful blonde the agency sent down from Washington to seduce the president, and everything else.

I knew almost from the beginning that he was married and that what I was doing was dangerous for me and for him, that it was against the unwritten code of the agency, and that, if this was Fate, maybe Fate was *not* on my side. But I was desperately in love, more in love than I could ever before have imagined possible. I did not know such love existed and here it was. I was carried away, swept away, out of control, head over heals, and everything else that we poor helpless mortals say about romantic love [Written by us at the time].

Tess's love is an example of pure romantic love.

The most extreme forms of love at first sight are reasonably easy to explain. They inspire us with a sense of mystery only because they are so unlike most of our everyday feelings and actions and so unlike the normally slow growth of love feelings—and because they are so contrary to modern rationalistic assumptions about human nature. One reason why the extremes of love at first sight and fascination at first sight involve a sense of fatedness is because in a way they generally *have* already happened. They are normally instances of the *déjà vu experience*, of seeing and responding to someone new in the same emotional way we did to someone else before. Once in a while, the remembered person and emotion are obvious to the lover. More commonly, they have only a vague sense that they have met and loved this person before. Even more commonly, they are not consciously aware that some earlier experience has produced an archetype in their subconscious memories that lies ready to spring into life when triggered by someone who looks, talks, acts, or feels the same as the original imprinter of the love archetype.

F. Scott Fitzgerald's love at first sight for Sheilah Graham is an obvious case of the triggering of dormant love. (He described it in *The Last Tycoon*, from which the opening quote to this chapter is taken.) He knew from the very beginning that he felt love at first sight for her because she reminded him in startling detail of his lost wife, Zelda. As soon as he saw Sheilah, his dormant love for Zelda was triggered. Zelda was a *specific loved archetype* lying dormant in his subconscious mind waiting to be triggered and when it was triggered by the sight of Sheilah Graham he knew it. No mystery there.

But most of us who have fallen in love at first sight or been seized at first sight by the less developed dimensions of love have not been aware of the presence of any archetype and, as a result, we have felt it to be mysterious, thus all the more magical and powerful, fated and unconquerable. (As Denis de Rougemont said, "The origin of a myth has to be *obsure*. . . . But the most profound characteristic of a myth is the power which it gains over us, usually without our knowing." Our individual archetypes of love are our individual myths of love: The more obscure, mysterious, and magical their origins are, the more power they have to cast a spell over our wills, to sweep us away.) Most of the time we have no sense at all of having seen the person before, or, rather, someone so like them that in the deepest realms, where our perceptions and emotions commune directly with each other, this new person is perceived and felt to be the same.

It is even more likely that a child who loses an adored parent at an early age will worship a secret archetype of him or her. The mother's death may leave the child with the conviction she still loves him from heaven, which may later nourish the conviction that the embodiment of this archetype is fated to love him. At a young age, the child's sense of self is still fused with the mother's self. Her death may prevent his ever becoming independent. If he does "rediscover" her love, he may well be incapable of feeling sexual at the same time.

Dante's mother died when he was a small boy. Even at his first sighting of Beatrice at the age of nine, his love was worshipful adoration. Throughout the rest of his life, the worship became stronger and any undertones of Eroticism disappeared. When, at 18, Beatrice first greeted him courteously, he returned home in the transports of worshipful ecstasy and fell asleep. He dreamed that the Lord of Love held Beatrice asleep in his arms and Dante's heart on fire in one hand. The Lord of Love told Dante that he would ever after be his Lord. Forever after, Dante did worship this Lord—Love—first in the flesh of Beatrice and then in the symbols of a religiously transfigured Beatrice. One day,

Beatrice did not return his greeting. He returned home in misery and "Fell asleep, like a little beaten child, in tears." Still later, at a wedding reception where Dante had no idea Beatrice might appear, he suddenly felt "a wonderful tremor begin in my breast on the left side, and extend suddenly through all parts of my body"—then he saw Beatrice. She saw his agitation and joined the other women laughing at him. He became ill and told a friend, "I have held my feet on that side of life beyond which no man can go with intent to return." Many years later, in the *Inferno*, he envisioned a sign over the gates of Hell: "Abandon hope, all ye who enter here." Her scorn had cast him into Hell: He lost all hope of winning Beatrice, but never lost his devotion and love.

When he was 48 (24 years after Beatrice's death), he wrote *The Divine Comedy* in which he ascends from hell, through purgatory to heaven. When he meets Beatrice in the Earthy Paradise, she reproaches him and he responds even more like a child who feels guilty and ashamed, with his "eyes upon the ground, listening and contrite and repentant." As he is about to ascend to heaven, Beatrice, "with a pitying sigh, directed her eyes toward me with that look which a mother turns upon her delirious child." In Heaven Beatrice takes her place with the Blessed Virgin Mary, Queen Mother of Heaven. The orphan love-possession syndrome seems clearly to be an individual instance of *mother worship* (Preston, 1982), which can be greatly encouraged and reinforced by culturally transmitted beliefs and rites, such as those of the worship of Mary.

We have found far more specific archetypes that trigger sexual feelings without love. These are often called "The Look," meaning the archetype of a face that triggers lust. But these sexual archetypes can be almost anything, from "uniforms" that turn a girl on immediately to the vast array of sexual fetishes to which some men are addicted. In some instances, the individuals can specify the origins of this transference of feeling in an earlier experience. Sometimes the sexual excitement can even be transferred to and imprinted upon a nonperson.

But certainly not all, or even most, of the triggers of love (or sex) at first sight are *primary archetypes* (that is, of one person only). Many, possibly most, are general archetypes of love (or sex). That is, there was never one single, specific person or partnership that became imprinted in the unconscious mind and later triggered love (or sex). Rather, some set of closely related perceptions and emotions, often associated with such a primary archetype, develop into a *generalized archetype of love* (or sex) that later respond to a broader spectrum of love (or sex) triggers than the primary archetypes seem to do. Very importantly, many of us seem to develop a *general archetype of beauty* (or more than one), which becomes an Inner Vision of Perfection for us. (This vision of beauty may include far more than physical appearance. It can include the gracefulness of movement, the tinkle of laughter, and character traits such as charity.) It seems likely that the strong love responses of Fitzgerald to Zelda and later his strong transference of those feelings to Graham were inspired by an even earlier, more generalized imprinting of a beauty archetype that both of them triggered. (In one of the notes that Fitzgerald labored over so lovingly, he even mentioned a woman's beauty that was like a painting and "evoked different dreams to every man, of the mother, of the nurse, of the lost childish sweetheart, of whatever had formed his first conception of beauty".)

While the Beatrices of lovers at first sight are not always beautiful, a strikingly high percentage of them are seen that way. Most are seen as more sexy than classically beautiful. This in itself is a clue to the fact that most of these "loves" are really intense lust with mere undertones of adoration love, given that sexy beauty is the most effective trigger of lust. But classical beauty also acts in another way to trigger even more intense—"real"—love at first sight. Anyone we have loved in the past, such as a mother or father, has been partly idealized so that our memories of them are more beautiful than other people would remember them. (See the discussion above of love mythification.) This idealization puts them closer to any beautiful person we might see in everyday life, so a beautiful person is more likely than most to trigger our earlier love feelings.

But there is another crucial factor involved as well. We do not fall in love at first sight in just any situation. We do not, for example, fall in love at first sight when we are already in romantic love with someone else, even if we see someone new who fits our archetype. If we are not highly aroused sexually by the person we are already in love with, someone representing our sexual archetypes might well trigger our sexual feelings, and we certainly have found people who are temporarily swept away by such sexual feelings when they are in love romantically with someone else; but they do not fall in-love with this new sex partner unless they go through unbonding from the earlier love. Being in-love (that is, with fusion) largely blocks the development of new romantic loves (see below). In order to fall in love at first sight (or crush, or fascination), it is necessary that the individual be *open* to the new love experience.

As long as the person is open to the experience, that is, not blocked, then the appearance of someone resembling the archetype can trigger the love and will tend to do so to the extent that he or she is emotionally primed for love, sex, and fascination. The emotional priming is experienced as the *craving* for love or sex. When someone says they are "lonely," they are primed to respond with love feelings to someone whom they can love; when they say they are desperately lonely or they are extremely sex starved, they mean that they are craving sex. And, of course, the more primed emotionally we are for love or sex, the more we tend to interpret our perceptions and evaluations of people to fit our preconceived archetypes. So when we are desperately lonely and sex starved, and bored with our lives (craving any excitement, mystery, fascination), we are extremely primed to see people as being just like our archtype(s)—and thus it is far more probable that someone will trigger our archetype-primal feelings and we will fall in love (or lust) at first sight.

When we have had little experience with love and sex to serve as archetypes that channel our love feelings, we respond to a far wider range of possible lovers. This is exactly the situation of the female adolescent: The new love and sex feelings prime her; she is not blocked to love (though she probably is, in our society, blocked to sex at that age); so she's ready to love easily. The result is "boy craziness," one crush after another until experience leads to discrimination in her responses and eventually to a blocking by romantic fusion love of further responses to new people (see Leilani in Chapter 4). Love at first sight does not seem to occur without a great deal of emotional priming. The normal instant lover is someone who is extremely lonely and sexually starved—that is, *craving* love and sex.

The less conscious we are of our emotional readiness and craving, the less able we are to guard our feelings by willpower. Thus, they are most apt to catch us off guard and sweep us away before we can try to impose willpower over them. This was most obvious in the girls like Leilani who went through one fantasy crush after another. When they finally found lovers, they started loving and stopped crushing. Sometimes this *drifting state* is consciously willed, or perhaps only subconsciously willed in the beginning and then forgotten. It is as if we consciously or semiconsciously put ourselves into a state of readiness and "psych" ourselves up (Adler, 1981), then get on with our lives as usual, but now with a new subconscious readiness ("set") to see possibilities of love where previously we did not. Once we begin to see with these new mythicizing eyes of craving, we suddenly "see" beauty where before we saw only another person, and we see emotional cues that before we "let pass."

People who crave romantic love commonly prime themselves by choosing to expose themselves to romantic love stories in movies, television, novels, and magazines. Young women often become highly addicted to stories in magazines and to "soap operas" on television that revolve around the quest for Romantic Love. As we noted, these stories provide partial gratification-venting for these powerful emotions, but they also build up emotions and expectancies that prime the addict to be ready to respond in specific ways. The stories are built on the basic outline of Romantic Love, so they commonly involve love at first sight (or fascination at first sight). Anyone who steeps herself in these stories becomes highly primed for love at first sight. This is seen very clearly in the case of Cheryl, who was highly tuned in to love stories and was completely convinced for a while that her Beatle, George Harrison, would fall in love with her at first sight—if only he would notice her among the thousands of other girls! (Schwartz et al., 1980). Angelina is an even clearer case. She sees herself as "the Ultimate Romantic Lover" and a "real Love-Nut." She has purposefully steeped herself in Romantic Love stories of all kinds since she was a young teenager and is now completely "in-love with Romantic Love":

> I was one of those little kids you see in front of the magazine racks, drooling over *True Confessions* while her mommy finished the grocery shopping. I quickly graduated to *Bonnie and Clyde*, *The Godfather*, and every Harold Robbins book ever written. The only type of love I thought there should be was an idealized romantic love. But I am the type of person that, if I had an appreciative partner, would happily play out all of those scenarios. By the summer after seventh grade I had my honeymoon all figured out, right down to the pink ostrich feathers that I would do my stripper dance in, to seduce my captivated and thoroughly charmed husband [Written by Angelina].

Angelina has been in love three times. Each time she has been fascinated at first sight and felt fated to love the man. In spite of the fact that the first two failed—in violation of the "Iron Law of Romantic Love"—she was completely convinced that the third love was "the ultimate love of my life" and would never fail. After three years, it did.

Do loves, crushes, or fascination at first sight work? It's obvious that they almost never work out, in the sense of becoming lasting romantic loves. Almost all of them fade away in the dawning light of one simple fact—the loved one is almost totally unknown. ("Alas, thou art in love, poor soul, and yet thou dost not know with whom!" as Boccaccio lamented of his love for Fiametta.) We do not know if they will love us in return. In fact, they rarely do, and some even use our love to manipulate us or taunt us, turning a blind mistake into palpable disaster. But, even if they do love us in return, the fact remains that we started loving them at first sight before we knew anything other than their archetypical characteristics. We rarely know anything about their character, and character is vital in maintaining the adoration at the core of our romantic love. We do not even know whether their total physical characteristics, once seen, will sustain our secret conviction that they fit our archetype. Our images of the ones we loved at first sight are more apparitions than realities, more inner visions of perfection mirroring our own deep cravings than perceptions of reality. And, very importantly, once we "fall," the idealization process goes into full swing: We focus only on the good qualities of the loved one until we learn the truth the hard way.

There are rare cases of love at first sight that work, that blossom and bear the lovely fruits of lasting romantic love. Sheilah Graham's love with Fitzgerald lasted for four years, until the day he died, but theirs was a love marred by ignorance. She fell in fascination at once, soon into love, and then discovered he was married to a schizophrenic he could not divorce and was himself an alcoholic given to outbursts of drunken violence, including Sheilah-battering. All love at first sight is a perilous flight into uncertainty and mystification. If there is something to the old adage, "Marry in haste, repent at leisure," there is far more to our new adage, "Fall in love at first sight, be glad of the last sight."

LESS HYSTERICAL LOVERS

One can go a long way in solitude, but alas one can go no further alone. Those things which make us more than animated and quarrelsome vegetables cannot be had by the imagination alone.

As for myself, I think you know that I am like a man who has seen in his mind's eye the glories of this existence, but had wandered through endless corridors, looking into empty rooms, till suddenly you unlocked the gate to the real world. . . .

Oh my dear, I could go on forever saying always the same thing in a thousand different ways. For you bind me and release me both, you bind

with the sweet grace of your love and release me with the sweet grace of
your love, and release me like an old bird who has flown wild, been long
caged and is once again on the wing [Walter Lippmann, letter to his love
and later, second wife; republished in Steel, 1980, p. 348].

Lippmann was 47 when he wrote this letter to Helen Byrne
Armstrong, the wife of his best friend. He had been married to a
beautiful woman for 20 years, had a princely income during the
depression, and was the most famous and influential journalist in the
world. He was wined, dined, and courted by the rich, the powerful, the
famous, and the beautiful. But beneath all the pomp and circumstance
of power, and all the shine and glitter of the gay social life, he was
secretly a deeply depressed man whose life felt empty, had no meaning,
no ultimate goal, no love. He had married a beautiful woman when he
was 27. For the first few years he believed his excitement and passion
was love. But his wife, Faye, had married him on the rebound,
apparently without love or passion. According to mutual friends, she
was the sort of woman who would adore a dancing, gay playmate; but
Lippmann was always a serious intellectual. She shared none of his
major interests and their tastes often clashed. He allowed her to have her
way to avoid arguments, which he dreaded. Their marriage settled into a
pleasant but dull routine. The gap between them yawned wider, but was
covered by sociability and some caring. No children came to bridge the
gap. It became an "OK" shell marriage. They never could talk about
much; in time they could hardly talk. "Finding the things that mattered
to me incommunicable, I have sought solitude behind a curtain of
depression." He resigned himself at an early age to a stoical existence—
endurance with grace. One of his greatest works, *A Preface to Morals*,
presented a general argument for stoically enduring, for walling the soul
off from the depression that was seeping in on him, even for living
without love. But it wasn't really working for him. He was sinking
beyond resignation and endurance into despair.

His best friend was Hamilton Armstrong. He and his wife, Helen, had
been close mutual friends with the Lippmann's for about 10 years. Helen
had secretly adored Lippmann since she first read *A Preface to Morals*,
but, while Lippmann always liked Helen, he never thought of their
relationship as anything other than friendship. She had taken his stoical
front to be the truth and believed him to be the supremely "adjusted"
man who could not be tempted by other women. After all, it seemed
obvious, and was true, that he had never had an affair, in spite of all the

women who wanted him. Then, one enchanted evening, they began talking and wound up communing:

> The music, the lights, the dancing couples floating past their table, the metallic brilliance of the art deco furnishings lent a strange excitement to the evening. Helen, for once, seemed oddly subdued. Each seemed to be waiting for the other to take the lead.
>
> Finally Walter took the initiative. Seized by an overwhelming compulsion, he began to talk of his feelings, and in a way he had never spoken to anyone. He began by telling her of his doubts about the value of the column and his temptation to quit daily journalism to write articles and books, and perhaps to teach. Feeling that she understood what he was trying to say, he lowered the barriers he had so carefully erected over the years. He spoke of the space he felt between himself and other people and how—although he had never had any desire to be psychoanalyzed—this probably came from a childhood in which he felt unloved. For the first time in his life he revealed his loneliness in growing up in a household of uncaring servants and parents too preoccupied with themselves to give him much attention. He told her how neglected he felt and unloved by his mother, of how this feeling had put a "chill" on his emotions and made him afraid of getting really close to anyone.
>
> He also talked about his life with Faye: how their marriage had become a habit, devoid of passion or even real affection; how lonely he had felt with Faye, even lonelier than being by himself; and how this made him pull back yet further into himself. His prescription for "disinterestedness" in *A Preface to Morals* was, he revealed, in part a way of dealing with that unhappiness. When he had written that "lovers who have nothing to do but love each other are not really to be envied; love and nothing else very soon is nothing else," he had been referring to his own marriage . . . she realized that he had torn down a barrier in speaking to her this way; he was treating her not as a confidante but as a woman. He was bringing her into his life. A sense of complicity had grown between them. He had allowed her into an inner sanctum where no one had ever before penetrated. He wanted something from her without quite knowing what it was. She did know. She listened gravely, asked questions delicately, softly laid her hand on his. They drank more wine than they were used to. They danced on the crowded floor, holding each other closer than they ever had before. By the time they left the Rainbow Room and he hailed a cab on Fifth Avenue to take her home, they both knew that something irrevocable had happened.
>
> The next day he called her. They arranged to have dinner again on a night when Hamilton would be away—this time not in a fashionable spot where

he was easily recognized, but in a quiet neighborhood restaurant. The relationship had changed. Their meeting had an air of conspiracy. During the twenty years of his marriage nothing like this had ever happened. Now for the first time in his life the rules seemed suspended. They held hands during dinner and spoke wonderingly of the strange thing happening to them. When they left the restaurant they went to a hotel.

They met the next day, and the next [Steel, 1980, pp. 345-346].

Walter Lippmann is a beautiful example of the *hysterical lover* who falls short of the mythical fall at first sight. Hysteria in general is "any outbreak of wild, uncontrolled excitement or feeling, such as fits of laughing and crying." Love hysteria, then, is a "fit of love," an outbreak of wild, uncontrolled, and, at its height, completely uncontrollable adoration love. Hysterical love comes suddenly. It may begin at once, with no warning to the inexperienced, who lack an inner ear for its first murmurs. These are the lovers at first sight who are the furthest extreme in hysterical love. The great majority of hysterical lovers fall in love suddenly in comparison to most lovers, but not as suddenly as their extreme brethren. Their love begins like the first crack in a dam signaling the awesome pressures built up behind it; then it rushes out with great intensity, as the water does through those first cracks; and soon it pours forth in a wild torrent and sweeps them away, as the water pours forth when the dam suddenly shatters and sweeps away every-thing in its path. Walter certainly did not fall in love with Helen at first sight. In all the years of their friendship, he had felt no hint of love beyond the tender liking of slightly intimate friendship. But suddenly, as his craving for love grew and a new situation arose, he saw something new in their relationship—a chance for *secure* romantic love. The first crack appeared in the dam he had built to wall back his love cravings. He looked at Helen with the craving look of love. She saw it and responded. A "spark" of romantic love jumped the gap of loneliness between them and they were transported into the realm of intensely intimate soul communion. Within days, the dam burst and Walter was swept away by love. In fact, he was wildly in-love, in a frenzy of love-possession so that he was ready to do all the things that before that enchanted evening seemed absurd. In the heat of this frenzied period of enchanted possession, he wrote a beautiful description of his condition. He wrote it about Amelia Earhart, a free spirit soaring into the heavens, but he meant it about himself and Helen, because he was now writing from his heart:

In such persons mankind overcomes the inertia which would keep it earthbound forever in its habitual ways. They have in them the free and useless energy with which alone men surpass themselves.

Such energy cannot be planned and managed. . . . It is wild and free. But all the heroes, the saints and the seers, the explorers and the creators, partake of it. They do not know where their impulse is taking them. . . . They have been possessed for a time with an extraordinary passion which is unintelligible in ordinary human terms. . . .

They do the useless, brave, noble, the divinely foolish and the very wisest things that are done by man. And what they prove to themselves and to others is that man is no mere automaton in his routine, no mere cog in the collective machine, but that in the dust of which he is made there is also fire, lighted now and then by great winds from the sky [Republished in Steel, 1980, p. 350].

Walter now felt the fire of love and knew it had been lit from a great wind in the sky—it came from nowhere, totally overpowered his will, was a heavenly force, and was fated. He and Helen had conspired to unchain the daimonic powers of romantic love trapped within him.

Walter Lippmann was an insecure love hysteric almost his entire life. Both his mother and father rejected him almost completely. Only the intermittent love of a grandmother saved him from the extreme miseries of primary insecurity. His dam burst first for his first wife, until he came to believe (out of insecurity?) she did not love him and was rejecting his love with her quiet awayness, which triggered his dread of being unlovable. He then quickly rebuilt his dam and walled his love off from the world, shielding himself behind a front of courageous stoicism that others must often have felt to be a lack of inner warmth, a lack of ability to love, a "cold heart."

Hysterical lovers seem to have a high degree of ambivalent conflict between primary security and secondary or tertiary insecurity. There are many different mixtures possible, with different effects, but great ambivalence in some degree and form is the hallmark of hysterical lovers. And the hallmark of ambivalence is the tendency to go from one extreme to the opposite, such as from coldness to wild love. Hysterical lovers are ambivalent about themselves, and about love, so they easily swing from one extreme to the opposite. The more ambivalent they are, the greater the swings can take, but the less commonly they swing at all.

The most ambivalent lovers are those who first receive the most complete love, thus learn to love most deeply, but then early in life experience some severe threat to their love feelings that produces a block or dam, a repression of love feelings that forces the love cravings to well up in the unconscious realm and thus to become ever more powerful, ever more ready to crack through, to shatter the dam and sweep the will away with waves of loving passion. The more secure a specific situation seems for their love, the more likely the dam is to crack and shatter. Both the growing craving and the great situational security are important in their cracking the dam.

As we can easily see from Janet's life story, she is a study in the ambivalent insecurities of beautiful women. Her mother has always been very loving and caring toward her and her two sisters. From her she learned to love intensely. But her father is a study in the aloof-and-cold syndrome, never kissing or showing affection for the girls in any way. Though a successful Army officer, he was also an alcoholic and when drunk would violently berate his wife. During these arguments he would refer to the girls as "Your children!" The girls could hear all of this from their closet, where they retreated during the arguments, clinging to each other and crying. Janet felt guilty, as if she were responsible for this rejection—unworthy and hatable. She developed the usual signs of insecurity, including that of embodying her insecurity in the feeling of being ugly, especially indicative for teenagers and overwhelmingly so for teenaged girls. But other people saw her as beautiful: She developed into the buxom, statuesque, beautiful woman at a very young age. So she became tremendously ambivalent in her feelings of confidence: At home she would look in the mirror and feel ugly and she would feel guilty and unloved because of her father's treatment of her; but she felt loved by her mother (hence lovable) and beautiful at school, thus socially competent. She turned more and more toward the boys in school as her source of confidence. Just as this was about to launch her into a career of casual sex, she was whisked away to the South, where the college boys protected her virginity with gallantry. She became the college beauty queen and fell desperately in love with the rich and handsome prince charming, Errol. She hardly realized at the time how deeply she was in love with Errol, how completely she was fused with him, how desperately dependent on him she was for everything. At the time it seemed like immensely exciting fun. But, as she now sees, "Errol had become my everything. He was my rock on which I could build my life." By hysterically fusing herself with his, she escaped that terrible sense of insecurity that lingered, in spite of all her social success as the Beauty Queen. He was her "rock of ages" and she could hide herself in the dependent security of that great strength. But her love made her blind to Errol's fatal flaw, his weakness and self-hatred, born of his father's crushing demands for a perfection he could never possibly attain. He had found in the beautiful woman—His Queen—an escape from his own basic insecurities and, unknown to her, found his rock even more in her, becoming desperately fused and dependent. When he volunteered for Vietnam in his quest for the escape of death, her world collapsed and she collapsed. She tried to free herself from her desperate love for him by escaping into marriage with someone she tried to convince herself she loved, but she could not escape.

When Errol returned and discovered her "betrayal," he was so shattered that he wound up in a mental institution and became obsessed with the thoughts of killing her and himself. Her ancient sense of guilt led her to see his killing her as just—as an escape from their communion in misery. At this point, they were very close to becoming the typical headline story of homicide and suicide: "War Hero Kills Beautiful Blonde in Jealous Rage, Then Turns Gun on Self," except this beautiful blonde would have died willingly. Escaping her soul-dependency on Errol took many months and involved some casual sex to counterweight her lingering love for him. This is the "wild period" of her life, her time of wandering in the wilderness, during which she was still so hurt by her lost love for Errol that she dreaded feeling love for anyone. But once the wound was healed, without knowing it, she once again craved love and began drifting toward it. She almost immediately fell into fascination with Jim—fascination at first date—and within a few days was falling in-love. She fell hysterically in-love with and was extremely dependent on him during the three years they lived together. Then, with no hint at all, he suddenly left her for a male lover, and cast her into her deepest despair. Her first rock crumbled slowly; her second disappeared instantaneously. Then her loved sister was killed the next day, raising the specter of ontological insecurity and casting her into mourning to multiply all of her other insecurities. If she had not had her mother's love to lean on, to bury her shattered self in during this period, she might well have committed suicide, just as so many other hysterical lovers have when they are deserted. Slowly Janet found a new rock in which to hide herself from her insecurities. She became a born-again Christian and this rock has sustained her. Her third love developed slowly. It was not without hints of her old insecurities. One day, during her lover's absence, she had a lunch date with a suitor. Suddenly, her undercurrent of guilt surfaced and she saw her lover's apparition pass through the restaurant. But for the most part she has not fallen back into deep dependency. Her love hysteria has withered as her new sense of security has grown. She married her lover and has had their first child. Janet's love with Errol is an instance of two hysterical lovers losing themselves in each other. Such hysterical love-duets are very powerful and, at their best, can be supremely beautiful for those involved. But the insecurities make the lovers immensely fearful and jealous. Each easily feels betrayed by the other, for each is really seeking both a lover and a Great Protector (Yalom, 1980).

THE SLOW TAKEOFF INTO ROMANTIC LOVE FUSION, AND THE MORE COMMON ABORTIONS OF TAKEOFFS

In the real world of today, love partnerships that grow over the years almost always begin amid the dross of everyday life. Their beginnings are as routine as those of most great friendships, so much so that individuals often do not remember when they first met, or find first and other early meetings quite unworthy of remarking, or are replaced in memory with mythical accounts that better befit—emotionally—the powerful outcomes that were totally unforeseen. (The Western myth of Romantic Love demands love at first lightening bolt, so when it does not happen that way people often reconstruct their memories to make it happen. The folk memory did some reconstructing of the first meeting of Wally Simpson with the Duke of Windsor to give it an air of fatedness.)

Love probably accelerates more rapidly than most friendships and is probably more apt to be punctuated with "crucial intuitions of specialness." (Again, we caution that these "guesstimates" are based, like almost all evidence about love partnerships, on memories of times past. Once adoration and sexual feelings begin to potentiate each other, mythification begins to take wing, and memories are among the more easily mythicized forms of experience. Once very much in-love, the memory is reconstructed mythically to validate the necessary, essential, timeless, and eternal nature of the partnership. Mythicized memories become the rosary beads of reassurance prefiguring the lasting nature of this most risky of human partnerships and every possible scrap of evidence is anxiously dredged up as a sign of the future beautification.

Diary accounts are far more reliable, but only direct, real-life observations will resolve many of the problems in such "guesstimates.") How rapidly such crucial intuitions and the overall partnerships develop depend predominantly on the situations. The main reason why most love partnerships develop slowly and at first largely imperceptibly is that almost all of our friendly encounters take place in humdrum, everyday situations in which little is revealed and much masked by pleasantries and role-play that hide the inner sense of self, which must be imputed (as in the case of the hysterical lovers) or, far more commonly, experienced and intuited before one feels the respect and liking that motivate the "getting to know you" from which adoration and identification will grow.

The vast majority of *interactions* never go beyond the externalities implied by that cold word. We act together, we do not really get to know much about each other's inner sense of self. We remain on the surface of social life, enacting role-plays, not revealing or sharing our senses of self, not ever becoming intimate with each other. Most of us maintain a shell of noninvolvement strategies around our lives to defend ourselves against overintimacies, if for no other reason than the practical ones of not having the time or emotional energies available for new commitments. The number of close and active friendships that we can maintain is extremely limited, rarely extending beyond five to ten and often falling short of five. (Of course, we can maintain a great many more dormant friendships that spring to life only intermittently when we can manage to get together across the vast distances of our modern lives.) Most of us are, then, pretty much closed to intimacies with new people most of the time, though the great majority of people maintain a slight openness for those extremely rare occasions when someone seems ideally suited to be our intimate friend.

Most of us are almost completely closed most of our adult lives to the beginning of a romantic love partnership because our emotions and identifications are preempted by already established partnerships and obligations, or because we know our situation makes a romantic partnership impossibly difficult (because, for example, we must endure years of penury in college) or dangerous (for those still recovering from love misery). Competent adults have a quick, intuitive, and rough sense of how *open* or *closed* someone else is to such intimate involvements. Sensing that someone else is closed off, they normally close themselves off in direct proportion to their degree of insecurity about love, even if in general they are quite open. This is the usual program of rejecting—or merely screening out—the potential rejector and is a vital defense against the excruciating pains of lost love—shame and embarrassment. People who are *open* for intimacies, and most especially those who feel lonely and crave intimacy, are continually scanning their social encounters for signs of openness from those not socially closed off by the unspoken rules concerning intimacy. When they sense openness in others and do not yet know enough about them to feel they should close themselves off, they engage them in brief forays of *feeling out* the others' senses of self by *progressively revealing and sharing* their own senses of self. These step-by-step, progressive intimacies are a drift process and proceed to the point where they encounter either a lack of interest or something negative, any rejected values or any repugnant or irksome mannerisms, and especially *distrust* of the other. The vast majority of these mutual feelings-out are aborted after the first few steps beyond superficiality, either because the other proves not as open as first sensed or because of encountering *negative signs*. Sociability gatherings— "parties"—are especially valuable to those craving intimacy because they relax the rules about intimacy, allowing more feeling out with less risk of embarrassment or shame than most other situations.

These intimacy feelings-out commonly proceed by a careful *manipulation of uncertainty* veiled by the attitude of play that allows the individual to retreat at any time behind a screen of implied unreality or professed misunderstanding. The individual who initiates a statement opens the possibility of an interpretation of his or her meaning as one involving more intimacy, without making it clear that he or she has committed him- or herself more intimately. Only if the other chooses the more intimate interpretation will he or she then proceed to offer an escalation in intimate possibilities. Otherwise, the individual retreats behind the screen of playful uncertainty, thereby largely protecting him- or herself from the painful shame and embarrassment.

The *ethos of openness* that has become so widespread among young people in the United States in recent years is not really an exception to these defensive strategies of closedness, though on the surface it appears to condemn them entirely. The reason is that this is openness without any real sharing of the sense of self, without sharing in the living of emotion that is the heart of intimate communing. The presenting of the bare outlines of the self—and even more the presenting of phony selves—is commonly wrapped in the ethos of coolness, that is, of nonemotional involvement of the sense of self (Lyman and Scott, 1970). This ethos is actually an excellent device for efficiently screening out the vast majority of people unfitted to be intimate friends in a highly pluralistic and conflictful society and, conversely, for admitting to the first inner circles of intimate involvement those who seem fitted. For the great majority of its practitioners in our urban youth subcultures, "openness" is merely a patina of intimacy, a simulation of friendliness that allows massive screening out with a minimum of pain. Unfortunately, it also allows more sexual predators to breech the traditional defense against overcloseness by fitting their self-presentations to the self-revelations of the others.

Of course, there have always been many very young ingenuous people, who are open in presenting their senses of selves and trying to share their emotional commitments with others. These were understood to be "innocent" of the dangerous wiles of so many social predators, such as sexual hunters waiting to seduce young girls who had not learned of seduction ploys and strategies in their families and cloistered schools run by nuns. But in all Western societies today, and most especially in the United States, the age of indiscriminate and sincere intimacy has been plummeting and by high school is now a rarity. (It is quite hilarious, and a true sign of Hollywood's surrealism, that all young actresses in Hollywood are still called *ingenues*—the centuries-old French term for an innocent and open young woman. Some young women used to arrive in Hollywood with innocence and indiscriminate openness, but no one who has read a Hollywood biography of any one of them would imagine following in their ingenuous footsteps. For an excellent presentation of the rites of passage out of innocence and ingenuousness, see Shulman, 1972.) As almost any high school student now takes for granted, those who are really friendly with strangers soon get "burned" and retreat into the patina of *pseudointimacy*, which invites others to be open for careful scrutiny but protects one's own sense of self from insecurity. This is not at all like being "other directed." Most young Americans are quite sociable on the surface, while being quite defensive until their feeling-out strategies lead them to believe someone is worthy of intimacy and a "good bet" for becoming friends. Their "social radars" are tuned to detect worthy and safe characters, not to tell their selves what to become. It is only absurd utopians, or would-be seducers, who insist that nondefensive, intimate community-spiritedness should replace these realistic strategies for interaction in a world in which sexual predators and worse roam freely.

By college age, many young Americans have learned from experience and from the pervasive cultural messages of sexual modernism to be somewhat cynical about Romantic Love and are far more apt to believe that "casual sex is all right if I really like someone, but I'm too young for love." Some really are casual and live by that ethos until they feel they are "ready," practically and emotionally, for romantic love. But most of these are merely cynical romantics, craving love without realizing it and deceiving themselves into thinking they merely crave sex. Many of them, especially many of the young women, are not very sexual at all but have been deceived by the sexual modernism they have been force-fed for years into believing that what they crave is sex, raw and simple.

Their craving for intimacy and love is probably greater than that of young people in the vast majority of cultures. This is not because of the lingering remnants of the Western Romantic Love Myth, which they pick up in the mass media. As with almost everything else in the media, the media are responding to their cravings and amplifying them, not creating them. Young people crave intimacy and romantic love because of the genetic primings at this age, but in our society these are greatly potentiated by the anxious craving for love that comes from the secondary and tertiary insecurities about lovability that are now so pervasive in our society, from the loneliness that comes with the often sudden breaking or distancing of family love and intimacy in adolescence and from the realization that many of those professing love and intimacy are really sexual hunters seeking only to use the unwary.

The defensive strategies, earlier experiences of "being burned" in love, and the dogmas of sexual modernism are often at war with this intense craving for romantic love. The intense craving for love is often suppressed or repressed because of the dreads of rejection, and when not is often ridiculed and suppressed, especially by the young college men and "liberated feminists" trained in the ethos of sexual modernism, as "soap-opera Romanticism." The result can be the rapid development of a sexual relationship and a slower, largely repressed falling in-love. "I'm not really in-love" has become a litany of self-reassurance among these young people who so confidently believe they can separate sex and "friendship" from romantic love and have begun to dread the prospect of losing the love and the misery that must immediately trigger. In our "elite" colleges, the repression of romantic love is probably far more common than the repression of sex was in the age of Victoria and Freud. Because love and intimacy are far more powerful, pervasive, and embedded in the sense of self, these repressions of love have produced an explosion of neurotic symptom formation. These "liberated" young people often live on high maintenance doses of therapy and drugs, both legal and illegal.

When they break under their emotional stresses, the true believers in sexual modernism redouble their efforts to be good sexual modernists, insisting on more casualness, not less. It does not occur to them that they are committing the modernist sin of repression in the very name of liberation from repression, because they do not believe love exists as something different from but interdependent with sex. When they experience sexual dysfunction because of the repressed love feelings and the depression that comes with the loss of the loved one they themselves have often left, they focus all their attention on their "sex problem," thereby failing to see that it is the result of a far more powerful, pervasive, and embedded love problem. A large minority of young people spend years floundering emotionally and thus in most other ways as well. They drift from one misery to another, from the serene misery of lonely craving to the intense misery of casual sex "relationships" that skim across the surface of life and cripple the possibility of deeper love partnerships, and back again to the insecure fortress of aloof coldness. As one pop singer/songwriter, Carly Simon, suggests in her 1985 song, "Floundering":

First she sees her hypnotist
Then she rushes to her psychiatrist
Then she sees her acupuncturist
She's got to got to get fixed

Then she sees her Scientologist
Gets fed by her nutritionist
She cannot seem to resist
Seeking cosmic consciousness
(chorus) Looks like she's floundering again
        Seems to be floundering again
        Looks like she's floundering again
        Seems to be floundering again

She swears by Jack La Lanne
Then she throws the I Ching again
She searches in the Himalayas
For somebody to ease the pain
(chorus)

She's looking for a cure
She does not know exactly what for
(chorus)

She's into political activism
Reading up on Tibetan Buddhism

Anna Freud's analyzed her dreams
And she's hoarse from primal screams
(chorus)
[Used by permission of C'est Music ASCAP]

Some of these are helped by the rapidly growing number of therapists who themselves have listened with the inner ear of common sense to the deep cravings for love and intimacy and have rejected the modernist dogmas. Far more literally grope their way to self-salvation ("spontaneous remission" to the experts). Their key to self-salvation comes in recognizing that love and intimacy are separate and more powerful, pervasive, and embedded in our senses of self than sexual "relating"; and that the "pleasurable skin sensations" of genital sex that so obsessed the behavioristic misinterpreters of Freud are also of minor importance in life compared to the daimonic creative powers of Eros.

BECOMING TRULY INTIMATE

Falling in-love comes only with the ripening and mellowing of true intimacy, which alone allows the intense fusion of selves to develop what is meant by "being in-love." That takes a great deal of time, communing, and doing together, except in those rare instances that cast our fates together on the edge of the abyss.

True intimacy is quite separate from and normally in considerable conflict with pseudointimacy. Anatole Broyard (1986) has noted that "it is the essence of the modern to say what one feels, to break an ancient silence into which we seem to have been shushed by church, state or society. More and more, we live by pronouncing ourselves." The fatal flaw in this dogma of the open self is the inevitable gap and commonly the wrenching conflict between our *purposefully presented sense of self*, which is commonly called our "self-definition," and our *true sense of self*. Much of what we purposefully present to strangers in public settings as being our selves is disinformation, that is, information intended to hide and mislead, for all the practical reasons just noted. But no amount of honesty and sincerity would ever allow many of us to bridge that gap completely between the presented self and the true self, even to one so adoring as to listen endlessly to our self-rhetoric. Though people differ greatly in how much of their real selves they are aware of and how much of it they can present, most of us are distinctly limited in these abilities. If that were not so, we would hardly find depth-psychology worthwhile, and understanding our experiences of love would not be nearly so problematic. "Know thyself" would hardly be a worthwhile injunction if people already complied with it. But it is the beginning and one of the ends of all honest pursuits of truth about human beings. And it is excruciatingly difficult. It is little wonder then that partnerships normally begin with the pseudointimacies of presenting self-ideals and slowly progress toward presenting sincere self-disclosures as we come to trust and respect the other people sufficiently to let down our moralistic defenses against public attack and to take them seriously. Putting the idealized front forward, sparring for defensive self-positions, and opening the other person up for our careful observation and analysis are the most common activities in the first buddings of communion and love partnerships. (The sociologists known as dramaturgists have given us a wealth of information on these many strategies, but err in believing these presentations are the whole human being. See Goffman, 1959.) When the dogma of openness and honesty in self-advertisements is in full force, even self-degradation becomes an ideal ploy in putting the most idealized front forward, in preparing to defend oneself against charges of not being open and honest, and in opening the other person up for inspection. Self-degradation also disarms anyone who might suspect us of harboring desires for dominance or success.

What matters most to true seekers of intimacy are not what others say. Silence often speaks the loudest about the self and endless prattle bores and distracts us from truth. What matters at the vastly complex subconscious level of intuition at which our sense of self operates is how we experience the "thou" in living together in doing and communing. It is the intuitively experienced sense of self, of our own self intertwined with and communing with others in action—the sense we have of our "fit" or "compatability" with others—that counts above all else in the sharing of our selves with them, that is, in the building of true intimacy. Meg Greenfield has stated very succinctly this vital truth about the "ring of truth," even concerning something inherently vastly complex, such as the public testimony given by technicians about the explosion of the space shuttle Challenger:

> Next, I think it is important to listen carefully to the testimony, not just in technological terms, but in terms of its ringing true. I know this will sound unprofessional and unsystematic. It is both, but it is also the way we all

make our most important and usually successful decisions every day. We determine the merit and nature of what we are hearing or are being asked to believe by its plausibility, and this we can measure only against our own experience in other situations and with other people. To me there has been something too carefully constructed, too clipped, too reluctant to add a single extra word in the testimony of those who were responsible for the launch. I am alternately put in mind during some of the testimony of the early Watergate holders-back and of a child who will answer when confronted with evidence he can no longer deny: "But you didn't ask me that." Quickly I add: I don't accuse the witnesses either of Watergate-type crimes or of kiddishness. I only say that to the normal listener, the testimony of a number of them has a ring of something funny to it, something not quite right . . . we don't need to be shy or scientifically insecure in saying that common, age-old human experience justifies our skepticism about much that has been said so far [Greenfield, 1986].

This *intuitive experiencing of selves* is how we go about sizing up the intentions of sexual hunters, status hunters, love-sick immatures, loving friends, and everyone else in everyday life. Our senses of their senses of selves are the outcome of our vastly complex programs for assessing human beings, all influenced by the emotions we experience at the time we are assessing. If we experience them as worthwhile and trustworthy— fitting—for our purposes, we proceed to engage our selves with theirs. If not, we disengage and begin to "tune out."

If our initial *sharing of our senses of our selves*—our communing— goes well, then we feel that we "fit" each other well, and we feel that our growing intimacy is "spontaneous" and "natural." We have a feeling of decreasing need to be "on our guard" and "controlled" in our revealing of our selves. We feel "relaxed" and "at ease," not tense. Falling in-love begins not with the tense and bothered feeling of lustful craving, but with the crumbling of our walls of public separation and the peaceful, free flowing communion of selves. It is only possible when we respect and trust our sense of the other. It continues to develop only so long as we sense in the other both fundamental similarities in our values and differences that we crave to make our own—to fuse with our selves. Intimate love grows because we see enough of our self in the other to trust and respect and because we sense in the other differences that we crave to share or become. The other must be enough like us to elicit the respect and trust that come only from shared basic values and to trigger our dormant archetypal feelings of love learned from earlier experiences, especially in communings with the members of our families who are so much like ourselves. These vital *similarities of love* are necessary to the development of friendly love, but more as the keys to love's gatekeepers—respect and trust. The first recognitions of them strike "sparks" of interest, but these arise from surprise and anticipation. They are not sufficient to trigger the romantic excitement necessary to begin the buildup to the critical range of falling in-love. *Positive differences* from the self are necessary to this buildup. Positive differences produce the uncertainty (mystery) and risk that inflame the positive emotions, all of which beyond a certain level produce romantic mythification (see above).

An individual's positive differences are those that outdo our characteristics and achievements along the same value dimensions, as we see with honesty or intelligence, or which complement our selves in ways we cannot hope to achieve, as we see in exclusive sexual differences. Differences along the same valued dimension are important in building love, but they involve possible envious conflicts. We may respect, admire, adore, or feel awed by the greater intelligence of someone and these may potentiate our growing adoration for her in general. But, because we value that for ourselves, there is always the possibility of envious competition for it, and thus for the negative emotional arousal and mythification (gray-lens effect) that entails. The more positive differences in the other *exclude* any possible achievement by us, the more inherently complementary to us they are and thus the more sure they are in arousing our positive emotions and eventually romantic mythifications. People the world over have intuited the vital importance of inherent sexual differences in producing these positively exciting complementarities. Thus they have strongly emphasized sexual differences and greatly amplified them culturally from early childhood on by dress, by cosmetics, by body decorations, by body movements, by ritual, by story, by separation of the sexes, by division of labor, by myth, and by almost every conceivable means. They have exulted in the difference. (As French romantics say, "Vive la différence!") Sexual modernists, of course, have revolted against this bit of human nature and cultural wisdom by creating the myth of androgyny and polymorphous perversity and by seeking to level all differences into a seamless "equality." They have, of course, produced rampant conflict and a stigmatic war of the sexes rarely before recorded in human history. The opposite of complementary differences is not sameness, but conflictful differences.

Once past the gatekeepers of positive similarities—respect and trust—the inherent and irreducible complementary differences of life—

the yin (female) and yang (maleness) of the Erotic—trigger the cravings to unite with the complementary opposite to become one whole Being. This craving is potentiatied both by our own feelings of deficiency and by our positive adoration of the differences. In cultural rituals around the world, the ritualized portrayals of yin and yang differences present them both as necessary and as adorable, each made the greater by the complementary differences and united equally in a greater Being.

There is an optimal range of these emotions and the complementary differences that potentiate them for the triggering of romantic love. Respect, admiration, adoration, and awe all constitute one dimension of increasing emotional response to persons who meet our positive evaluations. We refer to the entire dimension as adoration love, but the differences in degree are of vital importance, as seen in the categorical distinctions made by people commonsensically. Friends inspire respect and admiration. Lovers inspire adoration. Heroes, heroines, and God inspire awe. Anyone who inspires too little or too much of this positive evaluation and emotional arousal will fall outside the range of intimate communing and arousal necessary for romantic love to grow.

Once communers are past love's gatekeepers and have begun to experience adoration for the "thou," the buildup of romantic love accelerates steadily until for any.reason it is aborted. As it accelerates, the lovers often experience a sudden recognition that they are beginning to *fall* in-love, an awakening to the fact that Eros is "taking wing," for it is around this stage that the dimensions of the Erotic beyond sexuality begin to emerge strongly. These awakenings are seen as "turning points." After the fall, even those who did not awaken to what was happening commonly look back and "discover" turning points beyond which fate reigned over free choice. Most of this is probably Romantic Love mythification after the fact, but the idea encompasses a vital truth. There is at least a problematic range of emotional arousal beyond which the lover *falls* freely, swept away by the powerful emotions aroused and by the mythifications that "blind" reason. Once this range is reached, the individual cannot effectively manage his or her emotions to prevent the fall.

The effective management of one's emotions during the takeoff of love is based on the use of the basic properties of emotions, even though these properties are almost never recognized consciously. Above all, the successful emotion manager realizes that emotions can only be controlled by willpower at lower levels. Therefore, they follow the ancient tactics of commonsense wisdom summed up in such cultural injunctions as "Don't put off 'til tomorrow what can be done today," "Don't tempt fate," and, above all, "Don't play with fire." When a budding communion "goes sour," they abort and return to the search for new communion, rather than trying to launch a partnership that will almost certainly end in disaster. They realize that the longer they wait and let it drift, the more they are playing with the "fire" of powerful emotions that can be ignited into a conflagration that consumes their reason. Because the craving for love is so great today, there is a remarkably large number of people who "hang on" and "hope desperately" that "tomorrow" will bring a miraculous change in the loved one and the budding communion. (Popular books are written about them. See Norwood, 1986.) Caring and the morals of friendship, which mandate loyalty to the intimate, also encourage this perseverance in emotional gamesmanship. Those who have never been swept away by love and the Erotic find it so easy to believe that they can always control their emotions, especially if they also bear the burden of being rationalists, who deny the ancient wisdom that teaches that reason and "morals are as straw in the wind to the fire in the blood." They easily find themselves falling out of control into a love they knew rationally would end in disaster, before they passed the *critical range of emotional control* and began to see, think, and act in the glow of the pink-lens effect.

The *critical range of losing emotional control* is the range beyond which willpower, the emotion the self has direct control of to counter-weight other emotions, becomes less than the emotions opposed to it. Up to this critical range, the individual has free will to exercise his or her choices about continuing to develop, exit, or put on hold a budding love communion. (Up to this range, Ortega y Gassett, 1957, and others who argue we *choose* to fall in-love or not are right.) Once these other emotions reach this critical range, the individual's will is swept away, he or she is out of control, and he or she "falls" wither the dominant emotions direct. By this time, mythification has generally set in, so the controlling emotions are also focusing and changing perceptions and "rational" analyses to complement their goal orientation. Even the erstwhile love cynic now is converted into a born-again Romantic Lover with absolute faith that, "It *will* work—I *know* it must!" Most people who fall beyond the critical range do not continue onward and downward into love. Most unbond (see Chapter 6) soon after or find the loved one has not fallen so far and exits. But beyond this critical range where he or she loses self-control, the lover will grope in a "twilight zone" in which he or she makes decisions, wills, and acts, but, in matters of love, will do so as if he or she were being jerked around by a hidden Great Puppeteer. If he or she has gravely misintuited the loved one, and fallen under the willpower of (been *possessed by*) a nonloving manipulator, the individual will probably come to feel literally like he or she is being "jerked around" and will eventually unbond, but only after much anguish (see Chapter 6).

The mythification process and being swept away emotionally by the full panoply of romantic love produce the *fusion* of the sense of selves, which is what people now call *being in-love* (and used to call the *union of souls*). Because the mature and secure self has strong boundaries that define the self relative to all else, it takes the powerful craving and emotions of adoration love to open the self sufficiently to allow another self to become pervasively embedded in it, fused with it. The lesser emotions of respect to admiration are sufficient to produce the partial fusion found in friendly love partnerships. Extreme situations that involve high uncertainty and high potential payoffs, especially potential negative payoffs, break through the taken-for-grantedness of the everyday life attitude and the boundaries of their selves, triggering very powerful emotions that greatly increase the fusion of senses of selves of those involved. These extreme situations greatly speed up the "getting to know you" process and circumvent the natural caution and resistance to feeling much and identifying much with someone unknown. The foxhole situation of warfare and any similar fate-laden situation can lead to very rapid falling in-love and falling in-hatred, depending on what is revealed by actions about the inner senses of self. Soldiers easily fall in-love with those who share their extreme peril and who join with them in a fusion of common effort to avert death. The same is true of most people in perilous situations, and, though much less so, in more happy but exciting situations. Such situations, however, can also be very misleading by revealing only some aspects of the sense of self and by triggering the gratitude syndrome, which is a lesser, more situational form of adoration love and self-identification that can easily be mistaken for romantic love when in fact it lacks the Erotic. Exciting, happy experiences can be even more misleading by casting a *halo effect* of happy feeling over all those identified with the experience. The extreme adoration known as *awe* can almost instantly overwhelm and shatter the boundaries of the self, producing an implosive fusion with the greater self in which the imploded self is "lost" but thereby becomes part of the greater. This is what we see in religious *conversion experiences* and some extreme dependency-love experiences. All of these are preceded by a powerful buildup of insecurities and cravings for deliverance from the dreaded situation. Albert Speer has given a remarkable description of how he fell into a desperate dependency love with Adolph Hitler the first time he heard his sonorous paean to Germany's deliverance from the depths of despair (1970, pp. 43-47).

Once the fusion of selves has gone far, unbonding is extremely painful and necessarily involves the mourning process before one can free oneself enough to begin reconstructing it (see Chapter 6). This intense inner bonding of selves is the necessary foundation for the external bonding (partnership) of practical activities that is crucial to the optimal achievement of the growth of loving partnerships. It appears in full force only in infancy when the baby falls so deeply in-love with his mother and then in adulthood when adoration is powerfully potentiated by the Erotic. Once the Erotic wanes, beginning with the waning of sexuality (in the later forties and dwindling to embers by the sixties), individuals fall in-love less and less deeply. They build friendships, and may fall into dependency if they are highly insecure. They may still be sexual and may even act out fantasy romances. But they do not *fall in-love*. They are now much freer emotionally to concern themselves with the pursuit of wisdom, friendship, and leadership within their families and beyond, which have always been the special functions of the Elders.

The successful emotion manager also realizes that emotions not only wax and wane on their own but that they are triggered and inhibited by situations, by eidetic images and scenes, and by words. When they find an abyss of miserable love looming before them, they know that the best way to avoid the free-fall into love is to avoid all situations, images, and words that trigger the love feelings. Dieters quickly learn that the most important thing in successful dieting is staying away from food, especially from the smell of it, which triggers hunger. Just as food dieters must stay out of the kitchen and out of the candy stores, so the most important thing of all to the love dieter is to stay away from the loved person. During the buildup phase of love, love is like any other addiction. Being with the loved one gratifies the craving at the time, but afterward it leaves hungry where it most satisfied, that is, with a greater craving than before. Going "cold turkey" by staying completely away from the loved one triggers depression and mourning in the short run (once into the critical range of fusion), but it also does more than anything else (except arguments—see the next chapter) to abort the buildup of the love and to allow what has already built up to become dormant. *Dormant love* is still there in the subconscious program, but the conscious, *active feeling* itself is not there and the lack of gratification does not hurt. Once a love has become dormant, the erstwhile lover is free to love someone else. But the dormant love can be fanned into a flame by the mere sight of the once actively loved one, sometimes decades later. Wives and husbands know instinctively that the spouse's getting together with the ex-spouse for a friendly chat about old times can have disastrous consequences. Even when their love was turned to hate by prolonged arguments, there is often a great deal of dormant lust waiting to be inflamed. More important, most couples these days separate and divorce before they have completely unbonded emotionally, so they remain at least partly *in-dormant-love*. The dormant lover may be completely unaware that love is still there and easily saunter into a consuming conflagration.

Emotion management is extremely difficult at best. After all, the emotions are the generalized guides for human actions and, when inflamed, direct and control perception, reason, and will. Human reason and the willpower at its disposal for counterweighting emotions is a latecomer in the great tidal drift of evolution and is like a thin mantle of earth laid over molten lava—thus liable to be blown away at any time the lava heats up. In most cultures, there is a great deal of intended and unintended building of willpower throughout life, done largely by enduring pain. Building up your willpower to the point where you can go for days without eating or drinking water, walk over hot coals barefooted, fight lions with a dagger, or dangle for hours on leather thongs tied to eagle claws piercing your flesh are sure ways to build endurance for pain. The ancient Western ethos of submission to the will of God, of endurance in the face of suffering, of temperance and chastity in all emotions, and of resignation when suffering trained everyone in building their willpower. In the nineteenth century, the ethos of rugged individualism built on this foundation and enshrined in most hearts the moral compulsion of self-reliance and the desire to be "the captain of my ship, the master of my soul." In its extreme forms, this leads to a purposeful pursuit of extremely painful activities that "steeled" and "tempered"—chastened—the willpower to endure and overcome the pains of life. Abraham Lincoln and Teddy Roosevelt were adored national heroes in good part because their lives were shining monuments to this ethos.

A minority of Western people still live by this ethos, as we see in the lives of some athletes (but not the drug addicts), the widespread respect felt for the Kennedys' endurance and courageous struggle against adversity, and the great popularity of others who follow the Lincoln and Roosevelt regimen. Most people today, however, lead sheltered lives that do not train their willpower for much more than resisting the cravings of a sweet tooth. And those subjected to the preaching of the sexual modernists are routinely subjected to massive ridicule and stigmatization of "chastity" and any such "macho" spirit. They are trained in the ethos of instant gratification, vulnerability, sensitivity, complaint, shirking of responsibility, and letting it all hang out. (The very meaning of *chastity* has been perverted as part of the revolt against the myth of Victorianism. To "Victorians," and to early sexologists like Havelock Ellis, *chastity* meant self-control over the expression of emotions. *Chastity* now means celibacy. Victorians valued chaste sexuality, not celibacy.) People who have not built their willpower, and certainly those who love by the ethos of nonresistance to lust, can rationally expect they will be unable to control the powerful passions of romantic love, once sexual lust, dependency, status lust, or any other lusts are inflamed.

THE PEAKING-OUT OF
ROMANTIC LOVE

Falling in-love is normally a peak experience for anyone not suffering from basic insecurities. Even when the loved one does not reciprocate the adoration love or Erotic passion, this is normally hidden by the self-confirming myth once the lover has fallen deeply enough into real intimacy, adoration, caring, and the Erotic to be deeply in-love. At the peak of romantic love, the lover feels more completely alive than at any other time. He soars, floats on clouds, and dances the light fantastic. He or she is full of energy, exudes warmth, and gushes with optimism. He or she is in love with the world, smiles upon all, and dreams impossible dreams.

But why do all of the powerful emotions aroused by falling in-love peak? Why do they not soar onward and upward endlessly? Could they do so? Do they have to peak? We've never encountered anyone who asked these questions. Everyone seems to take it for granted that all good feelings, and certainly those of love, cannot go onward and upward forever. The obvious reason is that no one has ever heard of anyone who fell in love endlessly. Any commonsense experience with the emotions involved in falling in-love shows that it reaches a peak and then declines. But why?

The general reasons are not obvious, but we think they are clear. Beyond an upper threshold, which is probably different for each emotion and person, the central nervous system increasingly acts to dampen the feelings aroused by any stimulus. In the case of pain, we now know that beyond a certain limit the body manufactures its own natural opiates to dampen increases in the pain. Though we know of no physiological evidence of what happens to dampen the pleasurable feelings, it is only plausible to expect that something similar is done to dampen pleasures. In a similar way, the central nervous system acts to dampen the emotional effects triggered by any stimuli over time, so that the longer they are experienced the less emotional effect they have. This is known as the *adaptation-level* (or tolerance-level) *effect*. In commonsense terms, increased familiarity breeds decreasing emotional arousal (but by no means necessarily contempt). The general evolutionary explanation for these two seems clear as well. Living and passing one's genes on demands doing a great many things in very complex relations to each other. If any emotion kept increasing, it would soon come to dominate our whole lives and we would be stuck in a rut that would soon lead to death. (We might, for example, get more and more thirsty, so that we would soon spend all our time drinking water, thereby dying of starvation or drowning, or we might become so "lovesick" that we would "pine" away for the loved one.) Our bodies thus evolved in such a way that, beyond a certain upper limit, increased stimuli triggering one emotion increasingly trigger counterweighting emotions. Dampening the successive effects of stimuli allows us to avoid staying in a self-destructive rut because new stimuli arouse our emotions more and thus our attention and actions more.

More specifically, when someone falls into the nether reaches of romantic love, a number of counterweighting emotions are increasingly triggered. The mere fact of being so emotionally dependent on another person generally begins to arouse anxiety in even the most secure person. The intensity of the love, and especially of the fusion, makes the lover's general emotional state and sense of self highly dependent on the slightest action—or feared action—of the loved one. As these netherworld lovers have incanted throughout all the ages, a mere glance of love—a mere hint of interest—can instantly trigger the most sublime bliss; and the hint of a contemptuously down-turned lip can annihilate the world. Even if the sheer intensity of the emotional dependency does not trigger a counterweighting anxiety, and that in turn a curtailing of the plummet into the abyss, there are inevitably arguments, which trigger insecurities about the self and rage against the loved perpetrator (see Chapter 6). The fusing of the sense of self with that of the other makes the self extremely vulnerable to—dependent on—anything interpreted as an attack from the loved one and produces an extreme mythification of thinking that easily transmutes any disagreement into a "vicious attack" against the self. Everyone who has fallen deeply in-love is aware of how easily a small incident of disagreement over the salt shaker can lead to a full scale nuclear showdown and a night of deep despair. After a few of these brushes with rage and self-destructive despair, all sane people level off their plummet into the abyss of romantic love and begin to crawl back toward the more level plains of human existence in the everyday world.

Sexual ecstasies are especially subject to the *adaptation-level law of diminishing excitation*. The reason is very simple. Sexual desire and ecstasy are highly dependent on very specific perceptual inputs and the repetition of these quickly leads (especially in the case of visual stimuli for men) to the dampening of their emotional effects. Sexual lust is focused on the perceptions of the body (especially for men) and on the sensations of the genitalia and other erogenous zones. No matter how creative the sex partner is in coming up with new visual images and sexual activities, sexual excitation by that person is soon dampened and at an accelerating rate. The most beautiful body in the world is soon taken for granted when it is exposed to prolonged perception. That is one reason why the sex partners of the most beautiful bodies in the world soon drift away to search for new sexual stimuli. (Other reasons are that they were attracted to such celebrity bodies out of pure lust or, more commonly, out of lust for status to assuage their insecurities.)

The very high *newness premium of lust* makes it the first aspect of romantic love to peak and begin cooling. How quickly a sexual relationship peaks and cools depends on many things, so it varies widely. Those with a pornographic bent who are turned on sexually only by the newness of the body stimuli or the newness of the sexual conquest, and have little response even to variations in behavior, may peak and decline to coldness by the end of one or two sexual episodes. The ardor of the extreme Don Juan or Doña Juanita may even be extinguished by the acquiescence of the will and not endure to intercourse. At the other extreme, the sexually obsessed may remain obsessed with one person for many years. But these are quite rare. In the absence of any reliable statistical information, we "guesstimate" from all the good evidence available that the ubiquitous normal curve (the bell-shaped curve) reigns supreme. The first year is the time-honored "guesstimate" of how long intense sexual excitement lasts for those who enter a sexual relationship with mature and experienced responsiveness. During this "honeymoon" era of the pink haze, lust often so dominates that the "lovers" cannot tell whether there is much else involved. Only when lust cools can the highly aroused be sure whether they are growing in-love.

Adoration love normally peaks more slowly, though there are always the hysterics who can ignite so explosively and burn out so quickly. Once again, the reason is simple. Most lovers grow in adoration as they grow in intimate communion. You can see and feel just about all there is to a person sexually very quickly. You cannot join another in full, intimate communion in less than many months or years. Most people, of course, will never reach the upper limits possible for feeling adoration love, because they will find the loved one less adorable than that. Most people find themselves embroiled in arguments because of sexual differences or their own insecurities long before the full potential of adoration feelings is reached. This is especially common for the quick peakers in sexuality who soon start finding themselves sexually attracted to new sex objects, thereby creating conflicts with their love partners. The Appolonian lovers grow more slowly and commune more fully with each other over many months or years and then cool only very slowly.

This cooling does not have to reach absolute zero and rarely does for those who remain partners in life. This fact is most obvious in intimate friendships. Intimate friendships can remain in that lower level of adoration (respect) love, which normally characterizes them, for a lifetime. Most of the time, one will not actively experience the respect or adoration feelings for friends. Instead, they will be dormant. But whenever they are engaged in intimate communing, the feelings spring to life. They are probably more intense after 60 years than after a mere 20. Friendships normally grow in respect or adoration and intimate communing quite slowly, at least after an initial quick run up, and can go on growing for the rest of life. They are most commonly characterized by intermittent peaks of active feeling and troughs of dormant feeling when the thought of the friend will bring a minipeak and active communion will bring the maxipeaks characterizing friendships.

Romantic loves that have cooled from their peaks may also continue to grow in adoration over a lifetime. Normally, however, there is a peak in adoration that has resulted from the pink-lens effect, under the intense mythicizing influence of lust-potentiating adoration and the

Erotic, and a cooling to lower levels due to adaptation and arguments. If, however, the partners stop the cooling and unbonding process, they may resume intimate communing (if the scar tissue has not been too severe—see Chapter 6) and rebuild some of the respect or adoration feelings. They may then experience the same intermittent peaks and troughs of active and dormant feelings and the same very slow growth of adoration. Couples who when younger were so taken up with worldly problems of jobs and children that they never became very intimate with each other may even find that they experience the adoration peak very late in life, in the "we never really knew each other" pattern.

THE COOLING OF
ROMANTIC LOVE AND THE
GROWTH OF CARING LOVE

Traditional fairy tales assure us that the hero and heroine who have fallen madly in love with each other live happily ever after. They do not assure us that they remain in their state of romantic madness permanently. In fact, their love is not normally depicted as maddening even in the beginning. The madness of love is a relic of the nineteenth-century Myth of Romantic Love, especially of the Bacchanalian strain of the Myth found far more in France than anywhere else. The rage of love— the agony and ecstasy—is part of the torment of some of the Romantics, not part of the centuries-old Western tradition of romantic love. Romantic love has always been seen as very exciting once it has reached its peak. Sex alone would guarantee that for anyone capable of orgasmic ecstasy, at least briefly. But in all civilizations it has been depicted overwhelmingly in more chaste, more Apollonian terms. Eros is a sweeping, deep, and powerful force, but not in itself a maddening or tormenting one. Romeo and Juliet are tender and happy with each other, sweet and endearing, not wild and "crazy" about each other. We can feel sure that, however sexual they were (which was not likely to be terribly so when Juliet was only 14 and Romeo quite inexperienced), their most cherished moments were the tender and sweet moments of intimate communing that follow orgasmic delights for those who are truly, intimately in-love. The hero and heroine live "happily" ever after, not in a state of perennial stormy excitement.

Stormy romances only rarely involve more than a modicum of romantic love and most involve only lust. They are called "romances" only because of the confusion of sex with love. Even stormy romances must not be confused with the merely "stormy" relationships. There are relationships that endure for many reasons in spite of being filled with storm and struggle. There are even a small percentage of stormy partnerships in which the partners are mutually dependent on each other and may complement each other quite well in some vital respects. These may even involve some sadomasochistic excitement and satisfaction. There are also romantic love partnerships that are full of playful, simulated bickering, which is more like teasing than real conflict. Freud's analysis of such humor as "tendentious" wit, which argues that it is really an expression of aggression, is quite simplistic and quite wrong for some forms of teasing. As long as the emotion that forms the background context for the interaction is love and fun, the teasing is really only play aggression, not playfully real aggression. All true love partnerships probably involve teasing and, the more happily secure they are, the more the partners seem to enjoy it. Of course, if the framework of play is broken in any way, then the teasing hurts badly because of the love-dependency on the teaser. In general, the more insecure a person, the more easily the play framework is broken for him or her.

As adoration and sexual feelings cool, loving partnerships normally become both more caring and more happy. They become more caring because the intimate communing has led to a growth in the fusion of the senses of self. It is this fusion that leads to the feeling of caring for the other and to the acts of caring that express and fulfill it. Most striking of all is the fact that even those partnerships in which adoration has cooled to the level of respect (but not below that into the nether reaches of hateful disrespect, contempt, and revulsion) can experience growing caring, as long as the intimate communing grows. People who are very caring easily develop very caring partnerships with only a modicum of growth in the intimate communing, especially if the cared for one seems to need and depend on them greatly. This can even lead to feeling "trapped" in a caring relationship with little else. Angelina realized the day before her scheduled marriage that "It'll never work!" because her husband-to-be was so immensely insecure. But then she thought, in a flash of modernist inspiration, "Ah, but I can always get a divorce." As she now says, after years of anguish, "Hah! Hah!" Angelina is very, very caring and her husband's sense of security is desperately dependent on her.

In the happy love partnerships, the growth of caring love becomes a cornerstone of the emotional foundation on which the happiness is built. As we see in the mother and child love-duet, caring love becomes the emotion that pulls the partners together when other emotions— jealousy, hurt, anger—push them apart. Given that almost all love partnerships involve some painful and stormy periods, many of them triggered by lust for newly exciting stimuli, caring is vital to building them.

Caring is also of vital importance in and of itself, just as it is for children, in those situations in which we are suffering for some reason having nothing to do with the loved one. As John Bowlby (1979) has noted, no matter how old and mature and secure someone is, they still feel a great need for the supportive caring of a loved one during times of suffering and fear. In fact, it seems to be the most insecure individuals— those who have built a false sense of security in their defensive strategy of being cold and aloof—who reject caring when they are hurt and want to be alone to care for themselves, to "lick their wounds" and feel self-pity. In the moments of greatest hurt and fear, such as those of sickness and injury, the emotions and actions of romantic love would be about as appropriate and desired as hitting the victim. The wife who gives her husband a sexing-up kiss when he is being wheeled into the operating room is not likely to be appreciated, or long endured by either the surgeon or the husband. If it's done playfully, however, it *might* be a welcome distraction and a caring promise of better things to come.

The old refrain, "Will you love me in December as you did in May?," contains the germ of folk wisdom about the importance of caring love. Romantic love will pass rather quickly, at least in its more intense form potentiated by the newly stimulated sexual lust, so the building of a happy love partnership really depends far more over the years on the building of intimate communing, on the Erotic dimensions of pro- creating and creating, and on caring love. Those who concentrate only on the intensity of adoration and lust as the criteria for launching a would-be partnership are like investors who lock themselves into a set high interest rate for 30 years, not noticing that inflation might be so high 30 years down the road that their investment will be worth almost nothing. Powerful sex drives can be an immense pleasure when you want sex, but they are also far more apt to generate problems for you, especially because they are far more apt to be unsatisfied with one partner for many years. Adoration that flares up quickly—hysterically— is most likely to be a symptom of insecurity and, thereby, to lead to arguments that lead to the fizzling of the adoration.

Very importantly, the expression and acting out of caring love is itself an inspiration of adoration love. If we suffer and someone shows us happiness about this, our response is anger and hatred. If we suffer and someone shows caring love for us, our response is adoring love and gratitude. As we have already argued, the sharing of common suffering is probably the most potent form of intimate communing. The expression of adoration love in response complements the communing partnership and also inspires adoration in the caring lover.

The tremendous importance, and the problematic complexities of these caring bonds, was shown in the reactions of three young people to a serious operation on one of them.

I had met Steven early in my teens, quickly became his friend and lover and eventually married him after high school. We had a son, were married 2 years, then went through a terribly painful divorce. We managed to remain friends, but with great pains. Although Steven has never remarried, he was involved in the most serious of his relationships since our breakup when he learned of his illness. I had remarried years before and was securely rooted in my new family life. I had always just thought of Steven as my "ace in the hole." He was there whenever I, or our son, needed him for whatever reason. When he called to tell my husband and me that he was facing life-threatening surgery I remained calm on the phone, but after we hung up I literally collapsed in my husbands arms with fear and pain, somewhat akin to mourning.

Steven was uncertain as to whether to call his parents, but a reminder of how he might feel if our son failed to call him in just such a situation was all that he needed to understand that he should call. Steven asked me while on the phone if either or both of us would be able to come to the hospital. We had assured him that either I would be there or both of us would. He was upset because his girlfriend, with whom he shared a seemingly very serious relationship, was unsure that she would be able to take off from her professionally demanding job to attend his surgery. They in fact had even gotten into a very big argument the night before when he found out he'd have to have surgery, because she didn't want to come spend the night with him. He lives 25 minutes from her so it's not like it should have been a big deal. My husband, angry that Steven's girlfriend wasn't to be there, suggested that I spend the night with him, if he needed someone to be with him.

The next day he phoned us back to let us know that she would be able to attend the surgery and asked if I would please acquiesce and let her have the lead position at the hospital with all the other family members and friends present. He even asked if I would consider not coming down until the surgery was over. Although we would have been there from the moment he arrived at the hospital until he came out of the recovery room, I yielded and did not go until later in the day and then only for a few minutes [Written for us].

These reactions of caring love, adoration love, and intimate communing are, of course, first developed in the mother-child love-duet. The basic pattern does not seem to change significantly throughout the rest of life. As we grow older, the growing ontological insecurity makes them more important. Existential psychoanalysts, such as Irwin Yalom (1980), have found that the most profound emotional problems are grounded in failures to deal adequately with the dread of death. Many of these are the result of repressing the dread inspired by a threat, resulting in many forms of symptoms. It seems entirely likely that this repression and the many other problems are largely the result of the victims not having these normal caring love partners with whom they can commune about their dread and receive the caring love they crave. Yalom has found that the growing intimacy of a group in which all share this great threat is crucial in resolving the problems. This seems very much in line with what we would expect for individuals who do not have other caring love partnerships in which they can commune about their sense of dread and all the related problems of dying.

These are also most likely individuals who do not have the intimate communion with a group of caring people who commune in common with a caring God. For those who do, God is the ultimate provider of the all-caring, selfless love known in the Western world as *agape*. Many Western paintings have shown the extreme caring mingled with adoration of God for his "children" in their time of extreme dread and the extreme adoration and awe they have given in response. As James Preston has said of mother worship:

> The sacred mother . . . can act as protectress, source of ethnic identity, and nurturant healer. She is also capable of stirring the deepest levels of religious imagination by focusing human terror and assisting in its resolution. Ambivalence, awe, and terror are linked together at the most fundamental level of the human experience.
>
> What is this deeper element calling forth human ambivalence and resonating throughout the world in the form of mother worship? What is this mixture of terror and calm lurking in the shadows of our prehistory and persisting even in modern industrialized man? Humans are vulner-

able beings. Our elaborate civilizations are but recent experiments in a long evolutionary process. Mother worship is an ancient reminder for humans of their vulnerability and their earlier dependency on the earth; for we continue to be, in the words of W. H. Auden, "children afraid of the night." Everywhere the divine mother is a focus for this profound insecurity at the root of the human experience [Preston, 1982, p. 339].

THE EXCLUSIVENESS OF BEING IN-LOVE

Both the classical tradition of love and the Romantic Love tradition saw being in-love as an exclusive union with one unique person. Sexual modernism has denied both exclusiveness and uniqueness as properties of love. The extreme wing of the modernist movement has expanded the Freudian idea of polymorphous perversity into a universal ideology of casualness that sees exclusiveness and uniqueness as pathological symptoms of "bourgeoisness." The Bloomsbury group, for example, ardently embraced the Freudian liberation ethos and reveled in their own compulsive and exhibitionist homosexuality, bisexuality, and other combinatory permutations. The modernists find great delight in recounting the widespread cultural acceptance of polygamy for men and especially in the few misinterpreted accounts of the female variety of multiple mating, polyandry (see Fuller's, 1976, analysis of the ancient myths of polyandry among the Nayars). For the most extreme of the extreme, the sexual commune became the ultimate expression of "love."

As usual, much of the disagreements here spring from talking about different things while using the same words. It is obvious, in terms of our argument so far, that anyone capable of developing loving friendships is capable of loving more than one person—in fact, of loving as many as time allows—*at the lower levels of loving fusion*. It is also obvious to anyone who has closely observed—or even taken a brief look at—a boy crazy or girl crazy teenager like Leilani in her early teens that people can have bright flashes of intense adoration love—infatuations—for many people in rapid succession. Leilani did distinguish between her "one and only true love" and the rest of the massive pack, but she saw love for him as only one or two deci-hearts more intense than that for her many other not so true loves.

The uniqueness property does not seem to exist except at the extreme. It is clear that the proclamations of "you are the only one I can ever love," "undying devotion," and so on are very sincere expressions of the mythification effects of Romantic Love at its most intense. It is obvious that most people who feel in the aftermath of love depression that "I can never love again" do in fact love again, generally within a couple of years. In spite of this, there is clear evidence indicating that "Grand Passions" do exist. A "Grand Passion" is a very intense romantic love. Just as novelists have long maintained, especially in France, only a distinct minority of people ever experience such an intense—consuming— romantic love. Also as they argue, they seem to happen only once in a lifetime to even this minority. What we do not know is whether these appearances are only a result of the low frequencies making it hard to find many cases, and exceedingly hard to find people who repeat this spiral up and down, or whether there really are no repeats. Our "guesstimate" is that anyone who has had the most intense form of romantic love has been deeply fused-in-love and that the subsequent loss of this love—which alone makes a repeat possible—is so excruciatingly painful that the victim would always after be so love-shy as to prevent a repetition. Thus uniqueness may well characterize these most intense romantic loves, but certainly does not characterize the romantic loves of the great majority of people. The "utter despair" expressed after losing a romantic lover is almost always either the result of basic insecurities being triggered by the loss or will soon be seen as mythification inspired by misery.

While this indicates that there is not *only* one unique person whom an individual can love so intensely, this does not mean that there is no uniqueness involved in being in-love. Adoration love and Erotic love, without the fusion of the sense of self, can flare up repeatedly and be rather promiscuous. But anyone who has experienced an intense fusion of the sense of self with that of the "thou"—that is, has been deeply in-love—always retains an intense sense of that individual as unique. The popular notion that prostitutes must confuse sex partners to the point where they become at least largely exchangeable, if not indis- tinguishable, is largely correct. Prostitutes generally have little feeling about their sex partners as individuals. They commonly deindividualize and depersonalize them by giving them a generic term, such as the generic term of "John," which also stigmatizes them. Sexual modernists also depersonalize the individuals by talking about "object relations" and "sexual relationships." Both are excellent descriptions of the feelings involved in *casual* sexual relationships that involve little intimate communing and fusion of the sense of self with that of the "thou." But they are completely misleading about the nature of partnerships that do involve intimate communing and self-fusion. It is precisely the unique personhood that is involved in communing and fusing. It is the vastly complex, overall experience of the whole person and the overall communing together in unique life experiences, neither of which could ever be repeated with anyone else, not even with an "identical" twin, which are the heart of our love-gestalt for that person. Even when an outsider might see a remarkable—even total—similarity between the gesture of a lover and someone else, this might not seem so to the lover. Even such a very specific characteristic may be made different by the overall context in which it is ineluctably embedded. "It's different" is all most people who have been deeply in-love manage to say on this question.

Exclusiveness seems clearly to characterize all high degrees of romantic love that also involve an intense fusion of the sense of self, both after they have died or become dormant and *during the love partnerships*. The reason for this is almost obvious. Anyone very much in-love has little sense of self left over for anyone else. Even at the higher levels of romantic love, and especially during the time of the peak experience, the sheer intensity of the emotion focuses attention almost exclusively on the loved one (see Tennov, 1979). During this "I only have eyes for you" phase, even the closest of friends become largely irrelevant and almost all free time is spent with the loved one—or is spent talking to him or her on the phone in our modern version of near-nearness. As we have argued, great emotions focus attention intensely. When the fusion of selves is added to this, or even to a considerably lower level of it, the lover is "too much in love" to fall in love with anyone else.

This does not mean the lover is incapable of feeling sexual lust for others. Sex is the "wild card" in human love. It is highly responsive to external stimuli and thus to the situation. People who think they are very much in-love with more than one person are commonly confusing their lust feelings and other feelings of excitement and fun, status cravings, dependency cravings, and so on with being in-love. As usual, this is found predominantly in inexperienced young people. But people very much in-love do sometimes "stray" sexually. This happens primarily when they are away from the loved one for a long time and the love becomes partially dormant. This is especially likely to happen in very new situations where the situational stimuli do not arouse the feelings of love and do arouse sexual lust. The "love boat" romance has long been known commonsensically to be the perfect example of this. Of course, anyone very much in-love is not likely to want to take such a cruise without the loved one and such romantic attachments tend to be tightly bound to their situations of origin, quickly evaporating with the harsh realities of everyday life, especially with the harsh realization that the "lover" really is in-love with someone else—their spouse or partner (see Janine's description in Chapter 6 of Lee's cruise on the love boat).

The sexual betrayal of the loved one in these ways is normally experienced as a betrayal and induces intense guilt. This is especially true in our culture, where sexual exclusiveness is still very much a part of our inherited ideas about romantic love, but we suspect it is true in all other cultures as well. This, however, will not normally be seen as much in the marriages of other cultures because marriages are far more often contracted for reasons other than being in-love. (Anthropologists, historians, and others have sometimes failed to make the vital distinctions here. They have also too easily focused their attention on the exceptions to their own experience and fallen into the Bongo-Bongo trap.) The more identification of the self there is with the lover, the more a betrayal of the loved one is experienced as a betrayal of the self. These may be repressed, and sexual modernists who assume that all such ideas are merely hand-me-down repressions from Victorians routinely repress such guilt feelings. One young woman whose first love had left her for greener pastures summed this all up in her guidelines for fidelity for her second husband: "If I ever found out he'd been with someone else, I would nail him to the wall by his balls, hand him a knife and set the room on fire."

WORKING AT BUILDING
LOVE PARTNERSHIPS

As we made clear in our Preface, our focus in this book is on developing a theory that helps us to understand love, intimacy, and sex as cornerstones of human nature and of our Western cultures. Because of this, we cannot devote much of our precious space to analyzing those aspects that are peculiar to our extraordinary and, we suspect, temporary cultural situation. But one aspect of this situation is of such sweeping importance it demands at least a cursory analysis.

It is clear that the basic dimensions of love, intimacy, and sex are highly primed genetically. But this certainly does not mean that they can stand alone, independent of culture and community support. We are also cultural and social beings by genetic necessity. Love partnerships evolved in complementary dependency with cultural ideas, values, and institutions and with patterns of community action which strongly supported them. Love partnerships are the cornerstones of culture and society, but cultural and community supports are in turn cornerstones of love partnerships. Love partnerships unsupported by culture and society crumble, just as culture and society crumble when the love partnerships that form much of their foundation are eroded.

By one of the ironic twists of historical drift, the Romantic Love myth of the eternal and undying love, formed outside of cultural and social bounds, has worked hand in glove with the sexual modernist attack on everything but casual sexual relationships to undermine cultural and social support for love partnerships. The ideologue who attacks marital constancy and filial devotion out of repugnance finds the Romantic acquiescing because "Romance" supposedly transcends mere social institutions and filial obligations. (The American Romantic is also encouraged in this by the "rugged individualist" who places the emphasis on the cowboy individualist riding off alone into the setting sun.) As both Romantics and modernists might put it, "No one should be a martyr to a boring marriage or to illusions that children need stability in parental love." These strange bedfellows have teamed up with the mass media, the masses, and the politicians befuddled by such illusions to wither away most cultural and social supports for the love partnerships that are by far the most important in the development of our senses of selves and, thereby, to all of culture and society.

Anyone with much experience and a modicum of wisdom now recognizes that successful love partnerships of all forms are not made in heaven, nor do they just happen by genetic programming. They must be "worked at"—constructed—wisely and with perseverance by the partners. (Both heaven and the genes provide only open-ended, heuristic rules and rule programs. Adam and Eve must construct the specific meanings of these and the specific patterns of action to meet the concrete situations that emerge. We shall see more about how they do this in Chapter 6.) What even most experienced and wise people tend to overlook today, because of the complementary blandishments of the Romantics and the modernists, is that successful love partnerships are also the outcome of wise and persistent work by culture creators and by communities in support of them.

Today our cultural educators are busily analyzing parent-child love-duets in terms of incestuous lust and murderous rage; our journalists are extolling the latest "discoveries" of "creative divorce" and of how happy children are that it is finally over; our moviemakers are mass producing bright paeans to casualness; our sexual gurus on television are exorcising any remnants of "hang-ups" over devotion and self-sacrifice to love partnerships; and our politicians are knocking away the last legal impediments to the casual escape to the mythical delights of a Tahitian paradise. Certainly there are countertrends, including a great gnashing of collective teeth over our "cultural crisis" of love and our epidemics of sexual disease and psychic misery. But the dominant thrust is obviously the attack on the remaining cultural and social supports for love partnerships. Rather than "working at love," most of our cultural creators and social leaders are working against love partnerships even to the extreme of eliminating all linguistic reference in school textbooks to "marriage," "husband," and "wife." It is true that "mother" and "father" have not yet been replaced by "nurturer," by "money-object," or "legal dispenser of welfare payments," but the trend is clear.

In this "cultural crisis," even the wisest, most secure, and most loving individuals can easily fail in their most devoted love-work and find their most cherished partnerships—the cornerstones of their lives—crumbling away. Only the reconstruction of cultural and social supports fitting our situations will change that. Until that is done, our crisis and our epidemics will grow. Even more individuals will experience the awful miseries of falling out of love and slowly rediscover the joys of starting over.

NOTE

1. There were always a few dissonant notes sounded about the physical and cultural characteristics of the newly discovered peoples. Remarkably, the vast majority of these were sounded over one people, the Hottentots or Bushmen of southern Africa. They are probably the most unusual people in the world genetically, at least in their genetic inputs into physical appearance. Most peoples are not very different from the median human physical characteristics. The Hottentots probably have the widest variations. They were also very different culturally. When Europeans first discovered them by accident in the early seventeenth century, they found them very agreeable, but their striking differences focused attention on them. From the seventeenth century right up to today's anthropology texts, they became the favorite example of Bongo-Bongoism in matters of physical appearance and thus of the debate over whether beauty is universal or only in the culturally conditioned eye of the beholder.

6

FALLING OUT OF LOVE, DIVORCING, AND STARTING OVER

Love is an exquisite flower, but one must have the courage to go and gather it on the brink of a dreadful precipice.

Stendhal

"I never thought it could happen to us." "They seemed made for each other, but . . .." "Where did we go wrong?" "Was it something I did?" "We did everything we could for him, so why did he turn on his own parents?" On and on rolls the litany of perplexity over failed love. Falling out of love is probably more of a mystery to most people than falling in love. And the agony and sense of despair that normally accompany the falling out process make the questions about it far more strident and pressing. Before trying to answer why, let us look at how people fall out of love.

REAL "DE-FUSIONS" VERSUS DECEPTIVE BREAKS

"Falling in-love" is a nearly universally shared idea in our society because free choice and affluence have made romantic love a common experience. Why is "falling out of love" not heard? Probably because the actual experience is not so compellingly described in terms of "falling." Falling in-love normally involves a period of rapidly accelerating falling, during which the individual has some sense of the critical range, or "turning point," and losing control. Some falling out of love experiences are just like that, a reverse mirror image of falling in-love. But more of the downward slopes of partnerships might better be called "stumbling out of love" and some are already popularly called "growing apart" or "growing away from each other." Rather than being swept off a cliff into an abyss of despair, the opposite of being swept off one's feet into soaring ecstasy, most love partnerships gone awry stumble along from one minicrisis to growing minicrises; and it is not clear to those stumbling around in the dark, clashing in the "fogs of marital discord," until things are pretty bad indeed that they are careening downward. In fact, there are the experiences of "making up" and feeling "better than ever" (see below) that hide the steady downward drift process from them. And, of course, just as people are often set by ecstatic anticipation to see themselves falling in-love, even when they are not, so are they set defensively to deny they are falling out of love, because at the end of the fading rainbow lies a cauldron of misery. (The massive mythification normally involved in divorce processes is well understood by researchers. See Rasmussen and Ferraro, 1979; Kitson and Sussman, 1982; Booth et al., 1985; Menaghan, 1985.)

Let's note first that those who merely "grow apart" were never much in-love. Failing to distinguish them from those who really fall out of love obscures the process of falling out of love. Red-hot fires of lust may taper off and finally die away into cold embers of disinterest without precipitating the cooling ones into misery, depression, or anything else except possibly regret that the good times are gone. Those who were merely companionate spouses with a little sex thrown in for fun will normally part with a sense of sadness, such as you feel when you move to a new neighborhood and must leave your old friends. But there is no call for a great gnashing of teeth, searching of despairing souls, and emotional battering all around, unless there are children who must suffer a real falling out of love with an "abandoning" parent.

Of course, even casual sex couplers might go through some mutual battering. In fact, this emotional battering can sometimes be quite painful. This is normal when one or both of them feel betrayed sexually or otherwise by the other, thus feels more insecure about the sense of self. The betrayal makes them feel that something must be wrong with them sexually or otherwise, that they have been fools incapable of judging others, and so on. The victims commonly feel the intense situational insecurities of shame and embarrassment, roughly in direct proportion to their general sense of insecurity or security and to the degree to which they believe their status (reputation) is diminished with those from whom they crave prestige (esteem). This shame and embarrassment is often mistaken for jealousy because it springs indirectly from a sex partners' betrayal and leads to many of the same expressions of emotion and actions. Jealousy, however, is more directly aimed at controlling the love and Erotic emotions and actions of the loved one, or lusted-for one. The emotional expressions and actions springing from shame and embarrassment are more directly aimed at eliminating or compensating for the sense of being a *sexual failure* or *sexually submissive*. Lord Mountbatten apparently felt little jealousy over the sexual affairs his wife had, or, at the least, became quite resigned to his despised status as a sexual failure and cuckold. He even wrote a moving and intimate letter expressing deep caring love for her when one of her lovers died. But he was still haunted by the feelings of shame and embarrassment springing from his despised status and counterweighted these by his strenuous, often highly dangerous and completely successful pursuit of the apotheosized status of hero (see Ziegler, 1985).

Unbonding from a sexual obsession is normally far more painful and stormy, independent of any feelings of shame or embarrassment. A sexual obsession is a sexual addiction with powerful sexual cravings and withdrawal pains when the one lusted for is not available (see Chapter 5). Losing the lustee, especially if it is sudden—*going cold turkey sexually*—produces the usual withdrawal symptoms of depression and anxiety. Slowly growing apart sexually—*sexual detoxing*—can reduce these to manageable ranges, especially if the cravings are counterweighted with lust for new sexual objects. Sudden withdrawals mimic the emotional and behavioral characteristics of the catastrophic breaks in love partnerships, but generally at a lower level (unless basic insecurities are triggered) and last a much shorter period of time. Given that many cohabitations and marriages today are conceived far more in obsessive lust than love, while the participants mistake their feelings and relationships for those of love partnerships, observers are often led to believe that falling out of love and divorcing can be smooth, easy, and quick—a creative lark for some dull weekend. As Angelina said, "Hah! Hah!" (Almost all divorce researchers echo Angelina's balanced appraisal.)

Many people do not understand their emotions and are led by Romantic and modernist misunderstandings, and by the quickie "no-fault divorces," to break up almost instantaneously, without any of the unbonding process we shall see is normal. These *catastrophic breaks* are most commonly the result of one giant argument, but sometimes they are more the result of a misunderstanding of one's self and of all the fate-laden meanings of unbonding and divorce.

Over the years, we have closely observed several friends involved in these sudden, irrevocable breaks. They normally come when one partner feels betrayed by discovering the other is involved sexually with someone else or because one feels an "irresistible" craving for someone else. The stormy passions of these arguments hide from them the fact they are still in-love. Ratean was one young woman who discovered that a sudden break can leave the victim very much in-love:

I'd never been in love at all until this fall. I guess I was always too shy and too busy, since I work pretty hard in school. Anyhow, I always wanted to, but didn't. Then I met Tom. He's a lot older than I am, ten years older, in fact. I met him through a friend who knew him a little bit. We got along terrifically from the very first date. I don't know, he just seemed really neat, very intelligent, very caring, loving. He courted me completely and totally. I could feel he was really in love with me—he certainly acted like he was. So I knew this was it—I'd found the man for me.

I knew he'd been in love before. In fact, he was married for several years, then his wife ran away with some other guy, totally out of the blue, no warning, no idea that something was wrong. Just puuf—she was gone one day when he came home. He was really depressed for a long time. I was the first girl he'd dated since the Great Betrayal. Anyhow, I didn't care much about the earlier woman and it didn't seem to be his fault—it was her fault, not his. So I was really falling head over heels. I was really in love.

Then my parents went away for a few weeks' vacation in the desert. I'd never asked him to come over to the house before, but now we were real serious, so I asked him to come over for dinner. I put the dinner on first, before he got there. Then when he came I was so excited I just let it go—woosh! We made love for the first time—the first time EVER! Then, a lot later, I served dinner. I didn't feel hungry, but it was a special dinner, so I went ahead with it. It was very special, complete with champagne.

After dinner, we drank some more champagne. And some more. Tom just kept drinking and he started getting sadder and sadder. Then he started crying and, while I held his head to try to comfort him, and while I was worrying furiously about what I might have done to hurt him so badly, he blurted out, "I can't love you, I can't. I'm still in love with my wife. For the first time I can see that I never quit loving her, not at all. I love her as much as ever, just like the day she left me. Maybe I always will, I don't know, but I still do now. And I just can't make myself love you while I still love her."

I guess the champagne allowed him to feel what he couldn't feel when he was stone-sober. Anyhow, he meant it. He left right away and I haven't seen him since. It was terrible. I just cried and cried for days. I was depressed for a few months. I didn't know how bad it could hurt or that it could go on so long. Once I found out from my friend that he still felt the same after a few months, I became resigned. Then I would bury myself in my work and it wasn't so bad. But I sure wouldn't want to go through that again in one lifetime [From memory, written at the time].

These sudden breaks normally do not produce much unbonding by those who have been in-love. The love feelings and, especially, the fusion of selves remain largely intact. These are often denied or repressed in some other way, as a way of avoiding the feeling of having made a terrible and irreversible mistake, or to bury the pain. Some people, however, are very aware of what a terrible mistake they've made and are haunted by guilt for this. The inability to satisfy the demands of the remaining love and fusion produce protracted bouts of depression, craving, feeling lost, anxiety, panic, obsessive attention to the loved one, and counterweightings with sexual relationships and other "escapes" until they become dormant.

In some instances, the discovery of a great betrayal, especially the direct observation of a flagrant betrayal, seems to produce an inversion of feelings of adoration love into feelings of contempt. Just as one can suddenly fall into adoration love, as we see in the bright flashes of "infatuation" most common in adolescence, so one can suddenly *fall into contempt*. But this still leaves the fusion of the senses of selves. If there is only the fusion to contend with, the feelings of depression, craving, and so on will be much less, but the sense of being lost, of losing much of the sense of self, and even of being unreal will still be there, especially in those situations in which communion with the loved one took place. *Separation panics* seem to be agoraphobic panics and these seem especially common in those who suffer from early insecurity.

Most catastrophic breaks are precipitated by only one of the erstwhile partners. This is generally the *initiator of the unbonding process* who has been falling out of love with the other person at a more rapid pace than the other has been falling out of love (Rasmussen and Ferraro, 1979). This is seen most starkly in the classic scenario of the

"Dear John" (Jill) letter in which the partner still in-love has been unaware that the other was unbonding and heading for termination. Though they are commonly aware something was "wrong," the sudden revelation and departure of the loved one comes as a tremendous shock, both emotionally and cognitively. Because the "desertion" does not make sense rationally or emotionally, and because he has not been subconsciously preparing for it, he generally feels quite deranged mentally. What has happened does not seem real and, in his state of emotional shock, John often fears that he is literally going insane. The emotional shock involves filtering of the perceptions of reality to buffer their emotional effects and this produces a sense of derealization, making the world seem less real than normal. John casily fears that he is "losing contact" with reality. Our prototypical John described it for us:

I knew things weren't right—we were doing less and less together and she had grown very reluctant and passive sexually. I felt very isolated, especially since we lived in the small cottage on the ranch owned by her mother. It got so bad that I would go out and talk to the horses at night. At school, it was my first year of graduate work. People were friendly, but mostly new and submerged in a general ethos of competitiveness. I was popular with the female undergraduates, but was far too attached to [my wife] to pursue any of them. I actually turned down an open invitation with the "I love my wife" line. She left suddenly. I came home from a late evening seminar to a laconic note, saying that she had left, without saying why or for where. I went crazy. I couldn't believe it. I tried desperately to find her, change things, return together. I gave away my St. Bernard [a point of contention], I started reading the bible. [She had recently been "born again".] To no avail. My neighbors and good friends kept me from going crazy. Months went by before I realized it was over. I sold the horses and moved off the ranch. We were divorced that summer. She never even came down for it [Written for us. We observed John going through this state of shock].

In these asymmetric catastrophic breaks, the victim is often still suffering from the self-validating pink-lens effect, so he refuses to believe that the loved one does not love him in return, even if the loved one heaps scorn on him and shouts rejection of him from the rooftops. He may make repeated appeals to her to reconsider and "see" how she really feels before it is too late. He dreams obsessively, by day and by night, of her return and often refuses to remove himself from the site of communion—their erstwhile home—because he "knows deep down" that she "must" return to him. Sometimes his rational mind will "pooh-

pooh" such Romantic piffle, while his subconscious mind goes right on preparing for her return and performing magical rituals of loving endearment and propitiation. He sees inner and greater truths, which his friends see as only the illusions of *desperate love*. He "runs around in circles," trying desperately to figure out rationally what has happened, why she is acting in this absurd way, how he can convince her of the truth, but his obsessive cogitation only produces more confusion and despairing conviction that "she must really . . . "

Often the partners careening downward suffer *mutual unbonding madness* in which the initiator is just as subject to this obsessive mythification process in reverse, such as the conviction that "No, we never loved each other—the whole thing was a mistake from the word 'Go!'" The perpetrator of unbonding is often also involved in obsessive mythification of an idealized Romantic Lover waiting just beyond the magic portal of "Freedom"! These perpetrators suffer both guilt and the undertone agonies of unbonding, which seem to potentiate each other and produce massive mythification alternating between pink hopes for deliverance and gray dreads of doom. Most perpetrators are far more manipulative, but their guilt is normally not fully hidden by their mythical cloud of recrimination against the victim. The more guilt pricks them, the more they must attack the victim—"protest too much"—and deny any lingering love, or any love ever; and the more they must see deliverance just beyond the magic portal.

The desperate refusal to accept rejection does not seem to be increased by basic insecurity. Quite to the contrary, it seems clearly to be increased greatly by a basic sense of being lovable. The individual who is haunted by the feeling of being unlovable is not that surprised to discover that someone has rejected him or her—once again. When John (Jill) is convinced "deep down" that he is lovable, it does not seem to make sense that someone whom he loves so greatly and whom he would "do anything for" should reject him so painfully. Someone who was rejected or hated by a mother or father is very apt to feel, "There she (he) goes again!"

Catastrophic breaks do not produce de-fusion (or unfusion) because *protracted conflict is necessary to "free" the sense of self from the fusion with the other*. As we have seen, the mere passage of time, even of decades, only leads to the love fusion falling into dormancy, lying there ready to spring into life. Just as falling in-love at first sight does not involve a real fusion with the other's sense of self, so a sudden falling out of love does not involve a real de-fusion. De-fusion is largely independent of the losing of adoration love or the Erotic. Even when erstwhile lovers have gotten into the netherworld of mutual hatred, they may go on feeling very "close" to each other and caring for each other when they are endangered or hurt. Divorce researchers now commonly see this in Bowlby's ethological terms as *separation* anxiety and depression (Bohannan, 1971; Weiss, 1976; Trafford, 1982; Berman, 1985). This is seen most starkly in many cases of physically battered wives and emotionally battered spouses who "keep going back for more" even when they no longer have respect, adoration love, or lust for the batterer and have actual dread of him. One of the things they most commonly say to explain to the stunned onlookers why they are going back for more is "He needs me!" The fusion and caring have continued and carried the lover right into *hard love* (see Walker, 1979; Finkelhor et al., 1983; Denzin, 1984).

The most extreme instances are those of the battered child syndrome. People expect battered or abused children to be afraid of the parent and thus to show a desire to escape from him. But the exact opposite is commonly the case in the very young. The battered child tends to cling to the battering parent.

Some of these recalcitrant victims are participants in *caring love spirals downward*. The fusion of the sense of self with that of someone else is a one-way process. If left alone, it does not alter when it finds alteration in the situation or even in the self of the other. Because this is exactly what we have seen in parent-child love partnerships, it should not surprise us that the later love partnerships are basically the same. Mothers and fathers still normally identify with and care for their children when they have grown from tiny acorns into giant oaks, unless they go through protracted conflict and de-fuse. Romantic love partners can still identify with and care for each other even when they have changed from extremely indulgent honeymooners into bickering misfits for each other. The question is, what does produce the de-fusion of the sense of self from that of someone else?

Only the protracted conflict of repeated Big Arguments produces de-fusing. Everyone is vaguely aware that arguments—bitter conflicts—are the clashing cymbals of falling out of love and divorcing. But they are commonly seen as mere symbols—epiphenomena—of underlying differences of values and desires. While this is a partial truth, it also obscures the crucial truth. We have already noted that people can bicker with each other, or rave and rant, or batter and smash, without de-fusing. There is something special about the arguments that lead to de-fusing that separates them from the humdrum arguments that beset all intimate partnerships that last very long.

BIG ARGUMENTS AND DE-FUSING

The arguments that produce de-fusing of the sense of self from that of the love partner are those that are felt to threaten the basic sense of self itself (or its system of defenses, which in turn threatens the sense of self). The more arguments are felt to threaten the basic sense of self, the more de-fusing they tend to produce. The crucial thing is that the individual *feels* threatened in his or her basic sense of self. The greatest *feeling of threat* comes from those arguments in which the lover feels that the loved one *intends* to attack his or her basic sense of self. This is experienced as love *betrayal,* a betrayal of trust and of the intimate communing that is at the heart of being in-love. It is often referred to by expressions such as, "He really knows how to hit me where it hurts the most," and "She purposefully hits below the belt." John Johnson, who has worked extensively with violent men, found that counselors use the concept of "pushing buttons" to sensitize the men to those very issues that are most likely to threaten the self and produce a fight that can escalate into violence.

These Big Arguments are grounded in the vastly complex historical context of each love partnership. Outsiders commonly see them as highly bizarre, irrational, and even petty. This, however, is only because they do not really know the context and the emotions involved and thus cannot see why the individual feels so threatened. Very importantly, they cannot see that what is presented in an offhand manner, as if it were merely part of the everyday humdrum, is really a deadly thrust at the sense of self of the lover. Even very close friends watching the deadly duels that go on in the *endgames* of love (see below) are commonly not aware of these heart-thrusts when they go on in front of them, unless one of them intends to reveal the thrusts in order to shame, embarrass, or induce guilt in the other. The partners alone know each other well enough to craft the right emotional stilettos and they may know the friends well enough to veil their thrusts successfully. One highly observant student of the human heart told us of such a love duel between some close friends:

> I've known Jon extremely well for many years. He's a real open guy, even to the point of telling me, after we'd been friends for years, about his "Don

Juan complex." He and his wife fell in love way back in junior high and were real close. I think he was always much more in love with her than he realized. Anyhow, he went to graduate school and joined the ranks of the nouveau proletariat, while Wendy jumped on the fast track as a managerial yuppie. His profs were ego-bashing him, while her top managers were massaging her ego with raises, titles and perks. He couldn't handle it, so he set out to pump up his deflated ego by conquering beautiful young women. (I think he always felt insecure about himself—God knows why.) He'd been a good bit of a womanizer and boozer in college, almost losing Wendy over this wild oats period. I think he just fell back on this old tried and true ego builder when the going got rough with Wendy, but he never said that. He became a real Don Juan and eventually seemed to flaunt his conquests by letting Wendy see enough to know what was really going on. I think he was trying to put her down, deflate her ego so it'd be down to his own blow-out level. But he sure never said that. Anyhow, she must have gone through the wringer until she couldn't take it any longer.

She started hitting back with deadly accuracy. They had dinner with us one evening and everything seemed rosy. At one point we got to talking about sex and Wendy just said, very casually, "Jon's not much into sex." Considering his Don Juan trip, it seemed a strange thing to say, but I didn't make much of it. Jon went to the bathroom and then we continued dinner. It was months before he told me how devastated he'd been by her casual remark. He went to the bathroom to throw up. But he kept his cool—until months later she left him a "Dear John" note and set sail. He went into a tailspin of depression and guilt. That was about six years ago and he's into his third marriage, but I don't think he's gotten over it. It's not just that he got kicked in his ego-balls. I think he's long since over that, but I don't think he's got Wendy out of his system, probably never will [Written for us].

The lover with whom you have communed deeply is the person who knows intuitively the most about your innermost secrets, the secrets of your sense of insecurity and security, the secrets of your innermost self, the secrets of your security system of defenses, the secrets you hold most dear about your love partnership, and the secrets of your worldly affairs that can be used to undo you in your struggle with rivals and enemies. When your lover begins to use those secrets to attack in the ways that can hurt the most—the attack directed at the sense of self, either directly or indirectly by attacking your system of self-security defenses, it normally comes as a tremendous shock.

The threatening attack may be done as a provocation to goad you into counterattacking, thereby "justifying" escalation of the love-war by counterattacking with even more deadly weapons, all drifting toward unbonding and divorce (see the discussion of the endgame of love below). At the other extreme, it may be an accident, a chance statement or action, that is misinterpreted as an intended attack. Obviously, the more insecure an individual is in general, the more he or she will tend to interpret what is said and done by the lover as a threat. This is most pervasive and extreme with basic insecurities, but situational insecurities can also lead to such fatal misinterpretations. The young man who has just been fired from his job can see his pregnant wife's question, "What are we going to do now?," as an indictment of his whole manhood—"Oh, so you think I'm not man enough to find another job to support you and the baby?" Undiscounted insecurities mythically weight our cognitive interpretations in the direction of anticipating, and hence defending against, the thing feared. They then tip the whole partnership in the direction of unbonding, for defending against these misinterpretations sets in motion the fatal *self-reinforcing spiral downward.*

Regardless of whether the felt attack is intended, it is defended against in direct proportion to the victim's own insecurities, in the ways the individual normally defends his or her sense of self and self-security system. Ordinary arguments take sudden turns—"flare up"—when some thrusts "hit home" to the victims' sense of self or security defenses. Some people withdraw into splendid aloofness. Most counterattack against the attacker's sense of self and self-security system, which normally leads to an escalation of the love-war with more threatening attacks, which in turn leads to more of the same.

Because of this *vicious spiral into insecurity and defensive counterattack,* the seemingly most innocent comment at dinnertime about the salt shaker can soon lead to an all-out love war of mutual attrition. Once the self feels threatened enough, the counterattacks may become *quite* spiteful, that is, launched with almost no rational regard for their long-run effects. Contrary to what biologists often argue about "spitefulness," while the arguers do not think rationally at this point, spitefulness is not irrational. The attacks on the self and on the defensive self-security system can be so great a threat to the sense of self that protecting the sense of self and its security system in the immediate situation is the only rational course. This fact easily escapes cold technicians who have not experienced the immense pain of being attacked at this basic level by a greatly loved person. Anyone who is truly in-love is inherently vulnerable and in that sense emotionally dependent on the lover, and life itself is in the balance when arguments flare up. (We suspect that arguments with the most loved persons are the most common triggers of suicides, and arguments with the once most loved persons, a common trigger of homicides.)

The most explosive and self-destructive love partnerships are those in which both individuals are highly insecure from the beginning and through their arguments become mine fields of situated insecurities for each other. Each is primed by insecurities instantly to mythicize casual comments or offhand actions into deadly threats to the self. Either one who—perhaps in a moment of feeling especially vulnerable (open or dependent) and insecure—first launches a defensive foray is likely to precipitate a vicious spiral downward into all-out, spiteful attacks. Given that the insecure often attract each other and drift together as a last resort, there are always a great many of these mutual insecurity pacts waiting to self-destruct.

Partners who are both reasonably secure about themselves tend to *dampen* or buffer the potential threats launched by accident or because of temporary feelings of situational insecurity. The generally secure person who also feels secure and trusting in a love partnership may feel a twinge of anxiety and defensive anger when such a threat is made, yet contain it and respond in a way that dampens it, rather than reinforcing it. A simple statement, such as "You don't really mean that, do you?," may parry even a well-aimed thrust and elicit an apology or disclaimer from a secure partner that de-fuses the whole potential argument. An insecure person whose particular insecurities are counterbalanced (complemented) by the particular securities of a more secure partner may also achieve a quite stable partnership. This, in fact, was part of the traditional image of ideal married partnerships.

It is perfectly obvious that anyone struggling with the great risks involved in wresting a living from the soil, fighting enemies, struggling with rivals, or whatnot will suffer at times from great situational insecurities. The traditional theory of the secure family life, which seems to have reigned supreme for thousands of years in somewhat varying forms in all civilizations, was that the husband shouldered most of these outside insecurities, while the wife and children stayed largely clear of them and provided him with a safe harbor where he could withdraw from the world's outrageous misfortunes and recoup his sense of security. By not telling his wife and children much about those outside insecurities and putting on a happy front about them, he protected them from much insecurity. Meanwhile, the situational insecurities suffered by the wife and children in the more immediate home and garden environment were shouldered by them and the husband was largely protected from them by silence and a happy front. If we assume, as seems plausible, that, on average, half of life's situational insecurities would be experienced in the home and half outside, and that they were not likely to occur at the same time, this arrangement would seem to compartmentalize and stagger much of life's trials so that each person would have to bear only about half of them and would likely be supported by a situationally secure partner when suffering most of them.

At the same time, the high degree of separation of work roles along sexual lines found in all previous cultures, though with significant variations in degrees, meant that men and women love partners did not normally become sources of nonfamily status (dominance) or competence insecurity for each other. Men competed against men and women against women, but not against each other. They thus became complementary supports for each other. The man could cheer the woman on without posing any insecurity threat for himself and she could do the same for him. Because all cultures arrived at roughly the same general *complementary family balance* of this sort, with all civilizations merely developing it further, it must have worked tolerably well to express and fulfill human nature and cultural training (see Parsons and Bales, 1955; Payne, 1985).

This does not mean that we are about to start a great political crusade to return to extreme gender role differentiation. We are not involved in love politicizing and we frankly do not know whether the recent variations from the ancient security arrangement are merely temporary or will prove to be long-run solutions to new problems created by vast changes in technology. We suspect some major changes will be permanent. What we do know is that *young people who have veered most sharply away from this ancient complementary balance are suffering great insecurities that reinforce each other and tend very easily to become vicious spirals of love unbonding leading to shell relationships and divorce* (see Kitson and Sussman, 1982). This may simply be because the new patterns are so new that people have not learned how to recognize the insecurities they produce and then to prevent or dampen them. When both love partners are suffering the same kinds of insecurities at the same time and not complementing each other by compartmentalizing and providing safe harbors, and counterweighting each other's insecurities by providing securities, and when they are both competing for the same general status items (money and competence, prestige, fame, and power in work life), the insecurity spiral potentials are highly explosive. The astronomic rates of love misery, therapy, counseling, unbonding, and divorce found among these young people bear stark testimony to the mutually reinforcing insecurities they are suffering. (Because they commonly are educated modernists, they put off marriage until many years later than the nonmodernists who have not gone to college. The modernist miseries show up mainly in unbonding over the years before they actually get married. The official divorce statistics vastly underestimate the love miseries of these young modernists.)

FALLING INTO THE
DOWNWARD SPIRAL—
AND PULLING OUT

If arguments are the immediate cause of unbonding, it might seem simple enough to prevent unbonding by simply avoiding arguments. But that is obviously not the case. Why? Because some people want to "browbeat" their partners into submission; some want to goad their partners into counterattacking, so they can feel justified in leaving (see below); some are the victims of situated circumstances, as we have just argued; and most do not understand themselves or their partners well enough to avoid falling into arguments over and over again. The optimistic American view that all conflicts are the result of misunderstandings is a great misunderstanding of human beings, most obviously of those human beings who very systematically plan to degrade, use, domineer, injure, and destroy other human beings. But it contains an important nugget of truth for understanding conflicts between most love partners. In our society, at least, most arguments between lovers do spring from misunderstandings.

As we have argued, basic insecurities and great situational insecurities are very commonly not recognized as such by the individuals suffering them, at least until they are well past youthful loves. They commonly suppress them into their peripherally conscious or subconscious thoughts or repress them entirely. (Men are far more likely to do so because of our cultural rule of masculine strength and self-confidence). As a result, they do not understand that they are insecure, even when they feel the dread, anxiety, and depression—and show all of their symptoms—that are core aspects of the insecurity. (Psychiatrists find that even the severely depressed often do not know they are suffering depression.) Not understanding their insecurities, they are not generally very good at anticipating what will trigger their dread or rage, or at understanding that they have mythified minor events into monstrous threats to their selves—"made mountains out of molehills."

At the same time that people hide their insecurities from themselves, they are hiding them from others. Most people are even better at hiding their insecurities from all but the most experienced and wise observers than at hiding them from themselves. Those who are quite conscious of their great insecurities often become experts at hiding them from others. Beautiful women sometimes train themselves in front of mirrors to hide their insecurities, even to present the picture of the "supremely confident and coldly aloof beautiful woman" to the world in precisely those situations where they feel most insecure. Today there are millions of people engaged in formal training in how to hide and suppress—as well as to overcome—shyness, and in presenting the general picture of self-confidence that is so important in being or appearing to be a success. When all of this consciously deceitful self-presentation is combined with all of the lack of self-understanding, and these are filtered through the pink-lens of romantic love, it is not difficult to see why people are so commonly misled about the insecurities of the people with whom they fall in-love. The man who marries "the most beautiful woman in the world" may intend only to be helpful by pointing out to his new, "supremely confident" bride that she has a tiny pimple on her nose. If so, he will be genuinely shocked when she attacks him in a rage as a cruel wife batterer, or collapses into paroxysms of sobbing, or withdraws behind a wall of ice.

Because most people today enter into love partnerships without the long months of "getting to know" each other—that is, before love and lust mythification set in—that growing up together and long courtships used to provide, it is almost inevitable that they will trigger each other's insecurities at times and precipitate arguments. This is all the more likely because the commonsense knowledge of the astronomical rates of love failure makes most people situationally insecure about their partnerships in the early years and because most people still share enough of the Myth of Romantic Love to believe that true love can be—and should be—free of arguments. Every little argument easily seems like a betrayal of "true love" and the beginning of the end, thereby triggering more insecurity, thereby triggering mythification . . . and soon one of the partners is proclaiming, "I should have listened to my mother about you!," and thereby precipitating a spiraling plunge into the abyss.

These misunderstandings are multiplied greatly by the tremendous variety of cultural and family backgrounds now found in new American love partnerships. Even experts on love partnerships often do not anticipate some of the fateful consequences that such differences can have. The very meanings of "arguments" can differ wildly from one American subculture to another and lie in waiting as a thinly veiled abyss for young partners. In Woody Allen's famous movie, *Annie Hall*, he depicts the typical (if overdrawn) Eastern European Jewish family in New York having dinner in their apartment next to the subway. Throughout the meal, everyone is talking, shouting, gesticulating, sometimes even making what appear to most Americans as threatening gestures and tones of voice. The Jewish antihero then visits his very midwestern, Anglo-Saxon fiancée's home for dinner. No one shouts, gesticulates, or threatens. The quiet voices are deafening to him. Everyone seems to him to be mad at everyone else, refusing to say much or to express their emotions. He thinks something is all wrong and becomes very insecure. His fiancée would find his family's "wild" discussion equally disquieting. Most Anglo-Saxons react to such "wildly" expressive disagreements as monstrous arguments. In the same way, most Eastern European Jews, Southern Italians, and Irish Americans see the "restraint" of the Anglo-Saxons as extreme pouting and withdrawal, sure signs of monstrous arguments. "Getting one's signals crossed" on something this basic in life can lead to some extreme mutual reinforcements of insecurities.

Given all of these problems, how do love partners come to understand themselves, their partners, and the ways in which they are precipitating insecurities and arguments with each other? Ideally, they would read this book and figure it all out before arguments start. Realistically, no matter how much knowledge one has of such things, life is so complex and inherently uncertain, and the mythification process so potent, that nothing seems to prevent some arguments. And for the great majority of young people today, nothing prevents a great number of agonizing arguments. They learn how to avoid them, if at all, only in one way—the "hard way," through "hard knocks."

After having "run around the same track" of the same arguments quite a number of times, almost all couples gain a better understanding of their own insecurities, those of their partners, and how the arguments are precipitated by and cause insecurities. Most couples today do not arrive at these understandings until they have already spiraled downward in arguments and into considerable unbonding. Even most of those in which both have been very much in-love seem to suffer a great deal of unbonding before they reach this apex of commonsense wisdom.

Students of romantic love such as Eric Fromm (1956) and Nathaniel Branden (1980) have concluded that successful romantic loves are only possible for "mature" people, by which they seem to mean mainly people in their forties or beyond. If one first eliminates the highly insecure "many time losers" and those more willing to separate and divorce to "solve" problems, the chances of success in-love go up rapidly as people reach their forties (for complexities, see Hunt and Hunt, 1977; Udry, 1974). There seem to be a number of contributing factors to this. By that age, most people have overcome many of their situational insecurities and learned much about avoiding the triggering of their more embedded and pervasive insecurities. They have learned from the "hard knocks" not to expect Utopian Love in any partnership and that it is necessary to "work at making love successful." But the understandings they have gained of themselves, of love, and of their partners—especially of insecurities and their effects and causes—seem to be the most important sources of their success. Janine, whose life we have studied intensively for six years, recently showed how vital these understandings are when her husband took a cruise on a "love boat" and fell into vacation-love in the stereotyped manner:

> Lee and I had been married just over 5 years when he had the opportunity to go on his first real vacation ever. His work had been especially stressful and our relationship had been suffering for some time when the cruise to the Virgin Islands presented itself. Both of us felt strongly that he should go. Little did we realize what a turning point it was to be.
>
> Our relationship had undergone some very turbulent and rocky times. It was firmly rooted in trust and loyalty, but we were both well aware of the dying "fire" between us. I had come from a traumatic and disturbed childhood to a youthful first marriage. My husband sowed his wild oats and I eventually found myself divorced and alone with a small child. Lee had a very lonely and hardworking farm childhood. He felt ostracized from the community as a teenager. His high school sweetheart and first

wife suddenly deserted him for the contractor next door, leaving him with their two small children after 10 years of marriage. When we met and married we both were "surviving" with our children in our loneliness. Each of us had had relationships with people that for one reason or another had not satisfied us. I was particularly weak emotionally and very defensive on the outside. I was very supportive and loving of Lee, but never really gave myself to him intimately, sexually or emotionally. We simply went through the routines, each attempting to heal our own wounds. Repeatedly, I would say things to Lee like, "You don't know the person inside of me. I'm not the ogre you think I am." But I never let him see the real me. Although very much in love with Lee, I let my great insecurities and fears of rejection grow into a great monster between us, to the point at which I began to attack his ego, never explaining myself and never letting go. Slowly, Lee came to believe a false reality and respond to it in turn.

When Lee left on the cruise he was ready emotionally to break free of our relationship. Facing midlife, he felt a new season was upon him, his last chance at a more perfect relationship.

When Anne and Lee first met on the cruise there were no immediate "sparks" between them, but the more time they spent merely talking together the more sparks flew. Anne had divorced a year and a half earlier, after her husband had gone from mental to verbal and finally physical abuse. Anne read all Lee's signals of caring and warmth and resisted them, knowing he was a married man with children and not yet totally over her own hurts. They were simply drawn to each other and became intimate, although not sexually, within a few days.

Lee decided at that time that he knew his relationship with me was over. He felt that, although there would be great sadness and difficulty in executing the whole process, he wanted to be with Anne. We had even agreed at times that, if either of us "fell in love" with someone else, then the other would have to let go.

When Lee returned home and everything he had experienced with Anne was out in the open, I experienced a "rebirthing" of myself. My worst fears of losing him had finally manifested themselves. But, when faced with the actual situation my strength came forward and I let go of the fears just as my worst fears were being realized.

Within a few days of Lee's return, he began to see me in new and exciting ways as I began to respond to him more intimately, expressing myself freer sexually and to join him in activities never before shared. Lee began to realize that, although his love for Anne was real and strong, we shared a new sense of intimacy and love that had to be given a chance. Anne responded with hurt and anger that Lee was weak and unable to stand up for his love for her. At the time of this writing, the situation is resolving itself. I now know I am very much in love with Lee and will desperately cling to the chance to be with him. Lee, being the warm, caring, sensitive man that he is, feels torn between his loyalty to me, and all that we have together, and his sense of excitement and newness with Anne [Written for us].

And how do more secure and worldly wise lovers deal with the insecurities they still have that can endanger their love partnerships? If the Freudian theory of "abreaction" and "working through" one's insecurities were true, they would presumably talk endlessly about their insecurities and their sources until they had thoroughly exorcized them. Most people who have in fact worked their way through these mine fields would see that as absurd. That would be what is commonly called "picking at" your insecurities, or "rubbing the sore spots raw." There are times when *talking it out* can be invaluable in learning to recognize and deal with such insecurities. At their best, these can come as *revelations*, which throw light on the basic problems and prove invaluable in solving them. This is what Janine and Lee did. But those come only after long practical experience in working them out and only when the loving communion is still great, so the partners are *working at it together*.

The great practical secret to handling insecurities in love partnerships is to come to recognize them, especially what it is in the partnership that is triggering or causing them, and then to *evade them*. The great insecurities that wreck love partnerships are like deep abysses that cannot be filled up or papered over with rational discussions, but that can be avoided. Successful partners get so that they can almost instantly recognize when one of the abysses is looming on the horizon and they take instant evasionary action to skirt them. Successful love partnerships commonly have subjects that cannot be discussed, by mutual understanding. Much of wisdom in love-work consists in knowing what not to talk about, what not even to get near. It is quite true that this means that for those realms of life the love partnership is less intimate than close friendships in which they can be discussed. But these local nonintimacies are agreed upon in the service of the far greater overall intimacy of the love partnership.

THE SELF-REINFORCING
SPIRAL AND RATCHETING DOWN

The most fateful aspects of the spiral downward are that it accelerates, because arguments are self-reinforcing, and that each argument seems to produce a ratchet-down effect, so that it is not really possible to return to the level of adoration, intimate communing, and fusion the partners had earlier. The combined effects of this spiraling acceleration and this ratcheting down is that it is extremely important to partners to recognize that they are having arguments as early as possible so they can begin to understand them and evade them. But, as we have just seen, there are inherent aspects to romantic love partnerships today, including the common modernist misunderstandings of them, that tend to prevent this. The result is that, once arguments start, they tend to accelerate beyond the critical unbonding range where it is too late to remain in-love, even when the erstwhile partners remain in marriage or in a shell relationship.

The self-reinforcing nature of arguments is due to the simple fact that each argument itself becomes a new source of situated insecurity in the partnership, which can henceforth trigger further arguments, which then produce their own insecurities. Big Arguments are often talked about metaphorically as though they were like big storms, maybe like tornadoes that flatten everything around and leave pain, but quickly go away and are heard of no more. If we must limp along on physical metaphors, however, arguments should rather be talked about as nuclear blasts, some of which are localized (measuring in insecurity-kilotons) and some of which are generalized (measuring in insecurity-megatons). The crucial point is the Arguments do not just blow away like a storm. They litter the partnership-scape with abysses full of radioactive feelings of insecurity. The feelings they leave behind do tend to decay with time (as long as they are not restimulated), as feelings do in general, but they become dormant long before they disappear and, during that long period of dormancy, they can easily be triggered by any slight reference or situational similarity. As one life study of many years, Gail, explained

> We were having a party at our home for my husband's 40th birthday with lots of people and a great band so it was easy to get lost among the crowd. At one point of the evening I observed my husband talking intimately with one of the secretaries from his work. This distressed me but I let it go. Then a little later I saw he had his arm around her shoulder. I went over, grippingly took him by the arm and said "I need to speak with you now."

> We went in the bathroom where I closed the door and exploded accusatorily. He laughed and calmed me down, explaining she'd lost her job at work that week. I went on angrily at him until he shouted back at me "Why do I have to pay for [your first husband's] errors?" It hit me then

that this arm around the shoulder routine was the first thing I saw of my first husband's reaction to the woman he eventually ran away with. It was the situation I was hurting over, fearing; not Bill my present husband. [Written for us.]

These abysses have long half-lives and sometimes partners can feel pangs of pain 50 years later when they are reminded of the time one of them betrayed the other. (In another Woody Allen movie, *Hannah and Her Sisters*, an old married couple continually trigger these ancient feelings of betrayal and fall into "spats" over them.)

Each argument, then, tends to become in itself a future source of easily triggered insecurity, and anything that triggers it tends to trigger the original, greater insecurity. Also, whenever the original insecurity is triggered, it is easily channeled into the more recent arguments related to it. Thus a husband who once felt betrayed and initiated a terrible argument about it may feel a dread of new betrayal every time his wife does anything similar to what she did at that time (even looking at a man with the same color of hair, given that these feelings spread very widely to new stimuli); and, every time he feels insecure about her love or sexual faithfulness, he may tend to "fall into the rut" of the earlier argument, proclaiming, "Oh, so it's just like Tom all over again!" Moreover, each time the "old sore" (Argument) is reopened, the abyss becomes more pervasive—that is, it is widened (to more stimuli) and becomes more embedded—that is, deepened (so it more easily triggers greater insecurities and is harder to exorcise) and leaves more radioactive feelings behind to contaminate future experience.

After a number of Argument abysses have been exploded, widened, and deepened around the same general insecurity, the partners fall ever more easily into them, until in the endgame they feel like they are completely "stuck in a rut" or "sound like a broken phonograph record." Just about anything can trigger the basic insecurities and the situational ones of the many earlier arguments revolving around it, and they go "round and round the same track," exploding new abysses, digging the old abysses ever deeper and wider, and filling their lives with ever-more radioactive dust. The more Arguments they have, and the more intense (insecurity-triggering) they are, the more their spiral downward accelerates. The more they have and the more intense they are, the more they trigger each other, so that "getting stuck in one rut" soon gets them stuck in more than one. The original insecurity is reinforced by the more situational ones and they come to reinforce each other, as we saw in Gail's case.

Just as there appears to be a spark zone in the spiral upward of romantic love, beyond which the lovers' "fall" accelerates very quickly and they lose control of it, so there is a fatal zone in unbonding beyond which the accelerating spiral downward is very rapid and the erstwhile partners cannot control it, regardless of their best intentions. This critical range is the range beyond which the insecurity threats posed by the other person are so great that they quite outweigh the remaining love and other good feelings (such as fun), the remaining sense of common identity, and the pains of unbonding. As the erstwhile partners de-fuse their senses of self, the problems that once were felt to be *our* problems become *your* problems or *my* problems. As long as they still identified intensely with each other, even arguments commonly soon became "our problem" that "we must work at to solve." Once they have largely unbonded, Arguments pose separate and different problems for each against which they must defend their selves from the other.

Beyond this *fatal zone*, which erstwhile partners normally do not realize they have passed for a long time, each person is more concerned with defending him- or herself against the threats to his or her security posed by the other than in working at making the tattered partnership succeed. The erstwhile partners become more and more common enemies, locked increasingly into a love-war of attrition in which each is trying to win over the other or, at least, avoid losing to the other. The gray-lens effect comes increasingly into play and mythifies the erstwhile partnerships so that each seems far more threatening to the other than is really the case. In the end, they are so concerned with protecting their own selves and their own senses of security that they become very spiteful, striking out to destroy the other so the other cannot destroy them. That's when they spend hours arguing over who gets the bookends in the divorce settlement. The value of the bookends has nothing to do with it. The protection of the self has everything to do with it. In game theoretic terms, the relationship has gone from being a cooperative game, in which outcomes are shared outcomes, to being a zero-sum game, in which a victory by one means a loss to the other. Actually, arguments in love games remain mixed for a long time, with a shifting balance toward zero-sum games. Most never become entirely zero-sum, especially when there are children with whom they both identify, and thereby have a residue of common identity and common interests that make it necessary for them to reach a detente that allows them at least to "deal with" each other.

The victims of love warfare have evolved a vitally important conception about how they defend themselves against the insecurities produced by Arguments. It is based on the metaphor that depicts the memory of the Argument as a "sore spot." To overcome the constant pain of the insecurities aroused by the sore spot, the victim builds *emotional scar tissue*. The metaphor is tremendously apt. The body's scar tissue is a repair of injured tissue. Scar tissue is not as strong or as functional as the original tissue and it easily becomes a source of pain and other problems in itself. It is vital in allowing the body to go on functioning, but it is not the original and never will be, and it has its problems. Emotional scar tissue is also vital in going on, in not falling into continual pain. It covers up the sore spot so it does not hurt as badly. But it is not like the original and it creates its own problems. Scar tissue acts as a veil or protective layer over the sore spot, but in doing so it leaves the sore spot there as an abyss into which the individual can fall again in the future. (Once you break the body's tissue and scar tissue forms, that spot will always be far more subject to injury than before.)

This "emotional scar tissue" is the everyday metaphor depicting the ratchet-down effect. Once partners trigger insecurities in each other through Arguments, they develop emotional scar tissue to protect themselves against that sore spot and, thereby, against a part of the other that created the sore spot. Scar tissue prevents their getting back to where they once were in intimate fusion or adoration feelings. At this point, they commonly feel that a *wall separates them*. And there is a wall, a wall of "scar tissue." At this stage, they commonly feel irrevocably "isolated," and the coldness that characterized their brief periods of feeling isolated when the Arguments began becomes a "deep freeze" (see Weiss, 1976, on isolation). We have not found any cases, in spite of our active search, of people who have rebonded and reinspired mutual adoration once they have gone through much unbonding and built much emotional scar tissue to protect themselves. Considering the vast complexity and problematic nature of these assessments, maybe there are such people. We believe, however, that beyond that fatal zone of unbonding, you do not rebond. The partners can only avoid further unbonding by the best efforts of working at making the partnership a success at that level.

Unfortunately for us, as human beings, this tragic fact of life (if it is such) is hidden from us at the crucial times of the peak love experiences by the pink-lens effect and by the special "better than ever experience" that follows the "making up" after any but the most traumatic Arguments. In the most traumatic Arguments, the sense of insecurity triggered is so great that it does not dissipate enough to allow for the "better than ever experience." Big Arguments, especially at the peak of romantic love, call into question the whole partnership, our sense of self-confidence in our ability to understand and deal with people, and much else. It is like a death knell to everything. (Everything is black, life is over, the universe is collapsing—at the very least.) Once the partners make up, apologize, and vow never to let this injure their love or to happen again, the clouds clear, the sun rises from the ashes of despair, and the world is reborn. In short, there is a feeling of potentiated relief, very similar to what people feel when their death sentence is reprieved or when a terribly destructive war is won. The misery potentiates very powerful feelings of joy, and the individual who a moment ago was depressed and filled with dread explodes with bounding joy expressed in many ways, everything from weeping tears of joy to making ecstatic love and lust—often all together at once.

In these moments, days, or months of joyful relief and release, the partners are commonly filled with utopian thoughts. The pink lens is enveloped in a golden haze. They are sure everything is going to be wonderful because now everything is better than ever. They may indeed be among the fortunate few today who will not experience much more in the way of Arguments and will slowly decay in adoration love and grow into caring communion. Things for them will not remain better than ever, unless they were not really triggering each others' insecurities, but they will not get worse, only better in a different way. But, for most people today, the initial shots fired in Arguments are like the shot at Sarajevo, which produced anxiety and sadness that was followed by ecstatic war fever, only to be replaced soon by the utter misery of the war of attrition in the trenches of World War I. The "better than ever" feeling slowly wanes and is followed by an explosive Argument, or is itself exploded by an explosive Argument. Most people go through a good number of these falls into the abysses, soarings into the high of the "better than ever" feeling, plateauing, falling into the abysses, and so on before they realize that there is something more basic, more related to insecurities, going on between them. By then they are normally past the fatal zone of unbonding and arguments leave a residue of feeling "worse than ever." The Armageddon of love looms.

THE GREEN MONSTER

Jealousy has been the most terrifying of monsters to sexual modernists. Their reasoning has been impeccable. If jealousy is an inherent aspect of sexual relationships, then the casual ethos is doomed to produce suffering all around, suffering by the one who feels the jealous sense of betrayal and suffering by the betrayer when the betrayed strikes out. Therefore, they reason, because the exclusiveness and uniqueness of the Victorian Myth must be exorcized, jealousy must be a cultural delusion that can be exorcized (see Clanton and Smith, 1977).

The extremes to which at least the more utopian sexual modernists will go to exorcise jealousy is striking. Bennett Berger (1981) has described a communal ritual by which members of a sexual commune sought to "burn out" jealousy at a sexually "liberated" commune in California, which he calls the Ranch. Feeling jealousy is strictly forbidden, because it violates the rule of sexual freedom, to which all other freedoms are enchained. (One of the paradoxes of sexual modernism is that sexual "freedom" must be maintained by the repression of other freedoms.) Anyone who felt jealous because a "lover" had sexual relations with anyone else was expected to control it or to submit to the "burning out" ritual in which the "lover" had sex nearby with the new coupler while the communards consoled and supported the jealous one in his or her agony (see the case of Vickie, pp. 148-154).

We suspect this ritualized self-immolation would be very successful in providing an appearance of evidence supporting the modernist ethos. The intense suffering induced would most likely be the critical emotional wedge that leads the sufferer beyond the fatal zone of the unbonding process. In this instance, the jealous agony would normally be so intense that, at least if protracted, it would destroy the love partnership. The erstwhile love partners would then have much less jealousy, or none, if their partnership were totally destroyed, thereby making it look as if the ritual worked. As usual, the modernists were extremely confused in all of their thinking about these matters because they had abandoned the most elemental truths of our ancient common sense about love and sex. (Berger notes that many at the Ranch were acutely aware of their confusion, even to the point of feeling that "feelings" themselves were highly problematic—see 1981, pp. 155-156.)

There is no inherent interdependency between sexual activity and jealousy. The Don Juan often anxiously tries to shunt his latest conquest off on some new sex coupler, while he escapes. Prostitutes do not normally have a big problem with jealous customers. Jealousy is inherently interdependent with the intimate fusion of the sense of self with the loved one, not with sex. One may feel intense envy for others who get the sex they crave. This will be extreme and mimic jealousy if the craving comes from a sexual obsession. The impotent may even envy, hate, and sadistically attack the sexually successful, just as the poor may envy, hate, and sadistically attack the rich. Pangs of this sexual envy are quite common in frustrated adolescents. But sexual envy easily evaporates if some sexual conquests are made. Jealously over the betrayal of someone with whom you are in-love does not evaporate when your agony tempts you into a little counterweighting through casual sex. You might feel "sweet revenge," but your "sweetness" will still be tinged with bitterness, depression, and guilt once the rage subsides.

Jealousy, not envy, is one of many emotions that galvanize extreme actions to defend love partnerships. (Fear, even dread, of losing the loved one on whom one is dependent emotionally, materially, or otherwise is often confused with jealousy because it can lead to the same anger and defensive actions, though not to the desperate spitefulness jealousy can produce.) Jealousy, then, is universal whenever a real love-partnership is believed by one partner to be threatened by the other partner's commitment to a third party. The contention of the modernists that Bongo-Bongoers (usually the Eskimo) lend their wives to strangers and, therefore, jealousy is not an inherent aspect of love is a typical bit of modernist confusion. Wife-swapping is a rational tactic for men not in-love with their wives, especially for men who consider their wives to be like property ("Its," not "thous"). (As Berger notes, the hippies talked love and equality, but they exploited their "old ladies" sexually and in every other way, often getting them pregnant and leaving them. See 1981, p. 151; and see Davidson, 1977. Hippies normally had abysmal childhood relations with their families. The members of the "Manson Family" were only the extreme of an extreme in this regard. "Love" was a weapon they used against the people they hated but professed to love.) Swapping women-property is subject to the role of strict reciprocity the world over and is a fine tactic for buying casual sex objects. When the swap is not returned, envious outrage is the standard response (Romanucci-Ross, 1985, p. 95, gives a good example of this among the Manus).

The typical American teenager understands all of this subconsciously. Thus they play "jealousy games" in which they try to trigger jealousy in their beloveds by flirting with others to determine whether the beloveds really love them. If they do not, they feel jealousy and outrage. (Of course, a sufferer from extreme love insecurity might react with despairing aloofness and exit the reimagined, revivified primal scene of rejection.) Teenagers also know that it matters greatly to a lover whether a sexual betrayal is *merely* sex or *really* love. *Jealousy varies directly with the degree of perceived threat to the love partnership, thus with the degree of perceived threatening commitment to a third party.* Another love partnership is far more threatening than mere sex, except to someone whose very sense of self-security is threatened by sexual *deviance* in itself (as we see in the true Puritan). Similarly, a mere infatuation—adoration *without* the fusion of self—is far less threatening than falling in-love with someone else; and falling in-love with the full panoply of Erotic commitments, including procreation, is the most threatening of all.

We believe the popular view that women are less jealous (and merely more fearfully dependent) than men is a confusion resulting from the failure to understand these facts of jealousy. Men are far more apt than women to have (merely) casual sex. When they do, this does not trigger jealousy in their loving women nearly as much as when the men fall in-love. Of course, there are, as usual, complications in this. Having sex with someone else is normally a sign of not being very much in-love and normally comes in the endgame of love-partnerships. Thus husbands often *say* it was *only* sex, while wives are *convinced* otherwise. And, even if it were only sex to begin with, it normally involves some intimacy and can lead to falling deeply in-love, or can result in procreation with someone else, or can produce a sexual obsession. Also, if others know or might know of the sexual rejection, it is degrading and makes one look like a sexual failure, thus arouses angry defensiveness, even spiteful revenge. Life is not simple.

Sexual utopias—"communes"—have been found to be almost universal failures. In the nineteenth century, all of the sexual utopias failed quite quickly and were disbanded, in almost all instances, or were transformed into sexually conventional—Victorian—strongholds (Muncy, 1974). A century later, another wave of utopians, inspired by the same sexual revolutionary ethos and normally quite ignorant of their historical predecessors, repeated these experiments on a far vaster scale. Within a few brief years, almost all of them abandoned the experiments and their communalized misery. A high percentage turned to very conventional patterns, many becoming "Jesus Freaks" or other born-again Christians. Berger (1981), who was clearly extremely sympathetic to the Ranch, found that there was a continual turnover, that many of the communards stayed because their alternatives made divorce a dismal prospect, and that it drifted toward a dominance of bisexual feminists with a real scarcity of men.

In the past 20 years, some uncounted millions of Americans and other Western people carried out these same experiments in the self-reconstruction of human nature. In Southern California, especially, we have encountered many highly educated and intelligent people who are genuinely surprised even to hear the argument that jealousy is a powerful aspect of human nature. They have almost always picked up the modernist ethos from popular accounts in the mass media, from word of mouth, or from more serious arguments in college courses, such as those in Gordon Clanton and Lynn Smith's well-known book, *Jealousy* (1977). They believed them, carried out the exciting adventures in self-transcendence, and *drifted* or fell into confusion and misery.

Eric was a typical example of this very important pattern, but one who eventually became unusually honest with himself about the causes and consequences. Over several years, he had drifted away from the traditional Christian values and ideas of his childhood, largely as a result of the explosion of the casualness ethos around him in the late 1960s.

Although my behavior had proceeded on only a slightly different course, my idea of right and wrong (at least in some areas) had come about 180 degrees. The most pronounced change was that, where I never questioned before, I now questioned everything. I questioned and discovered I didn't like the answers I'd received before. Perhaps out of frustration from wanting to do something of social significance (always an underlying motivation as far as I can remember) or perhaps out of an unconscious desire to inflate an ego that had always been very low, I searched for an easy way to exercise my new-found self determination. I informed Linda [my wife] that, as soon as she thought it was OK, I was going to try to go to bed with another woman. She wasn't exactly bubbling with exuberance. Her lack of enthusiasm wasn't difficult to perceive and, being a loving husband able to appreciate the sensitivity of the situation, we decided that I should wait. And I did wait, about half a second. I went after everything in sight. That, coupled with the fact that I limited my wanderings to women who knew my wife, probably accounted, to a large degree, for my complete lack of success. My frustration grew when Linda finally accepted what I was doing and started playing the same game. Much to my chagrin, she was 100% successful. Isn't it funny how that works?

The first time she went to bed with another man I was actually very happy. I felt that I had been the instigator of all the changes we had made, changes she had accepted only reluctantly, and she had, by this act, finally caught up, or was actually leading the way. I saw her as an individual to be reckoned with now, no longer someone to be taken care of or who needed to be shown the way. She could find her own path. In the few seconds it took for her to tell me what she had done my respect for her increased immeasurably. After those two seconds, it was my jealousy that increased immeasurably.

The odd aspect of the entire affair is that in the midst of intense but hidden jealousy, I would encourage her to continue her "promiscuity." Even after arguments following my jealous outbursts, during which I always substituted some technicality for admitting (even to myself) the real reason for my anger, we would decide that we really believed in the individual's rights (even to this extent) and that we should continue this behavior, even if it was painful. We never expected that changing such deeply rooted values would be easy and we thought the prize (being able to do this sort of thing without any painful repercussions) worthwhile. What we were after was much broader than the sexual events. We sought an attitude that would permeate our lives and affect our social relations in all their aspects. We saw nothing but gain to be had from opening ourselves to the world around us. I commented to a friend once (this was not a casual acquaintance as witnessed by the fact that he later became and still is Linda's lover) that I wish I loved Linda enough so that if she ever wanted to leave me, I could let her go without remorse. I wished I loved her enough to want for her what she wanted for herself. Of course, if things worked out the way we wanted, her leaving would not be necessitated by her loving another man. She could love two men with no complications. Hell, I wasn't greedy. She could love three if she wanted! As we saw it, the real advantage was not the giving of oneself to others and receiving from them in return; rather, it was the attitude that one marriage partner must have to allow a spouse to become emotionally involved with another person. Or, on a less dramatic note, to simply have fun with members of the opposite (or same) sex. Everyone's heard of the husband's night out with the boys. This allows for the husband's night out with the girl friend, or vice versa. It also allows for the husband's and wife's evening at home with the husband's girl or with the husband's girl and her boyfriend or even the wife's night out with the husband's girl. The list could go on to get complicated, but what it amounts to is, anyone can be with anyone else, and everyone stands to benefit by it.

We sincerely believe that being able to get involved with members of either sex, not hesitating to become emotionally involved, even if it leads to copulation, will broaden us as individuals and enrich our marriage. We communicated to one another that it is desirable for each partner to welcome (but not go in search of) such friendships or in the case of the opposite sex, love affairs. We believe that one person can love, and be loved by, several people simultaneously. And if this philosophy is spread by our actions, the world may be a little better place to live in. In other words, sort of a "fuck for peace."

Not only did we both agree to its innocence, but we thought it was fun. There was also this nagging feeling, in the back of my head, that the whole scenario was a scheme, prompted by my not so subconscious, to enable me, with my wife's permission, to get into bed with a woman of my emotionally attached choice.

I especially felt this way since I usually philosophized in this manner equipped with an erection [Written for us several months after the events].

Eric's "philosophizing" soon led him to organize his own little swinging party. He, his wife, and another couple gathered at his apartment for dinner, proceeded to play strip poker, and wound up in bed with swapped mates. Perhaps he had finally conquered the Green Monster of Jealousy and would now launch a career of Erotic bliss, unmarred by marital conflict, jealousy, or guilt? Such was not to be his fate. Like so many before and after him, he soon discovered the hard way that he could not escape the Green Monster. No matter how he writhed, or whither he turned in his sexual labyrinth, there was the Monster ready to devour him. And it did, or, at least, it devoured his marriage. He got a divorce shortly after this moment of swapping bliss. (Actually, it wasn't very blissful. Eric spent much of the night trying to arouse his newfound mate, but, in spite of the supposed excitement of the "new partner," his new partner remained steadfastly loyal to frigidity and Eric wound up with little more than sore abdominal muscles and a state of confusion over a cool breakfast.)

Biologically, the function of jealousy is obvious. Jealousy inspires actions by the male that protect or increase the likely payoffs of his genetic investments and actions by the female that protect the support given her and her offspring by the male. This "genetic investment" is the only factor normally considered by biologists and anthropologists. For us human beings, however, the emotions involved in our love partnerships become extremely important in themselves and probably evolved in direct dependency with the protection of those partnerships (see Chapter 2). Jealousy protects our immense investment of our whole sense of self in our love partnerships.

In primates, the similar patterns of behavior vary widely. The males of at least one species kill off all the children of their predecessors when they become dominant. The males of most species rely on less drastic actions to increase the probability that their genes will be transmitted to the new generation. Most are quite vigilant in trying to keep other males from mating with the females when they are in heat. Even chimpanzees, who have often been touted by modernists as completely promiscuous, show this basic pattern (see de Waal, 1982).

Human beings are far more bonded together in love partnerships than most primates, and immensely more so than chimpanzees (except in the mother-child partnership). We are also very conscious of the relation between sexual activity and birth. In general, human beings seem to be extremely jealous compared to other primates. Just as we would expect from the fact that females can always be sure of the protection of their genetic investment in their offspring, while males cannot, human males show far more jealousy than females over relations that might produce pregnancy. (Having a child with a man other than the husband is an extreme betrayal. Even when the man acquiesces because he is infertile, it is extremely stressful for most of them.) This, however, does not mean that we subscribe to the modernist argument that women in polygamous cultures and "macho" cultures do not feel jealous when the men with whom they are in-love feel love for other women. As usual, the cultural training has far more effect in repressing feelings and actions from public view than in determining actual feelings or actions in private. Whenever women in cultures with "machismo" are actually in-love, they seem to feel the usual human jealousy. Mexican women may present a front of stoical aloofness when their "macho" Don Juans stray, but they feel the same hurt of insecurity and the same jealous rage as Americans when they are really in-love, though no doubt attenuated by past miseries of the same sort and by expectations of what lies in store for them in marriage. (The unexpected betrayal is always more shocking and painful.) Hortense Powdermaker (1933/1971, pp. 330-331) noted that even among the Lesu, who publicly allow both partners to have sexual episodes, jealousy frequently erupts:

> The expression of jealousy, and apparently the feeling of it too, is another temperamental or personality trait which differs from individual to individual, and which is an interesting variant from the usual social pattern. Extramarital relationships are the accepted social rule, and I heard of no relatively young married man or woman who did not follow this pattern, and therefore, logically, one would not expect to find jealousy. But jealous fights occur frequently.

Individuals vary widely in their tendency to respond with jealousy. Some lovers suffer from the extreme pattern psychiatrists call *conjugal paranoia,* which leads to the interpretation of the most innocent actions and body language in the most lurid terms. Some men literally lock their wives up when they leave the house and some women would no doubt love to be able to do so to their husbands. Far more see lovers under every bed. Individual genetic differences probably account for some of these differences. Far more seem clearly related to differences in the degrees and dimensions of insecurity. As common sense informs us, the jealous lover who has little realistic reason for his or her jealousy is an insecure lover. Basic insecurity seems to lie behind the more extreme patterns of jealousy. Basic insecurity in one's sense of lovability seems to lead to the most intense jealousy of all. The lover who feels he or she may not be lovable dreads this in more or less direct proportion to the intensity of love for someone. They may show no jealousy at all until they fall deeply in-love with someone, thereby triggering a jealousy felt for a new sibling or someone else who "took away" the love of the mother.

Unlike the basically insecure, the secure can see that those in-love with them are more or less *closed* to other loves and, though far less so, to other sexual temptations. They thus feel pretty secure in their love and trust their lovers. This leads to a pattern of *discounting* evidence of betrayal. It is very striking how blind to even otherwise obvious evidence lovers can be to the betrayals of their loved ones when the pink lens is refracting reality. When jealousy has been inflamed by insecurities or by real events, the green lens of jealousy espies threats everywhere, long before the gray lens is put in place by the rising hatred of the endgames of love. Those who feel secure in their loves see trustworthiness all around.

TURNING TO FRIENDS FOR
INSIGHT AND LOVING SUPPORT

As we have seen throughout this book, every love partnership is vastly complex and has its own peculiar history and its own distinctive interpretations of each major rational concept, such as "arguments." The abstract ideas of reason are extremely blunt instruments for probing such vast complexity and uniqueness. Just as it would be absurd to use a shovel to take a hair out of your eye, so it would be absurd to use a Freudian conception of the "libido" to understand your love partnership. Intuiting this basic truth, love partners come to understand each other's insecurities and to avoid them by *feeling their way* along many convoluted paths, stopping when they cause too much pain, proceeding when it helps, inching forward a step at a time in a *drift process*, not by leaping over tall problems in a single theoretical bound.

Today, a high percentage of people, especially the more educated, look to marriage counseling and other forms of counseling and therapy to solve their problems. Expert counselors can be extremely helpful in dealing with certain special problems that are not understood by most people today, especially when they do not have much experience or experienced friends and family members to whom they can turn for help. The deserted lover, who feels he is "going out of his mind" because he is confused and the world does not seem "real," can be vastly reassured to learn that this is a common effect of sudden, wrenching unbonding, and he will go away reassured enough to work through mourning and rebuild his sense of self (see below). But the great majority of people who go to counselors wind up unbonding anyway. There are people who benefit from therapy and counseling and people who seem to be made worse from it. There seems to be no way of telling who will benefit and who may be made worse, though good counselors and therapists certainly try to assess this. Studies of the outcomes of therapy in general indicate that they have no significant positive results beyond what would be expected by "spontaneous remission"—that is, by solving the problems on your own. In general, counseling and therapy seem to help in the same ways that intimate discussions with friends do and they help most when the practitioners are warm and friendly, just like friends. People who do not have intimate and understanding friends might benefit greatly from such professional help. (All of the questions involved here are quite complex. It seems clear to us, for example, that most people who go to counselors and therapists do so as part of the "endgame" of their partnership. Commonly, the initiator is looking for expert support to justify the final break and, thereby, prevent his or her feeling the agony of guilt. The world's greatest counselors will have a hard time coming up with much of a batting average in those cases, which is why we call it *hard therapy*.)

The close friend is the universal human counselor and therapist in times of love problems. In spite of the varying values and meanings of friendship, almost everyone who has close friends turns instinctively to them for help in understanding, bearing, and working through their love problems. Close friends have normally developed an intuitive grasp of the person and of his or her partner through years of intimate communing with them, yet, unlike the sufferer and his or her lover, the friend remains independent enough emotionally and in his or her identification with the sufferer to avoid the pink-lens and gray-lens effects. The friend has enough love and identification to motivate him or her intensely in seeking to grasp the situation and the problems and to help work through them. It is precisely this in-between status of the close friend—one who is very close and loving, but not so close and loving as to be emotionally blinded—that makes him or her the ideal helper in this time of peril.

Friends differ greatly in how intuitively understanding they are, how articulate they can be, how warm and loving they are, how much moralism will likely be mixed with their help, how free they are from their own problems at a given time, and how much experience they have with a specific problem. Most people have several close friends nearby and they pick and choose among them, often shifting back and forth, to find the right mix for their problems as they shift, soar, and plummet from moment to moment. Some people with a lot of interest and experience in love problems become almost full-time love nurses.

As the Arguments and their insecurities become intense, the lover normally becomes aware that he or she is confused. The lover senses that his or her own thinking is being intensely mythified, that the gray-lens effect may be distorting all of his or her thinking about feelings, about the partner, about everything. If the lover has begun to develop love or sexual feelings for someone else, he or she may sense that the pink-lens effect (and the green-lens effect of anticipated relief and potentiated optimism known as "greener pastures") is interacting with the gray-lens effect to produce multiperspectival distortions of everything. Up may come to feel like down, and inside like outside. Feelings seem to rebound around erratically, going from depression to ecstasy and back again in rapid succession. Being "all mixed up," the lover feels a desperate need for close friends who know him or her and the situation well, who love him or her enough to help all they can, but who are free enough of all the emotional fallout to "straighten things out."

One of the greatest problems of the lover is determining how he or she "really feels." Is he or she *really* still in-love or do the feelings of bitterness, emptiness, depression, hostility, and whatever else running through his or her consciousness mean that he or she is no longer in-love, that it's all over and time to leave and start over again? What most people do not realize very clearly is that this little "really" in their discussions about whether they are still in-love refers to the fusion of their sense of self with that of the loved one. The lover knows more or less what he or she is feeling right now, and what he or she felt last night and the night before. What the lover does not know, and normally becomes aware of once he or she starts thinking about whether or not to give up and leave, is how he or she will feel in the future when the present situation has changed. The lover probably feels a lot of anger at the partner as a result of insecurity wounds, or a lot of lust or love for someone new, or he or she would not be as likely to be thinking of leaving. But how will the lover feel when the nuclear dust settles and the new day dawns? That depends overwhelmingly on how much of a fusion of his or her sense of self there still is with that of the loved one. And that is what is normally so elusive, so inherently problematic, so obscured by fleeting passions, and so largely misunderstood in our modernist society. And that is where the wisdom of friends given in loving communion is the most important of all.

Once lovers pass the fatal zone in unbonding, they begin commonly to crave romantic love with someone else. Many people today, especially men, experience this more as craving sex with someone new. Others, especially women, experience it as craving adoration love and intimacy. They feel "drawn" toward new people and begin, subconsciously or consciously, to give off the signs of being "open" for romantic considerations. A high percentage of people today begin "love affairs" during this endgame phase of love partnerships. *Endgame affairs* come in all dimensions of emotion and commitment, from casual flings in states of liquored-up "abandon" (misconstrued as "freedom") to falling deeply in-love. The vast majority fall between these extremes and have the fateful effect of greatly distorting the individual's understanding of everything, especially of how much he or she is still in-love with the partner.

This problem in self-understanding is so common today that even teenagers speak offhandedly of it as one of the problems of the *rebound* period (though this would have to be considered early rebound, whereas teenagers are normally concerned with the rebounding after the breakup). The basketball term *rebound* has obviously been carefully chosen and crafted by generations of wise American teenagers, because it is one of the most apt phrases in the rich repertoire of physical metaphors for love experience. A rebounding basketball is hard to judge for two reasons. The angle of rebound is highly problematic because of the steel basket rim that may be in its way. The human being easily judges that the angle of rebound will be equal to the angle at which it hits the flat backboard (unless it is thrown with spin on it), but, unless the shooter is very bad, the ball also hits the rim—and thereby bounces in highly unpredictable ways. But there is another factor of great importance at work: the force with which it hits. The greater the force, the greater will be the rebound.

Lovers unbonding rebound in these same highly unpredictable ways, especially when there is a foreign object—a new lover or sex object—in the way. Nobody can be very sure where they will be tomorrow in their feelings and commitments. They bounce around. The person who can least predict these things is normally the person doing the rebounding, especially one rebounding from being deeply in-love, because the intense pain and craving for relief produce intense mythification.

Teenagers normally look at rebounding from the perspective of possibly getting involved with the person rebounding and issue a wise rule of thumb: "Steer clear of the rebounder." Adults speak similarly of the "Walking Wounded," or "zombies," and advise would-be lovers to weave a wide detour around them. Wise people take this for granted and add a vital corollary to it: "Rebounder, steer clear of other loves and lusts!" Their point is simply that adding a new love or lust to the old one during the rebound phase will multiply confusion and multiply the chances of making terrible mistakes. Few people of experience doubt that they are right. But there is also no doubt that, once they are largely or completely unbonded from an old love, a high percentage of people rebound into new loves and lusts. When both of the new lovers or lusters are rebounding, they are so unpredictable, so back and forth, so round and round, that they might better be called *love-ricochets* (because a bullet ricochets so fast and with such force that it is far more unpredictable than a basketball rebound—and far more deadly). Starting a new love or lust on the rebound is one of the most common reasons for breakups of budding love partnerships. The new love or lust feels so wonderful, because it is potentiated by the pain felt in the unbonding process, that even the most experienced are apt to fall into pseudolove or impossible love. Close friends can provide their greatest help by showing the dangers involved in rebounding and trying to show that the rebounder may be wrong in thinking he or she is "completely free," given that most never achieve that state of liberation. But doing so is extremely difficult even for the wisest of friends.

However devoted friends are to helping, and however much they realize their help is the vitally important help, a little experience in this netherworld of love quickly convinces them that helping someone in this phase of unbonding is painful for them and fraught with dangers for their friendship. Anyone caught in the iron grip of mythical thoughts easily misinterprets the best intended "advice" as not so well intended. Friends learn to tread cautiously here and commonly steer clear of giving advice directly. Their *indirect advice* is often given in *love parables and anecdotes* about what they themselves did or would do in a similar situation. Dealing with the new love involves dealing with an explosive mix of the old miseries and the new ecstasies, and it poses the possibility of opposing what just might turn out to be a successful new partnership for the friend. Friends caught between these multiplying dilemmas quickly recognize that Ulysses had it easy steering between a rock and a hard place in a bad storm at night with tattered sails and a broken rudder while the ship was sinking and the sirens were calling him to ecstatic escape. It is not surprising that so many subtly refuse to help, especially with advice, and many jump ship in midcrisis. Without the restraining reality testing of close friends, mistakes are far more likely in breaking up and in rebounding into new miseries. Regardless of what they think their values are, those who initiate the break from someone they still care for, and especially from someone who still cares for them, will almost always experience haunting guilt that will partially poison the best of new loves. Feeling guilt for hurting someone who loves us and for whom we care seems to be one of those basic genetic programs. Politicians may believe there is such a thing as "no-fault" divorce, but the human heart will tell lovers otherwise.

Aside from providing invaluable feedback on the realities, close friends provide the all-important caring love and respect that are needed to assuage the insecurities triggered by the arguments of unbonding and by the sense of being unlovable that come with rejection. Heterosexual communing can be the most assuaging of all (for heterosexuals), but does always run some danger of falling out of platonic communing and into love or lust before the rebounding is over. In some instances, the feelings of gratitude and peaceful relief gotten from platonic loves are so intense that they mimic romantic love, thus becoming pseudoloves, and lead to misalliances later regretted.

PERPETRATORS AND VICTIMS

The early stages of unbonding are normally roughly symmetrical in terms of who initiates the arguments and who merely suffers them. The exceptions clarify this important point. When one of the supposed partners "cools off" and discovers that he never felt anything much more than lust, he is very likely to initiate most or all of the arguments, or simply to slink off in the night via the "Dear Jill" note. Again, when one of the partners is highly insecure and, thereby, summons up jealous visions of betrayal that trigger his insecurities, then he is very likely to initiate the arguments. Most partners, however, drift into the downward spiral because of unintended and unexpected clashes in values, other fundamental aspects of their senses of selves, or more situated aspects of everyday life that wind up triggering insecurities. Each will tend to blame the other for "always starting these arguments," but that is because each is pretty much equally guilty on average and the dread of guilt encourages mythification in each. Sometimes he will start it, sometimes she will.

But as they spiral downward, approach or pass the fatal zone, and get into the endgame of love, the onus normally shifts strongly to one of them. One of them becomes the perpetrator of argument after argument against the other, the victim. The reason for this growing asymmetry is that one of them has normally unbonded far more than the other and is often rebounding into someone else's arms, or craving to do so. Long before the perpetrator normally becomes conscious of it, him- or herself, he or she is subconsciously making indirect attacks on the sense of self and self-security system of the victim, thereby precipitating arguments that push the partnership toward the breakup.

Paul Rasmussen and Kathy Ferraro (1979) have done the definitive analysis of the strategies of the endgame of love. They show that, at this stage, the feeling of guilt and the dread of guilt feelings, and the fear of shame and embarrassment in facing friends and family, become crucial blocks to further drift toward the breakup. The more conscious the perpetrator is of his or her desire to breakup and, above all, of the fact that he or she is doing the initiating of arguments that are hurting the partner and pushing him or her down the spiral, the more guilt the perpetrator will feel, either then or later when it is all over. This is why *indirection* is used in *drifting* toward the craved goal. The more the perpetrator can maneuver the other into position—*set him or her up*— so that the victim will overtly initiate the argument he or she wants and, above all, the more the perpetrator can set the victim up to make the final break, the less guilt the perpetrator will feel. The perpetrator may do this indirect *goading* very consciously, but most seem to repress their guilty schemes to the periphery of consciousness, thereby avoiding most of the guilt they would otherwise suffer. Their goading, then, is subconscious.

In addition to the terrifying possibilities of guilt they face, perpetrators have to be concerned about the shame and embarrassment that still come with the stigma of being a "loser" in sex relationships and, most especially, in marriage. Most perpetrators recognize the obvious fact that most of their problems of shame, embarrassment, and guilt will evaporate if their victims get involved sexually with someone else, use violence against them, or commit some other heinous crime of love betrayal. Thus many perpetrators slyly and indirectly set up their victims by creating situations in which they will be tempted to have a sexual affair or be goaded into hitting the perpetrators. Some perpetrators go so far as to taunt their victims into having an affair or hitting them.

After some months of this kind of emotional battering, victims have commonly unbonded a great deal more than at the beginning of the war. It is not uncommon then for victims to become perpetrators and engage the original perpetrator in a war of mutual recriminations in which each recognizes, at least subconsciously, that "it's all over but the shouting and tears" and each is trying to maneuver the other into taking the lion's share of shame, embarrassment, and guilt for making the open break.

Even with the worst of mutual intentions, some erstwhile partners never manage to overcome their complex mixes of dependency; their convictions that divorce is immoral; or their dreads of shame, embarrassment, and guilt. Some manage to declare peace, often by tacit understanding, before they completely unbond. If so, by cautious, mutual evasion of each other's insecurities, and by cultivating what they do share in identifications—especially the vital one of their children—and their common interests, they can develop a friendly partnership. In time, as the agony of the wounds goes dormant, they can nourish this partnership into a *cordial understanding* (what diplomats call an *entente cordial*). It is built first of all on an agreement to leave disagreements alone—out of sight and out of mind as much as possible. They agree to "let bygones be bygones," as must as possible anyway; "let sleeping dogs lie"; "hew to the straight and narrow" (that is, not hurt each other's vital interests, especially not betray each other); and "work for a brighter tomorrow." Common sense has many clichés for discussing the strategies and tactics necessary for making such cordial understandings possible, presumably because they have been so common throughout all the centuries when divorce was almost impossible for practical or religious and legal reasons. If there is a sincere desire to "make the best of it," even if it consists of "making the best of a bad marriage," and if the semipartners use caution ("feel their way") and intelligence to build upon all their shared identity and interests, it can certainly be done. What commonly begins in resignation—"giving up the Romantic Dream"—can end in real friendship, a loving partnership that will become ever more fulfilling as they grow beyond the youthful cravings for the thrills of sex and "pitty-pat" love.

Young people aflame with the craving for Romantic Love almost always see such compromises as plainly and simply "giving up" and living a "fate worse than divorce." The common attitude today is certainly that put so sharply by one disappointed young man, "I'm too young to live in a marriage without love." (He meant "without the thrills of romantic love," for his wife was certainly very caring toward him.) Some older people who have opted for compromise marriages, generally because of their shared love and identification for their children, do feel some pangs of nostalgic craving for "what might have been." But over the years, the cordial and friendly partnerships of companionship become more and more important, and the craving for the fires of romantic love die away.

MOURNING AND
STARTING OVER

As we have noted, sexual relaters and marital companions may unbond, separate, and divorce with little fanfare. Indeed, their creative liberation from the humdrum of burned-out or tinsel relationships can be liberating and creative, with few bad afterthoughts. These modernist heroes and heroines are rare specimens, however. Most people who look as if they feel *only* liberated and creative immediately after breaking up are merely playing the role for the modernist galleries, or whistling in the dark to psych-up their own courage, or refusing to give their spiteful ex-partners "the satisfaction" of seeing their misery over the loss.

Most people who have been in-love separate and divorce long before they have fully unbonded and must go through a prolonged mourning process when they break up and divorce. Each individual's mourning process will be somewhat unique, depending on the particular insecurities and securities, the particular emotions, morals and cognitions, and the situations involved. As people who have been through this wringer say, "You have to experience it to know what it's like." But, as usual in matters of love, intimacy, and sex, there is also a genetic core to this experience that gives it an archetypical human form upon which our culture and each individual elaborates.

Mourning over the loss of someone with whom you are to some degree still in-love is the same whether the loss is through separation and divorce or through death. In both cases, the remaining degree of fusion of self with the lost one is the most important determinant. The more fused, the more intense and prolonged mourning will be. Other factors, however, are also important. The degree of *closure* is clearly important. Closure is the degree of uncertainty over the loss. The more certain— closed—the loss of the partnership, the more mourning will be experienced, the more it will be worked through, and the more quickly the loser will become resigned to the loss; and conversely. A husband missing in action, but not known to be dead, leaves a loving wife "hanging in suspense" for years, because there is little closure and little resignation to the partnership loss. People who have little tolerance for suffering anxiety and depression, and all of the general chaos of emotion and life produced by mourning, often push unbondings to *premature closure*, that is, to losses before the situation otherwise rationally justifies giving up and becoming resigned. The prolonged agony of having your self torn apart piece by piece by the unbonding process always poses a great temptation to lunge toward premature closure.

Anguish, agony, misery, dread, terror—such are the awful words used to try to describe mourning over the loss of a greatly loved partner. *Depression* is the somewhat pallid psychiatric label used most often these days. Certainly depression is part of it for everyone, though probably more toward the acceptance of the loss in resignation than in the early stages. The emotional overtone of the first phase of mourning, which comes at the point one rationally—but not emotionally—believes in the loss tends to be that of *shocked numbness*. The rational mind now knows the loved one is lost, but the defensive security system goes into full-scale operation to defend the self from total annihilation. In one of the great mysteries of life, it does this by throwing up a glass wall between the innermost sense of self and the outside world, including the outer sense of self that must continue to interact, automatically, with the rest of the biosphere. The *glass wall* of the shock defense is only one of many metaphors used by people to try to describe this mysterious phenomenon, but it seems the most apt. People with basic insecurities commonly have a glass wall in place as a normal part of life, as Walter Lippmann described it so strikingly. Anyone experiencing a traumatic situational insecurity tends to throw up the glass wall instantaneously, without ever having experienced it before.

The glass wall of shock allows us to perceive the world, sometimes with laser-sharpness because time is slowed down and everything "drags" along so slowly, without feeling the full impact of the emotions affected. Thus we know how to interact with the world, but we do not experience the world as real. The world is derealized and depersonalized, to the degree we experience shock and thus to the thickness of the glass wall we throw up to defend ourselves. Only as the emotional reality of the loss begins to go dormant, and thus not be so threatening in its intensity, does the dampening effect of the glass wall begin to recede. The lover now feels more intensely the terror of the loss and learns to tolerate it (become adapted to it), and finally resigned to it. Eventually, generally after some years, the feelings go dormant almost completely, unless some contacts with the loved one continue to trigger them. As these feelings go more dormant, the self is progressively freed to re-create itself through initiatives in the world. (Probably the best description ever given of the sense of shock and the general mourning process is C. S. Lewis's *A Grief Observed*, 1980. See, also, Bowlby, 1971-1979, 1979; Furman, 1974; Parkes, 1972; Glick et al., 1974.)

Most love partnerships have unbonded over long periods of protracted conflict before separation and divorce, so that there is not enough fusion of the selves left to produce great shock and mourning. The mourning process has already been largely worked through piecemeal. There is also normally an overtone of lingering hatred and anger, so that depression, anxiety, and other negative emotions are mere undertones in the early stages of separation and divorce. It is often only later that the loser first experiences the great sense of loss and the anxiety and depression that are necessary parts of the whole mourning process. The mourner is only immobilized to the degree that shock and the depression and anxiety of mourning are actually experienced. When anger and hatred are the overtone, the sufferer may throw him- or herself more fully into mobilizing all resources to begin rebuilding the self and his or her life. Realizing this, people often psych themselves up to hate the erstwhile partner and try to goad him or her into doing hatable things, which also counterweight any feelings of guilt. This adds emotional fuel to the protracted conflict and helps to turn what had been peaceful détentes into spiteful all-out attacks.

Just how prolonged the period of mourning and hatred will be depends on how deeply one was in-love, how much fusion has remained, how much the attacks and loss have triggered insecurities in the loser, what the situation is, and the choices the individuals make in dealing with it all. For unknown reasons, the mourning phase normally lasts about a year and that seems to be the rule of thumb in many cultures. (Perhaps the fertility god must pass through one complete cycle, from the mourning of dying and death in the fall to rebirth in the spring and fruition in the summer? There would be mythopoetic resonances here, except that few people are ready for any Erotic fruition eight months after their traumatic loss.) After a year of retreat and re-creation of the sense of self ("R&R" for the divorced), mourners are generally over the "I'll kill him and become a nun" phase and ready to start over again. It will still normally take many months, however, for them to "pull themselves together again" (Weiss, 1976; Trafford, 1982).

The most traumatically insecure, those who suffer from some basic insecurity, do not ever fully recover and may well wither away and die or kill themselves outright. C. S. Lewis was reported by a close friend never to have fully recovered. From his earliest years, Lewis had felt terror over his father's unpredictable passions. He loved deeply and identified with his mother and probably never unbonded from her when she died of cancer when he was nine. Most of his adult life he lived with a much older woman he called his "mother." It is obvious that he identified in the extreme with his wife Joy, whom he married very late in life. When she died of cancer, he went into very deep shock. He recovered somewhat emotionally, but he withered away unto death (see Chad Walsh's "Afterword" to Lewis, 1980).

No one goes through the trauma of unbonding without winding up with emotional scar tissue that protects him or her from future traumas. But this protection is bought at the price of not being able to fuse as deeply the next time, and certainly not quickly or easily. Losers of great loves become more insecure about their lovability permanently, though the degree wanes over the years. Most people who suffer this trauma certainly start over again, and most of these come to love again, but never with as much loving communion and fusion of the sense of self. Certainly many people lose a minor love and, after going through the purgatory of mourning and hating, find a new love with whom they eventually create a greater love with more fusion of the sense of self. After all, the sufferings over the loss of "puppy love" and early romantic partners is nearly universal. People who merely slightly burn their lips with hot coffee do not give up hot coffee, but people who set themselves on fire while "free-basing" cocaine never seem to do so a second time, unless they are very suicidal. In the same way, those who have felt the agony Dante felt when Beatrice laughed at him are not likely to fall deeply in love again. As Dante said on that occasion, "I have held my feet on that side of life beyond which no man can go with intent to return." Those who have felt the fires of hell and returned to tell the tale are not likely to repeat the trip. Rather, they shy away from the deeper reaches of the netherworld of love. Many, especially those with basic insecurities, never really love again. Those who have loved and lost more than once find themselves spiraling downward into less and less intimate relationships in which they engage their cathexis-objects in the shadow dances now known as "role play" and "liberated relationships."

More and more losers today are insisting on staying at arms length, refusing to commit themselves even to the degree of a marriage partnership with the escape clause of no-fault divorce. More and more losers are refusing to take any big chances in love again and are hedging all of their security bets by having "live-in lovers" with a modicum of love, a lot of companionship and sex, and escape hatches all around. In doing so, they are repressing the daimonic urges of the Erotic passions and often find themselves with a more generalized sense of insecurity, which they evade through drug and therapy dependency. The Erotic passions are the wellsprings of human life. When we cut ourselves off from them, we lose touch with our innermost senses of our selves and of life itself. After surveying the agonizing and prolonged mourning through which C. S. Lewis (Jack) went over the loss of his wife (Joy), Chad Walsh reached the same conclusion we think human beings who understand love will reach about cutting oneself off from the Erotic netherworld:

> As I finish this little essay on Lewis and his Joy, I find my thoughts turning from literature to life. *A Grief Observed* points my memories to Jack and Joy, and their all too brief but gloriously meaningful marriage. Neither of them is a character straight out of a medieval courtly romance, but they learned from each other the mysteries of Friendship, Affection, Agape, and Eros at a depth that makes them kin to the great lovers found in literature and sometimes in life. *A Grief Observed* reveals the price paid for that knowledge. I do not think Lewis would have chosen to save the price and renounce the knowledge. In this most harrowing of his books, there is found also the radiance of a love that death itself could not dim. Lewis was indeed surprised by Joy—into his own self-knowledge and deepest fulfillment [Lewis, 1980, pp. 150-151].

"PROLOGUE"
The Eternal Quest

The first time ever I saw your face
I thought the sun rose in your cyes
And the moon and the stars were the gifts
    you gave to the dark
And the endless skies.

> "The First Time Ever I Saw Your Face"
> (Words and music by Ewan MacColl)

All great Romantic Love stories are tragedies. Their lovers are star-crossed, doomed to lovesickness and often worse. The tragic ends of almost all the great loves at first sight echo down through the centuries—Paris and Helen, Aeneas and Dido, Abelard and Heloise, Dante and Beatrice, Petrarch and Laura, Boccaccio and Fiametta, Troilus and Criseyde, Romeo and Juliet—all are stillborn, broken, or murdered. Today, even in America, the nation that most loves a happy ending, all of the most moving and memorable love stories are tragedies. *Camelot*, *West Side Story*, *Love Story*, and *The Other Side of the Mountain* have been the most popular love stories. They begin at first sight, or at first communion by other means, and all end tragically.

The great love stories that last over the centuries and eons are inspired fairy tales that enchant us with their magic just as they did the peoples of those ancient worlds. Like all great fairy tales, they have a powerful appeal to our emotions and a powerful effect on our thinking and actions. They tell us something vitally important about ourselves and our lives. Our deepest feelings hear those messages in the subconscious realm largely beyond the reach of words, the realm where the caress and grace of the body, the soft and lilting tones of the voice, the ethereal beauty of adoring smiles, and the rhythm of life's movements intimate far more than words can ever say.

Fairy tales must have happy endings because they are meant to inspire hope. The heroes and heroines, like all of us, must go forth and face the terrible challenges of life. They do face them, they prevail, they have a happy ending, and so we are inspired with hope that our strivings will overcome the terrors we too must face.

The great love stories at the very hearts of our greatest fairy tales end tragically. But they inspire a soaring hope within us that we will find the same magic power of love that has transformed the lives of our tragic heroes and heroines. When we have witnessed an inspired presentation of *Romeo and Juliet*, the most moving of all love stories, we feel sad, but, instead of despair, we feel a renewed hope for love in our own lives. Certainly these star-crossed love stories are "cautionary tales," incantations that warn us that the subterranean passions of Erotic love summoned from the vast deeps of our own souls by the magical power of other human beings are at war with other passions that can destroy us in a world where love is but one of many contending forces. The blind love of one soul for another—and what love is more blind than the Romantic ideal of love at first sight?—will almost certainly lead to tragedy. And yet this tragedy uplifts us and the cautionary note is drowned out by our revitalized hope for romantic love and for all of life.

This magic transformation of tragedy into hope is accomplished by showing us that true love triumphs even over death. True love is the eternal quest of life and out of that love springs new life to carry on the quest. Whoever would seek security by withdrawing into the cold aloofness of lonely solitude will lose his or her very self. We can only live fully, discover our innermost selves, and transcend the limits of our sterile loneliness by hearkening to the daimonic cravings of our innermost selves—the Erotic spirit of life—to find another human being whom we can love and with whom we can create new life. But when we have felt the transcendent hope inspired by the great tales of love, we know that the terrifying risks are worthwhile, that even the seeming end of love—death itself—is but a prologue to new love and life. Serenely soaring above the storms of life, transcending all the tragedies, shines the fixed star toward which we grope, however blindly.

Let me not to the marriage of true minds
Admit impediments, Love is not love
Which alters when it alternation finds,
Or bends with the remover to remove;
O, no! it is an ever-fixed mark,
That looks on Tempests and is never shaken.
It is the star to every wandering bark,
Whose worth's unknown, although his height be taken.
Love's not Time's fool, though rosy lips and cheeks
Within his bending sickle's compass come;
Love alters not with his brief hours and weeks,
But bears it out even to the edge of doom.
    If this be error, and upon me proved,
    I never writ, nor no man ever loved.

[William Shakespeare, Sonnet No. 116].

APPENDIX

The Freudian Theory of
Incest and the
Jealous Child

Because Freud's ideas about childhood sexuality have had such a profound impact on modern ideas about the development of love, intimacy, and sex in general, it is important to see precisely how they are wrong. The Freudian theory of human nature and the human condition is built on the theory of childhood sexuality, and that theory in turn is built on Freud's conception of human energy or emotion, the "sexual-libido." Freud fell victim to the Western conception and language of the "libido," which goes back to the ancient world and was clearly presented by Augustine. As Augustine said, the Roman word *libido* means both "desire" or "lust" in general and "sexual desire" or "sexual lust." In Western language, then, for eons there has been some deep conceptual identification of desire with sexual desire.

This is seen even more clearly in the ancient myth of Eros or Erotic love, which is seen to spring from, to express, and to act out all of the deep-lying, creative, and procreative urges—lusts—of human beings. We believe this mythical conception expresses a profound truth about the experience of love, intimacy, and sex at their impassioned extreme, that of romantic, Erotic love. In the full heat of obsessive passion, these powerful emotions trigger undertones of—or "irradiate"—any and all of the emotions and thoughts that involve joy and excitement. The Erotic, then, springs from and expresses much of our innermost sense of self, our largely subconscious passionate engagements in the world, our daimonic urges to procreate, to create, to build and expand in the world. As people have noted since the ancient world, and as Freud insisted, in the full heat of Erotic desire, we even have some desires that involve the oral responses, the lips, tongue, and mouth in general. In the full heat of

Erotic love, the beloved *tastes* wonderful. In any other life situation, the mere thought of imbibing someone's saliva is a bit disgusting, but, in the grip of Erotic love, we "hungrily drink" of this nectar secreted by our loved one. That is, we do not actually feel hungry or thirsty for the saliva, nor do we actually drink, though we will in fact ingest to some extent. The emotions are only undertones triggered by the overtones of Erotic love, and the actions are thus only partial actions from the full repertoire of actions expressing and acting out real hunger and thirst and the real consummation of good taste in drinking.

There is, then, some real experience and much more conceptual identification that inspired the ancient and subsequent ideas. Over many centuries, the "doctors of physick" developed ideas of the "balance of the humours," which involved an assumption of some kind of body passages that connected all of the "humours" together. These ideas were then incorporated in the eighteenth-century ideas of "vitalism," which looked at the "humours" as interconnected hydrodynamic pressures in the body, especially of blood (hence the practice of bleeding to relieve pressure, but also of the "pressures" of the menses and semen). This in turn was interpreted thermodynamically in the nineteenth century in terms of the emotional energy states of the body as a closed system. Freud took the idea pretty much whole from the biology of his day. But he gave it a revolutionary twist. Whereas most other Victorians emphasized the dangers of deflating or deenergizing the body by releasing too much of the sexual pressures or energies, Freud was dealing with patients who commonly had little or no release, so he emphasized the opposite, the miseries and dangers of damming up the energies of the libido. Because, he reasoned, the pressures are all part of a closed system, damming up one of them, such as sex, inevitably produces too much pressure. This must then be vented through other channels, hence "neurotic symptom formation."

But Freud's really radical leap into the headlines came from his "discovery" of the child's supposed Oedipal lust for the parent and jealous rage against and dread of retribution from the same-sex parent. It seems clear enough that he did not discover this from any of his life studies of his patients. He discovered it initially in his own tortured self-analysis. Masson (1985) has argued that Freud actually was told by the patients that they were subjected to incestuous seduction or rape and that Freud lied, making the child the one guilty of incestuous desire and murderous impulses toward the same-sex parent out of jealousy. It seems more likely that Freud first "discovered" the Oedipal complex from his self-analysis and then *imposed* it on his patients and the rest of the world. In his letter of October 8, 1897, to his good friend, Dr. Wilhelm Fliess, Freud revealed that his tortured self-analysis had led him to remember that, when two years old, he had taken a train trip with his mother, saw her "nudam" and his "libido toward matrem had awakened." Freud then revealed in the same letter that he had welcomed the death of his brother, born one year after him, with "wicked wishes and genuine infantile jealousy" (see Bonaparte et al., 1954). Freud clearly felt great guilt about this and no doubt dreaded the shame and embarrassment that revealing it would cause, even though when he wrote it he was 41. Gay has argued that this is why he put it in Latin—thereby distancing it from his Germanic self and audience—and why he remembered being two when he was really four—thereby making his childhood self less responsible for it (see Gay, 1978, pp. 10-11). The fact that it was not revealed for decades, and then only in the collection of letters carefully censored by his daughter, is more directly revealing of Freud's feelings.

Having "discovered" this great and sinful secret, Freud seems to have been increasingly possessed by the conviction that this was a universal secret of infantile sexual lust, murderous jealousy, and guilt. This, of course, would eliminate all responsibility on his own part, thus evading the dread of shame, embarrassment, and guilt. When he confronted his patients with this universal "truth," they clearly "resisted," but he insisted until they agreed. Paul Chodoff (1966) and other recent psychoanalysts have shown the extreme pressures Freud and later analysts used to wrench these confessions from these highly insecure (neurotic) patients of the famous doctor:

> Thus we have a situation in which the formidable force of Freud's drive and enthusiasm was focused upon patients suffering from hysteria and other psychoneurosis, from whom he believed certain material should be forthcoming.

> The possibility must be considered that, to some extent, Freud was unconsciously imposing his beliefs on these patients, especially the more suggestible among them. Supporting this possibility, in the 1896 paper, "The Etiology of Hysteria," Freud describes how immensely difficult it is to wrest the memories of seductions from his patients, how they protest and deny, and how they insist that they have no feeling of recollecting the traumatic scenes. In "Sexuality and the Etiology of the Neuroses," in 1889, he says: "Having accurately diagnosed a case of neurasthenic neurosis, one may proceed to transpose into etiology the symptomatical

knowledge so gained, and may fearlessly require the patient's confirmation of one's surmises. Denial at the beginning should not mislead the physician; every resistance is finally overcome by firmly insisting on what has been inferred, and by emphasizing the unshakable nature of one's 'convictions.'"

It is legitimate to suspect that the uniformity of the memories produced under such conditions, which Freud adduced as a proof of their universality in hysteria, was a product, rather, of the uniformity of Freud's "convictions." And, of course, Freud later had to acknowledge a considerable error in the formulation of hysteria which he had advanced with such certainty, while the evidence of later developments has resulted in the abandonment of Freud's explanations of the so-called actual neuroses [Chodoff, 1966].

All of the massive evidence in recent decades from social research methods, certainly including our own (Douglas, 1976, 1985), make it obvious that such methods in the service of a powerful conviction would bias *any* findings, and, when used by a great authority figure like Freud (or any German doctor at that time), would produce massive compliance. The cultist presumptions and organization of the Freudians then made this infantile sexual syndrome an article of faith that was transmitted faithfully to each new generation of the devoted (Chodoff, 1966). Anyone who dissented was ruthlessly excommunicated (Roazen, 1971). This tragic Freudian misinterpretation was partly the result of Western verbal confusions, his own guilt, his dread of shame and embarrassment, his cravings for absolution and fame, and some biologistic preconceptions. But it was greatly aided by some very real facts of childhood sexuality. Freud probably did feel great excitement at seeing the forbidden nude body of his mother and easily misremembered it 37 years later as sexual lust, a misinterpretation made easier by the fact he was already drifting into a linguistic confusion of sexual libido with all emotions.

The existence of fragments of sexual behavior in infants is commonsensically obvious to anyone caring for them. The infant boy's erections and the girl's genital caressings are obvious enough. The only difficult question is what they *mean* (Jackson, 1982). Infantile *fragments of emotion and behavior*, which will eventually be developed into complex adult systems of emotional behavior, are common in higher animals. In fact, the vastly complex play behavior of animals and human beings is largely made up of such fragments. Playing at reality is essential for fully developing and organizing into functioning systems the fragments of emotion and behavior. It does seem likely, in view of all the evidence, that these fragments are from their beginnings partially interdependent with fragments of the emotions they will eventually fully express, and act out. Young predators secretly stalking make-believe prey or engaging in fragments of mock-battle appear already to show some fragments of the signs of the immense excitement and aggression that will eventually be acted out in hunting and agonistic behavior (dominance battle). But these bodily signs of the emotions are only fragments and they are ephemeral. They show that there is something there that can be developed, not that the emotional state and the behavioral patterns expressing and acting them out are lying there full-blown like some high-pressure jack-in-the-box demanding release and only held in by some external pressure.

On this crucial matter, as on so many others, Freud was also betrayed by the simple model of biological determinism that served as the foundation for his whole theory of the human biosphere. The simplistic assumption of ancient common sense about inherited characteristics was that "from little acorns do mighty oaks grow." That is, the seed contains the complete pattern, or, as we would now say, the complete hard program, which will use the resources of nourishment to build around the pattern, or encode, the complete adult. In nineteenth-century biology, this was the nub of the basic principle that "ontogeny recapitulates phylogeny," that is, the developing child goes through all the developments of earlier evolutionary development to get to the adult stage. The correlate of this was the idea that ontogeny fully anticipates the future development of the adult, an idea that was developed to the extreme in social Darwinism and in many ideas of earlier centuries about "the bad seed" and about the constitution of the infant determining all of future development. Sulloway (1983) has shown how powerful a sway this simple idea had on Freud's theory.

Freud did see the situations encountered by the developing child as important determinants of the adult the child would become. But he did not realize how completely the early genetic primings of emotions and fragments of behavior he was observing are interdependent with social experience for their full development, because the study of animal and human behavior in natural settings was in its infancy. The human child is highly primed to smile. Even in the early weeks of extrauterine existence, the child shows fragments of smiles, but not the fully organized, sustained, and socially competent *interactive* smiling. The child can show disgust with distasteful food in a fully organized, sustained, meaningful, and effective way, presumably because bad food is so dangerous to the child's existence that human beings evolved (completely?) hard programs for communicating this to any caretaker very early in life. But this is not true of the human emotions of social bonding. As we saw, it is only around the sixth week that the child is able to begin fully organizing, sustaining, and developing smiling—and *the child does so only if he or she perceives other people smiling at him or her.*

Blind babies never see these smiles and so, while they show the early fragments of smiling, they never *fully* develop social smiling, a fact that is profoundly disturbing to their parents and later to others because they look like they do not feel loving, even when they have in fact developed love fully through the other human channels of emotional interaction. It is quite true that the child possesses the internal, genetic priming to emit fragments of smiles, and the child probably has some minimal emotion of liking when he or she does so, but this will never be developed fully if the child does not encounter other human beings who initiate and return smiles to him or her. The child has only the beginnings of a genetic program and must have external inputs to develop the rest of the internal programming to perform the full pattern of interactive expression. This is exactly the same pattern we see in the development of the love feelings in general. This is a crucial point we have presented earlier and will further develop in this Appendix.

There is every reason to believe that exactly the same thing is true of infant and child sexual feelings. The baby experiences pleasure from the soft caress of the sexual organ and this emotion is probably sexual in some fragmentary way. But to define this as sexual in the same sense as the full panoply of sexual feelings and cravings of adults is ridiculous and is utterly absurd when applied to the full-scale daimonic passions of the Erotic. Young men at the peak of their lustfulness get erections sometimes at the mere memory-image of a sexy girl, and the sight of the real thing, especially of the female sex organ, is enough to cause intense arousal with a full panoply of action systems to fulfill the desire and a full panoply of misery when desire is frustrated. These facts of life are quite obvious to any competent teenager, both male and female.

> With eyes gleaming with merriment over the tale, she related how she and another young woman were sitting . . . and had tossed up their straw aprons and so exposed themselves. A man came up to take a baked taro . . . and seeing them he immediately had an erection. He wanted to have intercourse with them, but they refused and said they were just playing.

They told him to come closer and take the taro, but he only swayed back and forth in pain. Later the women lay down on a path by the bush and exposed themselves again. Once more the man saw them, had an erection and wanted them. Again they refused and said they were only playing.

This tale was told to me without embarrassment, yet dramatically, and amid shouts of laughter [Powdermaker, 1971, pp. 239-240].

Not the slightest touch is necessary to arouse these passions and their behavior patterns in lusty young men. But extensive caressing is probably necessary to arouse even fragments of sexual feeling in babies or young boys and is generally necessary in aging men in whom the fires of sexual cravings have become slightly smoldering embers. In his own day, Freud's theory was generally seen as ridiculous by the doctors, sexologists, and anthropologists who directly observed and analyzed sexual behavior. His theory of incest, which was the cornerstone of his whole theory of the human biosphere, was seen as especially ridiculous. Doctors were quite aware that incest actually occurred, but, of course, it occurred normally when the child was fully developed in adolescence. Above all, it seemed to occur in instances in which the child had only distant relations with the other offending family member. Havelock Ellis was quite explicit on this point and stressed it repeatedly. He was quite aware from his own unrepressed experience of how it operated in general. He remembered fully that it was his mother's and nanny's secret urinating that he came to associate with sexual excitement, but that neither this nor anything else led him to desire them sexually. Rather, his only sexual desires within the family sphere were directed toward a much younger sister who grew up while he was away from home (Grosskurth, 1985). This led him to agree with the arguments of Westermarck and others that the child either does not develop sexual feelings and behavior toward those with whom he lives closely or else develops a stronger counterweighting emotional repression (an inhibition) against these. Biologists (Shepher, 1983) have recently extended this relatively simple theory and shown that the fragmentary reliable evidence from around the world fits a relatively simple model. As we argued in Chapter 2, they show that the closer and earlier a child's loving partnership with anyone, the more inhibited any sexual feeling is toward that person even later when the full sexual feelings grow intense in adolescence.

There is apparently some genetic priming that leads in normal situations to this buildup of sexual inhibitions in direct proportion to the earliness and intensity of caring love partnerships. The evidence supporting this is striking. Almost everywhere the most abhorred sexual contact is between mother and child, the next most abhorred is between father and child and the next is between siblings. As one goes from mother to father to sibling, the degree of abhorrence normally declines while the exceptions and violations increase. In our society today, mother-son incest is exceedingly rare, in spite of the growing distance of some mothers from their children. Father-daughter incest is very rare but many times more common, presumably because there are so many fathers who are so distant, completely absent, or unloving of their daughters in childhood. Because the mother is by far the closest to children and most loving, with fathers considerably more distant and less loving, and siblings next, the facts of incest are precisely what the theory of caring love inhibition predicts. The vast majority (approximately 90% to 95%) of legal cases of "incest" are perpetrated by stepfathers or mother's boyfriends who had no love with the girl as a small child. It has been found that even nonrelated children who are raised closely together, such as children in the kibbutzim of Israel, strongly resist parental pressures to marry and almost never do; and child marriages, such as in Taiwan, are far more likely not to work (see Talmon, 1964; Wolf, 1966, 1968, 1970, 1976; Rosenblatt and Anderson, 1981).

In our society, the clothing of the body and the strong taboos against exposing sex organs after the age of two or three (which varies considerably from one Western nation and ethnic group to another) make it very difficult to disentangle the excitement and behavior associated with the revelation of the forbidden from specifically sexual (lust) excitement and behavior. Even young children clearly show great curiosity and probably sometimes experience excitement over the revelation of the sexual secrets of the body. By the age of four or five, "doctor and nurse" games of "you show me yours and I'll show you mine" begin in earnest and fragments of embracing and even mounting make their appearances, commonly hidden behind "innocent" fronts like wrestling or even shoving and bear hugging. These *fragmentary sexual activities* are quite obvious in more relaxed societies such as the Lesu (Powdermaker, 1971) and the Trobriands (Malinowski, 1929). They seem to grow in direct proportion to the development of the far more massive, pervasive, and emotionally powerful forms of play love (see the next section). There is every reason to believe that the sexual feelings develop in roughly the same way but at a far lower level of intensity until around the age of eight to eleven (with wide variations) when the prepubertal buildup of sexual feelings, interests, and behavior begins.

Sexuality obviously pervades human life far more than it does the lives of any other animals. It has become interdependent with many other basic dimensions of our lives, most obviously with love and intimacy. Much of the development of sexual feeling and behavior has indeed been partially hidden from public view in the Northern European societies by parental and community suppression and this made their revelations exciting. But the modernist revolution overleaped the mark of truth in its attempts to right the balance between public visibility and private reality.[1]

One of the arguments used by the defenders of the Freudian theory of the universality of incestuous desires is that the powerful taboos against them the world over show that there must be some powerful desire. After all, societies do not normally taboo cuprophilia (feces-love) or self-mutilation, and many do not taboo anal intercourse, because they see such things not as tempting but as insane, absurd, beyond the pale of possibility in sane human life (see Romanucci-Ross, 1985, p. 147, for an example concerning homosexuality). This is a convincing argument. They also argue that the myths and other stories involving incestuous themes are pretty universal, indicating some kind of repressed "wishing." On this point, we believe the stories show far more repressed dread of violating the terrible taboos, something Freud completely misunderstood because his theory of the dream as always involving a wish led him to quite misunderstand the nature of mythical thought (see Chapter 5). But, overall, they have a good point here.

What they have failed to note is that the taboos and stories are concerned and directed overwhelmingly at prepubescent and older people, not at children. There are definitely exceptions, such as the intense taboo on brother-sister contact in the Trobriands and among the Lesu, but Powdermaker seems quite right in noting that this is a form of anticipatory socialization, aimed at preventing the development of behavior and feelings that could lead to violating the incest taboo when it becomes relevant at puberty. The people of Lesu obviously don't expect the child brother and sister to have sex, any more than we expect normal children to have sexual lust for their parents. But what people recognize commonsensically the world over is that, when children first develop powerful sexual feelings and the behavior associated with it, they develop pervasive desires that must be socially channeled away from and toward the socially approved people to reinforce the earlier inhibition. Incest stories are overwhelmingly about adolescents and adults, not about adolescents and children; and incest taboos are directed at adults, not children.

This does not mean that there are no *fragments* of incestuous desires in children. We argued above that children probably have some weak sexual feelings (especially genital skin sensations of pleasure) associated with the fragments of sexual behavior they practice. It is most likely that these are associated with the people most at hand within the family, especially the mother touching the genitals. But the feelings are weak and the inhibition against them grows much stronger than the sexual feelings, normally in direct proportion to the closeness of the other person. (Note also that childhood sexual feelings are triggered by direct caressing of the genitalia. They are not an independent *craving* for such caressing except as a counterweighting of depression and anxiety, such as we see in the compulsive masturbation of depressed and anxious children.) This is why there are few violations and why any that occur are easily suppressed by shaming. When the lust feelings explode at preadolescence and adolescence, they give rise to sexual cravings, for any nearby sexual cues, especially in boys because their sexual feelings are far more triggered by visual cues. These are in direct conflict with the incest inhibition. This conflict and the social taboos multiply to help produce the disidentification and distancing behavior so obvious in adolescent rebellion. Of course, there are many other sources of "adolescent rebellion," and this one may well not arise at all, but in some instances it adds to the conflict until enough emotional or physical distance is achieved to reduce it to levels at which it can be contained without emotional venting and acting out.

The Freudian myth of the incestuous and jealously murderous child has greatly distorted the scientific understanding of children and of their very complex and evolving partnerships with their families and the rest of their biospheres. In recent years, this myth has also given aid and succor to extremists of the modernist movement who spread distrust of the family to undermine it. Its greatest impact has been on the miseducated masses of the college teenagers and college graduates, few of whom are yet aware of all the evidence showing the real nature of the Freudian movement and the real nature of family life. Given the undertone of dread of incest obviously felt by some adolescents, drumming into young people the suspicion that their love for their parents might really be a sublimation of repressed incestuous desires is an excellent means of driving an emotional wedge between them and their parents. Because so many millions of them already have serious love insecurities and other insecurities, resulting from pervasive divorce and other disturbances of their earlier family lives, these wedges of self-doubt are likely to be highly destructive of family support and wisdom when they sorely need it, at a time of great situational insecurities and new beginnings in uncertain waters. Most remarkable of all, the modernist myth of incest has filled some miseducated parents with dread that they lust after their infants (Greenspan and Greenspan, 1985, try to ally this dread to prevent parents from becoming distant and unloving).

THE JEALOUS CHILD

One of the other bits of fact that could lead to the tragic Freudian misinterpretation is the powerful jealousy the child sometimes feels toward those who seem to take the mother's love away from him or her. In adults, powerful feelings of jealousy are a rough index of romantic love feelings: the more jealous, the more romantic love; the more romantic love, the more jealous. This rule-of-thumb index is especially helpful in spotting repressed romantic love or repressed jealousy: if you can definitely see the one, then the other is generally there in certain situations. (For the further complexities, especially the importance of insecurities, see Chapter 6.) But there is a catch in this. Individuals can feel intensely jealous over withdrawn (or feared withdrawal of) love without any sexual feelings or fears being involved. Freud probably did feel jealous rage toward his new brother, but not because the new brother received sexual favors from his mother.

The obvious instance of nonsexual jealousy is same-sex sibling jealousy. Parents with a number of children close in age to each other are almost always highly aware of the pervasive and powerful effects of sibling jealousy. It is almost impossible to prevent its arising intensely at least in situational forms in which one child feels slighted by comparison with the others. And in most multichild families, more pervasive and embedded forms of this love insecurity seem almost inevitable. A surprisingly large number of adults have lingering undertones of jealous hatred for their parents or siblings and some still have strong overtones.

To the best of our knowledge, no one commonsensically suspects a jealous child of being sexually jealous of his or her siblings. It is the feared loss of the mother's love that makes the child jealous of the sibling, or the feared loss of a particular valued object or activity that makes the child envious. *Jealousy* is the everyday word used to refer specifically to the feared loss of a loved person's love to someone else. *Envy* is used to refer to the feared loss of a valued object or activity to someone else. The experiences can overlap. For example, when a mother gives John's toy to Pam, John may fear that he is losing both the toy and some or all of the mother's love. Given that the core emotional experience is also the same, the use of the two words overlaps, thereby causing considerable confusion.

The child may feel jealous in exactly the same way toward the father or anyone else, with no sexual jealousy involved at all. Unlike sibling jealously, however, father jealousy is quite uncommon. There appear to be several reasons for this. Most obviously, jealousy and envy are both felt toward someone perceived to be a direct threat to one's love or valued object or activity. A threat to one's love is perceived roughly to the degree that the other person is seen as a substitute or replacement for the self in the mother's love. *Thus the more comparable the other person to the self, the more likely one is to perceive them as a threat and to feel jealousy toward them; and, more directly, the more the loved one treats the other in the same way as the self wishes to be treated, the more likely one is to perceive the other as a threat.* The father is not on these grounds very likely to arouse jealousy because he is not very comparable to the child's self and because the mother does different things with him, things the child does not value so highly as the father does. One of the crucial things the mother does with the father that the child does not feel very jealous or envious over is sexual things. The average two- or three-year-old boy may feel jealous if he never receives hugs and kisses from his mother, but the fact that his mother spends long periods sitting on daddy's lap and kissing him in a passionate way does not make him feel jealous because that is not what he wants from her. He is far more interested in running around and tumbling to show them both how strong and developed he is than in sitting pinned up in her arms like that. By the age of three, he might even start feeling some jealousy toward his mother over this because he wants his father to play ball with him or ride him on his shoulders, rather than playing in such a different and uninteresting way with mommy. By two or three, most boys want to spend more and more time with their fathers, and less with their mothers. They are not repressing murderous ideas about father. Instead, they are slowly falling out of love with mother in general and more in love with father and with child playmates (see Lamb and Campos, 1982, for some preliminary findings).

But the degree of identification and disidentification that one feels with the potential threat, the compared rival, is the most important determinant of the tendency to feel threatened and thus jealous. This is most obvious at the extremes. Twins, especially identical twins, normally identify with each other to an extreme degree. Therefore, they feel minimal jealousy toward each other when the loved mother shows her love for the other. If the loved one shows love for your enemy, the person with whom you disidentify and whom you hate, then you feel the most betrayed and the most jealous rage. Brothers are normally pretty closely identified with each other and are seen to be so by others. This is the basic reason why they are most likely to inherit each others' wives in polygamous societies and, in those rare occasions where it *might* occur, to marry one wife. Brotherly love, which includes considerable self-identification, is far more common than jealous hatred.

Most children also do not feel much jealousy toward the father because the child loves him second only to the mother. The boy also identifies himself with the father, only normally less so than with the mother until he is three or older. And the child identifies mother and father together to a high degree. Even when he becomes an adult, he will commonly identify them to the outside world as "my parents," but, of course, only to the degree that they remain identified in his mind, which is normally pretty much in line with the degree to which they identify with each other.

Though he normally increasingly identifies himself with his father, this does not mean that he compares what he gets from the outside world or from his mother with what his father gets, as he is far more likely to do with a brother near his own age. His identification with his father is a love identification, not an object identification. He may well assert that someday he will grow up to be just like daddy and do just what he does, maybe even marrying mommy, because that is what daddy did. But he is not confused about their vast differences. It has been found in the study of animals that the mere fact of being picked up and carried about has profound effects on what the animal does. Even in adults, size and physical strength differences are extremely important in arousing feelings of many sorts, especially those of dominance and submission, and in shaping one's entire network of background assumptions about other people. Kings were routinely painted as taller than their subjects, or as towering over them on thrones or horses or elephants, or as touching the heads of their subjects kneeling in obeisance or kowtowing or groveling on the floor. Kings were Big Men indeed, in conceptions and in their emotional impacts, regardless of mere physical realities.

Fathers are very much the same to little children. Mommy is big and picks him up, but daddy sometimes picks her up and that says a lot more than words can. He is not comparable to his father in terms of what he gets from mommy or the world, so when daddy gets a new car or a kiss from mommy those things do not have much to do with him, thus there is no basis for jealousy. The child identifies himself as a lesser part of the father and mother, as subsumed under them. Thus only a small part of what happens to them is identified by him as happening to him. The parents conceive of the very small child as still almost completely subsumed under them, as still part of their greater selves, as flesh of their larger flesh—offspring in which their blood flows. Thus what happens to him is far more likely to be important to them, to feel like it is happening to some part of them. Parents who love their child are very concerned with what happened when he played house with his little friend. The child has almost no concern with what happened to daddy at the office or out on the golf course, even when he has been there. It is not really relevant to him, while almost everything he does is relevant to them until he becomes more independent of them, that is, less subsumed by them.

While daddy is not very comparable to him, his siblings are highly comparable, especially before he has gained the ability to make more detailed distinctions between older and younger, boy and girl, the interests of one and the interests of others, and so on. To the extent that he identifies his sense of self with his siblings in his love of them, he does not feel jealous. But *the law of jealousy and envy* is "equal treatment to equals and unequal treatment to unequals." More specifically, the more comparable someone is to the self, the more equal the treatment of the two should be; and the greater the divergence of treatment of them relative to the degree of comparability, the greater the sense of jealous or envious outrage. But the *law of loving identification* says the *jealousy will be defused in direct proportion to the degree of fusion of selves.* As one identical twin said, he never felt jealousy toward or over his brother, until the brother, with whom he lived, started sleeping with a girlfriend and *shut him out.* Shutting the door on him came as a great shock and started a traumatic process of partial de-fusing (see Chapter 6). He obviously felt jealousy toward the girl, for reasons of intimacy having nothing to do with sex.

Because those more equal in age are more comparable, they tend to be more jealous of each other than of much older or much younger siblings. Given that exactly equal treatment is almost impossible, the comparability factor almost always leads to some jealous and envious rancor among close siblings, but with distant siblings (especially the "baby of the family") the love identification may completely overwhelm the comparability factor and produce very harmonious partnerships with easy acceptance of considerable unequal treatment—but not more than is due the relative degree of incomparability relative to the degree of self-identification.

NOTE

1. To us the most striking evidence of this is the fact that none of our own experience or that of our friendly life studies has brought to light any clear memories of lustful sexual experience from early childhood. Most of these people are quite unrepressed sexually. They have fond memories from early childhood of playing house and mommy-and-daddy. They have distinct memories of excitement associated with sexual exposure games, and with the beginning of the rampaging passions in prepubescence. Though there is very wide variation, from nothing to fondling and even oral sex, and from revulsion to excited curiosity, they do not believe they had what we adults know to be distinctly lustful sex feelings until roughly the prepubescent age when sex play (strip poker, circle jerks, and so on) commonly begins. In view of the fact that today most people would prefer to be able to brag about early sexual exploits and the fact that most educated people have been subjected to considerable socialization in Freudian ideas, it is striking indeed that people do not often resort to such bragging or to Freudian self-deceptions.

We must remember, however, that these retrospective life-studies and the problematic nature of emotional and cognitive experience make such inferences inherently risky. We have tried to be very cautious in probing such memories (see Douglas, 1985). But any retrospection on this is uncertain and even direct observation of children is fraught with difficulties in inferring the feelings involved. The difficulties and ambiguities are multiplied many times over by the linguistic confusions inherent in the Freudian theory. All of these are apparent in the massive critiques of the Freudian theories by Eysenck and Wilson (1973), and the partial defenses of the theory by Fisher and Greenberg (1977) and by Paul Kline (1972).

References

Adams, Paul L. 1984. *Fatherless Children*. New York: John Wiley.
Adler, Alfred. 1930. *The Neurotic Constitution*. New York: Dodd.
———. 1946. *Understanding Human Nature*. New York: Greenberg.
———. 1964. *Practice and Theory in Individual Psychology*. New York: Harcourt.
Adler, Patricia A. 1985. *Wheeling and Dealing*. New York: Columbia University Press.
Adler, Peter. 1981. *Momentum*. Beverly Hills, CA: Sage.
Ainsworth, M.D.S. 1967. *Infancy in Uganda*. Baltimore, MD: Johns Hopkins Press.
Altheide, David L. 1976. *Creating Reality*. Beverly Hills, CA: Sage.
———. and John M. Johnson. 1980. *Bureaucratic Propaganda*. Boston: Allyn & Bacon.
Anders, Gunther. 1960. *Kafka*.
Anonymous. 1966. *My Secret Life, Abridged But Unexpurgated*. New York: Grove Press.
Saint Augustine. 1950. *The City of God*. New York: Modern Library.
Bade, Patrick. 1979. *Femme Fatale*. New York: Mayflower.
Baker, Russell. 1984. *Growing Up*. New York: Signet.
Beach, F. A., ed. 1965. *Sex and Behavior*. New York: John Wiley.
———., ed. 1977. *Human Sexuality in Four Perspectives*. Baltimore, MD: Johns Hopkins University Press.
de Beauvoir, Simone. 1961. *The Second Sex*. New York: Bantam.
Bell, Robert R. and Kathleen Coughey. 1980. "Premarital Sexual Experience Among College Females, 1958, 1968, and 1978." *Family Relations* 29:353-357.
Benedict, Ruth. 1934. *Patterns of Culture*. Boston: Houghton Mifflin.
Berger, Bennett. 1981. *The Survival of a Counter-Culture*. Berkeley: University of California Press.
Berman, William. 1985. "Continued Attachment After Legal Divorce." *Journal of Family Issues* 6(September):375-392.
Bernard, Jessie. 1955. *Remarriage*. New York: Dryden.
———. 1972. *The Future of Marriage*. New York: Bantam.
Bersheid, Ellen. 1985. "Interpersonal Attraction." Pp. 413-484 in *Handbook of Social Psychology*. Vol. 2, edited by Gardner Lindzey and Elliot Aronson. New York: Random House.
Bersheid, Ellen and Elaine Walster. 1974. "A Little Bit About Love." In *Foundations of Interpersonal Attraction*, edited by T. L. Huston. New York: Academic Press.
Bettelheim, Bruno. 1950. *Love Is Not Enough*. New York: Free Press.
———. 1967. *The Empty Fortress*. New York: Free Press.
———. 1976. *The Uses of Enchantment*. New York: Vintage.
———. 1983. *Freud and Man's Soul*. New York: Knopf.
Billington, James H. 1980. *Fire in the Minds of Men*. New York: Basic Books.

Binion, Rudolph. 1968. *Frau Lou: Nietzsche's Wayward Disciple.* Princeton, NJ: Princeton University Press.

Bloch, Ivan. 1937. *The Sexual Life of Our Times.* New York: Falstaff. (Original work published 1907)

Blumstein, Philip and Pepper Schwartz. 1983. *American Couples.* New York: McGraw-Hill.

Bohannan, Paul. 1969. *Love, Sex and Being Human.* Garden City, NY: Doubleday.

———. 1971. *Divorce and After.* New York: Doubleday.

Bolton, Frank G. 1983. *When Bonding Fails.* Beverly Hills, CA: Sage.

Bonaparte, Marie, Anna Freud, and Ernst Kris, eds. 1954. *The Origins of Psychoanalysis: Letters to Wilhelm Fliess, Drafts and Notes, 1887-1902,* translated by E. Mosbacher and James Strachey. New York: Basic Books.

Bonner, John. 1980. *The Evolution of Culture in Animals.* Princeton, NJ: Princeton University Press.

Booth, A. et al. 1985. "Predicting Divorce and Permanent Separation." *Journal of Family Issues* 6:331-346.

Bornstein, M. H., ed. 1987. *Sensitive Periods in Development.* Hillsdale, NJ: Lawrence Erlbaum.

de Bougainville, Lewis. 1967. *A Voyage Around the World.* New York: DeCapo Press. (Original work published in English, 1772)

Bowlby, John. 1971-1979. *Attachment and Loss.* 3 vols. New York: Basic Books.

———. 1979. *The Making and Breaking of Affectional Bonds.* London: Tavistock.

Brain, Robert. 1979. *The Decorated Body.* London: Hutchison.

Branden, Nathaniel. 1980. *The Psychology of Romantic Love.* Los Angeles: Jeremy P. Tarcher.

Brazelton, T. B. 1963. "The Early Mother-Infant Adjustment." *Pediatrics* 32:931-938.

———. 1980. "Behavioral Competence of the Newborn Infant." In *Parent-Infant Relationships,* edited by P. Taylor. New York: Grune & Stratton.

———., B. Kowslowski, and M. Main. 1974. "The Origins of Reciprocity: The Early Mother-Infant Interaction." In *The Effect of the Infant on Its Caregiver,* edited by M. Lewis & L. Rosenbaum. New York: John Wiley.

Brazelton, T. B., E. Troncik, L. Adamson, H. Als, and S. Wise. 1975. "Early Mother-Infant Reciprocity." In *Parent-Infant Interaction,* edited by M. A. Hofer. Amsterdam: Elsevier.

Brinton, Crane. 1959. *A History of Morals in the Western World.* New York: Harcourt, Brace & World.

Brinton, Daniel G. 1886. "The Conception of Love in Some American Languages." *Proceedings of the American Philosophical Society* (Philadelphia).

Broyard, Anatole. 1986. "In and Out of Love and Faith." *New York Times Book Review* (March 9):7.

Brunner, Emil. 1947. *The Divine Imperative.* Philadelphia: Westminster Press.

Buber, Martin. 1970. *I and Thou,* translated by Walter Kaufmann. New York: Scribner.

Bullough, Vern L. 1976. *Sex and Variance in Society and History.* Chicago: University of Chicago Press.

———. and James Brundage. 1982. *Sexual Practices and the Medieval Church.* Buffalo, NY: Prometheus.

Bullough, Vern L. and Bonnie Bullough. 1977. *Sin, Sickness and Sanity.* New York: New American Library.

Burns, James MacGregor. 1978. *Leadership*. New York: Harper & Row.

Burr, Wesley et al. 1979. *Contemporary Theories About the Family*. Vols. 1 and 2. New York: Free Press.

Cahen, Alfred. 1968. *Statistical Analysis of American Divorce*. New York: AMS Press. (Original work published 1932)

Campbell, Joseph. 1968. *The Hero with a Thousand Faces*. Princeton, NJ: Princeton University Press.

Cantwell, D. P. and L. Baker. 1984. "Research Concerning Families of Children with Autism." In *The Effects of Autism on the Family*, edited by Eric Schopler and Gary B. Mesibou. New York: Plenum.

Carter, Hugh and Paul Glick. 1970. *Marriage and Divorce: A Social and Economic Study*. Cambridge, MA: Harvard University Press.

Cherlin, Andrew J. 1981. *Marriage, Divorce, Remarriage*. Cambridge, MA: Harvard University Press.

Chodoff, Paul. 1966. "A Critique of Freud's Theory of Infantile Sexuality." *American Journal of Psychiatry* 123:507-518.

Clanton, Gordon and Lynn Smith, eds. 1977. *Jealousy*. Englewood Cliffs, NJ: Prentice-Hall.

Cohn, Norman. 1975. *Europe's Inner Demons*. New York: New American Library.

Cook, Mark, ed. 1981. *The Bases of Human Sexual Attraction*. New York: Academic Press.

Cott, Nancy F. 1976. "Divorce and the Changing Status of Women in Eighteenth-Century Massachusetts." *William and Mary Quarterly* 3rd Series, 33(October):586-614.

Crosby, John, ed. 1985. *Reply to Myth*. New York: John Wiley.

d'Andrade, R. G. 1973. "Father-Absence, Identification and Identity." *Ethos* 38(Winter): 440-445.

Darwin, Charles. 1877. "A Biographical Sketch of an Infant." *Mind* 29:286-294.

Davidson, Sara. 1977. *Loose Change*. New York: Doubleday.

Davis, Clive, ed. 1983. *Challenges in Sexual Science*. Philadelphia: Society for the Scientific Study of Sex.

Davis, David Brion. 1984. *Slavery and Human Progress*. Oxford: Oxford University Press.

Davis, Keith. 1985. "Near and Dear: Friendship and Love Compared." *Psychology Today* 19(February):22-30.

Davis, Murray. 1973. *Intimate Relations*. New York: Free Press.

Dawkins, Richard. 1976. *The Selfish Gene*. New York: Oxford University Press.

Day, Max and E. V. Semrod. 1978. "Schizophrenic Reactions" and "Paranoia and Paranoid States." In *The Harvard Guide to Modern Psychiatry*, edited by Armand M. Nicholi, Jr. Cambridge, MA: The Belknap Press of Harvard University Press.

Delamater, John and Patricia MacCorquodale. 1979. *Premarital Sexuality*. Madison: University of Wisconsin Press.

Denzin, Norman. 1984. "Toward A Phenomenology of Domestic, Family Violence." *American Journal of Sociology* 90:483-513.

Deutsch, Helene. 1973. *Confrontations with Myself*. New York: Norton.

Dickerson, M. G. 1983. *Compulsive Gamblers*. New York: Longman.

Douglas, Jack D. 1967. *The Social Meaning of Suicide*. Princeton, NJ: Princeton University Press.

———. 1970. *American Social Order*. New York: Free Press.

————. 1976. *Investigative Social Research*. Beverly Hills, CA: Sage.

————. 1983. "Cooperative Paternalism Versus Conflictual Paternalism." In *Paternalism*, edited by Rolf Sartorius. Minneapolis: University of Minnesota Press.

————. 1984a. "The Emergence, Protection and Growth of the Sense of Self." In *Existential Studies of the Self*, edited by Joseph Kotarba and Andrea Fontana. Chicago: University of Chicago Press.

————. 1984b. "The Fundamental Processes of Becoming Deviant." Pp. 213-222 in *The Sociology of Deviance*, edited by Jack D. Douglas. Boston: Allyn & Bacon.

————. 1985. *Creative Interviewing*. Beverly Hills, CA: Sage.

————. In press. *The Myth of the Welfare State*.

————. et al. 1980. *Introduction to the Sociologies of Everyday Life*. Boston: Allyn & Bacon.

Douglas, Jack D. and Paul Rasmussen, with Carol Ann Flanagan. 1977. *The Nude Beach*. Beverly Hills, CA: Sage.

Douglas, Mary. 1973. *Natural Symbols*. New York: Vintage Books.

Dwyer, J. and J. Meyer. 1976. "Psychological Effects of Variations in Physical Appearance During Adolescence." *Adolescence* 11:353-376.

Edwards, Anne. 1981. *Sonya*. Simon & Schuster.

Eibl-Eibesfeldt, Irenaus. 1970. *Ethnology*. New York: Holt, Rinehart & Winston.

————. 1980. "Strategies of Social Interaction." Pp. 57-80 in *Emotion*, edited by Robert Plutchik and Henry Kellerman. New York: Academic Press.

Ekman, P. 1972. "Universal and Cultural Differences in Facial Expression of Emotion." In *Nebraska Symposium on Motivation 1971*, edited by J. K. Cole. Lincoln: University of Nebraska Press.

————. et al. 1972. *Emotion in the Human Face*. New York: Pergamon.

Ellenberger, Henri F. 1970. *The Discovery of the Unconscious*. New York: Basic Books.

Ellis, Albert. 1962. *The American Sexual Tragedy*. 2nd ed. New York: Stuart.

Ellis, Havelock. 1936. *Studies in the Psychology of Sex*. Vols. 1 and 2. New York: Random House.

————. 1939. *My Life*. Boston: Houghton Mifflin.

Erikson, E. H. 1963. *Childhood and Society*. New York: Norton.

Eysenck, H. J. and G. D. Wilson. 1973. *The Experimental Study of Freudian Theories*. London: Methuen.

Finkelhor, D. et al. 1983. *The Dark Side of Marriages*. Beverly Hills, CA: Sage.

Fisher, S. and P. R. Greenberg. 1977. *The Scientific Evaluation of Freud's Theories and Therapy*. Hassocks: Harvester Press.

Flaceliere, Robert. 1971. *L'Amour En Grece*. Paris: Hachette.

Fontana, Andrea. 1980. "The Mask and Beyond." Pp. 62-81 in *Introduction to the Sociologies of Everyday Life*, edited by Jack D. Douglas et al. Boston: Allyn & Bacon.

Ford, Clellan S. and Frank A. Beach. 1951. *Patterns of Sexual Behavior*. New York: Harper & Row.

Foucault, Michel. 1980. *The History of Sexuality*. New York: Vintage.

Freeman, Derek. 1983. *Margaret Mead and Samoa*. Cambridge, MA: Harvard University Press.

Freud, Anna and Dorothy Burlingham. 1943. *War and Children*. New York: International Universities Press.

————. 1944. *Infants Without Families*. New York: International University Press.

Freud, Sigmund. 1953-1974a. "Civilization and Its Discontents." Pp. 59-145 in *The*

Standard Edition of the Complete Psychological Works of Sigmund Freud. Vol. 21. London: Hogarth.

———. 1953-1974b. "'Civilized' Sexual Morality and Modern Nervous Illness." Pp. 179-204 in *The Standard Edition of the Complete Psychological Works of Sigmund Freud.* London: Hogarth.

———. 1953-1974c. "The Interpretation of Dreams." In *The Standard Edition of the Complete Psychological Works of Sigmund Freud.* Vols. 4-5. London: Hogarth.

———. 1953-1974d. "Three Essays on the Theory of Sexuality." Pp. 125-243 in *The Standard Edition of the Complete Psychological Works of Sigmund Freud.* Vol. 7. London: Hogarth.

———. 1953-1974e. "Totem and Taboo." Pp. 1-161 in *The Standard Edition of the Complete Psychological Works of Sigmund Freud.* Vol. 13. London: Hogarth. (Original work published 1912-1913)

Friedrich, O. 1979. *Clover.* New York: Simon & Schuster.

Fromm, Eric. 1974. *The Art of Loving.* New York: Harper & Row.

Fuller, C. J. 1976. *The Nayars Today.* New York: Cambridge University Press.

Furman, E. 1974. *A Child's Parent Dies: Studies in Childhood Bereavement.* New Haven, CT: Yale University Press.

Garmezy, N. 1985. *Child Psychiatry.* 2nd ed. Oxford: Blackwell Scientific.

Garmezy, N. and M. Rutter, eds. 1983. *Stress, Coping and Development in Children.* New York: McGraw-Hill.

Garnek, D. M. et al. 1980. "Cultural Expectation of Thinness in Women." *Psychological Reports* 47:438-491.

Gay, Peter. 1978. *Freud, Jews and Other Germans: Masters and Victims in Modernist Culture.* New York: Oxford University Press.

———. 1984-1986. *The Bourgeois Experience: The Education of the Senses.* Vols. 1 and 2. New York: Oxford University Press.

Gittelman, R. 1985. "Anxiety Disorders in Children." Pp. 65-67 in *Advances in Clinical Child Psychiatry,* edited by B. B. Lahey and A. E. Kazdin. New York: Plenum.

Glick, I. O. et al. 1974. *The First Year of Bereavement.* New York: John Wiley.

Goffman, Erving. 1959. *The Presentation of Self in Everyday Life.* New York: Anchor Books.

Goldfarb, W. 1943. "Infant Rearing and Problem Behavior." *American Journal of Orthopsychiatry* 13:249-265.

———. 1945. "Effects of Psychological Deprivation in Infancy and Subsequent Stimulation." *American Journal of Psychiatry* 102:18-23.

Goldstein, Daniel et al. 1977. *The Dance-Away Lover.* New York: Ballantine.

Goode, William J. 1959. "The Theoretical Importance of Love." *American Sociological Review* 24:38-47.

Greenfield, Meg. 1986. "We Must Get Straight Answers." *Newsweek* (March 10).

Greenspan, Stanley I. and Nancy T. Greenspan. 1985. *First Feelings.* New York: Viking.

Groos, Karl. 1898. *The Play of Animals.* New York: Appleton.

———. 1901. *The Play of Man.* New York: Appleton.

Grosskurth, Phyllis. 1985. *Havelock Ellis.* New York: New York University Press.

Hare, H. E. 1962. "Masturbation Insanity." *Journal of Mental Science* 452:2-25.

Harlow, H. F. and M. K. Harlow. 1965. "The Affectional System." In *Advances in the Study of Behavior,* edited by A. M. Schrier, H. F. Harlow, and E. Shore. New York: Academic Press.

————. 1969. "Effects of Various Mother-Infant Relationships in Rhesus Monkey Behavior." In *Determinants of Infant Behavior IV*, edited by B. M. Foss. Amsterdam: Methuen.

Hartung, J. 1982. "Polygyny and Inheritance." *Current Anthropology* 23:1-12.

Heath, Graham. 1978. *The Illusory Freedom*. London: Heinemann.

Heller, Peter. 1966. *Dialectics and Nihilism*. Amherst: University of Massachusetts Press.

Henderson, A. A. 1974. "Care-Eliciting Behaviour in Man." *Journal of Nervous and Mental Disease* 159:172-181.

Hess, Eckhard H. 1973. *Imprinting*. New York: Van Nostrand.

Hillebrand, John. In press. "Friendship: A Human Odyssey." Ph.D. Dissertation, Department of Sociology, University of California at San Diego.

Himmelfarb, Gertrude. 1986. *Marriage and Morals Among the Victorians*. New York: Knopf.

Hochschild, Arlie. 1979. "Emotion Work, Feeling Rules and Social Structure." *American Journal of Sociology* 85(November):551-575.

Hodgen, Margaret T. 1964. *Early Anthropology in the Sixteenth and Seventeenth Centuries*. Philadelphia: University of Pennsylvania Press.

Hofer, M. A., ed. 1975. *Parent-Infant Interaction*. Amsterdam: Elsevier.

Hoffman, M. L. 1976. "Empathy." In *Moral Development and Behavior*, edited by T. Lickona. New York: Holt, Rinehart.

————. 1978. "The Arousal and Development of Empathy." In *The Development of Affect*, edited by M. Lewis and L. A. Rosenblum. New York: Plenum.

Holbrook, David. 1972a. *The Masks of Hate*. New York: Pergamon.

————. 1972b. *Sex and Dehumanization*. Bristol: Pitman.

Holden, Constance. 1985. "Against All Odds." *Psychology Today* (December):31-36.

Horney, Karen. 1950. *Neurosis and Human Growth*. New York: Norton.

————. 1980. *The Adolescent Diaries of Karen Horney*. New York: Basic Books.

Huizinga, Johan. 1956. *The Waning of the Middle Ages*. Garden City, NY: Doubleday Anchor.

Humphreys, Laud. 1970. *Tearoom Trade*. Chicago: Aldine.

Hunt, Morton M. 1959. *The Natural History of Love*. New York: Knopf.

————. and Beatrice Hunt. 1977. *The Divorce Experience*. New York: McGraw-Hill.

Huston, Ted L., ed. 1974. *Foundations of Interpersonal Attraction*. New York: Academic Press.

Izard, C. E. 1971. *The Face of Emotion*. New York: Appleton-Century-Crofts.

————. 1980. "Aspects of Consciousness and Personality in Terms of Differential Emotions Theory." Pp. 165-187 in *Emotion*, edited by Robert Plutchik and Henry Kellerman. New York: Academic Press.

Jackson, Stevi. 1982. *Childhood and Sexuality*. Oxford: Blackwell.

Jewett, Robert and John S. Lawrence. 1977. *The American Monomyth*. Garden City, NY: Anchor.

Johnson, Paul. 1983. *Modern Times*. New York: Harper Colophon.

Kagan, J., R. Kearsley, and P. Zelazo. 1978. *Infancy*. Cambridge, MA: Harvard University Press.

Kanner, L. 1943. "Autistic Disturbances of Affective Contact." *Nervous Child* 2:217-250.

Katz, Richard. 1985. *Boiling Energy*. Cambridge, MA: Harvard University Press.

Kern, Stephen. 1973. "Freud and the Discovery of Childhood Sexuality." *History of Childhood Quarterly* 1:117-141.

Kern, Stephen. 1975. *Anatomy and Destiny: A Cultural History of the Human Body.* Indianapolis: Bobbs-Merrill.

Kiefer, Otto. 1934. *Sexual Life in Ancient Rome.* London: Abbey Library.

King, Lester S. 1958. *The Medical World of the Eighteenth Century.* Chicago: University of Chicago Press.

Kinsey, Alfred et al. 1948. *Sexual Behavior in the Human Male.* Philadelphia: W. B. Saunders.

―――. 1953. *Sexual Behavior in the Human Female.* Philadelphia: W. B. Saunders.

Kitson, Gay and Marvin Sussman. 1982. "Marital Complaints." *Journal of Marriage and the Family* 44:87-101.

Kitzinger, Sheila. 1974. *The Experience of Childbirth.* Baltimore: Penguin.

―――. 1979. *Women as Mothers.* New York: Vintage.

Klein, Carole. 1977. *How It Feels to Be a Child.* New York: Harper.

Kline, Paul. 1972. *Fact and Fantasy in Freudian Theory.* London: Methuen.

Komarovsky, Mirra. 1985. *Women in College.* New York: Basic Books.

Lamb, Michael E. and Marc H. Bornstein. 1987. *Development in Infancy.* New York: Random House.

Lamb, Michael E. and Joseph J. Campos. 1982. *Development in Infancy.* New York: Random House.

Landau, R. 1977. "Spontaneous and Elicited Smiles and Vocalizations of Infants in Four Israeli Environments." *Developmental Psychology* 13:389-400.

Laslett, Peter. 1984. *The World We Have Lost: Further Explored.* New York: Scribner.

Lasswell, Marcia and Norman Lobsenz. 1980. *Styles of Loving.* New York: Ballantine.

Lauer, Robert H. and Jeanette C. Lauer. 1983. *The Spirit and the Flesh: Sex in Utopian Communities.* Metuchen: Scarecrow Press.

Laurin, Janko. 1941. *Tolstoy: An Approach.* London: W. Collins.

Lecky, W.E.H. 1955. *History of European Morals from Augustus to Charlemagne.* New York: Braziller. (Original work published 1869)

―――. 1955. *History of the Rise and Influence of the Spirit of Rationalism in Europe.* New York: Braziller.

Leiderman, P. Herbert et al., eds. 1977. *Culture and Infancy.* New York: Academic Press.

Leites, Edmund. 1986. *The Puritan Conscience and Modern Sexuality.* New Haven, CT: Yale University Press.

Lenneberg, E. H. 1960. *Biological Foundations of Language.* New York: John Wiley.

Lenzner, Robert. 1985. *The Great Getty.* New York: Crown.

Leon, G. R. and P. W. Phelan. 1985. "Anorexia Nervosa." Pp. 81-111 in B. J. Lahey and A. E. Kazdin, eds. *Advances in Clinical Child Psychology.* New York: Plenum.

Levy, D. M. 1937. "Primary Affect Hunger." *American Journal of Psychiatry* 94:643-652.

―――. 1943. *Maternal Overprotection.* New York: Columbia University Press.

Levy, Robert. 1983. "The Attack on Mead." *Science* 20(May 20):829-832.

―――. 1984. "Mead, Freeman, and Samoa." *Ethos* 12(Spring):85-89.

Lewis, C. S. 1960. *The Four Loves.* New York: Harcourt.

―――. 1980. *A Grief Observed.* New York: Bantam.

Lewis, M. and L. Rosenbaum, eds. 1974. *The Effect of the Infant of Its Caregiver.* New York: John Wiley.

Libby, Roger and Robert Whitehurst, eds. 1977. *Marriage and Alternatives.* Glenview, Il: Scott, Foresman.

Licht, Hans. 1934. *Sexual Life in Ancient Greece.* London: Abbey Library.

Lichtenberger, J. P. 1931. *Divorce*. New York: Arno Press.

Liddell Hart, B. H. 1954. *Strategy*. New York: Praeger.

Liddy, G. Gordon. 1981. *Will*. New York: Dell.

Lyman, Stanford and Marvin Scott. 1970. *A Sociology of the Absurd*. New York: Appleton.

MacDonald, R. H. 1967. "The Frightful Consequences of Onanism: Notes on the History of a Delusion." *Journal of the History of Ideas* 28:423-431.

Mahler, Margaret. 1975. *The Psychological Birth of the Human Infant*. New York: Basic Books.

Malcolm, Janet. 1984. *In the Freud Archives*. New York: Knopf.

Malinowski, Bronislaw. 1929. *The Sexual Life of Savages* (Preface by Havelock Ellis). New York: Harcourt, Brace.

Manchester. 1983. *The Last Lion*. Boston: Little, Brown.

Mandler, George. 1980. "The Generation of Emotion." Pp. 219-244 in *Emotion*, edited by Robert Plutchik and Henry Kellerman. New York: Academic Press.

Manuel, Frank E. and Fritzie P. Manuel. 1979. *Utopian Thought in the Western World*. Cambridge, MA: Harvard University Press.

Marcuse, Herbert. 1966. *Eros and Civilization*. Boston: Little, Brown.

Maslow, Abraham. 1962. *Toward A Psychology of Being*. New York: D. Van Nostrand.

———. 1970. *Motivation and Personality*. New York: Harper & Row.

Masson, J. M. 1985. *The Assault on Truth: Freud's Suppression of the Seduction Theory*. New York: Penguin.

Masten, Ann S. and Norman Germezy. 1985. "Risk, Vulnerability and Protective Factors in Developmental Psychopathology." In *Advances in Clinical Child Psychology*, edited by B. B. Lahey and A. E. Kazdin. New York: Plenum.

Masters, William and Virginia Johnson. 1966. *Human Sexual Response*. Boston: Little, Brown.

———. 1970. *Human Sexual Inadequacy*. Boston: Little, Brown.

Maurois, Andre. 1944. *The Seven Faces of Love*. New York: Didier.

May, Elaine Tyler. 1980. *Great Expectations*. Chicago: University of Chicago Press.

May, Rollo. 1969. *Love and Will*. New York: Norton.

———. 1977. *The Meaning of Anxiety*. New York: Norton.

McDermott, J. F. 1970. "Divorce and Its Psychiatric Sequelae In Children." *Archives of General Psychiatry* 23:421-427.

McDougall, Joyce. 1986. *Theaters of the Mind: Illusion and Truth on the Psychoanalytic Stage*. New York: Basic Books.

McGrath, William. 1986. *Freud's Discovery of Psychoanalysis*. Ithaca, NY: Cornell University Press.

McNeill, William. 1976. *Plagues and People*. Garden City, NY: Anchor Press.

Mead, Margaret. 1928. *Coming of Age in Samoa*. New York: William Morrow.

Medawar, P. B. 1972. *The Hope of Progress*. London: Methuen.

Melichar, J. and D. Chitiboga. 1985. "Timetables in the Divorce Process." *Journal of Marriage and the Family* 47:701-708.

Menaghan, E. 1985 "Depressive Affect and Subsequent Divorce." *Journal of Family Issues* 6:295-306.

Michael, R. P. and J. H. Crook, eds. 1973. *Comparative Ecology and Behavior of Primates*. New York: Academic Press.

Milford, Nancy. 1970. *Zelda*. New York: Avon.

Minturn, L. et al. 1969. "Cultural Patterning of Sexual Beliefs and Behavior." *Ethnology* 8:301-318.

Mochulsky, K. 1967. *Dostoevsky*, translated by M. Minihan. Princeton, NJ: Princeton University Press.

Morgan, Edmund S. 1942. "The Puritans and Sex." *New England Quarterly* 15(December): 591-602.

Morris, Desmond. 1977. *Manwatching*. New York: Abrams.

Morris, Edmund. 1979. *The Rise of Theodore Roosevelt*. New York: Coward, McCann & Geoghegan.

Muncy, Raymond Lee. 1974. *Sex and Marriage in Utopian Communities*. Baltimore: Penguin.

Munroe, R. L. et al., eds. 1981. *Handbook of Cross-Cultural Human Development*. New York: Garland.

Murdock, George P. 1949. *Social Structure*. New York: Macmillan.

New York Times News Service. 1985. "Freud Unorthodox by Today's Standards, Papers Show." *San Diego Union* (November 28):8.

Nicholi, Armand M., Jr. 1978. *The Harvard Guide to Modern Psychiatry*. Cambridge, MA: The Belknap Press of Harvard University Press.

Norton, David. 1970. "Toward An Epistemology of Romantic Love." *Centennial Review* 14.

Norwood, Robin. 1986. *Women Who Love Too Much*. Pocket Books: New York.

O'Neill, William. 1967. *Divorce in the Progressive Era*. New Haven, CT: Yale University Press.

Ortega y Gasset, José. 1957. *On Love*, translated by Toby Talbor. New York: Meridian.

Parent-Duchatelet. 1836. *Prostitution*. Paris: J. B. Bailliere.

Parkes, C. M. 1972. *Bereavement: Studies of Grief in Adult Life*. New York: International Universities Press.

———. 1973. "Factors Determining the Persistence of Phantom Pain in the Amputee." *Journal of Psychosomatic Research* 17:97-108.

Parsons, Talcott and Robert F. Bales. 1955. *Family Socialization and Interaction Processes*. Glencoe, IL: Free Press.

Payne, Jaynann. 1985. "The Traditional Family with the Woman as Homemaker and the Man as Breadwinner Is Best for Most Families and for Society." In *Current Controversies in Marriage and the Family*, edited by H. Feldman and M. Feldman. Beverly Hills, CA: Sage.

Payne, Robert. 1961. *Dostoevsky*. New York: Knopf.

Peace, Richard. 1971. *Dostoevsky*. Cambridge: Cambridge University Press.

Pearce, Roy Harvey. 1965. *Savagism and Civilization*. Baltimore: Johns Hopkins University Press.

Peck, Scott. 1978. *The Road Less Traveled*. New York: Simon & Schuster.

Peele, Stanton. 1976. *Love and Addiction*. New York: Signet Books.

Pepys, Samuel. 1970. *The Diary of Samuel Pepys*, edited by Robert Latham and William Matthews. 11 vols. Berkeley: University of California Press.

Peters, H. F. 1962. *My Sister, My Spouse: A Biography of Lou Andres-Salome*. New York: Norton.

Pfeiffer, Ernst, ed. 1972. *Sigmund Freud and Lou Andres-Salome: Letters*. London: Hogarth.

Plutchik, Robert and Henry Kellerman, eds. 1980. *Emotion*. New York: Academic Press.

Pogrebin, Letty. 1987. *Among Friends*. New York: McGraw-Hill.

Powdermaker, Hortense. 1971. *Life in Lesu*. New York: Norton. (Original work published 1933)

Preston, James J., ed. 1982. *Mother Worship*. Chapel Hill, NC: University of North Carolina Press.

Rasmussen, Paul. 1978. "Massage Parlors." Ph.D. Dissertation, University of California, San Diego.

———. and Kathy J. Ferraro. 1979. "The Divorce Process." *Alternative Lifestyles* 2:443-460.

Reckless, W. 1933. *Vice in Chicago*. Chicago: University of Chicago Press.

Reich, Wilhelm. 1945. *The Sexual Revolution*. 3rd ed. New York: Orgone Institute Press.

Reik, Theodore. 1944. *A Psychologist Looks at Love*. New York: Farrar and Rinehart.

Reisman, John. 1979. *Anatomy of a Friendship*. New York: Irvington.

Richardson, Joanna. 1974. *Stendhal*. New York: Conard McCann and Geohegan.

Rimmer, Robert, ed. 1973. *Adventures in Loving*. New York: Signet.

Roazen, Paul. 1975. *Freud and His Followers*. New York: Knopf.

———. 1985. *Helene Deutsch*. New York: Doubleday.

Robinson, Paul. 1976. *The Modernization of Sex*. New York: Harper & Row.

Romanucci-Ross, Lola. 1985. *Mead's Other Manus*. South Hadley, MA: Bergin and Garvey.

Rosenblatt, P. C. and R. M. Anderson. 1981. "Human Sexuality in Cross-Cultural Perspective." Pp. 216-250 in *The Bases of Human Sexual Attraction*, edited by M. Cook. New York: Academic Press.

de Rougemont, Denis. 1940. *Love in the Western World*. New York: Harcourt.

———. 1963. *Love Declared*. New York: Pantheon.

Rowell, Thelma. 1972. *The Social Behavior of Monkeys*. Baltimore: Penguin.

Sameroff, A. J. 1975. "Early Influences on Development." *Merrill-Palmer Quarterly* 21:267-294.

Sameroff, A. J. and P. J. Cavanaugh. 1979. "Learning in Infancy." In *Handbook on Infant Development*, edited by J. D. Osofsky. New York: John Wiley.

Scheler, Max. 1961. *Ressentiment*. New York: Free Press.

Schnall, Maxine. 1981. *Limits: A Search for New Values*. New York: Clarkson N. Potter.

Schoenfeld, W. A. 1969. "The Body and Body Image in Adolescents." In *Adolescence*, edited by G. Caplan and L. Lebouici. New York: Basic Books.

Schopler, Eric and Gary B. Mesibov, eds. 1984. *The Effects of Autism on the Family*. New York: Plenum.

Schwartz, Gary et al. 1980. *Love and Commitment*. Beverly Hills, CA: Sage.

Sears, Robert R. et al. 1957. *Patterns of Child Rearing*. White Plains, NY: Row, Peterson.

Segal, Erich. 1985. "Heavy Breathing in Arcadia." *New York Times Book Review* (September 29).

Seigel, Jerrold. 1986. *Bohemian Paris: Culture, Politics and the Boundaries of Bourgeois Life, 1830-1930*. New York: Elisabeth Sifton Books/Viking.

Shelley, Percy Bysshe. 1975. *Epipsychidion*. New York: AMS Press.

Shepher, Joseph. 1983. *Incest*. New York: Academic Press.

Shulman, Alix Kates. 1972. *Memoirs of an Ex-Prom Queen*. New York: Knopf.

Smith, Daniel and Michael Hindus. 1975. "Premarital Pregnancy in America, 1640-1971: An Overview." *Journal of Interdisciplinary History* 5(Spring):537 ff.

Solomon, Robert C. 1981. *Love*. Garden City, NY: Anchor.

Sorokin, Pitirim A. 1956. *The American Sex Revolution*. Boston: Porter Sargent.

Speer, Albert. 1970. *Inside the Third Reich*. New York: Avon.

Spencer, Herbert. 1890. *The Principles of Psychology*. Edinburgh: Williams and Norgate.

Spiro, Melford E. 1979. *Gender and Culture*. New York: Schocken.

———. 1982. *Oedipus in the Trobriands*. Chicago: University of Chicago Press.

Spitz, R. A. and K. M. Wolf. 1946. "The Smiling Response." *Genetic Psychology Monographs* 34:57-125.

Steel, Ronald. 1980. *Walter Lippmann and the American Century*. Boston: Little, Brown.

Stendhal [Marie Henri-Beyle]. 1957. *Love*, translated by G. and S. Sale. Middlesex, England: Penguin.

Stern, Daniel. 1977. *The First Relationship*. Cambridge, MA: Harvard University Press.

Sternhell, Carol. 1986. "A Donkey Among Horses." *New York Times Book Review* (March 9):14.

Stone, Lawrence. 1977. *The Family, Sex and Marriage*. New York: Harper & Row.

Stuart, I. R. and L. E. Abt. 1981. *Children of Separation and Divorce*. New York: Van Nostrand.

Suggs, Robert C. 1966. *Marquesan Sexual Behavior*. New York: Harcourt, Brace and World.

Sulloway, Frank J. 1983. *Freud, Biologist of the Mind: Beyond the Psychoanalytic Legend*. New York: Basic Books.

Super, C. M. 1981. "Cross Cultural Studies of Infancy." In *Handbook of Cross-Cultural Psychology*, edited by H. Triandas. Vol. 4. Boston: Allyn & Bacon.

———. and S. Harkness. 1982. "The Development of Affect in Infancy and Early Childhood." Pp. 1-19 in *Cultural Perspectives on Child Development*, edited by D. A. Wagner and H. W. Stevenson. San Francisco: W. H. Freeman.

Talmon, Y. 1964. "Mate Selection In Collective Settlements." *American Sociological Review* 29:491-508.

Taylor, P., ed. 1980. *Parent-Infant Relationships*. New York: Grune & Stratton.

Tennov, Dorothy. 1979. *Love and Limerance*. New York: Stein and Day.

Thomas, A. and S. Chess. 1977. *Temperament and Development*. New York: Brunner Mazel.

Thompson, Andrew H. 1969. *The Feldman Method*. Lyndrook, NY: Farnsworth.

Trafford, Abigail. 1982. *Crazy Time*. New York: Harper.

Triandas, H., ed. 1980. *Handbook of Cross-Cultural Psychology*. Vols. 1-6. Boston: Allyn & Bacon.

Udry, J. Richard. 1974. *The Social Context of Marriage*. Philadelphia: Lippincott.

———. 1981. "Marriage Alternatives and Marital Disruption." *Journal of Marriage and the Family* 43(November):889-897.

Unwin, J. D. 1934. *Sex and Culture*. Oxford: Oxford University Press.

van Lawick-Goodall, Jane. 1971. *In the Shadow of Man*. New York: Dell.

Vitz, Paul. 1985. "Textbook Bias Isn't of a Fundamental Nature." *Wall Street Journal* (December 26).

de Waal, Frans. 1982. *Chimpanzee Politics*. New York: Harper & Row.

Wagenbach, Klaus. 1960. *Franz Kafka*. 2nd ed.

Wagner, D. A. and H. W. Stevenson, eds. 1982. *Cultural Perspectives on Child Development*. San Francisco: Freeman.

Walker, Lenore. 1979. *The Battered Woman*. New York: Harper.

Walsh, Froma, ed. 1982. *Normal Family Processes*. New York: Guilford.

Walster, Elaine and G. W. Walster. 1978. *A New Look at Love*. Reading, MA: Addison-Wesley.

Waterman, W. C. 1932. *Prostitution and Its Repression in New York City, 1900-1931*. New York: Columbia University Press.

Weiss, Robert. 1976. *Marital Separation*. New York: Basic Books.

———. 1979. *Going It Alone*. New York: Basic Books.

Weitzman, Lenore. 1985. *The Divorce Revolution*. New York: Free Press.

Weld, Jacqueline. 1986. *Peggy: The Wayward Guggenheim*. New York: Dutton.

Werner, E. E. 1977. *Kauai's Children Come of Age*. Honolulu: University of Hawaii Press.

———. 1979. *Cross-Cultural Child Development*. Belmont, CA: Wadsworth.

———. 1982. *Vulnerable But Invincible*. New York: McGraw-Hill.

———. et al. 1971. *The Children of Kauai: A Longitudinal Study from the Prenatal Period to Age 10*. Honolulu: University of Hawaii Press.

Westermarck, Edward A. 1921. *The History of Human Marriage*. 5th ed. London: Macmillan.

———. 1934a. "Recent Theories of Exogamy." *Sociological Review* 26:22-40.

———. 1934b. *Three Essays on Sex and Marriage*. London: Macmillan.

Willcox, Walter. 1969. *The Divorce Problem*. New York: AMS Press. (Original work published 1891)

Wilson, Edward. 1975. *Sociobiology*. Cambridge, MA: Harvard University Press.

———. 1978. *On Human Nature*. Cambridge, MA: Harvard University Press.

Wilson, James Q. and Richard J. Herrnstein. 1985. *Crime and Human Nature*. New York: Simon & Schuster.

Winch, Robert. 1958. *Mate Selection: A Study of Complementary Needs*. New York: Harper & Row.

Winnick, Charles and Paul Kinsie. 1971. *The Lively Commerce*. Chicago: Quadrangle.

Winnicott, D. W. 1965. *The Maturational Processes and the Facilitating Environment*. New York: International Universities Press.

———. 1971. *Playing and Reality*. New York: Basic Books.

Wolf, A. P. 1966. "Childhood Association, Sexual Attraction, and the Incest Taboo: A Chinese Case." *American Anthropologist* 68:883-898.

———. 1968. "Adopt a Daughter-in-Law, Marry a Sister: A Chinese Solution to the Problem of the Incest Taboo." *American Anthropologist* 70:864-874.

———. 1970. "Childhood Association and Sexual Attraction: A Further Test of the Westermarck Hypothesis." *American Anthropologist* 72:503-515.

———. 1976. "Childhood Association, Sexual Attraction and Fertility in Taiwan." In *Demographic Anthropology*, edited by E. Zubrow. Albuquerque: University of New Mexico Press.

Woodham-Smith, Cecil. 1972. *Queen Victoria*. New York: Dell.

Yalom, Irvin D. 1980. *Existential Psychotherapy*. New York: Basic Books.

Yarmolinsky, A. 1957. *Dostoevsky*. Rev. ed. New York: Funk and Wagnalls.

Yarrow, L. J. 1964. "Separation from Parents During Early Childhood." Pp. 89-136 in *Review of Child Development Research*, edited by M. L. Hoffman and L. W. Hoffman. Vol. 1. New York: Russell Sage.

Ziegler, Phillip. 1985. *Mountbatten*. New York: Knopf.

Zigler, Edward. 1984. "Handicapped Children and Their Families." Pp. 21-40 in *The Effects of Autism on the Family*, edited by Eric Schopler and Gary B. Mesibov. New York: Plenum.

About the Authors

Jack D. Douglas is married and the father of four young adults. His family and the lives of his friends which he has shared intimately are for him the most important sources of the ageless truths on which the more problematic truths of this work are built. Like everyone, he has learned much from his mistakes and misfortunes, but is glad indeed to have avoided the worst and to have learned about them only through the life studies of others. He has been developing basic ideas and models of human nature for many years and hopes this is only the first of the major works that will present those. He has published a number of books building up to this one, notably *Existential Sociology* (with John M. Johnson et al.), *The Sociology of Everyday Life* (with some close coworkers), *Investigative Social Research,* and *Creative Interviewing.* He professes the quest for truth about human life at the University of California at San Diego. Freda Cruse Atwell and her family have shared that quest as friends for 12 years.

Freda Cruse Atwell grew up on a cattle ranch in rural Arkansas. She began her studies in 1975 at the University of California, San Diego. In 1978, after two years of marriage, she found herself completely alone in the city with her toddler daughter and knowing only a handful of people. Choosing to adhere to the advice given by her friend and mentor, Dr. Jack Douglas—"You can either learn to understand it [divorce] and get on with your life, or you can let it devastate you"—she began assisting Dr. Douglas's teaching and research (most notably, *Creative Interviewing,* Sage Publications, 1985, and other works of her own such as *The Distorted Mirror, Love Obsessed,* and *The Recycling of Men*). She has received degrees in English, American literature, and sociology from UCSD. She dedicates a tremendous amount of time to family planning organizations such as Planned Parenthood. In 1984 she was awarded the honor of Outstanding Young Woman of America and in 1986 was appointed Associate Chairperson of the 1986 National United Nations (UN) Day Program. She lectures throughout the United States on family relations, love, intimacy and sex, and self-concepts and self-esteem.

John Hillebrand is a veteran of youthful involvements in the rock 'n' roll and motorcycle racing subcultures. His intense interests in existentialism and the sociologies of everyday life led him to San Diego, where he is completing his Ph.D. dissertation, *Friendship: A Human Odyssey,* an in-depth study of friendship experiences. A rare and creatively inspiring friendship with Dr. Jack D. Douglas resulted in his research contributions to Dr. Douglas's books *Creative Interviewing* and *The Myth of the Welfare State.* He contributes to the journals *Deviant Behavior, Journal of Contemporary Ethnography,* and *Sociological Inquiry.* He plans further work in the areas of deviance, marriage and the family, and the development of qualitative methods, although he is currently neither deviant nor married but is methodical.